Quantum Software Engineering

Manuel A. Serrano • Ricardo Pérez-Castillo •
Mario Piattini
Editors

Quantum
Software
Engineering

 Springer

Editors
Manuel A. Serrano (iD)
aQuantum
University of Castilla-La Mancha (UCLM)
Ciudad Real, Spain

Ricardo Pérez-Castillo (iD)
aQuantum
University of Castilla-La Mancha (UCLM)
Talavera de la Reina, Spain

Mario Piattini (iD)
aQuantum
University of Castilla-La Mancha (UCLM)
Ciudad Real, Spain

ISBN 978-3-031-05326-9   ISBN 978-3-031-05324-5   (eBook)
https://doi.org/10.1007/978-3-031-05324-5

This Springer imprint is published by the registered company Springer Nature Switzerland AG
The registered company address is: Gewerbestrasse 11, 6330 Cham, Switzerland

The editors want to dedicate this book to the aQuantum Team for their great work in Quantum Software Engineering research and practice.

To Laura and Maria Jose, we are entangled through the time

Manuel A. Serrano

To my loved ones, to whom I am entangled with

Ricardo Pérez-Castillo

To Terry and Peter Finch, a very "entangled" couple, with love

Mario Piattini

Preface

Overview

Historically, we can identify different industrial "revolutions": the first revolution that took place at the end of the eighteenth century with the creation of the steam engine and the telegraph; the second (in the first decade of the nineteenth century) with the oil-fueled combustion engine, electricity, the telephone, and the radio; and the third brought about by information technology and the spread of the Internet. In the last two decades, we have witnessed another confluence of technologies, social networks, mobile, big data and data analytics, cloud computing, artificial intelligence (AI), 3D printing, virtual and augmented reality, robotics, blockchain, Internet of things (IoT) and Internet of everything, etc., that have provoked a real digital "revolution/transformation" in organizations. Far from stopping, the next revolution is already looming, resulting from the combination of nano- and biotechnologies, genomics, and quantum-based technologies. In fact, if the nineteenth century was the "machine age," and the twentieth century was the "information age," the twenty-first century will probably be the "quantum age."

Quantum computing is gaining a lot of interest from governments, research agencies, companies, and investors alike. It is already possible to use various quantum computers, based on counterintuitive principles as superposition or entanglement, and take advantage of their bigger computing power to solve problems that cannot be addressed by "classical" computers in a reasonable timeframe. The application and usage of quantum computing require the use of completely different kinds of algorithms and programming languages. Several quantum platforms are already available for coding these new algorithms. So, it can be stated that: "The thing driving the hype is the realization that quantum computing is actually real. It is no longer a physicist's dream—it is an engineer's nightmare" [1].

As the IBM Institute for Business Value highlights: "We are living in the Quantum Decade, when quantum computers are getting ready to overperform their classical cousins in a meaningful task, achieving what we call Quantum Advantage" [2]. The same report remarks that: "The integration of quantum computing, AI, and classical computing into hybrid multi-cloud workflows will drive the most significant computing revolution in 60 years."

However, for quantum computing being a more effective reality, quantum computer science, hardware, and software are not enough, and a novel "Quantum Software Engineering" (QSE) is becoming a must. Recently, the Software Engineering Institute of the Carnegie Mellon University has published a "National Agenda for Software Engineering Research & Development" titled "Architecting the Future of Software Engineering" [3], which includes an "Engineering Quantum Computing Software Systems Research Focus Area," pointing out that "If we imagine that hardware advances that permit scaling are achieved, then advances in software and software engineering will also be needed." One of the "research recommendations" of this agenda is to "Catalyze Increased Attention on Engineering for New Computational Models, with a Focus on Quantum-enabled Software Systems. The software engineering community should collaborate with the quantum computing community to anticipate new architectural paradigms for quantum-enabled computing systems."

Precisely this book was conceived with this in mind, to gather a set of software engineering techniques and tools to improve the productivity and assure the quality in quantum software development. Thereby, quantum computing will be the main driver for a new software engineering golden age during the present decade [4].

Organization

The book is composed of 15 chapters structured as follows.

Chapter 1, written by Elías F. Combarro, introduces the main general concepts and foundations related to quantum computing.

Then a set of chapters deal with the quantum software engineering, methods, and techniques.

In Chap. 2, Mario Piattini and Juan Manuel Murillo present the quantum software engineering landscape and the main challenges that arise in this new computing paradigm. This chapter also briefly reviews the Talavera Manifesto for quantum software engineering and discusses the main problems in the field.

In Chap. 3, Miguel Ángel Blanco and Manuel A. Serrano propose a governance system adapted to quantum information systems, based on COBIT.

In Chap. 4, Benjamin Weder, Johanna Barzen, Frank Leymann, and Daniel Vietz show a quantum software life cycle for hybrid systems, proposing a new framework specially adapted to this kind of system.

Carmelo R. Cartiere is the author of Chap. 5, where he explores and defines a new formal method for quantum software engineering.

In Chap. 6, written by Carlos A. Pérez-Delgado, a quantum software modelling language is presented, and Q-UML is proposed in order to facilitate the modelling of quantum applications.

Chapter 7, by Iaakov Exman and Alon Tsalik Shmilovich, offers a rigorous formulation of the density matrix-based approach as a Universal Software Design procedure. It enables modularization of all software system types.

In Chap. 8, written by David Valencia, Enrique Moguel, Javier Rojo, Javier Berrocal, Jose Garcia-Alonso, and Juan M. Murillo an approximation to the development of hybrid quantum-classical services is proposed using service-oriented architectures, in order to tap on problems hard to deal with classical computing algorithms. From the experiments made and analysis carried out, several shortcomings of actual quantum computing are derived, allowing the proposal of some directions for future development of quantum service-oriented computing (QSOC).

Antonio García de la Barrera, Ignacio García-Rodríguez de Guzmán, Macario Polo, and José A. Cruz-Lemus show, in Chap. 9, the current trends and emerging proposals for quantum software testing.

In Chap. 10, Miguel-Angel Sicilia, Marçal Mora-Cantallops, Salvador Sánchez-Alonso, and Elena García-Barriocanal discuss the apparent differences and similarities of quantum software engineering as an emerging discipline with "classical" software engineering from the viewpoint of measurement and point to future research directions in that particular area.

Ricardo Pérez del Castillo and Luis Jiménez-Navajas present in Chap. 11 a software modernization process based on ADM, and, hence, on reengineering, which could be effective in situations resulting from the evolution of classical and quantum software.

Turning to the quantum software environments and tools, Chap. 12, by Jose Antonio Cruz and Manuel A. Serrano, presents an overview of the different quantum software layers and the existent quantum software tools and platforms.

Chapter 13, written by Guido Peterssen y Jose Luis Hevia, shows QuantumPath® (QPath®), which is a quantum software development platform to support the design, implementation, and execution of quantum software applications.

Nir Minerbi briefly explains, in Chap. 14, how quantum software development could be achieved with Classiq, a Quantum Algorithm Design (QAD) platform that automatically synthesizes complete quantum circuits from high-level functional models.

And finally, in Chap. 15, Filipa Ramos Ferreira, João Paulo Fernandes, and Rui Abreu present and overview of quantum software frameworks for deep learning.

Target Readership

The target readership for this book is assumed to have previous knowledge of information systems and software engineering. The book is aimed at academics, researchers, and practitioners involved in the creation of quantum information systems and software platforms.

It can also serve as a reference book for monographic courses on quantum software development, as well as for the subjects to be incorporated in the curricula of bachelor's and master's degree courses in the field of computer science.

Ciudad Real, Spain   Manuel A. Serrano
Talavera de la Reina, Spain   Ricardo Pérez-Castillo
Ciudad Real, Spain   Mario Piattini
February 2022

References

1. Knight W (2018) Serious quantum computers are finally here. What are we going to do with them? MIT Technol Rev
2. IBV (2021) The Quantum Decade. A playbook for achieving awareness, readiness, and advantage. IBM Institute for Business Value. https://www.ibm.com/downloads/cas/J25G35OK
3. SEI (2021) Architecting the future of software engineering. A national agenda for Software Engineering Research & Development. Carnegie Mellon University, Software Engineering Institute. https://resources.sei.cmu.edu/library/asset-view.cfm?assetid=741193
4. Piattini M, Peterssen G, Pérez-Castillo R (2020) Quantum Computing: a new Software Engineering golden age. ACM SIGSOFT Softw Eng Notes 45(3): 12–14. https://dl.acm.org/doi/10.1145/3402127.3402131

Acknowledgments

We would like to express our gratitude to all those individuals and parties who helped us produce this volume. In the first place, we would like to thank all the contributing authors and reviewers who helped improve the final version. Special thanks to Springer-Verlag and Ralf Gerstner for believing in us once again and for giving us the opportunity to publish this work.

We would also like to say how grateful we are to Natalia Pinilla of Universidad de Castilla-La Mancha for her support during the production of this book.

Finally, we wish to acknowledge the support of the "QHealth: Quantum Pharmacogenomics Applied to Aging" project, the 2020 CDTI (Center for the Development of Industrial Technology of the Ministry of Science and Innovation of Spain) Missions Program and FEDER, and the SMOQUIN project (PID2019-104791RB-I00) funded by the Spanish Ministry of Science and Innovation (MICINN).

Contents

10   Quantum Software Measurement 193
   Miguel-Angel Sicilia, Marçal Mora-Cantallops,
   Salvador Sánchez-Alonso, and Elena García-Barriocanal

List of Contributors

Rui Abreu Faculty of Engineering, University of Porto, Porto, Portugal
Instituto de Engenharia de Sistemas e Computadores: Investigacão e Desenvolvimento em Lisboa, Porto, Portugal

Antonio García de la Barrera aQuantum, Alarcos Research Group, Department of Technologies and Information Systems, Escuela Superior de Informática, University of Castilla-La Mancha, Ciudad Real, Spain

Johanna Barzen Institute of Architecture of Application Systems, University of Stuttgart, Stuttgart, Germany

Javier Berrocal University of Extremadura, Cáceres, Spain

Miguel Ángel Blanco Alarcos Research Group, Institute of Technologies and Information Systems, University of Castilla-La Mancha (UCLM), Ciudad Real, Spain

Carmelo R. Cartiere Kellogg College, University of Oxford, Oxford, UK

Elías F. Combarro Computer Science Department, University of Oviedo, Oviedo, Spain

José A. Cruz-Lemus aQuantum, Alarcos Research Group, Institute of Technologies and Information Systems, University of Castilla-La Mancha, Ciudad Real, Spain

Iaakov Exman Software Engineering Department, The Jerusalem College of Engineering – Azrieli, Jerusalem, Israel

João Paulo Fernandes Artificial Intelligence and Computer Science Laboratory, Faculty of Engineering, University of Porto, Porto, Portugal

Filipa Ramos Ferreira Faculty of Engineering, University of Porto, Porto, Portugal

Jose Garcia-Alonso University of Extremadura, Cáceres, Spain

Elena García-Barriocanal Computer Science Department, University of Alcalá, Alcalá de Henares, Spain

Ignacio García-Rodríguez de Guzmán aQuantum, Alarcos Research Group, Department of Technologies and Information Systems, Escuela Superior de Informática, University of Castilla-La Mancha, Ciudad Real, Spain

Jose Luis Hevia aQuantum, Alhambra IT, Madrid, Spain

Luis Jiménez-Navajas aQuantum, Alarcos Research Group, Institute of Technologies and Information Systems, University of Castilla-La Mancha (UCLM), Ciudad Real, Spain

Frank Leymann Institute of Architecture of Application Systems, University of Stuttgart, Stuttgart, Germany

Nir Minerbi Classiq Technologies, Tel Aviv, Israel

Enrique Moguel University of Extremadura, Cáceres, Spain

Marçal Mora-Cantallops Computer Science Department, University of Alcalá, Alcalá de Henares, Spain

Juan Manuel Murillo University of Extremadura, Cáceres, Spain

Ricardo Pérez-Castillo aQuantum, Alarcos Research Group, Institute of Technologies and Information Systems, University of Castilla-La Mancha (UCLM), Ciudad Real, Spain

Carlos A. Pérez-Delgado University of Kent, Canterbury, Kent, UK

Guido Peterssen aQuantum, Alhambra IT, Madrid, Spain

Mario Piattini aQuantum, Alarcos Research Group, Institute of Technologies and Information Systems, University of Castilla-La Mancha, Ciudad Real, Spain

Macario Polo aQuantum, Alarcos Research Group, Institute of Technologies and Information Systems, University of Castilla-La Mancha, Ciudad Real, Spain

Javier Rojo University of Extremadura, Cáceres, Spain

Salvador Sánchez-Alonso Computer Science Department, University of Alcalá, Alcalá de Henares, Spain

Manuel A. Serrano aQuantum, Alarcos Research Group, Escuela Superior de Informática & Instituto de Tecnologías y Sistemas de Información, University of Castilla-La Mancha, Ciudad Real, Spain

Alon Tsalik Shmilovich Software Engineering Department, The Jerusalem College of Engineering – Azrieli, Jerusalem, Israel

Miguel-Angel Sicilia Computer Science Department, University of Alcalá, Alcalá de Henares, Spain

David Valencia University of Extremadura, Cáceres, Spain

Daniel Vietz Institute of Architecture of Application Systems, University of Stuttgart, Stuttgart, Germany

Benjamin Weder Institute of Architecture of Application Systems, University of Stuttgart, Stuttgart, Germany

List of Abbreviations

ACM	Association for Computing Machinery
ADL	Architectural Description Language
ADM	Architecture-Driven Modernization
AG	Alignment Goal
AI	Artificial Intelligence
API	Application Programming Interface
APO	Align, Plan, and Organize
ATPG	Automatic Test Pattern Generation
AWS	Amazon Web Services
BAI	Build, Acquire, and Implement
BIST	Built-In Self-Test
BPEL	Business Process Execution Language
BPMN	Business Process Model and Notation
BQM	Binary Quadratic Model
CAD	Computer-Aided Design
CEN	European Committee for Standardization
CENELEC	European Committee for Electrotechnical Standardization
CIM	Computation Independent Model
CLQP	Categorical Logic of Quantum Programs
CNN	Convolutional Neural Networks
COBIT	Control Objectives for Information and Related Technologies
CPU	Central Processing Unit
CSA	Cloud Security Alliance
DBE	Deutsch, Barenco, and Ekert
DSL	Domain-Specific Language
DSM	Design Structure Matrix
DSS	Deliver, Service, and Support
EDM	Evaluate-Direct-Monitor
EG	Enterprise Goal
EP	Entanglement Principle

EPR	Einstein-Podolsky-Rosen
EQF	European Quantum Flagship
ETSI	European Telecommunications Standards Institute
F-QSE	Formal Quantum Software Engineering
FM	Formal Method
FPGA	Field-Programmable Gate Arrays
FS	Formal Specification
FV	Formal Verification
GAN	Generative Adversarial Neural
GHZ	Greenberger-Horne-Zeilinger
IBV	Institute for Business Value
IDB	Inter-American Development Bank
IEC	International Electrotechnical Commission
IEEE	Institute of Electrical and Electronics Engineers
IoT	Internet of Things
ISACA	Information Systems Audit and Control Association
ISO	International Organization for Standardization
IT	Information Technology
JSON	JavaScript Object Notation
KA	Knowledge Area
KDM	Knowledge Discovery Metamodel
LOC	Lines of Code
LSM	Linear Software Model
MDA	Model-Driven Architectures
MDE	Model-Driven Engineering
MEA	Monitor, Evaluate, and Assess
MNIST	Modified National Institute of Standards and Technology
NISQ	Noisy Intermediate-Scale Quantum
NIST	National Institute of Standards and Technology
OMG	Object Management Group
OOD	Object-Oriented Design
PaaS	Platform as a Service
PIM	Platform-Independent Model
PSM	Platform-Specific Model
PTM	Probabilistic Transfer Matrix
QaaS	Quantum as a Service
QAD	Quantum Algorithm Design
QAI	Quantum Artificial Intelligence/Quantum Algorithm Implementation
QALU	Quantum Arithmetic Logic Unit
QANSWER	Quantum Software Engineering and Programming
QAOA	Quantum Approximate Optimization Algorithm
QASM	Quantum Assembly Language
QC	Quantum Computing
QCE	Quantum Computing and Engineering

QCFG	Quantum Control Flow Graphs
QCP	Quantum Computing Platform
QDLC	Quantum Development Life Cycle
QDK	Quantum Development Kit
QEC	Quantum Error Correction
QFT	Quantum Fourier Transform
QHL	Quantum Hoare Logic
QIGTS	Quantum Information Technology Governance System
QIR	Quantum Intermediate Representation
QIS	Quantum Information Systems
QIT	Quantum Information Technology
QKD	Quantum Key Distribution
QML	Quantum Machine Learning
QRNG	Quantum Random Number Generator
QSOA	Quantum Service-Oriented Architecture
QSOC	Quantum Service-Oriented Computing
QuMA	Quantum Micro-Architecture
QoS	Quality of Service
QP	Quantum Programming
QPE	Quantum Phase Estimation
QPU	Quantum Processing Unit
QRAM	Quantum Random Access Memory
QS	Quantum Security
QSD	Quantum System Development
QSE	Quantum Software Engineering
QSOC	Quantum Service-Oriented Computing
QT	Quantum Technology
QTP	Quantum Teleportation Protocol
Q-UML	Quantum UML
QUBO	Quadratic Unconstrained Binary Optimization
QV	Quantum Volume
REST	Representational State Transfer
SDK	Software Development Kit
SDLC	Software Development Life Cycle
SEI	Software Engineering Institute
SOA	Services-Oriented Architecture
SUD	Systems Under Design
SWEBOK	Software Engineering Body of Knowledge
TOSCA	Topology and Orchestration Specification for Cloud Applications
TQF	Total Quantum Factor
TSP	Traveling Salesman Problem
UML	Unified Modelling Language

UP	Unified Process
VHDL	VHSIC (Very High-Speed Integrated Circuits) Hardware Description Language
VMS	Virtual Machine System
VQE	Variational Quantum Eigensolver
XACC	eXtreme-scale ACCelerator

Chapter 1
Quantum Computing Foundations

Elías F. Combarro

1.1 Introduction

Quantum computing [1] is a computational paradigm that explicitly uses properties of subatomic particles such as superposition, entanglement, and interference to achieve asymptotical speed-ups over classical algorithms on certain tasks. For instance, the famous Shor's algorithm [2] can factor an integer in polynomial time on its number of digits, while the best-known classical algorithm for the same problem is superpolynomial, and Grover's algorithm [3] achieves a quadratic speed-up over any possible classical algorithm (probabilistic or not) in the black-box search problem.

Until recently, implementing quantum algorithms on an actual quantum device required access to research lab prototypes. However, in the last few years, initiatives such as IBM Quantum [4] have made some quantum computers available on the cloud for free, creating a surge of interest in learning how to develop and execute quantum algorithms. This involves using concepts from quantum information processing theory (as, e.g., qubits, quantum gates, and measurements) that are not used in classical programming languages, as well as understanding some particular idiosyncrasies of quantum algorithms, such as reversibility, uncomputation, or the impossibility of cloning information.

This chapter introduces, from scratch, all the elements and concepts that are needed to understand and implement quantum algorithms in both quantum simulators and actual quantum computers and illustrates them with some simple examples. After this chapter, the reader will be equipped with all the quantum computing background needed to understand the challenges on quantum software engineering and to master the methods and techniques used in the field.

E. F. Combarro (✉)
Computer Science Department, University of Oviedo, Oviedo, Spain
e-mail: efernandezca@uniovi.es

M. A. Serrano et al. (eds.), *Quantum Software Engineering*,
https://doi.org/10.1007/978-3-031-05324-5_1

1

Throughout the chapter, we will use an axiomatic approach in which we only describe the kind of mathematical objects that we will use to represent information and data and the operations that we can perform on them in order to compute and obtain results. Little or no reference will be made to the physical implementation of these elements in actual quantum computers for, on the one hand, they can vary greatly from one device to another and, on the other, they are not really needed to understand how to process information and conduct computations with a quantum computer. This method is similar to the way in which modern computer programming courses are taught, with no need to explicitly mention how the computer stores and transforms data and has already been used with remarkable success to teach quantum computing courses (see [5]). Thus, in the following, we only assume from the reader some familiarity with linear algebra, in particular computing with matrices and vectors of complex numbers.

Although there are several different approaches to programming a quantum computer (cf. Sect. 1.2), we will focus mainly on the quantum circuit model, which we will introduce in Sect. 1.3. This is, by far, the most popular way of defining and implementing quantum algorithms and the one that is used in most quantum computers available today, and, for this reason, we will use it to introduce the fundamental ideas of quantum computing and to describe and analyze, in Sect. 1.4, some quantum algorithms. In addition to this, in Sect. 1.5, we also include a brief description of adiabatic quantum computing [6] and explain how this is particularized in quantum annealers (another popular type of quantum computers available today) to find approximate solutions of combinatorial optimization problems [7].

But before that, we will motivate the study of the quantum computing paradigm by presenting some of its applications.

1.1.1 Problems Quantum Computing Can Address and Some Applications

As a computational paradigm, quantum computing has exactly the same power as classical computing (as defined, for instance, by means of Turing machines). Thus, a quantum computer cannot solve any new problem that was not already solvable with traditional computers. However, we have evidence that quantum computers can solve some problems asymptotically faster than what is possible with just classical resources.

We still lack a complete characterization of the problems that are amenable to quantum speed-ups, but we have some prominent examples in several different fields of application. This includes tasks such as searching in unsorted databases quadratically faster (with the use of Grover's algorithm [3]) or factoring large integers with an exponential speed-up over the best, currently known classical algorithm, thanks to Shor's results [2].

In addition to this, quantum computers open the possibility of more efficient simulation of physical and chemical systems in which quantum properties are relevant. In fact, this was the original motivation (pointed out, among others, by Feynman [8]) of studying how to process information with quantum mechanical methods. Among the algorithms that have been proposed for this type of simulation, we can find methods based on quantum phase estimation [9, 10] or on variational circuits [11, 12].

Quantum computing also finds applications in the acceleration of classical machine learning algorithms (see [13]) as well as in the definition of new, purely quantum machine learning methods such as quantum neural networks [14]. The potential of this type of models is still not completely understood, but recent results [15] seem to indicate that they can offer an advantage in expressiveness when compared to classical neural networks.

In addition to this, several ways of applying quantum information processing techniques to finding approximate solutions of hard combinatorial optimization problems have been proposed. Some of the most widely used are adiabatic quantum computing and quantum annealing [7] and methods such as the quantum approximate optimization algorithm [16]. The possible fields of application are virtually endless and include finance [17], logistics [18], or transportation [19], to name but a few. Although no clear quantum advantage has been shown yet with these approaches, in recent years, a lot of research (both theoretical and in practice) has been conducted in order to determine their actual capabilities (see, e.g., [20]).

1.2 Models of Quantum Computing

As mentioned in the previous section, the main difference of quantum computing when compared to classical computing is the explicit use of properties such as superposition, entanglement, or interference. There are several ways to define models that take into account these properties in the computations, and, for instance, it is possible to define quantum Turing machines that can operate in superposition (see [21, 22]). However, the relevance of such a model is merely theoretical, and it seems almost impossible to implement in practice.

For this reason, in this chapter, we will roughly follow the classification of [23] and consider the three types of quantum computers described in the following subsections, as they are the ones that better describe the kind of quantum information processing devices currently available and those expected to be available in the short and medium term. Moreover, all of them are equally powerful (and also equivalent to the quantum Turing machine model) and represent the main different approaches existing nowadays to program quantum computers.

1.2.1 Gate-Based Quantum Computers

Gate-based quantum computers, also called digital quantum computers, follow the quantum circuit model of computation [24, 25]. This model somehow generalizes the classical model of Boolean circuits but uses quantum bits (or qubits) to store information. Then, unitary operations called quantum gates (in analogy to the logical gates used in classical circuits) can be applied to perform computations, and the results can be extracted by means of measurement of the qubit states.

This is, by far, the most widely used model of quantum computing, and most of the currently available quantum computers, such as those developed by companies like IBM, Google, Rigetti, Honeywell, or IonQ, are gate-based.

We will describe in detail all the elements of the quantum circuit model in Sect. 1.3.

1.2.2 Adiabatic Quantum Computers and Quantum Annealers

In contrast with the quantum circuit model, in which operations or gates are applied in discrete steps to modify the qubit states, adiabatic quantum computing [6] is based on the continuous evolution of a quantum state under the action of a Hamiltonian. That is, we encode some information on the state of a quantum system, act on it by some physical means (that depend on the actual implementation of the quantum computer), and, finally, measure the resulting state to obtain an output.

The main difference with the gate-based model is that, here, the Hamiltonian (that is usually time-dependent) acts continuously on the quantum state, while in digital quantum computers, we have a sequence of discrete actions that transform the quantum state step by step. If the Hamiltonian varies slowly enough (adiabaticity condition) and if we start in a ground state (i.e., state of minimum energy) of the initial Hamiltonian, it is guaranteed (see [6]) that the system remains always in a ground state. Thus, an adequate choice of the final Hamiltonian so that its ground state encodes a solution to a problem that we care about leads to a measurement that can be used to solve the problem, and, in fact, it can be shown that this model is equivalent to the quantum circuit one [26].

Ensuring adiabaticity (and even determining how slowly we should let the Hamiltonian change over time) is usually very difficult in practice. For this reason, quantum annealing has been proposed as a heuristic approach that follows the same scheme as quantum adiabatic computing but does not guarantee adiabaticity in general. This is the basis of commercial quantum computers such as the quantum annealers developed by D-Wave.

In Sect. 1.5, we will explain in more detail how to use this approach to solve combinatorial optimization problems.

1.2.3 Measurement-Based Quantum Computers

Measurement-based quantum computing (see [27]) is a way of doing computation starting from a highly entangled initial state and performing adaptive measurements on it. If the initial state is universal (such as is the case with, for instance, cluster states), then this model allows to perform any computation that is possible either with the quantum circuit model or with adiabatic quantum computing [28].

It is straightforward (see [29], e.g.) to simulate any quantum circuit in the measurement-based model and the other way around. In fact, the preparation of the initial highly entangled state can be done just by using one-qubit gates and two-qubit entangling gates, and the subsequent measurements can be implemented, again, with only one-qubit gates and measurements in the computational basis.

For this reason, in this chapter, we will focus mainly on gate-based quantum computers, and we refer the interested reader to [30, 31] for surveys of recent developments and proposals of practical implementations of the measurement-based model.

1.3 Elements of the Quantum Circuit Model

In this section, we will describe in detail the different elements of the quantum circuit model which, as mentioned in the previous section, are quantum bits (or qubits), quantum or unitary gates, and measurements. Then, we show how these elements can be combined in quantum circuits to conduct useful computations and highlight some differences of this model with classical computing approaches.

1.3.1 Qubits

A quantum bit or qubit is the smallest information unit in quantum computing. We can see a qubit as a mathematical abstraction that represents a quantum physical system that is capable of being in two different states that we usually denote by $|0\rangle$ and $|1\rangle$. In contrast with the situation in classical computing, where a bit can only take value 0 or value 1 at a given time, a qubit can be in what is called a superposition of the states $|0\rangle$ and $|1\rangle$, which in its most general form is

$$a|0\rangle + b|1\rangle$$

where a and b are complex numbers such that $|a|^2 + |b|^2 = 1$ (the reason for this normalization condition will become apparent in Sect. 1.3.2).

Thus, mathematically, we can represent the state of a qubit as a normalized vector in a vector complex space of dimension 2, and if we identify (as it is customary)

$|0\rangle$ with $\begin{pmatrix} 1 \\ 0 \end{pmatrix}$ and $|1\rangle$ with $\begin{pmatrix} 0 \\ 1 \end{pmatrix}$, we have that a state such as $a|0\rangle + b|1\rangle$ can be represented by the column vector

$$a\begin{pmatrix} 0 \\ 1 \end{pmatrix} + b\begin{pmatrix} 0 \\ 1 \end{pmatrix} = \begin{pmatrix} a \\ b \end{pmatrix}.$$

The reason for using this seemingly strange notation (known as Dirac notation) for column vectors is that, on the one hand, it can succinctly represent the kind of vectors in high-dimensional spaces that we will need in the following sections and, on the other, it simplifies some calculations. If we have a state $|\psi\rangle = a|0\rangle + b|1\rangle$, it is called *ket*, and its conjugate transpose, that is, the row vector $(a^* \ b^*)$, where a^* and b^* are the complex conjugates of a and b, is represented as $\langle\psi|$, and it is called a *bra*. Then, we can form the braket $\langle\psi|\psi\rangle$ which is just the inner product

$$(a^* \ b^*)\begin{pmatrix} a \\ b \end{pmatrix} = a^*a + b^*b = |a|^2 + |b|^2 = 1.$$

Another way of carrying out the same computing with Dirac notation is noting that $\langle\psi| = a^*\langle0| + b^*\langle1|$ and then

$$\langle\psi|\psi\rangle = (a^*\langle0|+b^*\langle1|)(a|0\rangle + b|1\rangle)$$
$$= a^*a\langle0|0\rangle + a^*b\langle0|1\rangle + b^*a\langle1|0\rangle + b^*b\langle1|1\rangle$$

which is equal to $a^*a + b^*b = |a|^2 + |b|^2 = 1$ because $\langle0|0\rangle = \langle1|1\rangle = 1$, and $\langle1|0\rangle = \langle1|0\rangle = 0$.

When we have more than one qubit, each of them can take values $|0\rangle$ and $|1\rangle$, and, thus, the whole system can be in states $|0\rangle \otimes |0\rangle \otimes \cdots \otimes |0\rangle$, $|0\rangle \otimes |0\rangle \otimes \cdots \otimes |1\rangle$, $\ldots$, $|1\rangle \otimes |1\rangle \otimes \cdots \otimes |1\rangle$ (which we call tensor products) and, in fact, in any superposition of them. We usually omit the tensor product symbol $\otimes$ and write, for instance, $|0\rangle|1\rangle|0\rangle$ or even $|010\rangle$ instead of $|0\rangle \otimes |1\rangle \otimes |0\rangle$. If the total number of qubits n that we are using is clear from context, we can further simplify the notation and write a decimal number instead of binary string so that, for instance, $|6\rangle = |0110\rangle$ when $n = 4$.

Then, the most general state of an n-qubit system is

$$\sum_{i=0}^{2^n-1} a_i|i\rangle$$

where each a_i is a complex number and it holds that $\sum_{i=0}^{2^n-1} |a_i|^2 = 1$. The a_i coefficients are usually called amplitudes.

We can identify each state $|i\rangle$ with the column vector of size 2^n which is all zeroes except in the i-th position where it is 1. For instance, when $n = 2$, we have

$$|0\rangle = \begin{pmatrix} 1 \\ 0 \\ 0 \\ 0 \end{pmatrix} \quad |1\rangle = \begin{pmatrix} 0 \\ 1 \\ 0 \\ 0 \end{pmatrix} \quad |2\rangle = \begin{pmatrix} 0 \\ 0 \\ 1 \\ 0 \end{pmatrix} \quad |3\rangle = \begin{pmatrix} 0 \\ 0 \\ 0 \\ 1 \end{pmatrix}.$$

The *bra* of an n-qubit *ket* is defined, again, as the conjugate transpose of the corresponding column vector, and, thus, we have the very useful identity

$$\langle i|j\rangle = \begin{cases} 1 \text{ if } i = j \\ 0 \text{ otherwise} \end{cases}$$

Notice that, then, $\{|i\rangle\}_{i=0}^{2^n-1}$ is an orthonormal basis of a 2^n-dimensional complex vector space that includes all possible n-qubit states. This exponential increase in the number of parameters needed to describe a general quantum state when we increase the number of qubits is one of the reasons behind the difficulty of simulating quantum computers with classical algorithms and behind the speed-ups that can be obtained with some quantum algorithms.

A very important notion when we are working with more than one qubit is that of entanglement. We say that an n-qubit state $|\psi\rangle$ is a *product state* if it can be written as a tensor product $|\psi_1\rangle|\psi_2\rangle$ where $|\psi_1\rangle$ and $|\psi_2\rangle$ are, respectively, n_1- and n_2-qubit states with $n_1, n_2 > 0$ and $n = n_1 + n_2$. If $|\psi\rangle$ is not a product state, then we say that it is *entangled*.

For instance, the state $\frac{1}{2}(|00\rangle - |01\rangle + |10\rangle - |11\rangle)$ is a product state because it can be written as

$$\frac{1}{\sqrt{2}}(|0\rangle + |1\rangle)\frac{1}{\sqrt{2}}(|0\rangle - |1\rangle)$$

while, as the reader can easily verify, the state $\frac{1}{\sqrt{2}}(|00\rangle + |11\rangle)$ is entangled, because it cannot be written as a product of any two one-qubit states. We will explore some uses of entanglement in Sect. 1.4.2.

1.3.2 Measurements

As we have seen in the previous section, the quantum state on an n-qubit system is implicitly defined by 2^n complex parameters that satisfy a normalization condition. However, according to the laws of quantum mechanics, there is no physical process that allows us to directly access those parameters (known as the wavefunction of the state). The only way in which we can obtain some information of this wavefunction is by performing a measurement that will alter the system state. In the quantum circuit model, measurements are usually performed in the computational basis and, thus, will probabilistically output results of the form i for some i between 0 and 2^n-1, leaving the system in state $|i\rangle$.

Let us explain this in more detail, by first focusing on the case in which $n = 1$, that is, when we only have one qubit. In the most general situation, we have a qubit in state $a|0\rangle + b|1\rangle$. If we measure it in the computational basis, we will obtain 0 with probability $|a|^2$ and 1 with probability $|b|^2$. In the first case, the state will change (we usually say that it collapses) to $|0\rangle$ and, in the second, to $|1\rangle$, so subsequent measures will output the same result with probability 1 (unless until we act on the state with a quantum gate, see next section).

The reason for imposing the normalization condition on a and b is now clear: since $|a|^2$ and $|b|^2$ are the probabilities of the two only possible measurement results, they need to add up to 1.

Similarly, when we have an n-qubit system in state $\sum_{i=0}^{2^n-1} a_i |i\rangle$ and we measure all of its qubits, we obtain i with probability $|a_i|^2$, and the state collapses to $|i\rangle$.

Alternatively, we can decide to measure just one qubit instead of all the n. Imagine, for instance, that we measure the j-th qubit. Then, we will obtain 0 with probability $\sum_{i\in A_0} |a_i|^2$ where A_0 is the set of integers $0 \le i \le 2^n - 1$ whose j-th bit is 0.

That is, we sum the probabilities of all the possible states which are compatible with measuring 0 on the j-th qubit. Moreover, the state will collapse to

$$\frac{\sum_{i\in A_0} a_i |i\rangle}{\sqrt{\sum_{i\in A_0} |a_i|^2}}$$

that is a normalized state. Analogously, the result of measuring the j-th qubit will be 1 with probability $\sum_{i\in A_1} |a_i|^2$ where A_1 is the set of integers $0 \le i \le 2^n - 1$ whose j-th bit is 1. In that case, the new state of the system will be

$$\frac{\sum_{i\in A_1} a_i |i\rangle}{\sqrt{\sum_{i\in A_1} |a_i|^2}}$$

For instance, if our state is $\frac{1}{\sqrt{3}} |001\rangle + \frac{1}{\sqrt{3}} |010\rangle + \frac{1}{\sqrt{3}} |100\rangle$, then the probability of measuring 0 on the middle qubit is $\frac{2}{3}$, in which case the state will collapse to $\frac{1}{\sqrt{2}} |001\rangle + \frac{1}{\sqrt{2}} |100\rangle$, and the probability of measuring 0 on the middle qubit is $\frac{1}{3}$, with resulting state $|010\rangle$.

Notice that the probability of obtaining i when measuring all the qubits of state $|\psi\rangle = \sum_{i=1}^{2^n-1} a_i |i\rangle$ can be expressed as

$$|a_i|^2 = |\langle i|\psi\rangle|^2 = \langle \psi|i\rangle\langle i|\psi\rangle.$$

Then, we can contemplate measuring the state in a different orthonormal basis $\{|\phi_i\rangle\}_{i=1}^{2^n-1}$, and the probability of obtaining the result associated with $|\phi_i\rangle$ (with subsequent collapse to $|\phi_i\rangle$) will be given by

$$\langle \psi|\phi_i\rangle\langle \phi_i|\psi\rangle = |\langle \phi_i|\psi\rangle|^2,$$

which is, indeed, the squared modulus of the coefficient of $|\phi_i\rangle$ when $|\psi\rangle$ is expressed in this new basis.

Thus, we can implement a measurement in a non-computational basis by first performing a change of basis (we will learn how in the following section) and then measuring in the computational basis.

1.3.3   Quantum Gates

So far, we have learned how an n-qubit system stores information in its state and how to access (part of) that information by performing measurements. In this section, we will introduce the kind of operations that we can use on qubits to modify their states and implement useful computations.

In general, transformations of (closed) quantum systems are solutions to the famous Schrödinger equation. Studying this equation and how to solve it is out of the scope of this chapter. But, for the purpose of learning how to program quantum computers, we only need to know that the evolution of a quantum system according to the laws of quantum mechanics is given by unitary transformations, that is, linear operations that preserve the state normalization condition. In the case of the quantum circuit model, operations are performed in discrete steps and on a finite number n of qubits. For this reason, these operations, known as quantum gates, can be identified with square matrices of size $2^n \times 2^n$. Since these matrices need to preserve the normalization constraint, they have to be unitary (cf. [1]), that is, their inverse must be their conjugate transpose.

Mathematically, a unitary matrix U is a square matrix of complex numbers such that

$$UU^\dagger = U^\dagger U = I,$$

where $U^\dagger$ is the matrix obtained by transposing U and conjugating all its entries and I is the identity matrix. Each quantum gate in the circuit model will be defined by a matrix of this kind, and we will devote the rest of this section to introducing the most important ones. Notice that these matrices can be interpreted as changes from one orthonormal basis to another.

Table 1.1 Most important one-qubit quantum gates

Gate name	Matrix	Symbol
I or identity	$\begin{pmatrix} 1 & 0 \\ 0 & 1 \end{pmatrix}$	$-\boxed{I}-$
H or Hadamard gate	$\begin{pmatrix} \dfrac{1}{\sqrt{2}} & \dfrac{1}{\sqrt{2}} \\ \dfrac{1}{\sqrt{2}} & -\dfrac{1}{\sqrt{2}} \end{pmatrix}$	$-\boxed{H}-$
X or NOT	$\begin{pmatrix} 0 & 1 \\ 1 & 0 \end{pmatrix}$	$-\boxed{X}-$
Y	$\begin{pmatrix} 0 & -i \\ i & 0 \end{pmatrix}$	$-\boxed{Y}-$
Z	$\begin{pmatrix} 1 & 0 \\ 0 & -1 \end{pmatrix}$	$-\boxed{Z}-$
S	$\begin{pmatrix} 1 & 0 \\ 0 & i \end{pmatrix}$	$-\boxed{S}-$
$S^\dagger$	$\begin{pmatrix} 1 & 0 \\ 0 & -i \end{pmatrix}$	$-\boxed{S^\dagger}-$
T	$\begin{pmatrix} 1 & 0 \\ 0 & e^{\frac{i\pi}{4}} \end{pmatrix}$	$-\boxed{T}-$
$T^\dagger$	$\begin{pmatrix} 1 & 0 \\ 0 & e^{\frac{-i\pi}{4}} \end{pmatrix}$	$-\boxed{T^\dagger}-$
Rotation of angle θ around the X axis	$\begin{pmatrix} \cos\dfrac{\theta}{2} & -i\sin\dfrac{\theta}{2} \\ -i\sin\dfrac{\theta}{2} & \cos\dfrac{\theta}{2} \end{pmatrix}$	$-\boxed{R_x(\theta)}-$
Rotation of angle θ around the Y axis	$\begin{pmatrix} \cos\dfrac{\theta}{2} & \sin\dfrac{\theta}{2} \\ \sin\dfrac{\theta}{2} & \cos\dfrac{\theta}{2} \end{pmatrix}$	$-\boxed{R_y(\theta)}-$
Rotation of angle θ around the Z axis	$\begin{pmatrix} e^{\frac{-i\theta}{2}} & 0 \\ 0 & e^{\frac{i\theta}{2}} \end{pmatrix}$	$-\boxed{R_z(\theta)}-$

We will start by analyzing the simplest case, that in which the system only has one qubit. Then, a one-qubit quantum gate will have an associated 2×2 unitary matrix that specifies how the gate acts on the basis vectors $|0\rangle$ and $|1\rangle$. One example is the X or NOT gate that takes $|0\rangle$ to $|1\rangle$ and $|1\rangle$ to $|0\rangle$ and thus is specified by the unitary matrix

$$\begin{pmatrix} 0 & 1 \\ 1 & 0 \end{pmatrix}.$$

For quick reference, the most common one-qubit quantum gates have been collected in Table 1.1. Notice that we have included the identity gate, which leaves the qubit state unchanged. Also, notice that there are three quantum gates, called rotations around the axes X, Y, and Z, that depend on a parameter θ. These gates are very important because it can be proved (see [1]) that any other one-qubit quantum gate can be decomposed as a product of these gates for an adequate choice of the angles. Also, the action of $R_x(\pi)$, $R_y(\pi)$, and $R_z(\pi)$ strongly resembles that of X, Y, and Z, respectively. In fact, the only difference is a complex number of modulus 1 that multiplies the whole state, called a global phase. But notice that this does not affect the measurement probabilities and, since all the gates are linear transformations, it does not change the subsequent application of quantum gates either. For this reason, states or gates that are equal up to a global phase can be considered equivalent.

Two-qubit gates can be identified with unitary matrices of size 4×4. Probably, the most important one is the *CNOT* or controlled-X gate which acts on basis states as follows:

$$|0\rangle\,|0\rangle \to |0\rangle\,|0\rangle \quad |0\rangle\,|1\rangle \to |0\rangle\,|1\rangle \quad |1\rangle\,|0\rangle \to |1\rangle\,|1\rangle \quad |1\rangle\,|1\rangle \to |1\rangle\,|0\rangle$$

Notice that when the first qubit is $|0\rangle$, the gate does not change the state of either qubit, but when the first qubit is $|1\rangle$, the second qubit is flipped (while the first one remains unchanged). That is, we are applying a *NOT* or X gate on the second qubit controlled by the value of the first one (hence, the controlled-X name). We can summarize this behavior for $x, y \in \{0, 1\}$ by

$$|x\rangle\,|y\rangle \to |x\rangle\,|x \oplus y\rangle$$

where $\oplus$ is the *XOR* operation on bits (or addition modulo 2).

This gate is collected, together with other important two-qubit gates, in Table 1.2, but notice that any qubit gate can be controlled to form a two-qubit gate as we have done with the X gate.

Another way of constructing two-qubit gates and, in fact, n-qubit gates for $n > 1$ is by means of the tensor product. If we have U and V, quantum gates acting on n_1 and n_2 qubits, respectively, then we can define the tensor product gate on $n = n_1 + n_2$ qubits $U \otimes V$, whose action is defined on basis states by

$$U \otimes V\,|x\rangle\,|y\rangle = U\,|x\rangle \otimes V\,|y\rangle$$

and extended linearly to all other states. We can simply think of $U \otimes V$ as U and V acting in parallel on two different sets of qubits.

The concepts we have introduced so far are already enough to construct any quantum circuit on an arbitrary number of qubits for it can be proved that, for instance, the one-qubit rotation gates together with the *CNOT* gate and the tensor product operation can be used to decompose any unitary gate of any size. In fact, actual computers usually implement that set of gates or a similarly reduced one and rely on decompositions to implement higher-order gates. However, we want to

Table 1.2 Some important two-qubit and three-qubit quantum gates

Gate name	Matrix	Symbol
CNOT or controlled-X	$\begin{pmatrix} 1 & 0 & 0 & 0 \\ 0 & 1 & 0 & 0 \\ 0 & 0 & 0 & 1 \\ 0 & 0 & 1 & 0 \end{pmatrix}$	
SWAP	$\begin{pmatrix} 1 & 0 & 0 & 0 \\ 0 & 0 & 1 & 0 \\ 0 & 1 & 0 & 0 \\ 0 & 0 & 0 & 1 \end{pmatrix}$	
Controlled-z	$\begin{pmatrix} 1 & 0 & 0 & 0 \\ 0 & 1 & 0 & 0 \\ 0 & 0 & 1 & 0 \\ 0 & 0 & 0 & -1 \end{pmatrix}$	or
Toffoli	$\begin{pmatrix} 1 & 0 & 0 & 0 & 0 & 0 & 0 & 0 \\ 0 & 1 & 0 & 0 & 0 & 0 & 0 & 0 \\ 0 & 0 & 1 & 0 & 0 & 0 & 0 & 0 \\ 0 & 0 & 0 & 1 & 0 & 0 & 0 & 0 \\ 0 & 0 & 0 & 0 & 1 & 0 & 0 & 0 \\ 0 & 0 & 0 & 0 & 0 & 1 & 0 & 0 \\ 0 & 0 & 0 & 0 & 0 & 0 & 0 & 1 \\ 0 & 0 & 0 & 0 & 0 & 0 & 1 & 0 \end{pmatrix}$	

introduce just one more gate because it will be important in our discussion on the relationship between classical and quantum computing of the following section.

The Toffoli gate or controlled-controlled-X gate is a three-qubit quantum gate whose action of basis states is given by

$$|x\rangle |y\rangle |z\rangle \rightarrow |x\rangle |y\rangle |z \oplus (x \wedge y)\rangle$$

where $x, y, z \in \{0, 1\}$ and $\wedge$ is the logical AND operation. The matrix of the Toffoli gate is presented in Table 1.2. As mentioned above, this gate can be decomposed in one- and two-qubit gates (see, for instance, [1]).

1.3.4 Quantum Circuits

We can now combine all the elements introduced in the previous sections to define what quantum circuits are and to explain how they can be used to perform computations.

A quantum circuit contains a fixed number n of qubits that we represent by n parallel lines or wires. Initially, the state of every qubit is $|0\rangle$ (and, hence, the initial

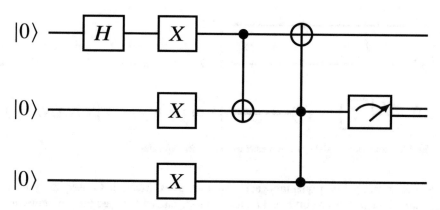

Fig. 1.1 Example of quantum circuit

state of the whole system is the product state $|0\rangle|0\rangle\ldots|0\rangle)$. Then, we sequentially apply quantum gates to one or more of the wires, and we can, eventually, also measure some of the qubits to obtain a result.

This is illustrated in Fig. 1.1, where we use the symbols from Tables 1.1 and 1.2 to represent the different gates and ⌐⌐⌐ to represent measurements. Gates are applied from left to right.

In the example circuit, we have three qubits initialized in state $|0\rangle$ so the whole system is in state $|000\rangle$. We start by applying an H gate to the top qubit (we should think of this as an application of the three qubit gates $H \otimes I \otimes I$) to obtain the state $\frac{1}{\sqrt{2}}(|000\rangle+|100\rangle)$. Then, we apply X gates to all the qubits to get $\frac{1}{\sqrt{2}}(|011\rangle+|111\rangle)$ which is transformed into $\frac{1}{\sqrt{2}}(|011\rangle+|101\rangle)$ after the application of the CNOT gate whose control is the top qubit and target is the middle qubit (again, think of this as the three-qubit gate CNOT$\otimes I$). Then, we apply a Toffoli gate whose target is the top qubit, and the state is transformed into $\frac{1}{\sqrt{2}}(|111\rangle+|101\rangle)$. Thus, when we measure the middle qubit, we obtain 0 with probability $\frac{1}{2}$ and 1 with probability $\frac{1}{2}$. After this measurement, the value of the second wire can be considered to be a classical bit, so it is customary to use a double wire instead of the single wire used for qubits.

There are several things that need to be taken into account when working with quantum circuits, especially because sometimes they are quite different from what we are used to with classical algorithms. Some of the most important ones are:

- *Probabilistic behavior.* In general, the result of the execution of a quantum circuit is not deterministic, and we will obtain different values with certain probabilities. Consequently, quantum algorithms usually involve a number of executions of one or more quantum circuits together with some statistical manipulation (such as considering the average or the mode) of the results obtained from the measurements.

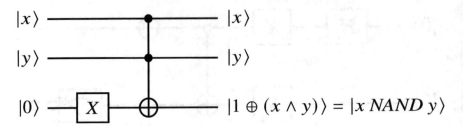

Fig. 1.2 Reversible NAND gate implemented with quantum gates

- *Reversibility.* Every quantum gate is a unitary transformation. Consequently, each quantum gate has an inverse, and its operation can be reversed (notice, however, that measurements cannot be reversed in general). This raises the question of whether quantum circuits can implement classical circuits composed of non-reversible gates such as AND, OR, NAND, or XOR. However, it is not difficult to show that the Toffoli and X gates, together with some ancillary qubits, can be used to simulate any classical Boolean gate. For instance, Fig. 1.2 shows how to implement a NAND gate. Notice that having the same number of inputs and outputs is a necessary condition for a gate to be reversible. Since NAND is universal for classical logic, it follows that we can simulate any classical circuit with quantum gates and little overhead in the number of qubits.

- *Hardness of classical simulation.* From what we have learned in the previous sections, it is easy to see that the execution of a quantum circuit is just a sequence of vector-matrix multiplications followed by sampling according to the squared moduli of the coefficients of the final vector. However, the size of the state vector is 2^n where n is the number of qubits, and we do not know of any classical method able to simulate general quantum circuits efficiently (i.e., in time polynomial in n). What is more, it is widely believed (see [32, 33], for instance) that such a method does not exist. Although we still do not understand completely what makes simulating quantum circuits hard for classical computers, there are several properties such as entanglement, superposition, and interference that seem to be the source of this difficulty.

- *Impossibility of copying quantum information.* Another particularity of quantum information processing is the impossibility of making independent copies of quantum states. In fact, it is not difficult to show (see [1]) that there is no quantum gate that takes as input $|\psi\rangle|0\rangle$, where $|\psi\rangle$ can be any arbitrary quantum state, and outputs $|\psi\rangle|\psi\rangle$. This fact, known as the no-cloning theorem, is a striking difference with classical algorithms and needs to be taken into account when programming quantum computers.

All these properties make quantum algorithms quite different from classical ones, so the design of useful quantum methods can become challenging in general. The next section is devoted to show some simple examples of how quantum circuits can be used to solve certain problems with an advantage over what is possible with just classical resources.

1.4   Some Quantum Algorithms

In this section, we describe some quantum algorithms to illustrate the concepts introduced in Sect. 1.3. Due to space constraints, we will focus only on some simple cases, and we refer the interested reader to quantum algorithms textbooks such as [1] or [34].

1.4.1   Generating Random Bits with a Quantum Circuit

Arguably, the simplest quantum circuit with a potential practical use is the one shown on Fig. 1.3. In fact, at least in theory, this circuit can be used to generate perfect random bits, something that is of vital relevance for cryptography, games, and simulation, among other applications. Indeed, the state after the application of the H gate is $\frac{1}{\sqrt{2}} (|0\rangle + |1\rangle)$ which, upon measurement, gives 0 with probability exactly $\frac{1}{2}$ and 1 with probability exactly $\frac{1}{2}$. Multiple, independent executions of the circuit would give a perfectly random binary string.

Alternatively, one can consider using several qubits in parallel, as in the circuit in Fig. 1.4. If we use n qubits, the state after the application of the H gates is

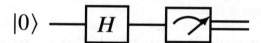

Fig. 1.3 Theoretical circuit to generate perfect random bits

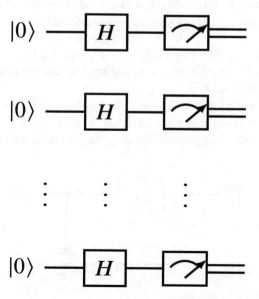

Fig. 1.4 Theoretical circuit to generate perfect random binary strings

$$\frac{1}{\sqrt{2}}(|0\rangle+|1\rangle)\ldots\frac{1}{\sqrt{2}}(|0\rangle+|1\rangle)=\frac{1}{\sqrt{2^n}}(|0\ldots0\rangle+|0\ldots1\rangle+\ldots+|1\ldots1\rangle)=\frac{1}{\sqrt{2^n}}\sum_{i=0}^{2^n-1}|i\rangle$$

which, when measured, gives a random uniform bitstring of length n. In fact, the application of a column of H gates to obtain an equal superposition of all n-bit strings is one the most widely used quantum computing primitives in the quantum circuit model, as it allows to apply an operation to all possible inputs of length n at the same time.

It must be noted, however, that the circuits presented in Figs. 1.3 and 1.4 are usually not enough to generate really uniform bitstrings in practice. As shown in [35], readout errors, noise, and imperfections in gate implementations present in current quantum computers can introduce biases in the outputs of these circuits.

1.4.2 Creating Entanglement

In the previous section, we have introduced quantum circuits to create superpositions. In this one, we show how to create entangled states, another powerful primitive that can be used in important protocols such as quantum teleportation [36], superdense coding [37], or the generation of certified random bits [38] and in quantum algorithms in general.

A simple way to create an entangled state is to use the circuit shown in Fig. 1.5. The final state obtained with the circuit is $\frac{1}{\sqrt{2}}(|00\rangle+|11\rangle)$ which is, indeed, entangled. This state is known as one of the Bell pairs or states, the other ones being $\frac{1}{\sqrt{2}}(|01\rangle+|10\rangle)$, $\frac{1}{\sqrt{2}}(|00\rangle+|11\rangle)$, and $\frac{1}{\sqrt{2}}(|01\rangle+|10\rangle)$. It is easy to see that these states can be obtained by adding an X gate, a Z gate, or both, to the top qubit of the circuit in Fig. 1.5.

The circuit in Fig. 1.6 also creates an entangled state, namely, $\frac{1}{2}(|00\rangle+|01\rangle+|10\rangle-|11\rangle)$. This kind of circuit and this type of entangled state (sometimes called a graph state) are widely used in measurement-based quantum computing (see Sect. 1.2.3).

Another widely used entangled state is the so-called GHZ state 7 given by $\frac{1}{\sqrt{2}}\times(|000\rangle+|111\rangle)$. It can be constructed with the circuit shown in Fig. 1.7, and it has applications, for instance, in protocols for the generation of certified random bits [38].

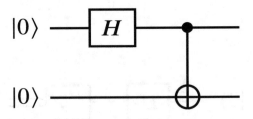

Fig. 1.5 Circuit to create a Bell pair

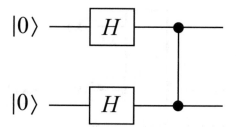

Fig. 1.6 Circuit to create a simple graph state

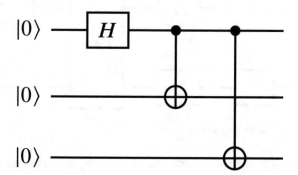

Fig. 1.7 Circuit to create a GHZ state

1.4.3 Deutsch's Algorithm

In the two previous sections, we have shown how to create superpositions and entangled states with quantum circuits. The third ingredient that is usually present in quantum algorithms is interference. Interference is produced when two quantum states are linearly combined so that the amplitudes of some basis states either reinforce (constructive interference) or cancel (destructive interference). For instance, if we apply an H gate to the state $|0\rangle$, we obtain $\frac{1}{\sqrt{2}}(|0\rangle+|1\rangle)$. If we now apply another H gate, by linearity, the resulting state is

$$H\frac{1}{\sqrt{2}}(|0\rangle+|1\rangle) = \frac{1}{\sqrt{2}}(H|0\rangle + H|1\rangle) = \frac{1}{\sqrt{2}}\left(\frac{1}{\sqrt{2}}(|0\rangle+|1\rangle) + \frac{1}{\sqrt{2}}(|0\rangle-|1\rangle)\right)$$

$$= \frac{1}{2}(|0\rangle+|1\rangle+|0\rangle-|1\rangle) = |0\rangle.$$

Notice that, in the last equality, the amplitudes of $|0\rangle$ have reinforced each other, while the amplitudes of $|1\rangle$ have canceled each other.

That the phenomenon of interference could be exploited to speed up some computations was first noticed by Deutsch. In [21], he proposed the following problem: we are given a black-box implementation of a certain Boolean function

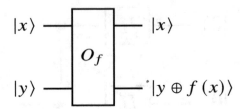

Fig. 1.8 Quantum oracle for a 1-bit Boolean function

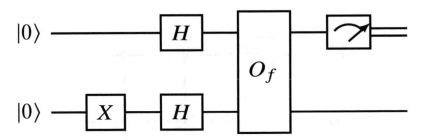

Fig. 1.9 Circuit for Deutsch's problem

f that takes one bit as input and returns one bit as its output, and we need to determine whether f is constant (it always returns the same output for any input) or balanced (it returns 0 for one input and 1 for the other). The goal is to minimize the number of queries to f.

In the classical setting, we need to query f on both 0 and 1, because the result of just one query is always compatible with the function being constant and with the function being balanced. However, there is a quantum algorithm that uses just one query to f and solves the problem exactly for each possible f. To be able to use the implementation of f in a quantum circuit, we need it to be reversible (cf. Sect. 1.3.4) so we assume that it is given by a black-box or oracle as the one presented in Fig. 1.8. Notice that the input is left unchanged in the top qubit and the output is added, modulo 2, to the bottom qubit. Thus, for input $|x\rangle|0\rangle$, we obtain $|x\rangle|f(x)\rangle$, successfully evaluating the function. The use of this type of oracle is common in many quantum algorithms.

We can solve Deutsch's problem with just one query to the oracle by using the circuit in Fig. 1.9. If f is constant, then we will measure 0. If f is balanced, the result will be 1. This can be easily proved because, just before the application of the oracle gate, we have

$$\frac{(|0\rangle+|1\rangle)(|0\rangle-|1\rangle)}{2}$$

which is the same as

$$\frac{|0\rangle(|0\rangle-|1\rangle)}{2} + \frac{|1\rangle(|0\rangle-|1\rangle)}{2}$$

When we apply the oracle, by linearity, we obtain

$$\frac{|0\rangle(|0\oplus f(0)\rangle-|1\oplus f(0)\rangle)}{2} + \frac{|1\rangle(|0\oplus f(1)\rangle-|1\oplus f(1)\rangle)}{2}$$

If $f(0) = 0$, we have

$$|0\oplus f(0)\rangle - |1\oplus f(0)\rangle = |0\rangle - |1\rangle$$

However, if $f(0) = 1$, we get

$$|0\oplus f(0)\rangle - |1\oplus f(0)\rangle = |0\oplus 1\rangle - |1\oplus 1\rangle = |1\rangle - |0\rangle = -(|0\rangle-|1\rangle)$$

For $f(1)$, the situation is the same, so the global state is

$$\frac{(-1)^{f(0)}|0\rangle(|0\rangle-|1\rangle)}{2} + \frac{(-1)^{f(1)}|1\rangle(|0\rangle-|1\rangle)}{2}$$

Because global phases are irrelevant (cf. Sect. 1.3.3), we can multiply the whole state by $(-1)^{f(0)}$ to get

$$\frac{|0\rangle(|0\rangle-|1\rangle)}{2} + \frac{(-1)^{f(0)+f(1)}|1\rangle(|0\rangle-|1\rangle)}{2}$$

So if $f(0) = f(1)$, we will have

$$\frac{|0\rangle(|0\rangle-|1\rangle)}{2} - \frac{|1\rangle(|0\rangle-|1\rangle)}{2} = \frac{(|0\rangle+|1\rangle)(|0\rangle-|1\rangle)}{2}$$

and when we apply the last H and measure, we obtain 0. But if $f(0) \neq f(1)$, the state is

$$\frac{|0\rangle(|0\rangle-|1\rangle)}{2} - \frac{|1\rangle(|0\rangle-|1\rangle)}{2} = \frac{(|0\rangle-|1\rangle)(|0\rangle-|1\rangle)}{2}$$

and then, we obtain 1. Notice that the application of the final H gate is creating the (constructive or destructive) interference that we need to obtain the correct result, exactly in the same way that we showed at the beginning of this section.

1.4.4   Advanced Algorithms

Space constraints prevent us from introducing more sophisticated algorithms in detail. We refer the interested reader to [1, 34]. However, in this section, we will briefly list and describe some quantum algorithms which are more advanced than the ones presented so far.

Deutsch-Jozsa's algorithm   Deutsch's problem can be generalized to n-bit Boolean functions. We need to restrict the possible functions f to those that are either constant or balanced (this is what we call a *promise problem*), and, again, we are asked to determine to which of the two groups f belongs. Any deterministic classical algorithm needs $2^{n-1} - 1$ queries to the oracle in the worst case, but, again, there is a quantum algorithm that solves the problem with just one query [39].

Grover's algorithm   Suppose we are given an unsorted list of N elements and we want to find one that satisfies a certain condition. In the classical case, we need to access the list a number of times that is $O(N)$. Grover's algorithm [3] can find the element with high probability with just $O(\sqrt{N})$ queries to the list.

Shor's algorithm   Finding non-trivial factors of large integers is widely considered to be hard with classical algorithms, and, in fact, this assumption supports the security of several well-known cryptographic schemes such as RSA [40]. Shor's algorithm [2] cleverly uses the so-called quantum Fourier transform (see [1]) to factor integers in time that is polynomial in the length of the binary expansion of the number.

Variational algorithms   In recent years, variational circuits (i.e., quantum circuits that use gates that depend on certain parameters as, for instance, the rotation gates introduced in Sect. 1.3.3) have been used to define a number of quantum algorithms that can address several different types of problems. For instance, the variational quantum eigensolver [12] can be used to study properties of physical and chemical systems, and the quantum approximate optimization algorithm [16] can be applied to obtain approximate solutions of combinatorial optimization problems. Variational circuits are also used as the basis of quantum machine learning methods such as quantum neural networks [14, 15].

1.5   Quantum Adiabatic Computing and Quantum Annealing

Quantum adiabatic computing is a computational model that uses quantum properties in a way different from the quantum circuit model (although it can be shown that both are equivalent [26]). Instead of applying quantum gates at discrete steps, the quantum state of the system at time t, denoted $|\psi(t)\rangle$, evolves according to the application of external forces given by a time-dependent Hamiltonian, i.e., a linear operator $H(t)$ such that $H(t)^\dagger = H(t)$ (matrices satisfying this property are called Hermitian).

Usually, the initial state $|\psi(0)\rangle$ is the ground state of a simple Hamiltonian $H(0) = H_0$, that is, a state such that $\langle\psi(0)|H_0|\psi(0)\rangle$ is minimum among all values $\langle\psi|H_0|\psi\rangle$. Notice that, because $H_0^\dagger = H_0$, it holds that

$$(\langle\psi|H_0|\rangle\psi)^* = \left\langle\psi|H_0^\dagger|\psi\right\rangle = \langle\psi|H_0|\psi\rangle$$

which is then a real value, so it makes sense to compare these quantities.

In addition, the final Hamiltonian at time T, $H(T) = H_f$, is set in a way that its ground state has some useful property (for instance, encodes a solution to a certain combinatorial problem). If the evolution from H_0 to H_f is slow enough, the adiabatic theorem guarantees (see [6]) that then $|\psi(T)\rangle$ is the ground state of H_f and, upon measurement, we can obtain information that can be used to solve our problem.

As an example, consider the well-known maximum cut or Max-Cut problem: we are given a graph $G = (V, E)$, and we need to obtain a partition of the vertex set $V = \{1,\ldots,n\}$ into two disjoint sets V_1 and V_2 such that the number of edges $(i,j) \in E$ such that i and j are one in V_1 and the other in V_2 is the maximum possible. This problem is known to be NP-hard [41].

To transform Max-Cut into the problem of finding the ground state of a Hamiltonian, we encode a partition V_1, V_2 of V as a basis state $|x\rangle$ with $x \in \{0, 1\}^n$ such that the i-th bit of x is 0 if $i \in V_1$ and 1 if $i \in V_2$. Then, we define the Hamiltonian

$$H_f = \sum_{(i,j)\in E} Z_i Z_j$$

where $Z_i Z_j$ is the tensor product of matrices $Z = \begin{pmatrix} 1 & 0 \\ 0 & -1 \end{pmatrix}$ in positions i and j and the identity in all other positions. Then, $\langle x|Z_iZ_j|x\rangle$ is 1 if $x_i = x_j$ and -1 if $x_i \neq x_j$. Consequently, $\langle x|H_f|x\rangle$ is minimized exactly when $|x\rangle$ encodes a partition that gives a maximum cut in the graph.

We can use this reduction to solve the Max-Cut problem via quantum adiabatic computing. We use the H_f defined above, we set H_i to a Hamiltonian whose ground state $|\psi_0\rangle$ we can easily prepare, and we evolve the system according to

$$H(t) = \left(1 - \frac{t}{T}\right)H_i + \frac{t}{T}H_f$$

where T is big enough that adiabaticity is ensured.

In practice, however, T can be prohibitively big (in fact, even determining T can be extremely difficult). For this reason, a heuristic version of quantum adiabatic computing called quantum annealing is used instead. With this approach, T is not necessarily set so that the evolution is ensured to be adiabatic, but the process is repeated a number of times, and the best solution is kept. This is the method used in the quantum computers developed by Canadian company D-Wave in which H_f is of the form

$$H_f = \sum_{i<j} J_{i,j} Z_i Z_j + \sum_i h_i Z_i$$

where the coefficients $J_{i,j}$ and h_i are tunable real numbers. This is called an Ising Hamiltonian, and it is easy to see that finding its ground state is *NP*-hard. In fact, if we set $J_{i,j} = 1$ for $(i,j) \in E$, $J_{i,j} = 0$ for $(i,j) \notin E$ and $h_i = 0$ for all i, we recover the Max-Cut problem, which we know is *NP*-hard.

These quantum annealers can, then, be used to obtain approximate solutions to combinatorial optimization problems, and the process of programming them reduces to finding a set of coefficients $J_{i,j}$ and h_i such that H_f adequately encodes our problem (see [42] for some recipes on how to do this for a big collection of common optimization problems).

1.6   Conclusions

In this chapter, we have introduced the paradigm of quantum computing with a special focus on the model of quantum circuits. We have explained the main elements of the model, namely, qubits, quantum gates, and measurements, and how to build quantum circuits with them. Then, we have shown some simple examples of quantum algorithms in which properties such as superposition, entanglement, and interference offer some advantage over what is possible with just classical resources. Finally, we have briefly introduced quantum adiabatic computing and quantum annealing and shown how these models can be used to obtain approximate solutions to hard combinatorial problems.

Acknowledgments This work was supported in part by the Spanish Ministry of Science and Innovation under grant PID2020-119082RB-C22.

References

1. Nielsen MA, Chuang IL (2011) Quantum computation and quantum information, 10th Anniversary edn. Cambridge University Press
2. Shor P (1994) Algorithms for quantum computation: discrete logarithms and factoring. In: Proceedings of FOCS, pp 124–134
3. Grover LK (1996) A fast quantum mechanical algorithm for database search. In: Proceedings of the Twenty-eighth Annual ACM Symposium on Theory of Computing, STOC '96. ACM, New York, NY, pp 212–219
4. IBM Quantum (2021) https://quantum-computing.ibm.com/

5. Combarro EF, Vallecorsa S, Rodríguez-Muñiz LJ, Aguilar-González Á, Ranilla J, Di Meglio A (2021) A report on teaching a series of online lectures on quantum computing from CERN. J Supercomputing:1–31
6. Farhi E, Goldstone J, Gutmann S, Lapan J, Lundgren A, Preda D (2001) A quantum adiabatic evolution algorithm applied to random instances of an NP-Complete problem. Science 292(5516):472–475
7. McGeoch CC (2014) Adiabatic Quantum Computation and Quantum Annealing. Synthesis Lectures on Quantum Computing. Morgan & Claypool Publishers
8. Feynman R (1982) Simulating physics with computers. Int J Theoretical Phys 21(6):467–488
9. Abrams DS, Lloyd S (1999) Quantum algorithm providing exponential speed increase for finding eigenvalues and eigenvectors. Phys Rev Lett 83(24):5162
10. Aspuru-Guzik A, Dutoi AD, Love PJ, Head-Gordon M (2005) Simulated quantum computation of molecular energies. Science 309(5741):1704–1707
11. Kandala A, Mezzacapo A, Temme K, Takita M, Brink M, Chow JM, Gambetta JM (2017) Hardware-efficient variational quantum eigensolver for small molecules and quantum magnets. Nature 549(7671):242–246
12. Peruzzo A, McClean J, Shadbolt P, Yung MH, Zhou XQ, Love PJ, Aspuru-Guzik A, O'brien, J.L. (2014) A variational eigenvalue solver on a photonic quantum processor. Nat Commun 5(1):1–7
13. Wittek P (2014) Quantum machine learning: what quantum computing means to data mining. Academic Press
14. Schuld M (2018) Supervised learning with quantum computers. Springer
15. Abbas A, Sutter D, Zoufal CZ, Lucchi A, Figalli AF, Woerner S (2021) The power of quantum neural networks. Nat Computational Sci 1:403–409
16. Farhi E, Goldstone J, Gutmann S (2014) A quantum approximate optimization algorithm. arXiv preprint arXiv:1411.4028
17. Orús R, Mugel S, Lizaso E (2019) Quantum computing for finance: overview and prospects. Rev Phys 4:100028. https://doi.org/10.1016/j.revip.2019.100028. https://www.sciencedirect.com/science/article/pii/S2405428318300571
18. Ding Y, Chen X, Lamata L, Solano E, Sanz M (2021) Implementation of a hybrid classical-quantum annealing algorithm for logistic network design. SN Comput Sci 2(2):1–9
19. Yarkoni S, Neukart F, Tagle EMG, Magiera N, Mehta B, Hire K, Narkhede S, Hofmann M (2020) Quantum shuttle: traffic navigation with quantum computing. In: Proceedings of the 1st ACM SIGSOFT International Workshop on Architectures and Paradigms for Engineering Quantum Software, pp 22–30
20. Hauke P, Katzgraber HG, Lechner W, Nishimori H, Oliver WD (2020) Perspectives of quantum annealing: methods and implementations. Rep Progr Phys 83(5):054401
21. Deutsch D (1985) Quantum theory, the Church-Turing principle and the universal quantum computer. Proc R Soc Lond A 400:97–117
22. Fortnow L (2003) One complexity theorist's view of quantum computing. Theoretical Comput Sci 292(3):597–610
23. Ding Y, Chong FT (2020) Quantum computer systems: research for noisy intermediate-scale quantum computers. Synthesis Lectures on Computer Architecture 15(2):1–227
24. Deutsch D (1989) Quantum computational networks. Proc R Soc Lond Ser A Math Phys Sci 425(1868):73–90. http://www.jstor.org/stable/2398494
25. Chi-Chih Yao A (1993) Quantum circuit complexity. In: Proceedings of 1993 IEEE 34th Annual Foundations of Computer Science, pp 352–361. https://doi.org/10.1109/SFCS.1993.366852
26. Aharonov D, van Dam W, Kempe J, Landau Z, Loyd S, Regev O (2004) Adiabatic quantum computation is equivalent to standard quantum computation. 45:42–51
27. Raussendorf R, Briegel HJ (2001) A one-way quantum computer. Phys Rev Lett 86(22):5188
28. Raussendorf R, Browne DE, Briegel HJ (2003) Measurement-based quantum computation on cluster states. Phys Rev A 68(2):022312

29. Childs AM, Leung DW, Nielsen MA (2005) Unified derivations of measurement-based schemes for quantum computation. Phys Rev A 71. https://doi.org/10.1103/PhysRevA.71.032318. http://arxiv.org/abs/quant-ph/0404132v2
30. Wei TC (2018) Quantum spin models for measurement-based quantum computation. Adv Phys X 3(1):1461026. https://doi.org/10.1080/23746149.2018.1461026
31. Wei TC (2021) Measurement-based quantum computation. https://doi.org/10.1093/acrefore/9780190871994.013.31. https://oxfordre.com/physics/view/10.1093/acrefore/9780190871994.001.0001/acrefore-9780190871994-e-31
32. Aaronson S (2010) BQP and the polynomial hierarchy. In: Proceedings of the Forty-Second ACM Symposium on Theory of Computing. pp 141–150
33. Arute F, Arya K, Babbush R, Bacon D, Bardin JC, Barends R, Biswas R, Boixo S, Brandao FG, Buell DA et al (2019) Quantum supremacy using a programmable superconducting processor. Nature 574(7779):505–510
34. Yanofsky NS, Mannucci MA (2008) Quantum computing for computer scientists. Cambridge University Press
35. Combarro EF, Carminati F, Vallecorsa S, Ranilla J, Rúa IF (2021) On protocols for increasing the uniformity of random bits generated with noisy quantum computers. J Supercomput 77 (8):8063–8081
36. Bennett CH, Brassard G, Crépeau C, Jozsa R, Peres A, Wootters WK (1993) Teleporting an unknown quantum state via dual classical and Einstein-Podolsky-Rosen channels. Phys Rev Lett 70:1895–1899. https://doi.org/10.1103/PhysRevLett.70.1895. https://link.aps.org/doi/10.1103/PhysRevLett.70.1895
37. Bennett CH, Wiesner SJ (1992) Communication via one- and two-particle operators on Einstein-Podolsky-Rosen states. Phys Rev Lett 69:2881–2884. https://doi.org/10.1103/PhysRevLett.69.2881. https://link.aps.org/doi/10.1103/PhysRevLett.69.2881
38. Acín A, Masanes L (2016) Certified randomness in quantum physics. Nature 540(7632):213–219
39. Deutsch D, Jozsa R (1992) Rapid solution of problems by quantum computation. Proc R Soc Lond A Math Phys Eng Sci 439(1907):553–558
40. Rivest RL, Shamir A, Adleman L (1978) A method for obtaining digital signatures and public-key cryptosystems. Commun ACM 21(2):120–126
41. Karp RM (1972) Reducibility among combinatorial problems. In: Complexity of Computer Computations. Springer, pp 85–103
42. Lucas A (2014) Ising formulations of many NP problems. Front Phys 2:5

Chapter 2
Quantum Software Engineering Landscape and Challenges

Mario Piattini and Juan Manuel Murillo

2.1 Introduction

The seed for the first quantum revolution is dated at the beginning of the last century, when many exceptional scientists (Planck, Einstein, Bohr, Schrödinger, Born, Dirac, De Broglie, Heisenberg, Pauli, etc.) settled the basis of a new physic theory: quantum mechanics. Quantum mechanics is the field of physics which describes the behavior of nature at subatomic levels (i.e., photons, electrons, etc.), for which classic mechanics cannot provide satisfactory explanations [1].

In 1982, Nobel laureate Richard Feynman in a visionary talk [2] asked: What kind of computer are we going to use to simulate physics? Also, in the 1980s, Paul Benioff [3] and Yuri Manin [4] laid the theoretical foundations of quantum computing, and David Deutsch [5] proposed the "universal quantum computer." So, the second quantum revolution was launched, in which the idea for a quantum computer was born, and quantum computer science started.

Over the last three decades, our understanding of "quantum computers" has expanded dramatically, as the efforts to realize such an exotic computer have made steady but remarkable progress [6]. Quantum computers will provide faster computing speed (key to provide high value in different important applications) through the usage of various "counterintuitive" principles of quantum mechanics such as superposition and entanglement, explained in the previous chapter. In fact,

M. Piattini (✉)
Alarcos Research Group, Institute of Technologies and Information Systems, University of Castilla-La Mancha (UCLM), Ciudad Real, Spain
e-mail: Mario.Piattini@uclm.es

J. M. Murillo
University of Extremadura, Cáceres, Spain
e-mail: juanmamu@unex.es

quantum computing is gaining a lot of interest since there are countless, cutting-edge applications in multiple areas [7]:

- Privacy and cryptography: certification of randomness and authentication
- Artificial intelligence: quantum machine learning, quantum deep learning, etc.
- Supply chain and logistics: optimization problems in procurement, production and distribution, vehicle routing optimization, etc.
- Chemistry: simulations of complex molecules, discovery of new materials, advanced molecular design, etc.
- Economics and financial services: portfolio risk optimization and fraud detection, actual randomness for financial models, simulations, scenario analysis, etc.
- Energy and agriculture: production of ammonia, better distribution of resources, asset degradation modeling, etc.
- Medicine and health: protein folding and drug discovery, disease detection, non-invasive and high-precision surgeries, targeted drug design, tailored medicine, improvement of the quality of life, prediction of therapeutic prescriptions, etc.
- Defense and national security programs

The achievement of such applications requires the use of a completely different kind of computers and algorithms, which have the potential to solve tasks that we do not even dare dream of today. And of course, as the Quantum Software Manifesto[1] underlines, "it is urgent that we step up our efforts in quantum software." Several quantum programming languages, software development kits, and platforms are already available for coding these new algorithms (see Chap. 12 "Quantum Software Tools Overview"). But all the existing and even planned quantum software is not enough.

In fact, it is necessary a new "quantum software engineering" (QSE). Clark and Stepney [8] in the "Grand Challenge for Computing Research" about QSE urge for "the development of a full discipline of Quantum Software Engineering, ready to exploit the full potential of commercial quantum computer hardware once it arrives.... This Challenge is to build the corresponding languages, tools and techniques for quantum software engineering," emphasizing the need to raise the level of thinking about quantum programs.

Quantum software need to be developed in an appropriate way, i.e., following software engineering best practices, adapting existing techniques, or creating new ones, with efficient software engineering environments. Fortunately, the development that this discipline has shown since the 1960s allows us to know which are the most appropriate ways of improvement. It is now up to software engineers, both in research and industry, to apply them.

The next section summarizes the software engineering evolution and how the quantum computing fits in it. Section 2.3 presents the *Talavera Manifesto for Quantum Software Engineering and Programming* that has been also endorsed by

---

[1] https://www.qusoft.org/quantum-software-manifesto/

various researchers and practitioners of different countries. Section 2.4 discusses software engineering techniques. Section 2.5 presents the challenges posed by software engineering environments, and Sect. 2.6 addresses the lack of standardization. In Sect. 2.7, the presence of quantum computing and QSE in current education curricula is discussed. Section 2.8 claims for the need for collaboration between industry and academy to maximize the impact of results. Finally, Sect. 2.9 summarizes the present chapter.

2.2 Software Engineering Evolution

Boehm [9] perfectly summarizes the evolution of software engineering as a process of continuous thesis, antithesis, and synthesis. The evolution of software engineering is "bottom-up" since it has been developed after computer science foundations. In 1931, Kurt Gödel [10] laid the foundation of computer science with his incompleteness theorem, and in 1936, Alan Turing and Alonzo Church [11] introduced the formalization of an algorithm, with limits on what can be computed (the Church-Turing thesis). In the late 1930s, the hardware base was developed, remember the first computers (such as Zuse's Z1), and in the 1940s, computers (e.g., IBM's Mark I) built with tubes and capacitors were built. These advances were complemented in the 1950s with the transistor-based computer and in the 1960s with the emergence of computers with integrated circuit boards.

With hardware, machine languages came up, and the first assembly programming languages come into view later. Maybe this is the closest point to the current development of QSE technologies. Likening those machine languages with the current circuit design for a quantum program and saving the differences with current programming environments, it could be said that the effort required of the programmer is of the same order of magnitude.

In the 1950s (e.g., FORTRAN) and 1960s (COBOL) the first high-level programming languages. With these languages arose the need of programming techniques; the most influential technique was the structured programming proposed by Dijkstra in 1968 [12, 13], as well as the techniques proposed by Warnier [14] and Jackson [15].

Based on those concepts, in the 1970s, structured design techniques were proposed by Myers, Yourdon, and Constantine, E/R model was defined by Chen [16], and, lately, Gane and Sarson [17], DeMarco, and Weinberg [18] came up with structured analysis. In the 1980s, comprehensive methodologies (Merise, SSADM, Information Engineering, etc.) were suggested. This is considered by Booch [19, 20], the first golden age of software engineering.

The same pattern was followed by object-oriented technologies. Different object-oriented programming languages appeared: in the 1960s (Simula), in the 1970s (Smalltalk), and in the 1980s (C++, Objective-C, Eiffel). In the 1990s, object-oriented is eventually considered "the" approach for developing information systems. Nearly 100 methodologies were proposed, first for object-oriented design and later for object-oriented analysis. The most important methodologies (those proposed by Booch, Rumbaugh, and Jacobson) were integrated in UML (Unified Modeling Language) [21] and UP (Unified Process). Booch [19, 20] named this the "second golden age of software engineering."

Also, in the 2000s, the need of an empirical and evidence-based software engineering was recognized, and several of the proposed techniques and methods were subjected to validation. In the past decade (2010s), DevOps and several associated techniques have been producing another golden age [19, 20].

At the same time, service-oriented computing [22] emerged as a paradigm that utilizes services as the fundamental elements for developing software. It proposes the implementation of complex software solutions through the use of a set of services that are composed and choreographed. Therefore, services can be invoked from another piece of code (potentially another service) agnostically with respect to the place, technology, or architecture of the invoked service. The services can thus be maintained, evolved, replaced, and reused independently without affecting the software that invokes them.

The success of service-oriented computing has been possible, thanks to the development of cloud computing. Current quantum computers, which are still a very expensive hardware to build and operate, are being offered following this model. In its current form, most quantum computers can be accessed through the cloud.

All signs point to that quantum computing will be the main driver for a new software engineering golden age during the present decade of the 2020s [23]. The question might be raised as to how far software engineering methods must be renewed to address the quantum era. Software engineering has built up a broad knowledge base and has learned many lessons that should be applied to the production of quantum software. The new quantum software engineering field needs to be considered as the application or adaptation of the well-known methods, techniques, and practices of software engineering. Some techniques can be used just as they are in classical computing. At the same time, however, new methods and techniques will be defined specifically for quantum software production. Think, for example, of the need to include in the software processes, together with business experts, scientists capable of providing the quantum formulation of problems. In formal methods, for example, model checking, the possibility of generating a target result and obtaining the trace that makes it possible, thanks to the reversible nature of quantum architectures instead of trying to demonstrate properties, many of them undecidable. Or thinking about modeling techniques, the need for new abstractions to model sequence diagrams in an architecture that no longer corresponds to the von Neumann model. The new needs are even more evident if one thinks about the treatment of concepts that are only present in quantum computing such as qubits superposition, entanglement, or collapse.

2.3 The Talavera Manifesto

In the "Talavera Manifesto," several principles and commitments for QSE have been gathered [24]. This Manifesto was developed because of the discussion and presentation of different viewpoints from academics and practitioners who joined in the 1st International Workshop on the Quantum Software Engineering and Programming (QANSWER'20). The nine principles referring to QSE are:

- QSE must be agnostic with respect to technologies and programming languages; it must use methods and processes that are understandable, controllable, and repeatable by broad communities.
- QSE must accept the coexistence of classical and quantum computing and promote the use of reengineering techniques that allow the integration of new quantum algorithms with existing classical information systems.
- QSE must enable the management of quantum software development projects, producing quantum software that satisfies business objectives and requirements, adequately meeting quality, time, and cost constraints. It will be necessary to provide methods for effort estimation in quantum software development.
- QSE deals with the evolution of quantum software, which must be maintained and evolved from its conception to its retirement; evolution must be addressed throughout the entire quantum software lifecycle.
- QSE must try to obtain quantum programs with zero defects, defining the testing techniques that allow to detect most of the defects before the program is released.
- QSE must be concerned with the quality of quantum software, both process and product management, developing new development processes/methodologies and new metrics for quantum programs.
- QSE must favor the reuse of quantum software, helping teams to share, index, and find quantum software that can be reused, creating reference libraries and application demonstrations.
- QSE should be aware of the need for security and privacy by design and should be applied from the early stages of quantum software development.
- QSE encompasses software governance and management. It must establish the processes, organizational structures, principles, policies, ethics, skills, competencies, etc. as well as the services, infrastructure, and applications associated with quantum software that must be provided by organizations.

This Manifesto also includes a call to action to all the stakeholders: software practitioners, researchers, educators, government and funding bodies, quantum technology vendors, professional associations, customers, and users.

2.4   Software Engineering Techniques

Quantum computing will affect all the areas of software engineering. As a matter of fact, most of the 14 areas in SWEBOK (Software Engineering Body of Knowledge) should be updated to include quantum issues.

It is necessary to reassess the software engineering techniques that are used today and to adapt them and create such new ones as are necessary to improve productivity and assure quality in quantum software development. In so doing, attention should be paid to all processes through the whole quantum software lifecycle [25] from "quantum-classical splitting," the first phase of the quantum software lifecycle in which "it is decided which parts of the problem to solve on a quantum computer and which on a classical computer depending on the requirements of the problem description," to the "result analysis" that can be done automatically or by the user, who has to decide whether an additional iteration is required to improve the results of the quantum software application or not. In fact, today's "NISQ" (noisy intermediate-scale quantum) computers are limited, and quantum computations are disturbed by errors [26].

Zhao [27] provides a comprehensive survey of the current state of the art in the field in the different phases of the quantum software lifecycle. Different researchers are already working on areas such as quantum software requirements analysis, quantum software design, quantum software implementation, quantum software testing, quantum software maintenance, or quantum software reuse. All these works reveal the need for a strong research effort on quantum software engineering techniques. As we already mentioned, the specific characteristics of quantum software, namely, quantum superposition and entanglement, but also the uncertainty associated with quantum measurements make necessary a new set of abstraction for quantum software.

As previously discussed regarding the evolution of software engineering in Sect. 2.2, every time new abstractions are introduced in software, they are accompanied by new software engineering techniques. The emergence of quantum computing and its associated abstractions will require a renovation of the existing software engineering techniques.

2.5   Software Engineering Environments

At the current state of quantum computing, there are two competing computational models for the development of quantum software: quantum circuit-based software and quantum annealing solutions. Since there is no dominant model yet and both approaches are completely different, software engineering environments should focus on one of them, assuming the risk that it will be deprecated later, or try to accommodate for both alternatives, duplicating the effort needed to provide a relevant environment.

We have also to be aware of the impact of quantum computing platforms on quality attributes and software development activities [28]:

1. The lower level of the programming abstractions increases code complexity impacting in maintainability, testability, reliability, and availability. Different abstractions are used for quantum circuits and quantum annealing, which would further increase complexity if both approaches were integrated.
2. Platform heterogeneity deteriorates software cohesion, affecting maintainability, reliability, robustness, reusability, and the manageability and testability of the system. Cohesion is deteriorated even further if both quantum computational models are to be supported.
3. Remote software development and deployment make programming, testing, and debugging quantum programs slower, affecting maintainability and testability.
4. The dependency on the known quantum algorithms affects the ability to perform enhancement and corrective maintenance and testability and interoperability (with classical software). Taking into account that algorithms for circuit-based and annealing machines are radically different, it complicates this problem even further to support both approaches.
5. The limited portability of quantum software affects availability, interoperability, maintainability, and scalability.
6. The lack of native quantum operating system decreases performance, manageability, reliability, scalability, and security.
7. The fundamentally different programming model increases code complexity, affecting maintainability, interoperability, security, and testability.

It is essential to have quantum software development environments not only oriented to conventional scientists (physicists, mathematicians, etc.) working in the field of quantum computing but that also satisfy the needs of software engineers. In fact, supporting quantum algorithm creation and design is very important, but also offering tools to design, program, test, and maintain quantum software programs is essential. Following the principles of the Talavera Manifesto [24], a quantum software development environment should:

- Support agnostic quantum software development. Ideally, quantum software (e.g., circuits, flows, etc.) should be visually designed, and the environment would oversee translating transparently to the software designer the quantum software definition in quantum software code, optimized for the specific target platform (quantum computer, quantum simulator, or both). This characteristic allows programmers to be independent of the specific details of each platform and language, obviating the need to understand the complexities of the different environments and specific quantum providers.
- Enable the integration of quantum/classical information systems, providing tools, services, and processes for the development of hybrid information systems and enabling classic development teams to manage the lifecycle of hybrid software projects. In fact, quantum computing will not replace classical computing, so it is necessary to integrate them using the appropriate service architectures.

- Allow developers to create and manage agnostic quantum services that can be composed with classical services for the creation of complex hybrid solutions and that brings all the advantages of service-oriented computing to the development of quantum software.
- Manage the lifecycle automatically, from the creation of the quantum algorithm through its development, testing, and implementation to its deployment and reuse.
- Handle and support overall modernization and reengineering efforts for quantum software [29], migrating from classical to quantum applications, based on extensions of standards such as KDM (Knowledge Discovery Metamodel) [30]. It should also transform or add new business operations supported by quantum software that will be integrated into the target hybrid systems.
- Provide techniques for quantum software testing, dealing with the inherent constraints of quantum computing to check intermediate states of quantum programs under execution, as well as the diversity of quantum platforms.
- Define layered quality models for quantum software, along with a set of metrics and knowledge to control quality, from circuit-based representation to the domain representation of a quantum program.
- Support quantum assets reuse, using a standardized, unified schema whatever the execution target and providing utilities to add, edit, and manage all the quantum assets: catalogues, circuit models, circuit flows, code, etc.
- Ensure, due to its own (environment) implementation and supported techniques, "secure and privacy by design" quantum information systems.
- Allow QSE to cover the governance and management of software—even offering the possibility of simultaneously launching the execution of the same quantum software in multiple targets (quantum computers and/or simulators) and collecting all the corresponding telemetry.

2.6 Lack of Standardization

In these moments of rapid evolution and a concomitant lack of standardization in quantum programming and tools, there is a logical fear of betting on a platform or language that in the end does not continue. This leads companies to hesitate over the adoption of quantum applications and places quantum software designers and programmers in the difficult position of having to simultaneously learn, train, and develop competencies for each of the existing and future languages and development kits.

There are several standardization efforts: ISO/IEC JTC1/WG14—Quantum Computing of International Organization for Standardization, Quantum Key Distribution (QKD) of ETSI (European Telecommunications Standards Institute), Quantum-Safe Security Working Group of CSA (Cloud Security Alliance), Focus Group on Quantum Technologies of CEN-CENELEC (European Committee for Standardization—European Committee for Electrotechnical Standardization),

Post-Quantum Cryptography of NIST (National Institute of Standards and Technology), Quantum Initiative Support for Standards of IEEE (Institute of Electrical and Electronics Engineers), etc. But at the moment there is no specific proposal on software engineering processes or products.

2.7 Software Engineering Education

Peterssen [31] highlights how limited is the quantity of workforce that has made quantum computing possible. This situation is even worse in the case of the invested in QSE. The urgency for growth requires some accelerators in the preparation of the quantum workforce, and one of them could be the training of engineers and programmers as specialists in quantum programming and software. Training of engineers and quantum programmers must be urgently approached by manufacturers, universities, and technical teaching to provide the quantum employment market with the essential qualified workforce.

In fact, as has happened in previous stages of software development, one of the major obstacles to the development of quality quantum software will be a shortage of skilled labor [31]. The use of quantum software (and its environment) can imply a relatively important period of learning and experimentation, so it is very important that academia provides industry with a highly competent software workforce, with specific quantum computing development skills.

Several online learning platforms offer different courses related to quantum computing. Some professional's organizations such as IEEE have created a new flagship Quantum Computing Education—Workforce Development Program "designed to empower our community of lifelong learners with quantum technology industry knowledge for global impact."[2]

There are also several universities and research centers which offer degrees, masters, and PhD courses related to quantum computing. However, the most prestigious computing curricula disregard quantum computing in general and QSE in particular. Piattini [32] proposes the inclusion of quantum courses in all the computing disciplines; through a cross-cutting "quantum technology" (QT), knowledge area (KA) could be created, including six different units with their topics: QC, quantum computing; QP, quantum programming; QSD, quantum system development; QAI, quantum artificial intelligence; QS, quantum security; and QIS, quantum information systems (see Table 2.1).

As universities, we must be very aware of the advice of Boehm [9]: "to keep courses and courseware continually refreshed and up-to-date, and to anticipate future trends and preparing students to deal with them" and so to incorporate in our curricula courses quantum technologies, quantum computing, and quantum software engineering.

---

[2] https://quantum.ieee.org/education/workforce-development

Table 2.1 Proposed quantum courses in the existing curricula

Computing curriculum	Subjects					
	QC	QP	QSD	QAI	QS	QIS
Computer Engineering	x	x				
Computer Science	x	x		x		
Information Systems			x		x	x
Information Technology		x	x			x
Software Engineering		x	x			x
Cybersecurity	x				x	x
Data Science	x	x		x		

2.8 Collaboration Between Industry and Academia

For the field of quantum technology to be as successful as possible, it is essential that there is close collaboration between industry and academia in several aspects. Applications and use-cases need to be developed in close cooperation between the two [33], and joint research efforts and projects are crucial to solving the problems that quantum computing still presents us with. In fact, in quantum computing, it is increased public and private sector investment which has enabled much of the recent progress [34]. So big "quantum ecosystems" are fostering by the main quantum software providers, such as the IBM Quantum Network,[3] the Google's Quantum AI's Summer Symposium,[4] or the Microsoft Quantum Network.[5]

Amazon, however, is following a different approach. As the dominant actor on the cloud computing market with AWS, it is also very interested in the possibilities of quantum computing. Nevertheless, instead of developing their own quantum computers, Amazon is acting as an integrator and through Amazon Braket provides centralized access to quantum hardware from different vendors. With this role, Amazon is acting toward an initial standardization of quantum computing software that can be run in different hardware. In this regard, to accelerate the development of quantum solutions and to engage in collaborative research projects with academia, Amazon has created the Amazon Quantum Solutions Lab[6] and a network of consulting and technology partners to provide expertise in quantum systems.

Another example of such a collaboration is "aQuantum", created in 2019 as a joint unit for research, development, consulting, and services in the fields of Quantum Software Engineering and Programming, by Alhambra IT (which belongs to the French Prologue Group) and the Alarcos Research Group of the University of Castilla La Mancha (UCLM). aQuantum follows a model of continuous co-experimentation, technology transfer 2.0, and co-production between industry and

---

[3] https://www.ibm.com/quantum-computing/ibm-q-network/

[4] https://events.withgoogle.com/2021-quantum-summer-symposium/

[5] https://azure.microsoft.com/en-us/solutions/quantum-computing/network/

[6] https://aws.amazon.com/es/quantum-solutions-lab/

academia [35, 36]. Additionally, some IT company partners and the members of the aQuantum Network[7] collaborate with aQuantum to pursue progress in the adoption of best practices in Quantum Software Engineering and Programming and the implementation of practical quantum products and services, training, competences, etc. aQuantum creates contributions to "quantum literacy" (especially in quantum software) and participates in informative activities such as giving introductory webinars on quantum computing, etc. We have also organized several international workshops and tracks (e.g., QANSWER,[8] QUATIC,[9,10] QSET[11,12]), which seek to bring together practitioners and researchers interested in quantum software engineering, quantum software quality, quantum systems development, and related topics. Such events play a vital role, as it is very important to know the real problems faced by practitioners when developing a quantum software project and how researchers can provide solutions to them. Also, aQuantum has started to provide different services related to the development of quantum software solutions and the QPath Platform.[13] Furthermore, we participate as part of a consortium with other companies and universities in a big project called "QHealth: Quantum pharmaco-genomics applied to ageing".[14] This will help, for example, to map onto quantum simulations the evolution of a patient in relation to their consumption of prescribed drugs as well as their genetic and environmental limitations. In conducting a project like this aimed at solving real problems, we came to understand some of the (remaining) shortcomings of software engineering in the quantum world.

2.9   Conclusions

Quantum computing speed up solutions to algorithms that require massive parallel computations (optimization, cryptography, machine learning, etc.) and allow us to simulate nature more (chemistry, materials, subatomic particles) [37]. However, for quantum computing to become a more effective reality, quantum computer science is not enough. Much more is needed; it is essential to promote a new field of "quantum software engineering" if all the real value of quantum applications and algorithms are to be achieved.

---

[7] https://www.aquantum.es/partner-network/

[8] https://www.qanswer.site/

[9] https://2020.quatic.org/thematic-tracks/quality-aspects-in-quantum-computing

[10] https://2021.quatic.org/thematic-tracks/quality-aspects-in-quantum-computing

[11] https://quset.github.io/

[12] https://quset.github.io/qset2021/

[13] https://www.quantumpath.es/

[14] https://www.aquantum.es/rdi/qhealth/

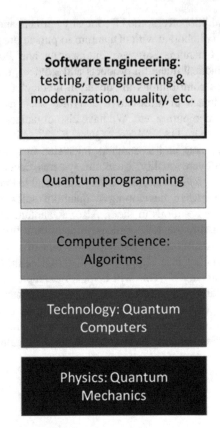

Fig. 2.1 Quantum disciplines

So, it is necessary to go further (see Fig. 2.1) and to develop a quantum software engineering body of knowledge and to focus efforts on software engineering methods and techniques applied to quantum computing. And this is a task for software engineers and researchers since several quantum computer scientists do not know the software engineering principles and techniques, so several errors could be done again, and some expensive "rediscoveries" could happen [38].

To achieve these aims, we recommend strengthening the relationship with academia in terms of both research and training of quantum software engineering and programming professionals.

References

1. Feynman RP (1959) Plenty of room at the bottom. Am Phys Soc 1959:1–7. https://web.pa.msu.edu/people/yang/RFeynman_plentySpace.pdf

2. Feynman RP (1982) Simulating physics with computers. Int J Theoretical Phys 21(6/7): 467–488
3. Benioff P (1980) The computer as a physical system: a microscopic quantum mechanical Hamiltonian model of computers as represented by Turing machines. J Statist Phys 1980: 563–591. https://doi.org/10.1007/BF01011339
4. Atiyah MF, Hitchin NJ, Drinfeld VG, Manin YI (1978) Construction of instantons. Phys Lett A 65(3):185–187. https://doi.org/10.1016/0375-9601(78)90141-X
5. Deutsch David (1985) Quantum theory, the Church–Turing principle and the universal quantum computer. Proc R Soc Lond A40097–117. https://doi.org/10.1098/rspa.1985.0070
6. Maslov D, Nam Y, Kim J (2019) An outlook for quantum computing. Proc IEEE 107(1):5–11
7. IDB (2019) Quantum technologies. Digital transformation, social impact, and cross-sector disruption. Interamerican Development Bank
8. Clark J, Stepney S (2002) Proposed "Grand Challenge for Computing Research" quantum software engineering. https://www.cs.york.ac.uk/quantum/sig/021108/qsegc.pdf
9. Boehm B (2006) A view of 20th and 21st century software engineering. ICSE'06, Shanghai, China, 20–28 May 2006. ACM
10. Gödel K (1931) Über formal unentscheidbare Sätze der Principia Mathematica und verwandter Systeme I. Monatshefte für Mathematik und Physik 38(1):173–198. https://doi.org/10.1007/BF01700692
11. Church A, Turing AM (1937) On computable numbers, with an application to the Entscheidungs problem. s2-42(1):230–265. https://doi.org/10.1112/plms/s2-42.1.230
12. Dijkstra EW (1968) Letters to the editor: Go to statement considered harmful. Commun ACM 11(3):147–148. https://doi.org/10.1145/362929.362947
13. Dijkstra EW (1972) Notes on Structured Programming. Structured programming. Academic Press, GBR, pp 1–82
14. Warnier JD (1976) Logical construction of programs. Van Nostrand Reinhold, New York. ISBN 0442291930
15. Jackson MA (1981) A system development method. In: Tools and notions for program construction: an advanced course. Cambridge University Press. ISBN 9780521248013
16. Chen PPS (1976) The entity-relationship model—toward a unified view of data. ACM Trans Database Syst. https://doi.org/10.1145/320434.320440
17. Gane C, Sarson T (1977) Structured systems analysis: tools & techniques. Comput J 23(3):255. https://doi.org/10.1093/comjnl/23.3.255-a
18. DeMarco T (1979) Structured analysis and system specification. Prentice Hall PTR, Upper Saddle River, NJ. ISBN 978-0-13-854380-8
19. Booch G (2018) The history of software engineering. IEEE Softw 35(5):108–114
20. Creswell J (2014) Research design: qualitative, quantitative and mixed methods approaches, 4th edn. Sage Publications
21. Booch G, Rumbaugh J, Jacobson I (1999) The unified modeling language user guide. Addison Wesley Longman, USA. ISBN 978-0-201-57168-4
22. Papazoglou MP, Georgakopoulos D (2003) Introduction: Service-oriented computing. Commun ACM 46(10):24–28. https://doi.org/10.1145/944217.944233
23. Piattini M, Peterssen G, Pérez-Castillo R (2020) Quantum computing: a new software engineering golden age. ACM SIGSOFT Softw Eng Newsl 45(3):12–14
24. Piattini M et al (2020) The Talavera manifesto for quantum software engineering and programming. In: Proceedings of the 1st International Workshop on the QuANtum SoftWare Engineering & pRogramming (QANSWER 2020). Talavera de la Reina, Toledo, Spain, 11–12 February 2020. http://ceur-ws.org/Vol-2561/paper0.pdf
25. Weder B, Barzen J, Leymann F, Salm M, Vietz D (2020) The quantum software lifecycle. In: Proceedings of the 1st ACM SIGSOFT International Workshop on Architectures and Paradigms for Engineering Quantum Software. pp 2–9
26. Preskill J (2018) Quantum computing in the NISQ era and beyond. Quantum 2:79
27. Zhao J (2020) Quantum software engineering landscapes and horizons. arXiv:2007.07047v1

28. Sodhi B, Kapur R (2021) Quantum computing platforms: assessing impact on quality attributes and SDLC activities (Accepted in ICSA 2021). https://doi.org/10.13140/RG.2.2.20190.66886/1
29. Pérez-Castillo R, Serrano MA, Piattini M (2021) Software modernization to embrace quantum technology. Adv Eng Softw 151:102933
30. OMG O (2016) Architecture-driven modernization: knowledge discovery meta-model (KDM) https://www.omg.org/spec/KDM/1.4/About-KDM/
31. Peterssen G (2020) Quantum technology impact: the necessary workforce for developing quantum software. In: Proceedings of the 1st International Workshop on the QuANtum SoftWare Engineering & pRogramming, Talavera de la Reina, Spain, 11–12 February 2020 (QANSWER 2020). pp 6–22. http://ceur-ws.org/Vol-2561/paper1.pdf
32. Piattini M (2020) Training e. In: Proceedings of the 1st International Workshop on the QuANtum SoftWare Engineering & pRogramming, Talavera de la Reina, Spain, 11–12 February 2020. CEUR Workshop Proceedings 2561, CEUR-WS.org 2020, 23–30. http://ceur-ws.org/Vol-2561/paper2.pdf
33. EQF (2020) Strategic research agenda. European Quantum Flagship
34. Grumbling E, Horowitz M (eds) (2019) Quantum computing: progress and prospects. The National Academies Press, Washington, DC
35. Mikkonen T, Lassenius C, Männistö T, Oivo M, Järvinen J (2018) Continuous and collaborative technology transfer: software engineering research with real-time industry impact. Inf Softw Technol 95:34–45
36. Sannö A, Öberg AE, Flores-Garcia E, Jackson M (2019) Increasing the impact of industry–academia collaboration through co-production. Technol Innov Manag Rev 9(4)
37. Bozzo-Rey M, Longbotton J, Müller HA (2019) Quantum computing: challenges and opportunities. Proc. CASCON 19, Toronto, Canada, November 2019. pp 393–394
38. Moguel E, Berrocal J, García-Alonso J, Murillo JM (2020) A Roadmap for Quantum Software Engineering: applying the lessons learned from the classics. In: 1st Quantum Software Engineering and Technology Workshop. Q-SET'20 co-located with the IEEE Quantum Week. IEEE International Conference on Quantum Computing and Engineering (QCE20), 13 October 2020. http://ceur-ws.org/Vol-2705/short1.pdf

Chapter 3
Quantum Information Technology Governance System

Miguel Ángel Blanco and Manuel Serrano

3.1 Quantum Technology and IT Governance

Quantum computing and quantum technology use different quantum phenomena [1] to solve various types of problems more efficiently than current technology is able to do [2, 3]. Some of the many applications of quantum technology are sensors, security, communications, and quantum simulation.

It is interesting to analyze the impact of these technologies in several industrial sectors [4, 5]: finance (where they are employed to optimize the asset price portfolio and to conduct risk analysis and fraud detection); insurance (to evaluate financial instruments, options, and guarantees in insurance products and to measure operational risk); energy (where these technologies can optimize current networks and suggest an appropriate use of energy); transport (where optimization is the most tangible application in this sector); logistics (the main use of quantum technology here is the optimization of operations related to the supply chain); automobiles and aerospace (where the management and optimization of large fleets of cars or autonomous planes are the main challenges); and chemist and pharmaceuticals (in which the main application is the simulation of molecules in the discovery of new compounds and materials, as well as to discover new materials to improve batteries, microcircuits, or network architectures). Table 3.1 shows the relation between these industries and their investment in different types of quantum technologies [6].

For a company to be able to pay off the cost of an investment in quantum technology, it is important that it be able to maximize value, minimize risk, and

M. Á. Blanco · M. Serrano (✉)
Alarcos Research Group, Institute of Technologies and Information Systems, University of Castilla-La Mancha (UCLM), Ciudad Real, Spain
e-mail: Manuel.Serrano@uclm.es; miguelangel.blanco@alu.uclm.es

© The Author(s), under exclusive license to Springer Nature Switzerland AG 2022   39
M. A. Serrano et al. (eds.), *Quantum Software Engineering*,
https://doi.org/10.1007/978-3-031-05324-5_3

Table 3.1 Relation between industry sector and quantum technology

Sector	Computing	Communication	Simulation	Security	Sensors
Finance	X			X	
Insurance	X			X	
Energy	X	X	X	X	X
Transport	X	X			
Automobile	X	X	X	X	X
Aerospace	X	X	X	X	X
Logistics	X			X	
Chemist	X		X		
Pharmacist	X		X		
Materials	X		X		

optimize resources. To achieve these objectives, it is essential to "govern" the quantum technology [6].

The definition of "IT Governance" has changed and evolved over time and has been adapted to the changing needs of companies. This evolution began with the "classic" definition of [7] as being a "Framework for specifying decision rights and responsibilities to promote desirable behavior in the use of Information Systems Technology" and has since moved on to encompass the "comprehensive" definition of [8]: "Information System Technologies Governance is the strategic alignment of the Information System Technologies with the organization so as to achieve maximum business value through the development and maintenance of effective control and responsibilities, performance management and risk."

More recent definitions emphasize that IT Governance is an integral part of corporate governance, exercised by the Board [9], and that its importance lies in directing and controlling IT [10]. As the Information Systems Audit and Control Association (ISACA) highlights: "Enterprise Governance of IT is concerned with value delivery from digital transformation and the mitigation of business risk that results from digital transformation" [11]. For this reason, it is very important to provide a Quantum Information Technology Governance Framework that can be used to design and implement the appropriate Quantum Information Technology Governance System.

The rest of this chapter sets forth our proposals for the development of a Quantum Information Technology Governance System which uses the COBIT 2019 [11] as its Information Technology Governance Framework and then proceeds to detail its limitations. This is followed by our conclusions from the work undertaken and suggestions for the next steps in our research.

3.2 Quantum Information Technology Governance System Design

ISACA has recently released COBIT 2019, which consists of:

- The COBIT 2019 Framework: Introduction and Methodology [11]
- The COBIT 2019 Framework: Governance and Management Objectives [12]
- The COBIT 2019 Design Guide: Designing an Information and Technology Governance Solution [13]
- The COBIT 2019 Implementation Guide: Implementing and Optimizing an Information and Technology Governance Solution [14]

The main objective of COBIT 2019 is to design an Information Technology Governance System that will best fit a company's strategy and will allow the delivery of value to be maximized, risks to be minimized, and resources to be optimized. To achieve this objective, COBIT 2019 includes the COBIT Core Model, which contains a set of Governance and Management Objectives, and considers different design factors and focus areas that should be used to build a best-fit IT Governance System. We have built a Quantum Information Technology Governance System (QITGS) by applying the methodology proposed by COBIT 2019 [13].

3.2.1 Step 1: Understand the Enterprise Context and Strategy

The objective of this step is to define the environment of the given company: its Enterprise Strategy, Enterprise Goals, Risk Category, and all issues related to Information Technology.

3.2.1.1 Enterprise Strategy

The strategy of companies that decide to invest in Quantum IT (QIT) is nowadays focused on "innovation or differentiation," since they are now beginning to invest in and create strategic lines [15], with only slight differences depending on their sector [6].

3.2.1.2 Enterprise Goals

When designing a QITGS, the most important enterprise goals to be chosen are those that are aligned with the company strategy, and, following COBIT 2019 [13], those primary enterprise goals are "EG01.—Portfolio of competitive products and services" and "EG13.—Product and business innovation." This is because, with an "innovation and grow" strategy, it is extremely important for the product and business innovation portfolio to be very clear and competitive. A secondary objective could, meanwhile, be "EG12.—Managed digital transformation program."

3.2.1.3   Risk Category

Another important key element to the design of a QITGS as proposed by COBIT 2019 is that of understanding the company's risk profile. COBIT 2019 defines different risk categories and identifies several examples of risks for each category that can be used to identify the priority of the risk categories. When designing a QITGS, the most important risk categories (with their corresponding COBIT 2019 identification shown between parentheses) are:

- QIT investment decision-making, portfolio definition, and maintenance (RISKCAT01). When investing in quantum technology, the selection of the infrastructure implies certain risks, because it is not a mature technology and there is a wide variety of types [16].
- QIT cost and oversight (RISKCAT03). QIT is currently very expensive, and it is necessary to invest to build a sustainable quantum industry [15]. Many public organizations from different countries are, therefore, investing large amounts of money in QIT [17].
- QIT expertise, skills, and behavior (RISKCAT04). In [18], the problem related to the lack of a quantum workforce is examined, while [19] highlights the lack of quantum technology in computer science curricula. A serious mismatch related to the skills required within Quantum IT could, therefore, appear.
- Quantum software adoption/usage problems (RISKCAT08). The application of QIT to new use cases can generate new problems as regards the use of quantum software. To solve these problems, it is necessary to confront new challenges in quantum software development, such as the creation of new quantum algorithms or the integration of quantum computing into current computing [15].
- Quantum software failures (RISKCAT10). To implement QIT in industrial and business sectors, it is necessary to resolve the impact of noise or decoherence that can provoke errors in quantum computation [20]. The computers that currently solve the noise problem are "noisy intermediate-scale quantum (NISQ)" computers [21, 22] and will probably have a high commercial value [23].
- Third-party/supplier incidents (RISKCAT12). Not all quantum technology vendors currently provide adequate support and services, although third-party companies that do provide quantum services are on the rise [17].

3.2.1.4   Quantum Information Technology: Related Issues

The immaturity of quantum information technology (QIT) has led to several issues:

- Significant quantum QIT-related incidents, such as data loss, security breaches, project failure, application errors, etc. (TRI01)
- QIT outsourcers having problems delivering the service. (TRI02)
- Reluctance by board members, executives, or senior management to engage with QIT or a lack of committed business sponsors. (TRI03)
- A complex QIT operating model and/or unclear decision mechanisms for QIT-related decisions. (TRI04)
- The excessively high cost of QIT. (TRI05)
- The gap between business and technical knowledge, which leads business users and QIT and/or technology specialists to speak different languages. (TRI06)
- The inability to exploit new technologies or to innovate using QIT. (TRI07)

3.2.2   Step 2: Determine the Initial Scope of the QITGS

This step translates the different pieces of information collected in the previous step into a set of prioritized governance components [13], i.e., the QITGS's Initial Scope.

The first Governance and Management Objectives to be chosen are those that, according to COBIT 2019 [13], cover the particular enterprise strategy identified in the Enterprise Strategy section, which are "APO02.—Managed Strategy," "APO04.—Managed Innovation," "APO05.—Managed Portfolio," "BAI08.—Managed Knowledge," and "BAI11.—Managed Projects."

The selected enterprise goals are then mapped onto the corresponding "alignment goals" (AG). Table 3.2 shows the AGs selected for the QITGS that have a primary (P) or secondary (S) importance.

COBIT 2019 also relates the alignment goals to a list of Governance and Management Objectives, as shown in Table 3.3.

The risk appetite defined in the Risk Category section also must be mapped onto priorities for Governance and Management Objectives. In the case of COBIT 2019 [13], the risk mitigation is implemented as Governance and Management Objectives that need to be achieved. Their relations are shown in Table 3.4.

Moreover, the diagnosis of quantum information technology-related issues influences the Governance and each Management Objective, as defined in Table 3.5.

3.2.3   Step 3: Refine the Scope of the QITGS

In this step, the Initial Scope is refined based on the assessment of the remaining design factors [13].

Table 3.2 Mapping of the Governance and Management Objectives onto the Alignment Objectives

	EG01.— Portfolio of competitive products and services	EG12.— Managed digital transformation programs	EG13.— Product and business innovation
AG03.—Realized benefits from I&T-enabled investments and services portfolio	S	P	
AG05.—Delivery of I&T services in line with business requirements	P	S	
AG06.—Agility to turn business requirements into operational solutions	P	S	S
AG08.—Enabling and supporting business processes by integrating applications and technology	P	P	S
AG09.—Delivering programs on time and on budget and meeting require-ments and quality standards	P	P	S
AG13.—Knowledge, expertise, and initiatives for business innovation	P	S	P

3.2.3.1 Threat Landscape

Companies that need to invest in QIT currently find themselves in a highly competitive environment, which is the main reason why the level of the threat landscape in which they operate could be considered as "high." In the context of COBIT 2019, the important Governance and Management Objectives which should be implemented by companies that operate in this high level are shown in Column 1 of Table 3.6.

3.2.3.2 Compliance Requirements

COBIT 2019 [13] defines three levels of compliance requirements: "low," "normal," and "high." According to [6], the companies that decide to invest in QIT mostly belong to the industrial sectors of finance, insurance, energy, transport, automobile, aerospace, logistics, pharmaceuticals, and materials. Companies in these sectors compete in markets with a high level of regulation, with the result that the level of compliance requirements of companies interested in the design of a QITGS could be considered as "high."

In the case of COBIT 2019, Column 2 in Table 3.6 (above) shows the list of Governance and Management Objectives that should be considered if companies have "high" compliance requirements.

Table 3.3 Mapping of the Governance and Management Objectives onto the Alignment Objectives

	AG03	AG05	AG06	AG08	AG09	AG13
EDM01.—Ensured Governance Framework Setting and Maintenance	P			S		
EDM02.—Ensured Benefits Delivery	P	S	S	S		S
EDM04.—Ensured Resource Optimization	S	S	S	S	P	
APO01.—Managed I&T Management Framework	P	S		S	S	
APO02.—Managed Strategy	S	S	S	P		S
APO03.—Managed Enterprise Architecture	S	S	P	P		
APO04.—Managed Innovation	S		P	S		P
APO05.—Managed Portfolio	P	P	S	S	S	
APO06.—Managed Budget and Costs	S				P	
APO07.—Managed Human Resources	S	S			S	P
APO08.—Managed Relationships	S	P	P	S	S	P
APO09.—Managed Service Agreements		P		S		
APO10.—Managed Vendors		P	S		S	
APO11.—Managed Quality	S	S			P	
APO14.—Managed Data					P	
BAI01.—Managed Programs	P		S	S	P	
BAI02.—Managed Requirements Definition	S	P	P	S	P	
BAI03.—Managed Solutions Identification and Build	S	P	P	S	P	
BAI04.—Managed Availability and Capacity		P			S	
BAI05.—Managed Organizational Change	P	S	S	P	P	
BAI06.—Managed IT Changes		S	P	S		
BAI07.—Managed IT Change Acceptance and Transitioning			P		S	
BAI08.—Managed Knowledge	S		S	S	S	P
BAI10.—Managed Configuration		S				
BAI11.—Managed Projects	P	S	P		P	
DSS01.—Managed Operations		P		S		
DSS02.—Managed Service Requests and Incident		P				
DSS03.—Managed Problems		P				
DSS04.—Managed Continuity		P				
DSS05.—Managed Security Services		S				
DSS06.—Managed Business Process Controls		S		P		
MEA01.—Managed Performance and Conformance Monitoring	S	P			S	
MEA02.—Managed System of Internal Control		S			S	
MEA04.—Managed Assurance		S				

Table 3.4 Mapping of the Governance and Management Objectives onto the risk categories

	RISKCAT01	RISKCAT03	RISKCAT04	RISKCAT08	RISKCAT10	RISKCAT12
EDM01.—Ensured Governance Framework Setting and Maintenance	X	X				
EDM02.—Ensured Benefits Delivery	X					
EDM04.—Ensured Resource Optimization	X	X	X			
EDM05.—Ensured Stakeholder Engagement	X	X				
APO01.—Managed I&T Management Framework						X
APO05.—Managed Portfolio	X					
APO06.—Managed Budget and Costs		X				
APO07.—Managed Human Resources			X	X		
APO08.—Managed Relationships				X		
APO09.—Managed Service Agreements				X		X
APO10.—Managed Vendors		X				X
APO11.—Managed Quality					X	
BAI01.—Managed Programs				X		
BAI02.—Managed Requirements Definition				X		
BAI03.—Managed Solutions Identification and Build					X	
BAI05.—Managed Organizational Change				X		
BAI07.—Managed IT Change Acceptance and Transitioning					X	
BAI08.—Managed Knowledge				X	X	
DSS02.—Managed Service Requests and Incidents				X		
DSS03.—Managed Problems				X	X	

Table 3.5 Mapping of the Governance and Management Objectives onto the technology-related issues

	TRI01	TRI02	TRI03	TRI04	TRI05	TRI06	TRI07
EDM01.—Ensured Governance Framework Setting and Maintenance			X	X			
EDM02.—Ensured Benefits Delivery					X		
EDM04.—Ensured Resource Optimization					X		
EDM05.—Ensured Stakeholder Engagement			X				
APO01.—Managed I&T Management Framework				X			
APO04.—Managed Innovation							X
APO06.—Managed Budget and Costs					X		
APO07.—Managed Human Resources						X	
APO08.—Managed Relationships			X			X	
APO09.—Managed Service Agreements		X					
APO10.—Managed Vendors		X					
APO11.—Managed Quality	X						
APO13.—Managed Security	X						
APO14.—Managed Data	X						
BAI04.—Managed Availability and Capacity		X					
BAI08.—Managed Knowledge						X	
DSS02.—Managed Service Requests and Incidents	X	X					
DSS03.—Managed Problems	X	X					
DSS04.—Managed Continuity	X						
DSS05.—Managed Security Services	X						
MEA04.—Managed Assurance	X						

3.2.3.3 Role of Technology

The role played by QIT is one of "turnaround" because its role is that of a driver for the innovation of business processes and services [13]. The most important Governance and Management Objectives to consider during the design of the QITGS are shown in Column 3 of Table 3.6.

Table 3.6 Governance and Management Objectives selected for each design factor

	Threat landscape	Compliance requirements	Role of technology	Sourcing model for technology	Technology implementation methods	Technology adoption strategy
EDM01.—Ensured Governance Framework Setting and Maintenance	X	X				X
EDM02.—Ensured Benefits Delivery						X
EDM03.—Ensured Risk Optimization	X	X				
EDM04.—Ensured Resource Optimization						
EDM05.—Ensured Stakeholder Engagement						
APO01.—Managed I&T Management Framework	X					
APO02.—Managed Strategy			X			X
APO03.—Managed Enterprise Architecture	X					
APO04.—Managed Innovation			X			X
APO05.—Managed Portfolio						X
APO06.—Managed Budget and Costs						
APO07.—Managed Human Resources						
APO08.—Managed Relationships						X
APO09.—Managed Service Agreements				X		
APO10.—Managed Vendors	X			X		
APO11.—Managed Quality						
APO12.—Managed Risk	X	X				
APO13.—Managed Security	X					
APO14.—Managed Data	X					
BAI01.—Managed Programs						
BAI02.—Managed Requirements Definition			X		X	X
BAI03.—Managed Solutions Identification and Build			X		X	X

Process						
BAI04.—Managed Availability and Capacity						
BAI05.—Managed Organizational Change						X
BAI06.—Managed IT Changes	X				X	
BAI07.—Managed IT Change Acceptance and Transitioning						X
BAI08.—Managed Knowledge						
BAI09.—Managed Assets						
BAI10.—Managed Configuration	X					
BAI11.—Managed Projects						X
DSS01.—Managed Operations	X					X
DSS02.—Managed Service Requests and Incidents				X		
DSS03.—Managed Problems	X					
DSS04.—Managed Continuity	X					
DSS05.—Managed Security Services						
DSS06.—Managed Business Process Controls	X					
MEA01.—Managed Performance and Conformance Monitoring						
MEA02.—Managed System of Internal Control	X					
MEA03.—Managed Compliance with External Requirements	X					
MEA04.—Managed Assurance	X					

3.2.3.4   Sourcing Model for Technology

The best source model to choose is the "cloud," the main reason being that QIT is currently very expensive to acquire and maintain, and it is generally provided by suppliers. Column 4 of Table 3.6 shows the most important Governance and Management Objectives to select from COBIT 2019 [13] when using a "cloud" sourcing model.

3.2.3.5   Technology Implementation Methods

Companies that decide to invest in QIT will have to integrate it with classic technology, because certain business processes are still supported by classic technology, with the result that these companies have to ensure that both technologies can coexist. In this respect, the best option to choose is a "Hybrid" method, such as that proposed by [24]. The Governance and Management Objectives are listed in Column 5 of Table 3.6.

3.2.3.6   Technology Adoption Strategy

Another important decision to consider is the appropriate technology adoption strategy. Currently, any company that decides to invest in QIT will have a "first mover" strategy, because the technology on the market is, at present, very immature, and they should consequently implement the Governance and Management Objectives listed in Column 6 of Table 3.6.

3.2.4   Step 4: Conclude the QITGS

The objective of this step is to specify the elements in the QITGS, considering the various decisions already made in the previous steps. This step is carried out using the Excel sheet provided by COBIT 2019 [13].

Figure 3.1 shows the Governance and Management Objectives that correspond to the Enterprise Strategy (Fig. 3.1, upper left), the Enterprise Goals (Fig. 3.1, upper right), the Technology Risk Profile (Fig. 3.1, lower left), and the Technology-Related Issues (Fig. 3.1, lower right).

An analysis of the impact and likelihood of each risk scenario category for the QITGS is shown in Fig. 3.2.

The initial priorities for Governance and Management Objectives in the QITGS are shown in Fig. 3.3.

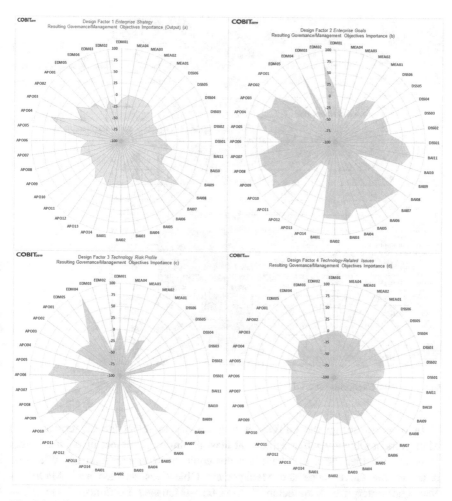

Fig. 3.1 Influence of the design factors on Governance and Management Objectives

3.2.4.1   Refine the Scope of the Governance System

A summary of the value of each design factor and the figure showing the graphical representation of its influence on the different Governance and Management Objectives is shown in Table 3.7.

3.3   Quantum Information Technology Governance System

The final QITGS, considering all the design factors that use COBIT 2019 as a proposal to design the IT Governance System, is shown in Fig. 3.6.

Risk Scenario Category	Impact (1-5)	Likelihood (1-5)	Risk Rating
Quantum Technology investment decision making, portfolio definition & maintenance	5	4	●
Program & projects life cycle management	1	1	●
Quantum Technology cost & oversight	5	5	●
Quantum Technology expertise, skills & behavior	5	5	●
Enterprise/Quantum Technology architecture	1	1	●
Quantum Technology operational infrastructure incidents	1	1	●
Unauthorized actions	1	1	●
Software adoption/usage problems	3	4	○
Hardware incidents	1	1	●
Software failures	4	4	◐
Logical attacks (hacking, malware, etc.)	1	1	●
Third-party/supplier incidents	4	5	◐
Noncompliance	1	1	●
Geopolitical Issues	1	1	●
Industrial action	1	1	●
Acts of nature	1	1	●
Technology-based innovation	1	1	●
Environmental	1	1	●
Data & information management	1	1	●

●	Very High Risk
○	High Risk
◐	Normal Risk
●	Low Risk

Fig. 3.2 Risk categories for a QITGS

In order to design the QITGS, it is necessary to select the Governance and Management Objectives that achieve at least a minimum number of points. In this case, we consider those that have a score equal to or greater than 65. With this criterion, the Governance and Management Objectives selected are "APO03.—Managed Enterprise Architecture," "APO05.—Managed Portfolio," "APO07.—Managed Human Resources," "APO09.—Managed Service Agreements," "APO10.—Managed Vendors," "BAI03.—Managed Solutions Identification and Build," "BAI05.—Managed Organizational Change," and "BAI08.—Managed Knowledge."

3.4 Limitations

Some characteristics of Quantum IT are not covered by COBIT 2019, and so it will be necessary to develop them for the design of the QITGS. The following two issues can be highlighted: the development of new enterprise or technical architectures that affect only the new design factors for quantum information technology and the impact of the coexistence of "classic" technology with quantum information

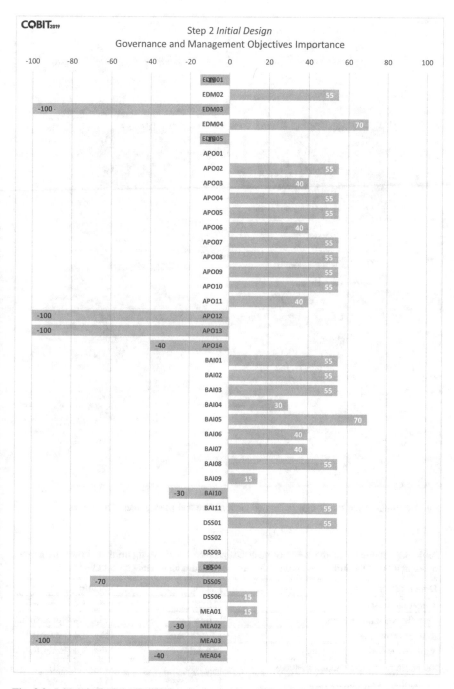

Fig. 3.3 Initial design of QITGS

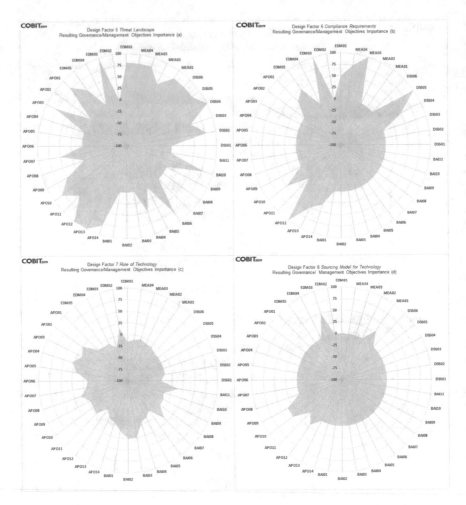

Fig. 3.4 Influence of the design factors on Governance and Management Objectives

Table 3.7 Summary of the value of each design factor and the figure that shows the graphic representation of the influence on the different Governance and Management Objectives

Design factor	Value	Figure
Threat landscape	High	Fig. 3.4 (upper left)
Compliance requirements	High	Fig. 3.4 (upper right)
Role of technology	Turnaround	Fig. 3.4 (lower left)
Sourcing model for technology	Cloud	Fig. 3.4 (lower light)
Technology implementation methods	Hybrid	Fig. 3.5 (left)
Technology adoption strategy	First mover	Fig. 3.5 (right)

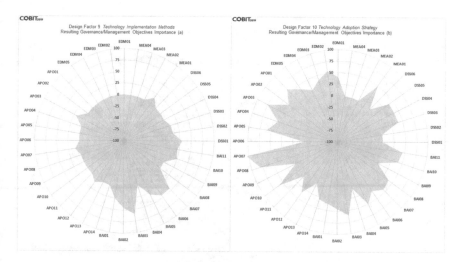

Fig. 3.5 Influence of the design factors on Governance and Management Objectives

technology. There are many COBIT 2019 design factors that do not apply to quantum information technology and apply only to "classical" technology. These design factors are shown in Table 3.8.

COBIT 2019 contains other elements, which are "processes," "organizational structures," "policies and procedures," "information items," "culture and behavior," "skills and competencies," and "services, infrastructure, and applications" and which could be used to implement in companies the Governance and Management Objectives identified in the QITGS. The adaptation of these elements for the implementation of QITGS has not been analyzed in this chapter.

3.5 Conclusions

Quantum technology can solve several problems more efficiently than "classic" technology. It is highly recommended that any company that decides to implement quantum technology should first design a Quantum Information Technology Governance System (QITGS) that will allow them to manage quantum technology investments, thus enabling them to achieve strategic goals, minimize risks, and optimize resources. A good starting point for the design of a QITGS is to use COBIT 2019. While designing the QITGS, we identified certain issues related to the use of COBIT 2019, and, although we consider it to be a good starting point from which to design a QITGS, it should be borne in mind that it is necessary to have a Quantum Governance Framework that covers all the characteristics and specifications of the current quantum industry, both as it stands at present and as it evolves in the future.

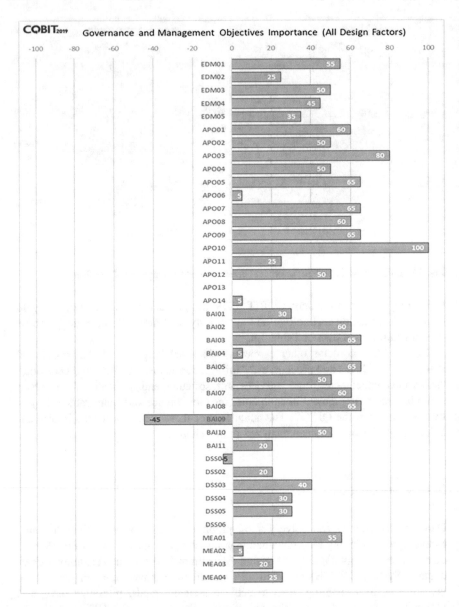

Fig. 3.6 Quantum Information Technology Governance System

Table 3.8 COBIT 2019 design factors that are not used to design the QITGS

Design factor	Classification
Enterprise strategy design factor	- Growth or acquisition - Cost leadership - Client service/stability
Enterprise goals design factor	- EG02.—Managed business risk - EG03.—Compliance with external laws and regulations - EG04.—Quality of financial information - EG05.—Customer-oriented service culture - EG06.—Business service continuity and availability - EG07.—Quality of management information - EG08.—Optimization of internal business process functionality - EG09.—Optimization of business process costs - EG10.—Staff skills, motivation, and productivity - EG11.—Compliance with internal policies
Risk profile design factor	- Program and projects life cycle management - Enterprise/IT architecture - IT operational infrastructure incidents - Unauthorized actions - Hardware incidents - Logical attacks (hacking, malware, etc.) - Noncompliance - Geopolitical issues - Industrial action - Acts of nature - Technology-based innovation - Environmental - Data and information management
Quantum information technology-related issues	- Frustration between different IT entities across the organization because of a perception of low contribution to business value - Frustration between business departments (i.e., the IT customer) and the IT department because of failed initiatives or a perception of low contribution to business value - Failures to meet IT-related regulatory or contractual requirements - Regular audit findings or other assessment reports about poor IT performance or reported IT quality or service problems - Substantial hidden and rogue IT spending, that is, I&T spending by user departments outside the control of the normal I&T investment decision mechanisms and approved budgets - Duplications or overlaps between various initiatives or other forms of wasted resources - Insufficient IT resources, staff with inadequate skills, or staff burnout/dissatisfaction - IT-enabled changes or projects frequently failing to meet business needs and delivered late or over budget - Obstructed or failed implementation of new initiatives or innovations caused by the current IT architecture and systems - Regular issues with data quality and integration of data across

(continued)

Table 3.8 (continued)

Design factor	Classification
	various sources
	- High level of end-user computing, creating (among other problems) a lack of oversight and quality control over the applications that are being developed and put into operation
	- Business departments implementing their own information solutions with little or no involvement of the enterprise IT department (related to end-user computing, which often stems from dissatisfaction with IT solutions and services)
	- Ignorance of and/or noncompliance with privacy regulations
Threat landscape	- Normal
compliance requirements	- Normal
	- Low
Role of technology	- Support
	- Factory
	- Strategic
Sourcing model for technology	- Outsourcing
	- Insourced
Technology adoption strategy	- Follower
	- Slow adopter

References

1. Mykhailova M, Svore KM (2020) Teaching quantum computing through a practical software-driven approach. In: 51st ACM Technical Symposium on Computer Science Education (SIGCSE'20). ACM, Portland, OR, pp 1019–1025
2. Humble TS, DeBenedictis EP (2019) Quantum realism. IEEE Computer 52(6)
3. MIT Technology Review. https://www.technologyreview.com/s/610250/serious-quantum-computers-are-finally-here-what-are-we-going-to-do-with-them/. Accessed 14 Jun 2020
4. Efe A (2020) Anticipating the disruptive and incremental innovations brought by quantum computing. ISACA J 1:26–32
5. Boston Consulting Group. https://www.bcg.com/publications/2019/quantum-computers-create-value-when.aspx. Accessed 14 Jun 2020
6. Blanco MÁ, Piattini M (2020) Adapting COBIT for quantum computing governance. In: Shepperd M, e Abreu FB, da Silva AR, Pérez-Castillo R (eds) Quality of information and communications technology. Springer International Publishing, pp 274–283. https://doi.org/10.1007/978-3-030-58793-2_22
7. Weill P, Ross JW (2004) IT Governance: how top performers manage IT decision rights for superior results. Harvard Business Press
8. Webb P, Pollard C, Ridley G (2006) Attempting to define IT Governance: wisdom or folly? Proceedings of the 39th Annual Hawaii International Conference on System Sciences (HICSS'06), 8, p 194a https://doi.org/10.1109/HICSS.2006.68
9. De Haes S, Van Grembergen W (2015) Enterprise Governance of IT. In: De Haes S, Van Grembergen W (eds) Enterprise Governance of Information Technology: achieving alignment and value, featuring COBIT 5. Springer International Publishing, pp 11–43. https://doi.org/10.1007/978-3-319-14547-1_2
10. ISO/IEC (2015) ISO/IEC 38500:2015. Information technology—Governance of IT for the organization

11. ISACA (2018) COBIT® 2019 framework: introduction and methodology. ISACA
12. ISACA (2018) COBIT® 2019 framework: Governance and Management Objectives. ISACA
13. ISACA (2018) COBIT® 2019 design guide: designing an Information and Technology Governance solution. ISACA
14. ISACA (2018) COBIT® 2019 implementation guide: implementing and optimizing an Information and Technology Governance solution. ISACA
15. European Quantum Flagship (2020) Strategic research agenda. European Quantum Flagship
16. Gerbert P, Ruess F (2018) The next decade in quantum computing—and how to play. BCG Global. https://www.bcg.com/publications/2018/next-decade-quantum-computing-how-play
17. Wachsman MW (2020) The CIO's guide to quantum computing. ZDNet
18. Peterssen Nodarse G (2020) Quantum technology impact: the necessary workforce for developing quantum software (ws.org/Vol)
19. Piattini M (2020) Training needs in quantum computing. QANSWER
20. Gill SS, Kumar A, Singh H, Singh M, Kaur K, Usman M, Buyya R (2020) Quantum computing: a taxonomy, Systematic Review and Future Directions
21. National Academies of Sciences E (2018) Quantum computing: progress and prospects. https://doi.org/10.17226/25196
22. Preskill J (2018) Quantum Computing in the NISQ era and beyond. Quantum 2:79. https://doi.org/10.22331/q-2018-08-06-79
23. Stewart D (2018) Quantum computers: the next supercomputers, but not the next laptops. https://www2.deloitte.com/uk/en/insights/industry/technology/technology-media-and-telecom-predictions/quantum-computing-supremacy.html
24. Pérez-Castillo R, Serrano MA, Piattini M (2021) Software modernization to embrace quantum technology. Adv Eng Softw 151:102933. https://doi.org/10.1016/j.advengsoft.2020.102933

Chapter 4
Quantum Software Development Lifecycle

Benjamin Weder, Johanna Barzen, Frank Leymann, and Daniel Vietz

4.1 Introduction

Quantum computing promises to solve many problems more efficiently or precisely than possible with classical computers, e.g., simulating complex physical systems or applying machine learning techniques [1–3]. With recent advances in developing more powerful quantum computers, also the development of corresponding quantum software and applications and their integration into existing software architectures are becoming increasingly important [4, 5]. However, the development of such quantum applications is complex and requires the knowledge of experts from various fields, e.g., physics, mathematics, and computer science [6–8].

Quantum software engineering is an emerging research area investigating concepts, principles, and guidelines to develop, maintain, and evolve quantum applications [5, 9, 10]. Thereby, it has the goal to increase the quality and reusability of the resulting quantum applications by systematically applying software engineering principles during all development phases from the initial requirement analysis to the retirement of the software [8, 11]. In classical software engineering, *software development lifecycles* are often used to document the different development phases a software artifact or application goes through [12, 13]. Furthermore, such software development lifecycles also summarize best practices and methods that can be applied in the various phases, as well as corresponding tools [8, 10]. Hence, they can be used for educating new developers by providing an overview of the development process or serve as a basis for the cooperation of experts from different fields [14].

B. Weder (✉) · J. Barzen · F. Leymann · D. Vietz
Institute of Architecture of Application Systems, University of Stuttgart, Stuttgart, Germany
e-mail: benjamin.weder@iaas.uni-stuttgart.de; johanna.barzen@iaas.uni-stuttgart.de;
frank.leymann@iaas.uni-stuttgart.de; daniel.vietz@iaas.uni-stuttgart.de

Today's quantum applications are most often hybrid, consisting of quantum and classical programs [15, 16]. Thus, the lifecycle for quantum applications involves the development and operation of both kinds of programs. However, existing lifecycles from classical software engineering [12, 17], as well as quantum software lifecycles [6, 8], only target one of these kinds and do not address the resulting integration challenges. Furthermore, the execution of the quantum and classical programs must be orchestrated, and data has to be passed between them [18]. *Workflow technology* is a means for these orchestrations providing benefits, such as scalability, reliability, and robustness [19, 20]. Therefore, also the workflow lifecycle must be integrated into the overall lifecycle for developing quantum applications.

To address this, we introduce a *quantum software development lifecycle* describing the different relevant phases when developing and operating quantum applications. Thereby, we analyze the purpose of each phase, as well as available concepts and tools. Furthermore, we discuss the different software artifacts usually constituting a quantum application and present their corresponding lifecycles. Finally, we identify the plug points between the various lifecycles to enable their integration into our overall lifecycle for the development of hybrid quantum applications.

The remainder of this chapter is structured as follows: Sect. 4.2 introduces fundamentals about hybrid quantum applications. In Sect. 4.3, we present our quantum software development lifecycle, as well as the lifecycles of the different software artifacts constituting a hybrid quantum application. Afterward, Sect. 4.4 describes assumptions and possible limitations of the introduced lifecycle. Finally, Sect. 4.5 discusses related work, and a conclusion and outlook are given in Sect. 4.6.

4.2 Hybrid Quantum Applications

Nowadays, quantum applications are, in most cases, hybrid, i.e., they consist of *quantum algorithm implementations (QAIs)* and *classical programs*, as depicted in Fig. 4.1 [15, 21, 22]. Thereby, the hybrid quantum application may comprise multiple QAIs, e.g., first performing clustering and then training a classifier based on the clustering results [1]. Furthermore, classical programs might be used to load data, transform it into another format, or visualize it for the user [21, 23].

But even a single QAI is often hybrid, comprising *quantum programs* and classical programs [15, 24]. The general structure of a gate-based QAI, i.e., quantum programs are realized as *quantum circuits*, is shown at the bottom of Fig. 4.1 [15, 22]. Thereby, the *pre-processing* tasks are implemented by classical programs and executed on classical computers. Pre-processing, e.g., includes generating *state preparation* circuits based on input data to initialize the register of the quantum computer when executing the quantum programs [25, 26]. The quantum programs are executed on a quantum computer, first preparing the required state in the register depending on the generated state preparation circuit [7, 15]. Afterward, the *unitary transformation* specified by the proper quantum algorithm is performed, and finally,

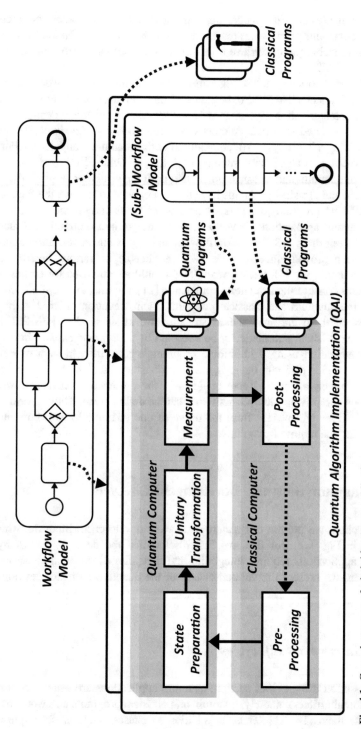

Fig. 4.1 General structure of a hybrid quantum application

the result is measured. *Post-processing*, e.g., on a classical computer, interprets the measurement results or mitigates readout errors in the result distribution by applying an unfolding technique to retrieve a less disturbed distribution from the measured distribution [27, 28].

In addition, various quantum algorithms also require algorithm-specific pre- or post-processing steps that have to be executed on a classical computer [21, 24]. For example, the factorization algorithm of *Shor* [29] relies on classical post-processing to analyze continued fractions. Another example is *Simon's algorithm* [30], which requires solving a linear system of equations after the quantum computation. Further, different variational algorithms, such as *VQE* [31] or *QAOA* [32], perform several iterations of quantum and classical processing until the result converges [24]. Thus, the quantum and classical programs have to be integrated to retrieve the final result.

The different programs of QAIs, as well as the QAIs and classical programs of hybrid quantum applications, have to be orchestrated, and required data must be passed between them [18, 33]. Workflow technology is an orchestration approach that has been proven since decades to be applicable in various heterogeneous application areas [34, 35]. Hence, workflows should also be used for orchestrating the programs constituting a quantum application [21]. For this, the required *activities* invoking the quantum and classical programs, their execution order, and the data flow between them are specified in so-called workflow models [19, 20]. Such workflow models can automatically be executed by a *workflow engine*. In contrast to the orchestration using a traditional program, e.g., written in Java or Python, workflows provide different benefits, such as robustness, scalability, or persistence [18, 20]. Further, alternative control flows in the presence of errors, as well as transactions comprising multiple activities, can be defined [36]. Thus, hybrid quantum applications will benefit from the usage of one or multiple workflow models orchestrating the required programs.

4.3   Quantum Software Development Lifecycle

In this section, we present our quantum software development lifecycle, which is depicted in Fig. 4.2. For this, we first discuss that the development of hybrid quantum applications requires integrating the lifecycles of different software artifacts. Then, we present the various phases of the quantum software development lifecycle.

4.3.1   *Interwoven Lifecycles*

As discussed in the previous section, quantum applications are usually compound from different artifacts, namely, quantum and classical programs and workflows, to orchestrate them [18, 21]. Thus, in addition to phases, such as the requirement

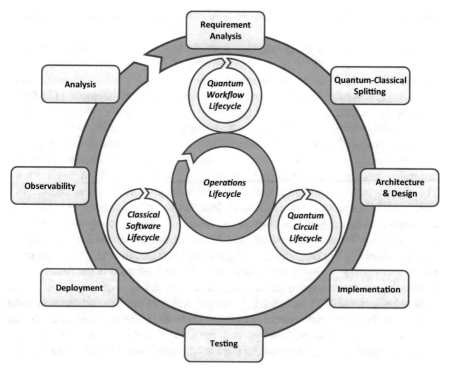

Fig. 4.2 Overview of the quantum software development lifecycle

analysis or the design of the application, the development of a quantum application also comprises the development of the constituting software artifacts. Hence, the quantum software development lifecycle incorporates multiple lifecycles that are interwoven, as depicted in Fig. 4.2: (1) *the quantum workflow lifecycle*, (2) *the classical software lifecycle*, and (3) *the quantum circuit lifecycle*. Further, the various software artifacts also have to be managed, which is prepared and done in the (4) *operations lifecycle*. Thereby, developers and operations personnel should be tightly integrated following the widely used *DevOps paradigm* [37, 38] to enable fast and frequent releases [39]. This is especially important in the quantum computing domain with the rapid development of new quantum computers or software tools, which may require adapting the quantum applications regularly [40]. Hence, these lifecycles have to be integrated into the overall lifecycle, and concepts, best practices, and tools used in the various lifecycles must be considered when developing hybrid quantum applications.

There are various lifecycles for business process management and workflows proposed by different works [11, 20, 41]. We base our lifecycle for quantum workflows on the lifecycles presented by Leymann and Roller [20], as well as Dumas et al. [41]. Furthermore, we added required phases specific to the quantum computing domain. The quantum workflow lifecycle is discussed in detail in Sect. 4.3.3.

Similar to workflow lifecycles, also multiple lifecycles for the development of classical software artifacts have been introduced [12, 13, 17]. A widely used software lifecycle is the *waterfall model*, comprising five phases: (1) requirement analysis, (2) design, (3) implementation, (4) testing, and (5) maintenance [13]. Other lifecycles or software development models are the *spiral model* [42], the *V-model* [17], and the *prototype model* [43]. However, the detailed discussion of lifecycles for the development of classical software artifacts is out of the scope of this chapter.

Additionally, a lifecycle for the development of quantum circuits has to be integrated into the overall lifecycle for the development of quantum applications. Thereby, we use the quantum circuit lifecycle that we proposed in previous work [8], which will be discussed in more detail in Sect. 4.3.4. Although there are some other lifecycles [6, 10], they are still abstract and need to be refined to capture all relevant details to guide developers (see Sect. 4.5). However, also lifecycles documenting the relevant phases in the development of quantum programs for other quantum computing models, e.g., the adiabatic model [44], can be integrated in the future.

Finally, all the developed software artifacts constituting a quantum application have to be operated. This includes, e.g., the packaging of the quantum application to ship it into the target environment or its deployment [37]. The required concepts and tools differ from classical DevOps and have to be extended for the quantum computing domain [38]. Section 4.3.5 presents the operations lifecycle exhaustively.

4.3.2   Enclosing Lifecycle

In the following, we introduce the enclosing lifecycle depicted in Fig. 4.2, defining how the different lifecycles must be interwoven. Thus, various phases require entering the lifecycles of the software artifacts constituting the quantum application, e.g., the implementation phase. Other phases rely on the interplay of the corresponding phases from the different lifecycles, e.g., the testing and deployment phases. Hence, the goal of these phases is summarized, and the phases that must be integrated are discussed.

4.3.2.1   Requirement Analysis

For both classical and quantum application development, the different interested stakeholders must identify their requirements first [6, 45]. Thereby, the requirements can be functional, i.e., defining the problems to solve, and non-functional, i.e., specifying quality attributes of the resulting quantum application, such as availability, scalability, performance, or maintainability [22]. The requirements are documented measurably to enable the evaluation of the resulting quantum application in the later lifecycle phases, e.g., the analysis phase (see Sect. 4.3.2.8)

[10]. Further, the different requirements are prioritized, and the overall project schedule is elaborated [37, 45].

4.3.2.2 Quantum-Classical Splitting

The *quantum-classical* splitting phase is intended to decide which parts of the quantum application to execute on a quantum computer and which on a classical computer [8, 46]. For the quantum parts, it is also determined if, e.g., a gate-based quantum computer [47] or a quantum annealer [44] should be used. The splitting is based on the requirements from the previous phase, i.e., it is evaluated for which parts suited quantum algorithms exist [6]. Furthermore, it is verified if the non-functional requirements can be satisfied by a quantum program considering the capabilities of the available quantum computers [48]. The splitting can, e.g., be done by quantum experts based on their knowledge and experience [8]. However, this task is complex, time-consuming, and error-prone. Therefore, it should be automated or supported by a recommendation system, which can be based on *patterns* [26, 49] and best practices or so-called provenance data [50, 51] about other quantum applications.

4.3.2.3 Architecture and Design

The result of the previous phase is a collection of quantum and classical parts. In the *architecture* and *design* phase, an architecture is conceptualized by using these parts and specifying corresponding software components with their functionality and interfaces [13, 37]. Then, the architecture is refined with the internals of the different software components, e.g., the used data structures [10]. The resulting description should provide enough details for the implementation of the various components in the next phase. Thereby, it can, e.g., be specified using the *Unified Modeling Language (UML)*, for which an extension for quantum computing exists [16, 52].

4.3.2.4 Implementation

In the next phase, the quantum application is implemented based on the requirements and design from the previous phases. Thereby, the implementation includes the development of the different constituting software artifacts. This means the lifecycles for classical programs and quantum programs (see Sect. 4.3.4) are entered in this phase. Furthermore, workflows should be used for orchestrating the control and data flow between these programs [18, 21]. Thus, also the quantum workflow lifecycle is interwoven into this phase (see Sect. 4.3.3). The reuse of existing code and programs is one of the major goals of quantum software engineering [5, 9]. Hence, before entering the lifecycles to develop the required software artifacts, existing code and implementations are searched, e.g., using an API manager [53], a service registry [54], or a platform for sharing quantum software [4, 55].

4.3.2.5 Testing

After the implementation, the quantum application is tested to verify the intended behavior according to the specified requirements before delivering it to the users [10, 13]. Similar to the implementation phase, it includes the testing of all constituting software artifacts, i.e., quantum programs, classical programs, and workflows. Therefore, the testing of these artifacts is also located in their corresponding lifecycles (e.g., see Sect. 4.3.4.3). In addition to testing the artifacts in isolation, so-called integration tests should be performed to verify if the independently developed artifacts work together correctly [56]. Although there are some testing and verification approaches for quantum circuits, the development of a holistic testing strategy for hybrid quantum applications is still an open research question [57–59].

4.3.2.6 Deployment

During the *deployment* phase, everything is prepared to enable the execution of the quantum application [60, 61]. Thus, the execution environment for the classical programs is set up, e.g., for a Python script, a virtual machine may be created, and the required Python runtime is installed on it [23]. Similarly, also the quantum programs and the workflows must be deployed. However, some of the required functionality may also be available as a service or API and require no deployment [62]. The deployment is part of the operations lifecycle and is discussed in detail in Sect. 4.3.5.4.

4.3.2.7 Observability

In the next phase, the quantum application and its execution environment are monitored. Thereby, data is collected for two different purposes: (1) observing the current state of a running quantum application and (2) storing the data in the long term to enable its analysis, e.g., to improve the quantum application or to enable traceability, comprehensibility, and reproducibility [20, 50]. This phase requires the collection of data about all software artifacts comprising the hybrid quantum application [51]. Hence, it must be defined in the different development lifecycles what data to collect, which is then gathered at runtime in the operations lifecycle.

4.3.2.8   Analysis

In the last phase of the lifecycle, the collected data from the observability phase is analyzed. The goals of this phase are to find bugs that have to be fixed or possible improvements for the quantum application [21, 51]. For example, if the quantum programs frequently produce erroneous results, a sub-optimal splitting for today's limited quantum computers could be the reason [8, 63]. Therefore, after the analysis phase, the next iteration of the lifecycle can be entered, e.g., adapting the requirements to perform an improved splitting and realize the other found optimizations.

4.3.3   Quantum Workflow Lifecycle

As discussed in Sect. 4.2, the different programs realizing a quantum application have to be orchestrated, which should be done using workflows to benefit from their advantages [21, 23]. Next, we present the quantum workflow lifecycle (see Fig. 4.3).

4.3.3.1   Modeling

In the *modeling* phase, the collection of activities implementing the quantum application and their partial order are defined in a workflow model depending on the result of the architecture and design phase (see Sect. 4.3.2.3) [20, 21]. Furthermore, also the data flow between the activities is specified [19, 36]. Thereby, a standardized workflow language, such as the *Business Process Model and Notation (BPMN)* [64] or the *Business Process Execution Language (BPEL)* [65], should be used to simplify the reuse of workflow models across different workflow engines [20, 34].

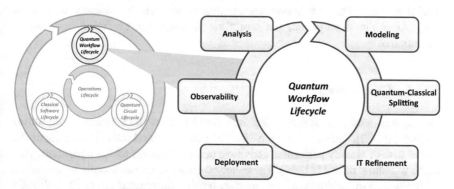

Fig. 4.3 Detailed view of the quantum workflow lifecycle

4.3.3.2 Quantum-Classical Splitting

Similar to the quantum-classical splitting of the enclosing lifecycle (see Sect. 4.3.2.2), a splitting is also performed in the quantum workflow lifecycle. Thereby, the goal is to decide which of the activities of the workflow model from the previous phase are implemented classically and which require the execution of a quantum algorithm or program. For this, corresponding extensions for workflow languages have been proposed providing explicit modeling constructs for the execution of quantum circuits, as well as frequently occurring pre- and post-processing tasks [18, 33].

4.3.3.3 IT Refinement

The IT *refinement* phase is intended to transform the abstract workflow model from the previous phases into an executable workflow model [20]. For this, the contained activities are refined regarding three dimensions: (1) *what* has to be done within the activity, (2) *with* which programs is the activity performed, and (3) *who* is responsible for the activity. Thereby, existing implementations for the activities should be searched first, e.g., quantum and classical programs or workflow models that can be used as sub-workflows to increase the software reuse [5, 53, 54]. If no suited implementation to reuse is found, it must be implemented in this phase by entering the corresponding lifecycle, e.g., the quantum circuit lifecycle (see Sect. 4.3.4).

4.3.3.4 Deployment

In the *deployment* phase, the modeled and refined workflow model is uploaded to the workflow engine [20, 41]. Thereby, the workflow model is usually frozen, i.e., it can no longer be changed. Thus, the upload of a changed workflow model from another iteration of the lifecycle results in a new version of the workflow model and does not affect running instances. The implementations of the different activities in the workflow can either be bound during deployment or dynamically at runtime [54]. After the deployment, the workflow is ready for execution and can be instantiated.

4.3.3.5 Observability

The created workflow instances are monitored to track their current state during runtime [19, 20]. This includes, e.g., the currently executed activities, the input and output data of already performed activities, or the reason for taking a particular path in the workflow model [21, 34]. The collected information can usually be visualized by the workflow engine and, e.g., used to handle unexpected errors [20]. When a workflow instance terminates, the collected data is moved to the *audit trail*, a separate database comprising the information about completed workflow instances [66, 67].

4.3.3.6   Analysis

In the last phase, the data stored in the audit trail is analyzed, e.g., using process mining or machine learning techniques [66, 68]. Thereby, statistics about the various paths taken through the workflow model or the average execution times can be used as a basis for redesigning and improving the workflow model in the next iteration [20]. This redesign, e.g., includes parallelizing activities, adding automated error handling for frequently occurring errors, or improving slow activity implementations.

4.3.4   *Quantum Circuit Lifecycle*

In the following, we discuss our quantum circuit lifecycle [8], as depicted in Fig. 4.4. This lifecycle is, e.g., entered if a quantum circuit is required as part of a quantum application, and no suitable implementation can be found (see Sect. 4.3.2.4).

4.3.4.1   Quantum-Classical Splitting

The splitting in the quantum circuit lifecycle is the splitting at the lowest granularity compared to the splitting of quantum applications and quantum workflows. It is entered with a description of the problem to solve and is intended to decide if a pure quantum algorithm or a hybrid quantum algorithm should be used [8]. For example,

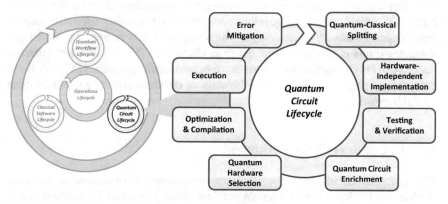

Fig. 4.4 Detailed view of the quantum circuit lifecycle

if the problem is to find eigenvalues, the *quantum phase estimation (QPE)* as a pure quantum algorithm or the *variational quantum eigensolver (VQE)* as a hybrid algorithm can be used [69], and the decision is done in this lifecycle phase.

4.3.4.2 Hardware-Independent Implementation

After deciding which quantum algorithm to use, the corresponding quantum circuit must be implemented. Thereby, the implementation should be hardware-independent to enable a later hardware selection based on the current characteristics of the different available quantum computers (see Sect. 4.3.4.5) [33, 48, 70]. Furthermore, the quantum circuit should also be defined independent of specific input data, which is encoded in the next phase by prepending a suited state preparation circuit to the beginning of the implemented circuit [25, 26]. Thus, the quantum circuit can be reused for different instances of the problem to solve [8]. For the implementation of the quantum circuit, a plethora of technologies can be utilized, for example, (1) quantum programming languages, such as *Q#* or *Quipper*; (2) quantum assembly languages, such as *OpenQASM* or *Quil*; and (3) quantum libraries that are embedded into classical programming languages, such as *Qiskit* or *Forest* in *Python* [15, 40, 71].

4.3.4.3 Testing and Verification

Next, the quantum circuit is tested and verified to ensure its correct behavior. One approach is to add statistical assertions to the quantum circuit [72]. Then, it is verified that the specified state is measured when executing the quantum circuit until the point where the assertion is defined. Thus, the results of the assertions guide programmers in finding bugs. However, this requires the execution of the circuit for each assertion, which is only feasible for small quantum circuits and few assertions. Additionally, first approaches try to check assertions dynamically at runtime [73]. But then additional ancilla qubits and gates are required, limiting the applicability with today's restricted quantum computers [63]. Another approach adapted from classical software engineering is white- and black-box testing, e.g., utilizing a simulator if this is feasible for the quantum circuit size [58, 74]. Further, quantum circuits can also be verified by experts or using automated approaches [57, 59]. However, the debugging, testing, and verification of quantum circuits are still an open research question.

4.3.4.4 Quantum Circuit Enrichment

The quantum circuit from the hardware-independent implementation phase is implemented independent of a certain problem instance to solve. Thus, it is enriched with the details required to solve a particular instance of the problem in this phase

[8]. This enrichment comprises two steps: (1) *state preparation* [25, 26] and (2) *oracle expansion* [75]. For the state preparation step, a circuit initializing the register of the quantum computer with the required state is generated based on the input data [15, 26]. The resulting state preparation circuit is then prepended to the original circuit. Thereby, different encodings exist, such as the *angle, amplitude,* or *basis encoding* [26]. These encodings provide different characteristics, e.g., the number of required qubits or gates. Furthermore, different quantum algorithms rely on black-box functions, so-called oracles [15, 75]. However, these oracles have to be implemented or loaded from a corresponding library before executing the quantum circuit.

4.3.4.5 Quantum Hardware Selection

Quantum computers that are available during the *noisy intermediate-scale quantum (NISQ)* [63] era are error-prone and provide only limited capabilities [15, 48]. Additionally, periodic re-calibrations change their characteristics, e.g., the decoherence times of the qubits, over time [51, 70]. Thus, the selection of a suitable quantum computer to execute a given quantum circuit is a complex task [33, 48]. To overcome this issue, different metrics, such as *quantum volume (QV)* [76] or the *total quantum factor (TQF)* [77], and various benchmarks [78, 79] have been introduced to assess the capabilities of the available quantum computers. Further, there are some tools, such as the *QuRE Toolbox* [80], to estimate the required resources to execute a quantum algorithm on given input data. Finally, the *NISQ Analyzer* [48] automatically selects a suitable quantum computer based on properties of the quantum circuit, such as width or depth, and the current characteristics of the available quantum computers.

4.3.4.6 Optimization and Compilation

After selecting a suitable quantum computer for the execution of the quantum circuit, it has to be optimized and compiled to the machine instructions that can be executed by the selected quantum computer [81, 82]. For this, a quantum compiler assigns the qubits of the quantum circuit to the physical qubits of the quantum computer [15, 83, 84]. Due to the different characteristics of the qubits, e.g., their decoherence times or connectivity, the assignments influence the error probability of the quantum circuit execution [15]. Therefore, the assignments should be optimized based on current provenance data about the qubit characteristics [51]. Similarly, the gates used in the quantum circuit must be mapped to gates physically implemented by the selected quantum computer [81]. If one of the gates is not physically implemented, it has to be replaced by a corresponding subroutine of implemented gates [51, 82].

4.3.4.7 Execution

In the next phase, the compiled quantum circuit is executed on the selected quantum computer. Depending on the quantum cloud offering used, this is done by submitting a corresponding job to a queue or reserving a time slice for the execution [4, 47]. The quantum circuit is usually executed multiple times, referred to as the number of shots, to reduce the impact of statistical errors [15, 51]. Furthermore, if a variational algorithm is selected in the quantum-classical splitting phase, the execution may comprise multiple iterations of quantum and classical processing [8, 15].

4.3.4.8 Error Mitigation

In contrast to full *error correction* [85, 86], which is unfeasible on today's NISQ machines, *error mitigation* [87] has the goal to reduce the impact of noise in the results of quantum circuit executions [15]. Some of these error mitigation techniques require adding additional gates or adapting existing ones while using much fewer qubits than needed for error correction [88]. However, the circuit then has to be adapted before the execution. After the execution, classical post-processing is used to mitigate the errors [87]. Some techniques also solely rely on classical post-processing and do not require changes in the circuits [89]. A subset of these techniques is so-called readout error mitigation or unfolding techniques [27, 28]. Thereby, depending on the used technique, different states are periodically prepared and subsequently measured on the quantum computer [8]. Based on the retrieved data, the impact of readout errors can then be reduced in the result distribution of a circuit execution [27].

4.3.5 Operations Lifecycle

The last lifecycle integrated into the quantum software development lifecycle is the operations lifecycle, for which the different phases are depicted in Fig. 4.5. It is intended to operate all the software artifacts comprising a quantum application.

4.3.5.1 Topology Modeling

The operations personnel performing the phases in this lifecycle are in charge of deploying and managing all software artifacts of the hybrid quantum application (see Sect. 4.3.5.4). However, a manual deployment and management are time-consuming and error-prone [62, 90]. Thus, it must be automated using so-called provisioning or deployment technologies, such as Kubernetes or Terraform [60, 61]. For this, all necessary software artifacts and their dependencies are described by a directed

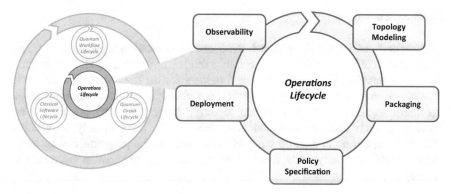

Fig. 4.5 Detailed view of the operations lifecycle

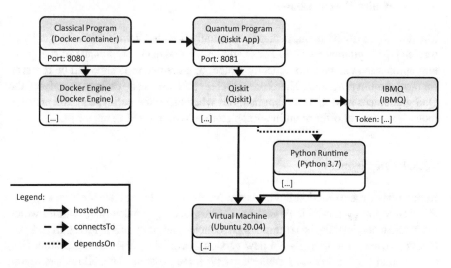

Fig. 4.6 Exemplary topology model for a hybrid quantum application (based on [60])

acyclic graph, called the *topology model* [91]. In addition to the proprietary languages provided by the different provisioning technologies, there are also standardized languages such as *TOSCA* [92] to define topology models [60]. Figure 4.6 depicts an exemplary topology model for a hybrid quantum application. Thereby, the nodes in the topology model represent the different software artifacts, e.g., the classical and quantum programs [23]. Further, the edges specify the relations between the artifacts, e.g., that the classical program is hosted on a docker engine or connects to a quantum program after performing some pre-processing. The semantics of the nodes is defined by reusable types shown in brackets [61], e.g., the quantum program is implemented as a Qiskit app and executed using the IBMQ quantum cloud offering. Finally, the nodes in the topology model can be configured using so-called properties, e.g., the token to access IBMQ at runtime as shown at the corresponding node [60].

4.3.5.2   Packaging

After specifying the topology model, the quantum application is packaged as a self-contained archive [21, 38]. Therefore, only a single entity including all dependencies has to be transferred into the target environment for the execution [62]. This self-contained archive contains the quantum and classical programs comprising the quantum application, as well as the topology model from the previous phase describing their dependencies and how they can be automatically provisioned [21, 62]. Furthermore, workflow models to orchestrate the programs can be added to the archive. Finally, data required by the quantum application may also be packaged [93].

4.3.5.3   Policy Specification

The developed quantum application can usually be offered with different quality of service (QoS) guarantees [94]. For example, the classical components of the quantum application can be automatically scaled, or a defined time slice can be reserved for the quantum programs. Therefore, different policies can be defined specifying the QoS guarantees as well as the implications when using the policy, e.g., the incurred monetary costs, to offer them in an app store or over an API manager [4, 53].

4.3.5.4   Deployment

In this phase, the execution environment for the quantum application is set up. For this, the topology model is passed to a corresponding provisioning engine, which interprets it and installs the required dependencies and programs [21, 61]. In addition to a deployment for all users if a new version is available, also advanced strategies, such as performing a *canary deployment* [95], are possible. This allows deploying the new version for a subset of users to evaluate it before rolling it out for all users.

4.3.5.5   Observability

During runtime, the deployed software artifacts are monitored to verify their correct behavior or to visualize their current state for the user (see Sect. 4.3.3.5). Thereby, the collected data for all software artifacts constituting the quantum application must be consolidated to enable a unified view [51]. This comprises, e.g., the logs of a virtual machine executing a classical program, the logs of a workflow instance, or the current characteristics of the used quantum computers. Furthermore, this data is stored in the long term to enable the analysis of the quantum application (see Sect. 4.3.2.8).

4.4   Discussion

The introduced quantum software development lifecycle integrates the quantum workflow lifecycle, implying that most non-trivial quantum applications should be implemented using workflow technology [18, 21]. Thereby, workflow technology enables benefiting from robust, proven, and mature solutions that have been applied in various heterogeneous application areas, such as *e-Science* [35] or *business process management* [34]. Furthermore, there are already the first commercial workflow offerings specialized for quantum computing like Zapata *Orquestra* [96]. Finally, IBM announced workflows as one of the major building blocks in their roadmap [97]. However, our lifecycle can also be used without workflows if it turns out in the architecture and design phase that workflows are not required for the application.

The presented quantum circuit lifecycle (see Sect. 4.3.4) is designated for the development and execution of quantum circuits during the NISQ era [8, 63]. Therefore, it contains some phases that can be skipped if fully error-corrected quantum computers are available, e.g., the hardware selection or error mitigation phase. Furthermore, other lifecycle phases might change significantly due to new developments. For example, the quantum circuit enrichment phase must be adapted if an efficient *quantum random access memory (QRAM)* [98] implementation is available [8, 26]. Additionally, the quantum software development lifecycle is assuming gate-based quantum algorithm implementations. However, it can be easily adapted by integrating a lifecycle for quantum programs relying on other quantum computing models, e.g., the adiabatic model [44], as discussed in Sect. 4.3.1. To the best of our knowledge, there exists currently no lifecycle for quantum programs using another model.

Finally, there are a lot of open research questions and possibilities to improve the lifecycle phases, for example, developing a holistic test strategy for hybrid quantum applications, the proposal of new metrics to assess and compare quantum computers, or designing a recommendation system for the quantum-classical splitting phases.

4.5   Related Work

Different research works proposed lifecycles, methodologies, or workflows for the development of quantum applications which will be discussed in this section.

Zhao [10] performed a comprehensive survey about quantum software engineering, presenting different methods, tools, and open questions in this research area. Additionally, he also introduces a quantum software lifecycle based on the classical waterfall model, consisting of five phases: (1) *quantum software requirements analysis*, (2) *quantum software design*, (3) *quantum software implementation*, (4) *quantum software testing*, and (5) *quantum software maintenance*. Thereby, the different phases are reused from the classical lifecycle, but the tools and methods for the phases are adapted to the quantum computing domain. However, it misses the discussion of some important aspects, such as the deployment of quantum applications, the orchestration of the quantum and classical programs, and the packaging of all required artifacts, e.g., to store and sell the quantum application in an app store.

A quantum software lifecycle similar to Zhao's is also proposed by Dey et al. [6]. Thereby, they include the same five phases but add an additional *quantum feasibility study* phase to the beginning of the lifecycle. This phase is intended to evaluate the availability of suited quantum algorithms, as well as powerful enough quantum computers. In our lifecycle, this is included in the quantum-classical splitting phase of the enclosing lifecycle, which separates the problem into classical parts and quantum parts that can be successfully executed on an available quantum computer. However, it also does not include some important phases, e.g., the monitoring of the running quantum application or their packaging as a self-contained archive and deployment.

Quantum DevOps was proposed by Gheorghe-Pop et al. [38], motivating the need to apply the DevOps paradigm in the quantum computing domain. Thereby, they analyze the different phases of the traditional DevOps process and extend them correspondingly. Further, they focus on the evaluation of the available quantum computers in each iteration, to enable the selection of a suitable one for the execution.

Sodhi et al. [22] analyzed the characteristics of different quantum computing platforms, e.g., from IBM and Rigetti. Based on this analysis, they examined how the characteristics affect quality attributes of quantum applications, such as maintainability, usability, or performance. Further, the impact on the various lifecycle phases and required steps to achieve the quality attributes in these phases are discussed.

4.6   Conclusion and Outlook

Quantum computers are rapidly evolving in terms of qubit counts, decoherence times, and lower error rates. Thus, problems in more and more application areas can be solved by quantum applications. Hence, the need for high-quality quantum applications will increase dramatically in the next years. However, the development of such applications is complex and incorporates experts from various fields. To enable their successful cooperation and ease the education of new developers, a common understanding of the development process of quantum applications is needed. In this chapter, we introduced a quantum software development lifecycle summarizing eight phases comprising this development process. Furthermore, we discussed the different software artifacts usually realizing a quantum application, i.e., quantum programs, classical programs, and workflows. We presented the lifecycles of these artifacts and showed how they are integrated into the overall lifecycle of quantum applications.

Quantum computing in general, and also quantum software engineering, is a very active research area where new concepts and tools are published regularly. Therefore, the quantum software development lifecycle is a living document, which can be adapted and extended with new developments. This comprises, e.g., the addition of new concepts and tools or the extension with another development phase.

Acknowledgments This work was funded by the BMWi project PlanQK (01MK20005N), the DFG's Excellence Initiative project SimTech (EXC 2075 – 390740016), and the project SEQUOIA funded by the Baden-Wuerttemberg Ministry of the Economy, Labour and Housing.

References[1]

1. Barzen J (2021) From digital humanities to quantum humanities: potentials and applications. In: Quantum computing in the arts and humanities. Springer. arXiv:2103.11825
2. Barzen J, Leymann F, Falkenthal M, Vietz D, Weder B, Wild K (2021) Relevance of near-term quantum computing in the cloud: a humanities perspective. Cloud Comput Serv Sci 1399:25–58
3. Gabor T et al (2020) The holy grail of quantum artificial intelligence: major challenges in accelerating the machine learning pipeline. arXiv:2004.14035
4. Leymann F, Barzen J, Falkenthal M, Vietz D, Weder B, Wild K (2020) Quantum in the cloud: application potentials and research opportunities. In: Proceedings of the 10th International Conference on Cloud Computing and Services Science (CLOSER). SciTePress, pp 9–24
5. Piattini M, Peterssen G, Pérez-Castillo R (2020) Quantum computing: a new software engineering golden age. ACM SIGSOFT Softw Eng Notes 45(3):12–14
6. Dey N, Ghosh M, Kundu SS, Chakrabarti A (2020) QDLC–the quantum development life cycle. arXiv:2010.08053
7. Nielsen MA, Chuang I (2002) Quantum computation and quantum information
8. Weder B, Barzen J, Leymann F, Salm M, Vietz D (2020) The quantum software lifecycle. In: Proceedings of the 1st ACM SIGSOFT International Workshop on Architectures and Paradigms for Engineering Quantum Software (APEQS). ACM, pp 2–9
9. Piattini M, Serrano M, Perez-Castillo R, Petersen G, Hevia JL (2021) Toward a quantum software engineering. IT Prof 23(1):62–66
10. Zhao J (2020) Quantum software engineering: landscapes and horizons. arXiv:2007.07047
11. Kohlborn T, Korthaus A, Rosemann M (2009) Business and software service lifecycle management. In: Proceedings of the 13th International Enterprise Distributed Object Computing Conference (EDOC). IEEE, pp 87–96
12. Canós JH, Penadés MC, Carsí JÁ (1999) From software process to workflow process: the workflow lifecycle. In: Proceedings of the International Process Technology Workshop
13. Munassar NMA, Govardhan A (2010) A comparison between five models of software engineering. Int J Comput Sci Issues (IJCSI) 7(5):94
14. Ghezzi C, Jazayeri M, Mandrioli D (2002) Fundamentals of software engineering
15. Leymann F, Barzen J (2020) The bitter truth about gate-based quantum algorithms in the nisq era. Quantum Sci Technol 5(4):044007
16. Pérez-Delgado CA, Perez-Gonzalez HG (2020) Towards a quantum software modeling language. In: Proceedings of the IEEE/ACM 42nd International Conference on Software Engineering Workshops, pp 442–444

---

[1] All links were last followed on June 15, 2021.

17. Mathur S, Malik S (2010) Advancements in the V-Model. Int J Comput Applications 1(12): 29–34
18. Weder B, Breitenbücher U, Leymann F, Wild K (2020) Integrating quantum computing into workflow modeling and execution. In: Proceedings of the 13th IEEE/ACM International Conference on Utility and Cloud Computing (UCC). IEEE, pp 279–291
19. Ellis CA (1999) Workflow technology. Computer supported cooperative work, trends in software series 7:29–54
20. Leymann F, Roller D (2000) Production workflow: concepts and techniques. Prentice Hall PTR
21. Leymann F, Barzen J (2021) Hybrid quantum applications need two orchestrations in super-position: a software architecture perspective. arXiv:2103.04320
22. Sodhi B, Kapur R (2021) Quantum computing platforms: assessing the impact on quality attributes and SDLC activities. arXiv:2104.14261
23. Weder B, Barzen J, Leymann F, Zimmermann M (2021) Hybrid quantum applications need two orchestrations in superposition: a software architecture perspective. In: Proceedings of the IEEE International Conference on Web Services (ICWS). IEEE
24. McClean JR, Romero J, Babbush R, Aspuru-Guzik A (2016) The theory of variational hybrid quantum-classical algorithms. New J Phys 18(2):023023
25. Cortese JA, Braje TM (2018) Loading classical data into a quantum computer. arXiv:1807.02500
26. Weigold M et al (2021) Data encoding patterns for quantum computing. In: Proceedings of the 27th Conference on Pattern Languages of Programs. The Hillside Group
27. Brenner L, Verschuuren P, Balasubramanian R, Burgard C, Croft V, Cowan G, Verkerke W (2019) Comparison of unfolding methods using RooFitUnfold. arXiv:1910.14654
28. Maciejewski FB et al (2020) Mitigation of readout noise in near-term quantum devices by classical post-processing based on detector tomography. Quantum 4
29. Shor PW (1997) Polynomial-time algorithms for prime factorization and discrete logarithms on a quantum computer. SIAM J Comput 26(5):1484–1509
30. Simon DR (1994) On the power of quantum cryptography. In: 35th Annual Symposium on Foundations of Computer Science, pp 116–123
31. Kandala A et al (2017) Hardware-efficient variational quantum eigensolver for small molecules and quantum magnets. Nature 549(7671):242–246
32. Farhi E, Goldstone J, Gutmann S (2014) A quantum approximate optimization algorithm. arXiv:1411.4028
33. Weder B, Barzen J, Leymann F, Salm M (2021) Automated quantum hardware selection for quantum workflows. Electronics 10(8)
34. Leymann F, Roller D (1997) Workflow-based applications. IBM Syst J 36(1):102–123
35. Liu J, Pacitti E, Valduriez P, Mattoso M (2015) A survey of data-intensive scientific workflow management. J Grid Comput 13(4):457–493
36. Eder J, Liebhart W (1997) Workflow transactions. Workflow Handb:195–202
37. Bass L, Weber I, Zhu L (2015) DevOps: a software architect's perspective. Addison-Wesley Professional
38. Gheorghe-Pop ID, Tcholtchev N, Ritter T, Hauswirth M (2020) Quantum DevOps: towards reliable and applicable NISQ quantum computing. In: IEEE Globecom Workshops. IEEE, pp 1–6
39. Wettinger J, Breitenbücher U, Kopp O, Leymann F (2016) Streamlining DevOps automation for Cloud applications using TOSCA as standardized metamodel. Future Gen Comput Syst 56: 317–332
40. Vietz D et al (2021) On decision support for quantum application developers: categorization, comparison, and analysis of existing technologies. In: Proceedings of the 21st International Conference on Computational Science (ICCS). Springer, pp 127–141
41. Dumas M, La Rosa M, Mendling J, Reijers HA (2013) Fundamentals of business process management, vol 1. Springer

42. Boehm BW (1988) A spiral model of software development and enhancement. Computer 21(5): 61–72
43. Kumar N, Zadgaonkar A, Shukla A (2013) Evolving a new software development life cycle model SDLC-2013 with client satisfaction. Int J Soft Comput Eng (IJSCE) 3(1):2231–2307
44. Aharonov D, Van Dam W, Kempe J, Landau Z, Lloyd S, Regev O (2008) Adiabatic quantum computation is equivalent to standard quantum computation. SIAM Rev 50(4):755–787
45. Grady JO (2010) System requirements analysis. Elsevier
46. Pérez-Castillo R, Serrano MA, Piattini M (2021) Software modernization to embrace quantum technology. Adv Eng Softw 151:102933
47. LaRose R (2019) Overview and comparison of gate level quantum software platforms. Quantum 3:130
48. Salm M, Barzen J, Breitenbücher U, Leymann F, Weder B, Wild K (2020) The NISQ analyzer: automating the selection of quantum computers for quantum algorithms. In: Proceedings of the 14th Symposium and Summer School on Service-Oriented Computing (SummerSOC). Springer, pp 66–85
49. Leymann F (2019) Towards a pattern language for quantum algorithms. In: Quantum technology and optimization problems. Springer International Publishing, pp 218–230
50. Herschel M, Diestelkämper R, Ben Lahmar H (2017) A survey on provenance: what for? What form? What from? VLDB J 26(6):881–906
51. Weder B, Barzen J, Leymann F, Salm M, Wild K (2021) QProv: a provenance system for quantum computing. IET Quantum Commun
52. Gemeinhardt F, Garmendia A, Wimmer M (2021) Towards model-driven quantum software engineering. In: Proceedings of the 2nd International Workshop on Quantum Software Engineering (Q-SE). ACM
53. De B (2017) API management. In: API management. Springer, pp 15–28
54. Garofalakis J, Panagis Y, Sakkopoulos E, Tsakalidis A (2006) Contemporary web service discovery mechanisms. J Web Eng 5(3):265–290
55. Leymann F, Barzen J, Falkenthal M (2019) Towards a platform for sharing quantum software. In: Proceedings of the 13th Advanced Summer School on Service-Oriented Computing (SummerSOC), IBM Technical Report. IBM Research Division, pp 70–74
56. Wu Y et al (2003) UML-based integration testing for component-based software. In: International Conference on COTS-Based Software Systems. Springer, pp 251–260
57. Amy M (2018) Towards large-scale functional verification of universal quantum circuits. arXiv:1805.06908
58. Miranskyy A, Zhang L, Doliskani J (2020) Is your quantum program bug-free? In: Proceedings of the ACM/IEEE 42nd International Conference on Software Engineering: New Ideas and Emerging Results (ICSE-NIER). ACM, pp 29–32
59. Wang SA, Lu CY, Tsai IM, Kuo SY (2008) An XQDD-Based verification method for quantum circuits. IEICE Trans Fundamentals Electr Commun Comput Sci 91(2):584–594
60. Wild K et al (2020) TOSCA4QC: two modeling styles for TOSCA to automate the deployment and orchestration of quantum applications. In: Proceedings of the 24th International Enterprise Distributed Object Computing Conference (EDOC). IEEE, pp 125–134
61. Wurster M et al (2019) The essential deployment metamodel: a systematic review of deployment automation technologies. Software-Intensive Cyber-Physical Systems
62. Weder B, Breitenbücher U, Képes K, Leymann F, Zimmermann M (2020) Deployable self-contained workflow models. In: Proceedings of the 8th European Conference on Service-Oriented and Cloud Computing (ESOCC). Springer, pp 85–96
63. Preskill J (2018) Quantum Computing in the NISQ era and beyond. Quantum 2:79
64. OMG (2011) Business Process Model and Notation (BPMN) version 2.0. Object Management Group
65. OASIS (2007) Web Services Business Process Execution Language (WS-BPEL) version 2.0. Organization for the Advancement of Structured Information Standards

66. Agrawal R, Gunopulos D, Leymann F (1998) Mining process models from workflow logs. In: International Conference on Extending Database Technology. Springer, pp 467–483
67. Waters BR, Balfanz D, Durfee G, Smetters DK (2004) Building an encrypted and searchable audit log. In: NDSS, vol 4. Citeseer, pp 5–6
68. Pinter SS, Golani M (2004) Discovering workflow models from activities' lifespans. Comput Indus 53(3):283–296
69. Wang D, Higgott O, Brierley S (2019) Accelerated variational quantum eigensolver. Phys Rev Lett 122(14):140504
70. Tannu SS, Qureshi MK (2019) Not all qubits are created equal: a case for variability-aware policies for nisq-era quantum computers. In: Proceedings of the 24th International Conference on Architectural Support for Programming Languages and Operating Systems, pp 987–999
71. Fingerhuth M, Babej T, Wittek P (2018) Open source software in quantum computing. PLoS One 13(12)
72. Huang Y, Martonosi M (2019) Statistical assertions for validating patterns and finding bugs in quantum programs. In: Proceedings of the 46th International Symposium on Computer Architecture. ACM, pp 541–553
73. Liu J, Byrd GT, Zhou H (2020) Quantum circuits for dynamic runtime assertions in quantum computation. In: Proceedings of the 25th International Conference on Architectural Support for Programming Languages and Operating Systems. ACM, pp 1017–1030
74. Usaola MP (2020) Quantum Software Testing. In: Proceedings of the 1st International Workshop on the Quantum Software Engineering & Programming, pp 57–63
75. Kashefi E, Kent A, Vedral V, Banaszek K (2002) Comparison of quantum oracles. Phys Rev A 65(5):050304
76. Bishop LS et al (2017) Quantum volume. Technical Report
77. Sete EA, Zeng WJ, Rigetti CT (2016) A functional architecture for scalable quantum computing. In: IEEE International Conference on Rebooting Computing, pp 1–6
78. Knill E, Laflamme R, Martinez R, Negrevergne C (2001) Benchmarking quantum computers: the five-qubit error correcting code. Phys Rev Lett 86:5811–5814
79. Michielsen K, Nocon M, Willsch D, Jin F, Lippert T, De Raedt H (2017) Benchmarking gate-based quantum computers. Comput Phys Commun 220:44–55
80. Suchara M, Kubiatowicz J, Faruque A, Chong FT, Lai CY, Paz G (2013) QuRE: the quantum resource estimator toolbox. In: Proceedings of the 31st International Conference on Computer Design (ICCD). IEEE, pp 419–426
81. Booth J Jr (2012) Quantum compiler optimizations. arXiv:1206.3348
82. Sivarajah S, Dilkes S, Cowtan A, Simmons W, Edgington A, Duncan R (2020) t| ket>: a retargetable compiler for NISQ devices. Quantum Sci Technol
83. Heyfron LE, Campbell ET (2018) An efficient quantum compiler that reduces T count. Quantum Sci Technol 4(1):015004
84. Javadi Abhari A et al (2014) ScaffCC: a framework for compilation and analysis of quantum computing programs. In: Proceedings of the 11th Conference on Computing Frontiers. ACM, pp 1–10
85. Gaitan F (2008) Quantum error correction and fault tolerant quantum computing. CRC Press
86. Reed MD et al (2012) Realization of three-qubit quantum error correction with superconducting circuits. Nature 482(7385):382–385
87. Song C, Cui J, Wang H, Hao J, Feng H, Li Y (2019) Quantum computation with universal error mitigation on a superconducting quantum processor. Sci Adv 5(9)
88. Endo S, Benjamin SC, Li Y (2018) Practical quantum error mitigation for near-future applications. Phys Rev X 8(3):031027
89. Endo S, Cai Z, Benjamin SC, Yuan X (2021) Hybrid quantum-classical algorithms and quantum error mitigation. J Phys Soc Japan 90(3):032001
90. Breitenbücher U, Binz T, Képes K, Kopp O, Leymann F, Wettinger J (2014) Combining declarative and imperative cloud application provisioning based on TOSCA. In: International Conference on Cloud Engineering (IC2E). IEEE, pp 87–96

91. Binz T, Breiter G, Leymann F, Spatzier T (2012) Portable cloud services using TOSCA. IEEE Internet Comput 16(3):80–85
92. OASIS (2013) Topology and Orchestration Specification for Cloud Applications (TOSCA) version 1.0. Organization for the Advancement of Structured Information Standards
93. Zimmermann M et al (2018) Towards deployable research object archives based on TOSCA. In: Papers from the 12th Advanced Summer School on Service-Oriented Computing (SummerSoC). IBM Research Division, pp 31–42
94. Cardoso J, Sheth A, Miller J, Arnold J, Kochut K (2004) Quality of service for workflows and web service processes. J Web Semantics 1(3):281–308
95. Ahmadighohandizi F, Systä K (2016) Application development and deployment for IoT devices. In: Proceedings of the 4th European Conference on Service-Oriented and Cloud Computing (ESOCC). Springer, pp 74–85
96. Zapata: Orquestra (2021) https://www.zapatacomputing.com/orquestra
97. IBM (2021) IBM's roadmap for building an open quantum software ecosystem. https://www.ibm.com/blogs/research/2021/02/quantum-development-roadmap
98. Giovannetti V, Lloyd S, Maccone L (2008) Quantum random access memory. Phys Rev Lett 100(16):160501

Chapter 5
Formal Methods for Quantum Software Engineering

Carmelo R. Cartiere

5.1 Introduction

Although quantum computing (QC) is the future of computing systems, the tools for reasoning about the quantum model of computation, in which the laws obeyed are those on the quantum mechanical scale, are still a mix of linear algebra and Dirac notation—two subjects more suitable for physicists rather than computer scientists and software engineers [17, 18]. On this ground, we believe it is possible to provide a more intuitive but still high-integrity approach to thinking and writing about quantum computing systems, not only to foster the design of quantum algorithms but also to simplify the development of quantum software. Here, we move the first step in such a direction, introducing the Zed (Z) specification language as the means to represent the operations of a quantum computer via axiomatic definitions, also hiring the same symbolisms, semantics, and reasoning principles to which classical software engineers are already used to. We name this novel branch *formal quantum software engineering* (F-QSE) [1].

5.2 Overture to Formal Methods

Formal methods (FM) are a tool of classical software engineering, the distinguishing feature of which is the ability to model and work with complex systems by considering them as mathematical entities.

C. R. Cartiere (✉)
Kellogg College, University of Oxford, Oxford, UK
e-mail: carmelo.cartiere@oxon.org

© The Author(s), under exclusive license to Springer Nature Switzerland AG 2022
M. A. Serrano et al. (eds.), *Quantum Software Engineering*,
https://doi.org/10.1007/978-3-031-05324-5_5

With FM, systems are represented with a rigorous mathematical model, which has not only the advantage of having its properties thoroughly verified but also of having its behavior tested via mathematical proof.

Indeed, the use of formal methods in a QC setting can help those who roam the world of computing to both (a) better "understanding and reasoning about the properties of quantum systems" with the adoption of a classical tool of software engineering [2] and (b) describe quantum structures and design quantum algorithms in a more spontaneous way while still adopting a particular form of a mathematically rigorous system [3].

Plus, if we design a QC system using formal specifications (FS), we are developing a set of theorems about that system which, by being proved correct, shall ensure the correct behavior of the system [20].

This is because the trait of FS is to adopt mathematical notations to accurately describe the characteristic properties of a system, without overly limiting how these properties are met, as well as describing the system's behavior, but without dictating how it should do it.

And FSs are helpful during the development process of a system for the reason that they allow to confidently answer the key questions regarding the functions of the system, without neither having to decipher any kind of information by immense amounts of code nor having to investigate the meaning of more or less detailed comments scattered across either the documentation or the code itself.

Since it is detached from the programming code, the guidelines of a FS can already be fulfilled at the early stages of development. Nevertheless, there may be a need to modify it along the way with any design change or addition, as well as when customer requests are changed. But, beyond everything, it is a valuable tool to promote a shared understanding of the system among all people involved in the project.

To say it with Jacky's words, "Using formal methods can be more difficult than programming in the usual way—because formal methods aim higher. Describing exactly what your program does is more difficult than letting testers or users figure it out for themselves. Making your program do the right thing in every situation is more difficult than just handling some typical cases. Any method that can handle hard problems will sometimes be hard to carry out; only superficial methods can be easy all the time. [. . .]. Formal methods make us confront the hard problems early. The difficulties cannot be escaped, only deferred. Superficial methods put off the hard parts until coding and testing—but then they appear with a vengeance. News stories about stressful projects tell of programmers who work eighty-hour weeks, sleep under their desks, punch holes in walls, have nervous breakdowns, and commit suicide [Markoff, 1993; Zachary, 1994]. Compared to that, formal methods don't seem so difficult after all. By making difficult issues more visible, formal methods encourage us to seek a more thorough understanding of the problem we are trying to solve. They require us to express our intentions with exceptional simplicity and clarity. They help us resist the usual tendency in programming to make things too complicated and therefore error-prone and difficult to use" [4].

5.3   The Z Specification Language

In our work, we adopted Z as the FS language of choice: not only because it is already the most (or one of the most) widely used formal languages for describing and modeling the classical computing systems[1] but also because, as Jacky pointed out: "Fortunately, most of the mathematics we need for formal methods is not terribly difficult. The discrete mathematics used in most practical applications of formal methods is easier than much of the calculus that students in the sciences and engineering must study" [4].

The Z specification language permits to build detailed and unambiguous specifications of the behavior of a system. Based on type theory, a branch of symbolic logic that not only formalizes mathematical entities like variables, functions, and operations on them but also formalizes the idea that each entity is of some definite type (e.g., the type $\mathbb{N}$ of natural numbers), it allows to reasoning over the properties of a system (e.g., inputs, transformations, outputs, boundaries) by adopting a *detailed mathematical notation* based on well-defined data structures (e.g., sets, relations, functions) and *logical expressions* written in first-order predicate logic.

It was Jean-Raymond Abrial that in 1977 originally proposed the Z specification language. And when in the 1980s Abrial started working with the Programming Research Group at the University of Oxford, the language was more substantially developed.

Abrial alleged that Z is so named because "it is the ultimate language," but we can also assume that the Z specification language is so-called because it is based on a minimal-typed version of Zermelo-Fraenkel's set theory.

In our description of the F-QSE tools, we shall mainly use Z's *axiomatic definitions*, which are a formal description of the behavior of the system, or part of it, by the means of *declarations* and predicates [19].

An axiomatic definition is drafted in the following form:

$$\begin{array}{|l}
x : S \\
\hline
p
\end{array}$$

In it, we can distinguish the two parts: the *declaration*, made up of the variable x and *basic* type S, and the *predicate* p.

The *declaration* (or signature) is the simplest way to define an object and can be expressed in two ways: if the object corresponds to an original set of elements, or basic type, then either we will write its name in brackets or, if the object is a variable of an already defined set, we shall give it the name of the set that it comes from (with no brackets). For example, the declaration [*Type*] establishes an original basic type

---

[1]The most widely used notations for developing model-based languages are Vienna Development Method (VDM), Zed (Z), and Bi (B) [5].

called *Type*. The other way is the declaration *x:A*, which establishes a new variable x drawn from the set A (but with the limitation that if this set is not the set $\mathbb{Z}$—i.e., the set of integers—then, in that case, the set must be defined somewhere in the specification) [2].

The *predicate* describes the behavior of the system: it takes as input one or more entities from the domain in question and returns an output that is either True or False [2]. In it, we can find the following logic symbols: $\forall$ (for all), $\exists$ (exists), $\in$ (belongs to), • (such as), $\wedge$ (and), $\vee$ (or), $\Leftrightarrow$ (if ... and only if ...), and $\Rightarrow$ (if ... then ...).

It is worth mentioning that the *basic type S* shall identify the *maximal set* of the system, that is, a set as much complete as possible within the boundaries of the given specification. This has the effect of making sure that any given value x in the specification shall be associated with exactly one type, that is, the largest set S for which $x \in S$ [2].

So, the adoption of Z for modeling a system requires the formalization of the building blocks of that system, which, in the case of a QC system, are the *observable* and the *observable operators*.

For the sake of simplicity, you can think about the *observable* as the data type that we shall use to declare qubits and about the *observable operators* as the operations that can be performed on qubits.

Once that the *observable* and the *observable operators* have been formalized, it is possible to proceed with the design and implementation of any QC model, i.e., the abstract representation of a QC system, and with its formal verification (FV), through a sequence of four rigorous yet intuitive steps: (a) the *specification*, which is the narrative of the QC system and describes what the system should do; (b) the *refinement*, which is an iterative fine-tuning of the FS and produces the polished QC system; (c) the *proof*, which walks us through the process to prove, or disprove, the properties of the QC system against its FS and demonstrate that the candidate system's design is correct; and, finally, (d) the *implementation*, which is the conversion of the specification into working code.[2]

5.4 An Introduction to the Quantum Computing Observable

Observables (or basis) can be considered the most significant entities of QM. Given that a quantum object (QO) holds many attributes (e.g., position, momentum, energy), one observable completely describes one attribute by conserving all of that attribute's possible states, or eigenstates, in a superposed configuration. In QC systems, QOs have only one observable, the *qubit*, which superposed configuration is the linear combination of its two possible eigenstates. Its quantum state vector,

---

[2]"The trick of using formal methods effectively is to know when proofs are worth doing and when they are not" [2].

commonly expressed in Dirac's bra-ket notation [6], is, therefore, the linear combination of the two eigenstates' associated eigenvectors $|0\rangle$, $|1\rangle$ ket, which corresponding measurable eigenvalues (the scalars) are 0, 1:

$$\vec{\psi} = |0\rangle + |1\rangle$$

As per its QM counterpart, measuring an observable in a QC system will collapse that observable into one of its eigenstates that for a qubit are those corresponding to either $|0\rangle$ or $|1\rangle$, with probabilities c_0, c_1 [3] [7]:

An easy way to illustrate the concept of an unknown state of an observable (i.e., when the basis' states are in superposition) is by describing Schrödinger's cat: if we receive a cat in a closed box, it can be both dead and alive, with given probabilities, until we open the box (i.e., we observe it). In bra-ket notation, it is simply written:

$$\overrightarrow{cat} = c_0 |\text{ alive}\rangle + c_1 |\text{ dead}\rangle$$

5.4.1 Formalizing the Observable

By the third postulate of QM, an observable that has a finite number of quantum states can be represented via a Hermitian matrix.[4] As such, the three requirements that it must have can be described, with a sound formalism, by adopting strongly typed data and first-order logic [3]; i.e.:

1. It must be a complex square matrix of order n:

$$|\ \mathbb{O}^n : \mathbb{C}^{n \times n}$$

---

[3] The probability for an observable to collapse into any of its states is the squared modulus of the states' corresponding probability amplitudes, which are complex numbers that weight each eigenvector and such that it is $|c_0|^2 + \dots + |c_n|^2 = 1$.

[4] But if the Hilbert space $\mathcal{H}$ is infinite-dimensional, the observable is described by a *symmetric operator*, which is represented as a map f between two domains of basis' states D and D^* dense in $\mathcal{H}$, such that $\forall x : D, y : D^* \exists f : D \mapsto D^* \bullet \langle f(x), y \rangle = \langle x, f(y) \rangle$. This is a *bijective function* (injective-surjective), in the sense that it cannot map two distinct states of the domain D onto the same state of the co-domain D^*, thus preserving its unitary quality. However, because an infinite-dimensional space is unbounded, also the operator is unbounded; therefore, it does not have a largest eigenvalue, leaving us with the conclusion that it might not be defined everywhere and, as such, classifying it as a *partial bijective* function, which implies graph inclusion: $D \leq D^*$.

2. It must be equivalent to its conjugate transpose:

$$\forall c : \mathbb{O}^n \; \exists_1 \; c' : \overline{\mathbb{O}^n}^T \bullet \left(c_{ij} = c'_{ij}\right)$$

3. For every eigenvector (or column) of the matrix, the eigenvalue must be a real number; and such that it is the element on the main diagonal of the matrix:

$$\forall V^{n \times 1} : \mathbb{PO}^n \; \exists_1 \; \lambda : \mathbb{R} \; \bullet \lambda = c_{jj} \epsilon \mathbb{O}^n$$

In Z, all three requirements can be summarized with the following axiomatic definition satisfying the principle of soundness promoted by FM [2]:

$$
\begin{array}{|l}
\mathbb{O}^n : \mathbb{C}^{n \times n} \\
\hline
\forall c : \mathbb{O}^n \; \exists_1 \; c' : \overline{\mathbb{O}^n}^T \bullet \left(c_{ij} = c'_{ij}\right) \epsilon \mathbb{C} \wedge c_{jj} \epsilon \mathbb{R}
\end{array}
$$

5.4.2 The Observable Operators

After having introduced the new type $\mathbb{O}^n$, it is now possible to define the observable operators. They are elementary quantum gates that perform unitary transformations U_f (i.e., reversible computations) and that, applied to an observable, make it possible to write quantum programs.

As we will see, most of quantum gates only need to perform one operation during a transformation, for example, when they make a classical state into a superposition state, while only two operations are needed to form an entanglement between two qubits.

In the following paragraphs, we introduce the axiomatic definition of the most common quantum gates: *Identity, Pauli-X, Phase Shift, Pauli-Z, Hadamard,* and *C-Not.* In this way, we shall have the necessary mathematical toolkit to design quantum software in Z.

Identity Gate. It is the simplest, single qubit, quantum operator that maps the input to the output unchanged. It is required by any operation where the same qubits that are passed as arguments must be returned:

$$I : \mathbb{O}^2 \twoheadrightarrow \mathbb{O}^2$$

$$\forall x : \{0,1\} \, \exists r \, : \, \{|x\rangle \mapsto |x\rangle\} \bullet r \in I \iff (|0\rangle \mapsto |0\rangle \land |1\rangle \mapsto |1\rangle) \in r$$

Pauli-X (or Bit-Flip) Gate. It is the quantum equivalent of the classical NOT gate:

$$X : \mathbb{O}^2 \twoheadrightarrow \mathbb{O}^2$$

$$\forall x : \{0,1\} \, \exists r \, : \, \{|x\rangle \mapsto |x'\rangle\} \bullet r \in X \iff (|0\rangle \mapsto |1\rangle \land |1\rangle \mapsto |0\rangle) \in r$$

Phase Shift Gate. It represents a family of gates that rotate the basis' state $|1\rangle$ of any arbitrary angle ϕ:

$$R_\phi : \mathbb{O}^2 \twoheadrightarrow \mathbb{O}^2$$

$$\forall x : \{0,1\} \, \exists r \, : \, \{|x\rangle \mapsto |x'\rangle\} \bullet r \in R_\phi \iff (|0\rangle \mapsto |0\rangle \land |1\rangle \mapsto |e^{i\phi}\rangle) \in r$$

Pauli-Z (or π Phase Shift) Gate. It is a special case of the Phase Shift gate that rotates the basis' state $|1\rangle$ a π angle:

$$Z : \mathbb{O}^2 \twoheadrightarrow \mathbb{O}^2$$

$$\forall x : \{0,1\} \, \exists r \, : \, \{|x\rangle \mapsto |x'\rangle\} \bullet r \in Z \iff (|0\rangle \mapsto |0\rangle \land |1\rangle \mapsto -|1\rangle) \in r$$

Hadamard Gate. It is perhaps the most useful quantum operator because it maps any basis' state to one qubit with balanced superposition and vice versa:

$$H : \mathbb{O}^2 \twoheadrightarrow \mathbb{O}^2$$

$$\forall x : \{0,+,1,-\} \, \exists r \, : \, \{|x\rangle \mapsto |x'\rangle\} \bullet r \in H \iff (|0\rangle \mapsto |+\rangle \land |+\rangle \mapsto$$
$$-|0\rangle) \in r \land (|1\rangle \mapsto |-\rangle \land |-\rangle \mapsto -|1\rangle) \in r$$

C-Not Gate. The Controlled Not gate is the most popular two-qubit operator because it puts two qubits in a separable state, where a tensor product pairs the first qubit with the result of an addition modulo-2 between both. As such, it is used to entangle two qubits or disentangle the EPR pair:

$$N : \mathbb{O}^4 \rightarrowtail \mathbb{O}^4$$

$$\forall x, y : \{0,1\} \, \exists r : \{|xy\rangle \mapsto |xy'\rangle\} \bullet r \in N \Leftrightarrow (|0y\rangle \mapsto |0y\rangle \wedge |1y\rangle \mapsto -|1\bar{y}\rangle) \in r$$

Similar to what happens in any conventional computation, quantum computations are just a sequence of gates applied in a particular order: each gate takes an input and, after having performed its operation on that input, returns an output. However, in QC, the single use of an operator simultaneously applies to all basis' states [8].

5.5 A Practical Example of F-QSE: Programming the Deutsch Algorithm from Specifications

By using FM, it is possible to describing and implementing quantum algorithms despite their complexity.

The Deutsch algorithm, the foundation model of QC [9, 10, 16], proves if a quantum oracle, i.e., a black box that performs a unitary transformation U_f on a qubit, is either *constant* (always maximizing the same state) or *balanced* (returning each state half of the time). It exploits the quantum entanglement principle [9] and requires the use of two quantum operators: a Hadamard gate, for preparing two qubits in balanced superposition, and a C-Not gate, for entangling the two qubits.

In Dirac notation, it is represented as a ket taking a pair of qubits, prepared from two different basis' states (x and y), and mapping them to an entangled pair where the second qubit performs as the register storing the state (solution) that will be set on the first qubit by the quantum oracle. The observation (measurement) of the first qubit shall, therefore, make it collapse into the state ($|0\rangle$ for *constant*, $|1\rangle$ for *balanced*) that is held by the second qubit, to which it is entangled:

$$| x, y \rangle \xrightarrow{U_f} | x, f(x) \oplus y \rangle$$

With the Z notation, the algorithm can be described through axiomatic definitions, either by importing within the constraining predicate the conventional Dirac representation (which is sound but doesn't add much in a SE perspective) (Fig. 5.1):

Fig. 5.1 The quantum circuit for the Deutsch algorithm

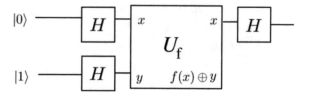

$$deutsch : (\mathbb{Z}_2 \rightarrow \mathbb{Z}_2) \rightarrow \mathbb{Z}_2$$

$$\forall f : (\mathbb{Z}_2 \rightarrow \mathbb{Z}_2); x, y : \{0,1\} \bullet deutsch\ (f) = |x, f\ (x) \oplus y\rangle$$

or by taking advantage of the axiomatic definitions already shaped for the observable operators, writing:

$$deutsch : (\mathbb{Z}_2 \rightarrow \mathbb{Z}_2) \rightarrow \mathbb{Z}_2$$

$$\forall f : (\mathbb{Z}_2 \rightarrow \mathbb{Z}_2); x, y : \{0,1\} \bullet deutsch\ (f) = N_f\ |\ x \leftarrow H\ |0\rangle, y$$
$$\leftarrow H\ |1\rangle\rangle \wedge H\ |x\rangle$$

rather than:

$$deutsch : (\mathbb{Z}_2 \rightarrow \mathbb{Z}_2) \rightarrow \mathbb{Z}_2$$

$$\forall f : (\mathbb{Z}_2 \rightarrow \mathbb{Z}_2); x, y : \{0,1\} \bullet deutsch\ (f) = x \leftarrow H\ |0\rangle \wedge y$$
$$\leftarrow H\ |1\rangle \wedge N_f\ |x, y\rangle \wedge H\ |x\rangle$$

Indeed, with the last two definitions, by describing the algorithm through a sequence of formal operators, we offer guidance for coding it by directly following the stepwise logic represented.

Of course, the coding part can be done in any quantum programming language. For our case, to match the formal definitions introduced, we worked out an instructions' set in Haskell that leans on Green's QIO library [11].

The Deutsch algorithm can now be, straightforwardly, translated into the following QC program:

```
deutsch :: (Bool → Bool) → QIO ( Bool )
deutsch f = do
x ⟵ qb("H|0⟩")
```

$$y \longleftarrow qb(\,"H|\,1\rangle"\,)$$
$$qN(f)\,x\,y$$
$$qH(x)$$
$$mq(x)$$

5.6 Another Practical Example of F-QSE: The Quantum Teleportation Protocol

The Quantum Teleportation Protocol (QTP) is an algorithm that was firstly published by Bennett et al. in 1993 and which can be used to transfer a quantum state between two remote endpoints A and B (say, Alice and Bob).

The QTP is at the base of the so-called superdense coding; that is, you communicate two bits of classical information by only sending out one single qubit.

The foundation of the QTP is the entanglement principle (EP): when two remote and not physically connected objects have in the past interacted within the same local system, they remain linked forever; and each modification of the state of one of them induces a modification into the state of the other one.

One practical use of the QTP is the possibility to carry out secure communications in such a way that the cryptographic key does not need to be transferred between the two endpoints but can just be teleported. By doing this, any risk of eavesdropping is completely cancelled.

Now, with the help of a short storytelling, we will show a handy example of how to implement the QTP with the use of FM.

Alice and Bob are two secret agents who met a long time ago but now live far apart. During the time spent together, they generated an EPR (Einstein-Podolsky-Rosen) pair or Bell state[5] [13]:

$$| \beta_{00} \rangle = \frac{1}{\sqrt{2}} \, | \, 00 \rangle + \frac{1}{\sqrt{2}} \, | \, 11 \rangle$$

The simplest way to do it is to set one qubit in superposition with the use of a Hadamard gate and, applying a C-Not gate, entangle it with a second qubit of known state:

---

[5]Bell states represent the simplest example of quantum entanglement and are a form of two maximally entangled basis' state vectors (qubits) which are pure (cannot be represented as a combination of other basis' states) and normalized (the overall probability of the particle to be in one of the two basis' states is 1): $\langle \Phi | \Phi \rangle = 1$.

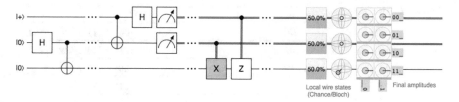

Fig. 5.2 The quantum teleportation circuit proposed by Bennett et al. [12]

$$|\beta_{xy}\rangle \xrightarrow{U_f} |x\rangle \oplus y$$

As already seen in Deutsch's algorithm, thanks to the use of Zed's axiomatic definition, we can express the constraining predicate with the conventional Dirac form as:

$$\begin{array}{l} bell : \mathbb{Z}_2 \rightarrow (\mathbb{O}^2 \rightarrow \mathbb{O}^2) \\ \forall f \in bell;\ x: \{0,1\};\ y: \{0\} \bullet f = |x\rangle \oplus y \end{array}$$

However, our aim is to provide a clearer definition of the algorithm for SE: something that can help the classically trained base of software engineers to go from zero (the definition) to hero (the code). And it can be easily done by recruiting the observable operators already defined, as:

$$\begin{array}{l} bell : \mathbb{Z}_2 \rightarrow (\mathbb{O}^2 \rightarrow \mathbb{O}^2) \\ \forall f \in bell;\ x: \{0,1\};\ y: \{0\} \bullet f = N\,|\,qa \leftarrow H\,|x\rangle, qb \leftarrow |y\rangle\,) \end{array}$$

rather than as:

$$\begin{array}{l} bell : \mathbb{Z}_2 \rightarrow (\mathbb{O}^2 \rightarrow \mathbb{O}^2) \\ \forall f \in bell;\ x: \{0,1\};\ y: \{0\} \bullet f = qa \leftarrow H\,|x\rangle \wedge qb \leftarrow |y\rangle \wedge N\,|\,qa, qb\,) \end{array}$$

When Alice and Bob had to part away, each of them took one piece of the EPR pair (*qa* and *qb*). At some point in his life, Bob has to hide himself, and Alice's mission is to deliver a message to Bob (*qdata*). This must be done by both preventing that the message can be eavesdropped and that anybody can use the transmission to track down Bob's location.

Alice does pair *qa* and *qdata*, performs a joint measurement with the intention of detecting on which of the four Bell states they have been projected, and sends (somewhere) to Bob the two classical bits obtained (*cdata*):

Table 5.1 The *cdata* map

In	Out
00	$(\lvert 00 \rangle + \lvert 11 \rangle)/\sqrt{2}\,) \equiv \lvert \beta_{00} \rangle$
01	$(\lvert 01 \rangle + \lvert 10 \rangle)/\sqrt{2}\,) \equiv \lvert \beta_{01} \rangle$
10	$(\lvert 00 \rangle - \lvert 11 \rangle)/\sqrt{2}\,) \equiv \lvert \beta_{10} \rangle$
11	$(\lvert 01 \rangle - \lvert 10 \rangle)/\sqrt{2}\,) \equiv \lvert \beta_{11} \rangle$

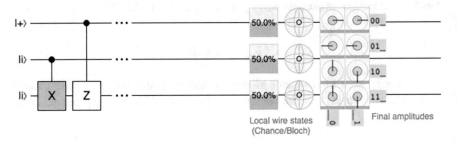

Fig. 5.3 The unitary operations that Bob must perform, controlled by *cdata*

$$alice : \mathbb{O}^2 \longrightarrow \mathbb{O}^2 \longrightarrow (\mathbb{Z}_2 \longrightarrow \mathbb{Z}_2)$$
$$\forall f \in alice;\ qa, qdata : \mathbb{O}^2 \bullet f = N\,\lvert qdata, qa \rangle \wedge H\,\lvert qdata \rangle$$

For his part, Bob, who possesses a qubit of the EPR pair, that is now collapsed due to the measurement performed by Alice, receives the two classical bits that will let him to conditionally apply any of four given quantum gates to his part of the (collapsed) EPR pair, obtaining in return the original message (Table 5.1).

$$bobcond : (\mathbb{Z}_2 \longrightarrow \mathbb{Z}_2) \rightarrow \mathbb{O}^2$$
$$\forall f \in bobcond;\ qb : \mathbb{O}^2 \bullet f = (\lvert 00 \rangle \Rightarrow I(qb)) \vee (\lvert 01 \rangle \Rightarrow X(qb)) \vee (\lvert 10 \rangle$$
$$\Rightarrow Z(qb)) \vee (\lvert 11 \rangle \Rightarrow X(z(qb)))$$

$$bob : \mathbb{O}^2 \rightarrow (\mathbb{Z}_2 \longrightarrow \mathbb{Z}_2) \rightarrow \mathbb{O}^2$$
$$\forall f \in bob;\ qb : \mathbb{O}^2, cdata : (\mathbb{Z}_2 \longrightarrow \mathbb{Z}_2) \bullet f = bobcond\ cdata\ qb$$

The Quantum Teleportation Protocol is now completely described, and we can translate it into an axiomatic definition and a corresponding QC program:[6]

---

[6]This program will not break the no-cloning theorem, because the state of the original qubit shall be lost during the process.

$$qtp : \mathbb{O}^2 \rightarrow \mathbb{O}^2$$

$\forall f \in qtp;\ qdata, qa,$

$\quad\quad\quad qb : \mathbb{O}^2 \bullet f\ =\ (qa, qb)\ \leftarrow bell\ (0) \wedge cdata$
$\quad\quad\quad\quad\quad \leftarrow alice\ (qa)\ qdata \wedge tdata\ \leftarrow bob\ (qb)\ cdata$

$qtp :: Qbit \rightarrow QIO\ (Qbit)$
$qtp\ qdata = do$
$(qa, qb) \leftarrow bell\ (b0)$
$cdata \leftarrow alice\ (qa)\ qdata$
$tdata \leftarrow bob\ (qb)\ cdata$
$return\ (tdata)$

From the point of view of a classical software engineer, the QTP circuit is intrinsically complex in order to be used as a guide for coding, but even by following the verbal description of the QTP, it is not easy to interpret and transform the algorithm into code.

Therefore, we cannot fail to appreciate both the clarity of the axiomatic definition to describe the QTP and the guidance it offers to write the code needed to perform such a powerful quantum function. And, with it, we also have the advantage of eliminating (or, at least, minimizing) the risk of introducing either conceptual errors during the drafting of the algorithm or coding errors during the transformation of the algorithm into a working program.

Finally, the formalization of the algorithm produced by Z can help to reason beyond its primitive use, with the possibility to extend the same logical structure for identifying use cases that go beyond the particular instance, as, for example, in the QTP paradigm, to describe the operations required to teleport matter and energy [21]. But this is a topic for another study.

5.7 Conclusions and Outlooks

The diffusion of QC cannot be forever relegated within a narrow circle of experts, but many computer scientists and software engineers entering the field of QC are quickly put off by the existing conceptual and notational barriers [14]. This is not only due to the intrinsic difficulty of the subject but also because it can only be seen through a dark glass (as the complete knowledge of the state of a quantum system is forbidden) [15].

Not only does QC require a completely different mindset, but in order to make quantum computers available to everyone, we need to prepare a QC-ready workforce capable of translating old and new challenges into problems that quantum computers can understand.

One possible way to overcome this stasis is to tap into the existing broad base of software engineers, introducing a vocabulary inspired by formal SE tools. In this work, you learned how the main notions of QC can take the form of axiomatic definitions in Z notation so that they can be used throughout specifications [2]. The result is a notational system that, ideally, can open the doors of QC to the wider audience of players, helping them to understand, describe, and, ultimately, translate the structure of a quantum algorithm into fully working code, adopting any quantum programming language that is available.

Appendix

A.1 Coding of Typical Quantum Operators

In the following sections, you will find the complete implementation of the quantum operators (QO) required to run the code used in the proposed examples.

These QO have been designed based on the QIO Monad, which is a Haskell library of purely functional interfaces for quantum programming [11].

A.1.1 QO for the Deutsch Algorithm

— return a qubit in a specified state
```
qb :: [Char] -> QIO ( Qbit )
qb qstate
  | qstate = = "|0>" = mkQ ( False )
  | qstate = = "|1>" = mkQ ( True )
  | qstate = = "|+>" || qstate = = "H|0>" = do
          qBit <- qb ( "|0>" )
          applyU ( uhad ( qBit ) )
          return ( qBit )
  | qstate = = "|->" || qstate = = "H|1>" = do
          qBit <- qb ( "|1>" )
          applyU ( uhad ( qBit ) )
          return ( qBit )
  | otherwise = error "qb: wrong argument"
```

— apply the C-Not (N) gate to a qubit
```
qN :: (Bool -> Bool) -> Qbit -> Qbit -> QIO ()
qN f qx qy = applyU ( cond (qx) (\ a → if f (a) then unot (qy) else mempty ))
```

— apply the Hadamard (H) gate to a qubit
```
qH :: Qbit -> QIO ()
qH qbit = applyU ( uhad ( qbit ) )
```

— measure a qubit
```
mq :: Qbit -> QIO ( Bool )
mq qbit = measQ ( qbit )
```

A.1.2 QO for the Quantum Teleportation Protocol

— return False
```
b0 :: Bool
b0 = (0==1)
```

— return True
```
b1 :: Bool
b1 = (1==1)
```

— apply the C-Not (N) gate to a qubit
```
qN :: Qbit -> Qbit -> QIO ()
qN qx qy = applyU ( cond ( qx ) (\ a -> if a then unot ( qy ) else mempty ) )
```

— apply the Hadamard (H) gate to a qubit
```
qH :: Qbit -> QIO ()
qH qb = applyU ( uhad ( qb ) )
```

— apply the Identity (I) gate to a qubit
```
qI :: Qbit -> U
qI qb = mempty
```

— apply the Not (X) gate to a qubit
```
qX :: Qbit -> U
qX qb = unot ( qb )
```

— apply the Pi Phase Shift (Z) gate to a qubit
```
qZ :: Qbit -> U
qZ qb = (uphase qb pi)
```

— apply the ZX sequence of gates to a qubit
```
qZX :: Qbit -> U
qZX qb = qX ( qb ) `mappend` qZ ( qb )
```

— create a Bell state by sharing a qubit in superposition with a qubit in given state
```
bell :: Bool -> QIO (Qbit,Qbit)
bell qf = do
    qa <- if not qf then qb("|+>") else qb("|->")
    qb <- qb("|0>")
    qN qa qb
    return (qa,qb)
alice :: Qbit -> Qbit -> QIO (Bool,Bool)
alice qa qdata = do
```

— Alice applies the C-Not gate to qa, controlled by qdata (the information to be sent)
```
qN (qdata) qa
```

— Alice applies the Hadamard gate to qdata
```
qH (qdata)
```

— Alice measures her qubits, collapsing them; and stores the result in two classical bits

```
cdata <- mq (qdata,qa)
return (cdata)

bobcond :: (Bool, Bool) -> Qbit -> U
```

bobcond (False, False) qb = qI qb *— do nothing*

bobcond (False, True) qb = qX qb *— apply the X gate (not gate)*

bobcond (True , False) qb = qZ qb *— apply the Z gate (pi phase shift gate)*

bobcond (True , True) qb = qZX qb *— apply the ZX sequence of gates*

```
bob :: Qbit -> (Bool, Bool) -> QIO ( Qbit )
bob qb cdata = do
```

— Bob applies the relevant gate to qb, which choice is controlled by the classical bits received

```
applyU (bobcond cdata qb)
```

— Bob now finally has the result of the manipulation of qb

```
return (qb)
```

References[7]

1. Cartiere CR (2020) Formal quantum software engineering: introducing the formal methods of software engineering to quantum computing. https://doi.org/10.13140/RG.2.2.26157.10725/2
2. Woodcock J, Davies J (1996) Using Z. Specification, refinement, and proof. Prentice Hall
3. Cartiere CR (2013) Quantum software engineering: bringing the classical software engineering into the quantum domain. Master's Thesis, University of Oxford, Department of Computer Science, Software Engineering Programme
4. Jacky J (1996) The way of Z: practical programming with formal methods. Cambridge University Press
5. Ruhela V (2012) Z formal specification language – an overview. Int J Eng Res Technol (IJERT) 01(06)
6. Dirac P (1958) The principles of quantum mechanics, 4th edn. Oxford University Press
7. Mateus P, Sernadas A (2004) Reasoning about quantum systems. In: Alferes JJ, Leite J (eds) Logics in artificial intelligence. JELIA 2004. Lecture Notes in Computer Science, vol 3229. Springer, Berlin

---

[7]The quantum circuits of Figs. 5.2 and 5.3 have been drawn with the help of quirk, the quantum circuit simulator by Craig Gidney (https://algassert.com/quirk).

8. Barenco A (1998) Quantum computation: an introduction. In: Lo H, Popescu S, Spiller T (eds) Introduction to quantum computation and information. World Scientific
9. Feynman R (1982) Simulating physics with computers. Int J Theor Phys 21:467–488
10. Deutsch D (1985) Quantum theory, the church-turing principle and the universal quantum computer. Proc R Soc Lond A 400:97–117
11. Green AS. The QIO package. Haskell community's central package archive of open source soft. https://hackage.haskell.org/package/QIO, v1.3
12. Bennett CH, Brassard G, Crépeau C, Jozsa R, Peres A, Wootters WK (1993) Teleporting an unknown quantum state via dual classical and Einstein-Podolsky-Rosen channels. Phys Rev Lett 70:1895
13. Nielsen M, Chuang I (2010) Quantum computation and quantum information: 10th Anniversary Edition. Cambridge University Press, Cambridge. https://doi.org/10.1017/CBO9780511976667
14. Greenwood GW (2001) Finding solutions to NP problems: philosophical difference between quantum and evolutionary search algorithms. Portland State University, Portland, OR
15. Gross AM, Stallard J (2007) Implementing Grover's algorithm using linear transformations in Haskell. In: Proceedings of the Eighth Symposium on Trends in Functional Programming, vol 8. p XXV
16. Deutsch D, Jozsa R (1992) Rapid solutions of problems by quantum computation. Proc R Soc Lond A 439:553
17. Simon DR (1997) On the power of quantum computation. SIAM J Comput 26(5):1474–1483
18. Kaye P, Laflamme R, Mosca M (2007) An introduction to quantum computing. Oxford University Press
19. Spivey JM (1992) The Z notation: a reference manual. Prentice Hall International
20. Saaltink M (1993) Z and EVES. Technical Report TR-91-5449-02
21. Roberts D, Nelms J, Starkey D, Thomas S (2012) Travelling by teleportation. Phys Spl Top J. University of Leicester

Chapter 6
A Quantum Software Modeling Language

Carlos A. Pérez-Delgado

6.1 Introduction

Modeling languages are useful tools for designing, discussing, and presenting new software, hardware, and complete systems. Software modeling languages, in particular, have been so useful that they can be partially credited with transforming the discipline of computer science (CS). Software modeling has helped CS to grow from a solely mathematical research area in the mid-twentieth century to a multi-disciplinary field that spans the entirety of the theory to end-product spectrum, employs millions worldwide, produces ubiquitous and pervasive technology, and has revolutionized every aspect of the human experience at the beginning of the twenty-first century.

The key insight behind software modeling, and software engineering in general, is that as long as any one person is required to understand the entirety of a project, the complexity of projects that can be undertaken by *homo sapiens* will be severely curtailed. The keys to surpassing the said limitations are *encapsulation* and *abstraction*. Together these allow large groups of humans to collaborate on projects whose complexities are too high to be understood by any one person alone.

It is thus natural to expect *quantum* software modeling to similarly help quantum computation in its evolution. Today, quantum computation is studied and developed almost exclusively by very highly trained specialists: mostly mathematicians, computer scientists, quantum chemists, and theoretical and experimental physicists.

If quantum information technologies are to achieve even a fraction of the ubiquity of their classical brethren, then the stage must be opened to a broader set of professionals. To achieve this, it will be necessary to be able to understand, and discuss, quantum software without having to delve down to the (atomic) details.

C. A. Pérez-Delgado (✉)
University of Kent, Canterbury, Kent, UK
e-mail: c.perez@kent.ac.uk

Software engineers today do not (usually) develop, discuss, or analyze their work at a level of abstraction that includes half-adders and flip-flops, let alone voltages or resistances. Similarly, we will need a language that allows us to discuss quantum software that does not concern itself with Hamiltonians, unitary gates, or even quantum circuits.

In the year 2021, there aren't many, if any, large-scale quantum software projects. So, it may seem premature to develop a quantum software modeling language. This brings us to next reason why software modeling languages are important: they act as an *intuition pump*. Language can indeed influence our ability to craft new ideas [1] and not just communicate them effectively [2]. All computer scientists are familiar with how different programming paradigms and their associated languages allow us to think about and tackle problems in different ways. All physicists are similarly familiar with Dirac notation and Feynman diagrams. And most mathematicians will be equally fluent in category and type theories—all to name but a few examples.

Software modeling languages have been amply credited as powerful intuition pumps in the past. Software modeling, and more generally software engineering, has had a large measurable influence on lower abstraction level research in computer science, such as programming languages [3]. It therefore stands to reason that the development of a proper quantum software modeling language can also help in the development of lower abstraction level tools—like quantum programming languages.

What then does a "proper" quantum software modeling language look like? That is the topic of the next section.

6.2   Fundamental Axiom of Quantum Software Engineering

A software modeling language is, above all, a *language*. As such, its utility is directly proportional to the square of the number of people that "speak" it. Therefore, while it may have some benefits, one should resist the temptation to start completely anew when developing a quantum software modeling language. On the contrary, it is quite clear that in order to derive the maximum possible value of a new quantum software modeling language, one should aim to make it as close as possible to existing classical modeling languages. We can explicitly state this requirement as the first part of our Fundamental Axiom of Quantum Software Engineering: *quantum software engineering should be as similar to classical software engineering as possible.*

Is it possible then that a specific *quantum* software modeling language may be entirely superfluous and a purely classical one would suffice? No. Quantum software and classical software, while they may share many important similarities, are different in fundamental ways. More importantly, they are different in fundamental ways that *need to be reflected in a design document*. In the section, we will discuss exactly how so.

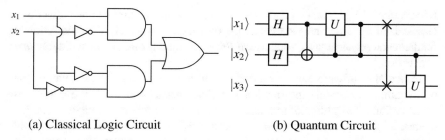

(a) Classical Logic Circuit   (b) Quantum Circuit

Fig. 6.1 Two logic circuits, each depicting a software program. The one on the left is classical logical circuit, whereas the one on the right is a quantum circuit. Note how, at least superficially, there is little to tell each one apart

Before we consider how they are different, however, let us first consider how quantum and classical software are similar or even the same. What sets quantum software apart from its classical counterpart is, of course, the use of quantum algorithms. However, despite the name, quantum algorithms are not, in themselves, quantum objects. Consider Fig. 6.1. Part A shows a classical algorithm, while Part B shows a quantum algorithm. In both cases, we have an ordered set of operations, taken from a larger set, that are applied to some data called the *input*.

What distinguishes classical circuit from quantum circuits are two things. The first is the set of permissible operations. Classical gates are usually taken to come from a standard set of universal logical bit operations, such as {AND, NOT} or simply {NAND}. Quantum gates, on the other hand, are taken from a universal set of *unitary* operators, such as {CNOT, H, S, T}.

The second distinction is deeply connected to the first (and is what gives rise to the operator disparity): quantum and classical algorithms (and software) operate on different types of *information*. This is both an obvious and a subtle point. It is obvious that quantum algorithms (and software) operate on quantum information, while classical algorithms (and software) operate on classical information.

As a software engineer, this distinction can be treated much in the same way that other, more traditional, data-type distinctions are treated. In traditional software engineering, it would not be uncommon to deal with modules that, say, operate on string or integer types. Specifying that a function/module/method takes as input a string rather than an integer is a well-understood design decision.

However, in classical software engineering, this distinction is completely *artificial*. There is, fundamentally, no real distinction between a string and an integer. Both are merely an ordered set of *bits*. It is true that we often create an abstraction layer, on top of bits, that contains objects such as strings and integers, each such object with its set of permissible operations, and so on. However, this abstraction is there only for the benefit of the programmer or software engineer.

Quantum information, on the other hand, is *fundamentally* different from classical information. Fundamental laws of physics dictate different sets of permissible operations for each. Quantum information can be put in *superposition*; classical information cannot. Classical information can be *cloned* or copied; quantum information—in general—cannot. While quantum information can be converted to classical information and vice versa, the operation is constrained to the following fundamental physical laws, such as the *Born rule*, and is often an unavoidably *lossy* conversion.[1]

Hence, the software engineer's decision to have a module/function/etc. operate on quantum or classical information is a *fundamental* one. And, it has immense repercussions. Quantum information can only be stored in a quantum module, operated by a quantum module, and can only be sent/communicated to other quantum modules. And these are all *fundamental* requirements, rather than engineering limitations. Even if quantum computers become as cheap and easy to operate as classical ones, for the reasons stated above, it will *always* be necessary to distinguish the use of classical from quantum information in a software design document.

This brings us to the second part of the Fundamental Axiom of Quantum Software Engineering which we can now state in full: quantum software engineering should be as similar to classical software engineering as possible, *but no more*.

! Fundamental Axiom of Quantum Software Engineering

Quantum software engineering should be as similar to classical software engineering as possible, but no more.

In the next section, we discuss precisely how quantum software modeling needs to be different from classical.

6.3 Design Principles for a Quantum Software Modeling Language

In the previous section, we discussed the fundamental axiom behind our approach to software modeling and software engineering in general. In this section, we will describe a set of *guiding principles* that we argue are both necessary and sufficient for a quantum software modeling language to achieve the aforementioned central axiom.

We will introduce five design principles. Each principle establishes a way in which *quantum* software modeling must differentiate itself from classical software modeling. For each principle, we will discuss why it is an essential feature of a quantum software modeling language. Finally, we will make the argument as to why these are the *only* five ways in which a quantum software modeling language should differentiate itself from a classical one.

---

[1]For a full discussion on the nature of quantum information, please see a proper introductory text, such as Nielsen and Chuang's classic *Quantum Computation and Quantum Information* [4].

From here forth, we will adopt the language of object-oriented design when appropriate. This is to ensure a consistent nomenclature throughout this chapter and because we will be extending an existing classical object-oriented software modeling language in the next section.

- **Quantum Classes**. Whenever a software module makes use of quantum information, either as part of its internal state/implementation or as part of its interface, this must be clearly established in a design document. The first and most obvious requirement is the proper labeling of modules or classes. As discussed in the previous section, whether a particular module is classical or quantum is an important design consideration, with important ramifications. A quantum module will operate on quantum information, using quantum functions/methods. It will need to run on quantum hardware that allows for the storing of the said quantum information and is capable of executing the said quantum operations. Classical modules do not have any of these requirements. While classical modules can be, in general, run on the same quantum hardware as the quantum modules, not doing so offers several strong advantages. As such, it must be explicitly specified in any design document. Below, we will discuss some guidelines that are helpful to a software designer when deciding whether a particular module is classical or quantum.
- **Quantum Elements**. Each module interface element (e.g., public functions/ methods, public variables) and internal state variables can be either classical or quantum and must be labeled accordingly.
- **Quantum Variables.** Each variable should be labeled as classical or quantum. If the model represents data types, the variables should also specify the classical (e.g., integer, string) or quantum (e.g., qubit, qubit array, quantum graph state) data type.
- **Quantum Operations**. For each operation, both the input and output should be clearly labeled as either classical or quantum. Whether the operation internally operates quantumly should also be labeled.

On a more basic level, data (variables) and operations that act on the data are, as discussed at length in the previous section, either classical or quantum. Quantum information can generally *only* be stored in a quantum variable. And, while classical information can be stored in a quantum variable, this would be both wasteful and overly restrictive if the information to be stored is known to always be classical (e.g., while the information could be potentially cloned, since it is classical, the design document would imply that, in general, it cannot).

Likewise, software operations (functions, methods) are either meant to operate on classical or quantum data and are, in general, not interchangeable. As such, it is important to label what kind of data the function takes as input and produces as output.

- **Quantum Supremacy.** A module that has at least one quantum element is to be considered a quantum software module; otherwise, it is a classical module. Quantum and classical modules should be clearly labeled as such. One of the major considerations of any quantum software design is which modules are to be quantum and which are classical. This principle states, in accordance with the central axiom stated in the previous section, that a module is to be quantum if and only if it contains quantum elements. Stated differently, a quantum module can contain both classical and quantum (interface) elements. A classical module can only have classical elements. A module having only classical elements will always be a classical module unless it is "upgraded" by the next principle: quantum aggregation.

- **Quantum Aggregation.** Any module that is composed of one or more quantum modules will itself be considered a quantum module and must be labeled as such. In a similar way to the "quantum supremacy" principle, if a software module aggregates (is composed of) at least one quantum module, then it itself will also be labeled as a quantum module. It could be argued that the previous two principles ought to be treated as a single, more general, principle: if a module uses quantum information, in any way, as part of its implementation, then it is to be considered a quantum module. Otherwise, it is a classical one.

There are two reasons to state the two principles separately. First, in most software modeling languages, aggregation is considered and represented in separate and distinct ways from other internal elements. Figure 6.3 gives an example of how aggregated sub-modules (sub-classes) are represented differently from other internal elements in both the quantum software modeling language Q-UML and the original modeling language upon which it is based, UML.

A second important reason is that it allows us to explicitly make the distinction between aggregation and *communication*, which is the next principle discussed.

- **Quantum Communication**. Quantum and classical modules can communicate with each other as long as their interfaces are compatible, i.e., the quantum module has classical inputs and/or outputs that can interface with the classical module.

In classical software engineering, there are two different ways in which two distinct modules can interact. The first one is the aforementioned *aggregation*. This occurs when one module is subsumed as part of another module. The second is *communication*. This allows two separate modules (classes) to work together without one being an internal part of the other.

In classical software engineering, there is really little distinction between the two. In either case, there are two modules that need to be aware of each other's interfaces and are expected to *couple* or work well together. The major consideration for a software engineer when deciding whether class B is an internal class of A or both classes A and B merely communicate with each other is whether packages/modules/ classes other than A need to be aware of class B. If none do, then it makes sense to hide class B as an inner, aggregated, class of A.

In QSE, there is another, more important, consideration. As noted earlier, a quantum class is one that makes use of quantum resources. It is important to note whether or not a class is quantum because that determines, among other things, what type of hardware resources is needed to run the module.

Let us suppose that class A is (otherwise) classical and B is intrinsically quantum. By making B an aggregated internal class of A, the software engineer is making the implementer of class A responsible for any and all quantum resources incurred by class B. In short, the designer is making the statement that quantum hardware and resources are needed to implement A. Hence, although A has no quantum elements of its own, it itself becomes a quantum class.

In contrast, if the designer chooses to make both A and B distinct classes that merely communicate with one another, then class A can be implemented/run on fully classical hardware. Any communication between A and B must then happen through purely classical communication channels—given that A is classical, it has no quantum interfaces and can therefore neither send nor receive quantum information messages. Class B is then responsible for transforming any quantum information meant for class A into classical (generally via measurement).

This consideration goes well beyond the differentiation between module aggregation and communication in classical software engineering; and it is a clear example of how and when QSE needs to go beyond its classical counterpart.

This concludes our discussion on the fundamental principles behind quantum software modeling language design. We present all five principles on Table 6.1 for easy reference.

The principles discussed in this section are the immediate consequences of precisely two things. The first is the maxim we introduced in the previous section: that quantum software engineering should differ from classical software engineering only inasmuch as is absolutely necessary. The second is the intrinsic nature of quantum information and its fundamental features that distinguish it from classical information.

Table 6.1 Quantum software modeling language core design principles

Quantum Classes Whenever a software module makes use of quantum information, either as part of its internal state/implementation or as part of its interface, this must be clearly established in a design document
Quantum Elements Each module interface element (e.g., public functions/methods, public variables) and internal state variables can be either classical or quantum and must be labeled accordingly
Quantum Variables Each variable should be labeled as classical or quantum. If the model represents data types, the variables should also specify the classical (e.g., integer, string) or quantum (e.g., qubit, qubit array, quantum graph state) data type
Quantum Operations For each operation, both the input and output should be clearly labeled as either classical or quantum. Whether the operation internally operates quantumly should also be labeled
Quantum Supremacy A module that has at *least* one quantum element is to be considered a quantum software module; otherwise, it is a classical module. Quantum and classical modules should be clearly labeled as such
Quantum Aggregation Any module that is composed of one or more quantum modules will itself be considered a quantum module and must be labeled as such
Quantum Communication Quantum and classical modules can communicate with each other as long as their interfaces are compatible, i.e., the quantum module has classical inputs and/or outputs that can interface with the classical module

These principles can—and we argue should—be applied when developing *any* kind of quantum software modeling language, regardless of its level of formality, or mathematical rigor. In the following section, we will put these principles into practice with the presentation of a particular quantum software modeling language: Q-UML.

6.4   Q-UML

In this section, we present Q-UML. Q-UML is an extension of the Unified Modeling Language (UML) that allows it to properly model quantum software. It was first introduced, alongside several other ideas covered in this chapter, at the Quantum Software Engineering Workshop of the ACM/IEEE International Conference on Software Engineering (ICSE) 2020 [5].

UML was chosen as the "base" classical modeling language for this first quantum modeling language for two closely related reasons. The first is that UML is an exceptionally easy to learn and use software modeling language, requiring very little training and background knowledge to understand. The second is its consequently large user base. By using UML as our basis, we can easily focus on developing and discussing the quantum extensions.

These extensions aim to *minimally* change base UML. A direct line can be drawn from each change to base UML to principle discussed in the previous section. The changes are also implemented in a way as to make Q-UML maximally *backwards compatible* with base UML. The goal is that for a purely classical piece of software, both the UML and Q-UML models ought to be identical. And, indeed, that is the case.

It did not, however, must be this way, nor is this a direct result of the principles detail in the previous section or the maxim (axiom) from two sections past. The first QSE principle discussed in the previous section states that quantum classes (modules) and classical ones need to be differentiated from one another. In Q-UML, we choose to make that distinction by presenting classical classes just as they would appear in base UML and adding new notation for quantum classes.

6.4.1   UML

UML (base) is a visual language that represents and models software via diagrams. UML is agnostic with respect to programming languages tools, platforms, and software development processes. That said, UML is an *object-oriented* modeling language.

As its name suggests, UML attempts to be usable in any complex system design and engineering. In many such systems, software may be merely a small component of the overall whole. There are in total 14 different types of UML diagrams, split into two general categories: *structure* and *behavior* diagrams.

Structure diagrams are used to model and represent the static elements of a (software) system. The seven structure diagram types are *class*, *package*, *object*, *component*, *profile*, *composition structure*, and *deployment*.

Behavior diagrams are used to model and represent the dynamic elements of a (software) system. The seven behavior diagram types are *state machine*, *use case*, *activity*, *sequence*, *interaction overview*, *communication*, and *timing*. These last four are commonly referred to as interaction diagrams.

Of these 14 diagram types, the most widely used (and hence important) diagrams are use case, class, object, state machine, sequence, and activity diagrams. Use case diagrams are used to specify the functionality of a (software) system.

Class and object diagrams, as their names suggest, show the classes and objects of the system, including their internal members, and their relationships (inheritance, aggregation, communication) with each other. State diagrams are used to represent the intra-object dynamics of the software system. Activity diagrams represent the general logical and control flow of the entire system.[2]

6.4.2 Q-UML Extensions

Following the aforementioned QSE axiom and our design principles, all Q-UML diagrams are identical to (base) UML diagrams, except for one thing: all instances of quantum information, whether it is being stored, communicated, or processed, are to be clearly labeled as such. Since UML is a graphical language, the Q-UML extensions are also graphical.

There are two ways in which UML presents information in its diagrams. The first is pictorially. Classes and objects are represented by rectangles, in class/object diagrams, and their relationships to one another are represented via connecting lines/arrows/etc. The second is via text, usually used as labels, for instance, the names of classes and objects and the internal members of either.

Quantum information can be represented either pictorially or textually in Q-UML. When it represented textually, quantum information will be typeset in **bold** font, to distinguish it from classical. When quantum information is represented pictorially, double lines will be used to set it apart. Whenever possible, *both* bold font *and* double lines are used to represent quantum objects/processes/etc. This covers the *syntax* of Q-UML.

As for the semantic rules, these follow from the previously discussed principles. All static structures and dynamic processes in Q-UML are by default classical. A

---

[2]There are many good introductory texts to UML. That said, the text *UML @Classroom: An introduction to object-oriented modeling* by Seidl et al. [6] is not only excellent; it happens to cover in-depth precisely the UML diagrams discussed here.

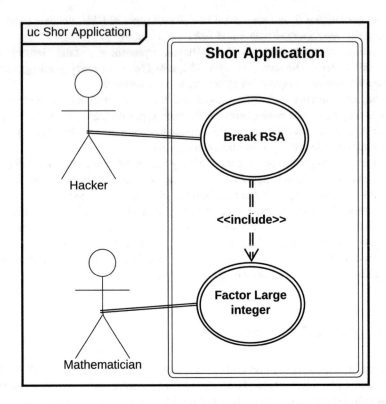

Fig. 6.2 Q-UML use case diagram of Shor Application. Note how any use case of the software that requires quantum resources (in this case, all of them) is distinguished by use of a double line

static structure (e.g., class) is set to quantum *if and only if* (a) it directly stores quantum information or (b) one of its constituent structures (a variable, aggregated class, etc.) stores quantum information. Likewise, a dynamic structure (e.g., process) is quantum if and only if it is itself a quantum information process or one of its own sub-processes is a quantum information process.

The rules are best presented through example. For this purpose, we present Shor Application: a quantum software implementation of the well-known Shor's algorithm [7]. This software system would have obvious applications in cybersecurity: Shor's algorithm can be used to easily break RSA2048 encryption. Of course, there are other more benign applications: factoring large integers is useful in many number-theoretic, combinatorial, and optimization problems. There are likely many more use cases for this software system, but we can focus on these two and provide a Q-UML *use case diagram* that details them—see Fig. 6.2.

Use case diagrams in Q-UML are a bit subtle and slightly different from other diagrams in their portrayal of quantum information resources. Obviously, human actors (users of the system) cannot be quantum in nature.[3] Further, no quantum communication is sent to/from the user. Rather, the double lines in the use case diagram are meant to denote the *use* of quantum resources, by the software system, in satisfying the use case requirements.

A more common portrayal of quantum information in Q-UML is in class and object diagrams, which we discuss next.

6.4.2.1   Class and Object Diagrams

Class (object) diagrams in Q-UML, as in base UML, denote not just classes (objects) in the software system but also their internal elements and the relationships (communication, aggregation, inheritance) between them.

Figure 6.3 showcases a Q-UML class diagram of our Shor Application. We can use it to showcase the rules as they apply to both class and object diagrams. Shor Application makes use of six classes—five of them quantum. The class Euclidean is the only non-quantum one. The classes **ShorApplication**, **ShorFactor**, **ShorOrder**, and **QFT_n** are all quantum. Note how their names are all typeset in bold to emphasize this fact. The class ***QFT*** is both quantum and abstract; as such, its name is typeset in both bold and italics, the latter following the (base) UML rule to italicize abstract class names.

Finally, note how for all quantum classes the border of the rectangle denoting the class uses a double line. This is a departure from the previous version of Q-UML [5], which used only bold typeface to denote quantum classes.

This change was made for three reasons. The first reason is consistency. Q-UML has—*essentially*—two syntactic rules, one for pictorial and one for text representations. Since classes in class diagrams (and objects in object diagrams) are represented in *both* ways (a rectangle and a name), it makes sense that they follow *both* sets of rules.

The second reason is readability and clarity. It is common for the class names to be typeset with a slightly larger font than class elements. Merely using bold typeface for quantum classes may not be clear or readable enough in some conditions.

Third, the use of double-lined borders for quantum classes does not seem to add much visual clutter. Hence, both mentioned advantages can be achieved without any discernible disadvantage.

Bold text is also applied to class members. Any attributes that store quantum information will have their name typeset in bold. Representing quantum methods is slightly more complex. If any of the inputs are quantum, these are bold. If the output or data type of the method is quantum, then the data type should also be bold. For

---

[3] Putting aside any philosophical discussions about the quantum nature of the universe, here, we use quantum as a shorthand for non-classical or coherent information.

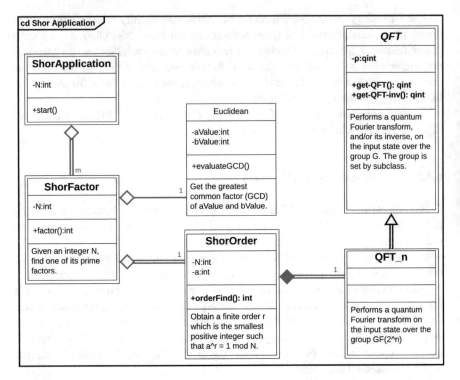

Fig. 6.3 Q-UML class diagram of Shor Application. Quantum classes and elements are presented in bold text, while quantum classes and relationships use double lines

backward compatibility with regular UML, whenever the input or output data types of a method are omitted, these will be assumed to be classical in nature. In accordance with the previously established rules, if a class/object has any quantum attributes or methods, then it itself is considered quantum. In this case, its name shall also be bold, and its border will use double lines.

Finally, relationships between classes follow the same rules, using double lines whenever the relationship is quantum in nature. For inheritance, if the superclass is quantum, then the sub-class, and the inheritance relationship, will also be quantum—however, the converse is not necessarily true. In the case of aggregation and composition, if a class/object being aggregated/composed is quantum, then the class/object to which it is aggregated/composed into, as well as that relationship, will also be quantum.

In contrast to the above, association relationships do not have any special rules. Two classes can communicate together regardless of whether one, both, or none is quantum. However, a classical class cannot (as already established) have the capacity to receive, send, or store quantum information. Hence, any communication between a quantum and a classical class must be through purely classical channels.

All of these rules translate directly to objects, their members and relationships, in object diagrams. Next, we move onto the features of behavior Q-UML diagrams.

6.4.3   Activity and State Diagrams

Much in the same way that class and object diagrams are so closely related that they merit being discussed together, so do activity and state diagrams. However, while state and object diagrams are so similar that presenting one is sufficient to understand both, activity and state diagrams have subtle and important difference between them in Q-UML. Hence, it is important to detail them both with examples. Figure 6.4 presents a state diagram of an object belonging to the class **QFT_n**. Figure 6.5 presents a flowchart of the main algorithm followed by Shor Application.

Both follow the same basic rules: quantum information states and processes are denoted through the use of bold text and double lines.

In our state diagram (Fig. 6.4), we have two quantum states: a computational basis state and a Fourier basis state. Each is properly denoted as being quantum states. The operation that transforms one into the other is necessarily a quantum operator.

Hence, the transitions between both states—the arrows—are denoted as quantum states using double lines.

Now consider the activity diagram in Fig. 6.5. Once again, the only quantum operation—the period-finding step—is properly denoted as a quantum operation using both double lines and bold text. However, note the complete lack of double-lined arrows throughout the diagram. Why is this the case?

In Q-UML diagrams, as in base UML, activity diagrams represent multi-step processes. Each rectangle (node) represents an activity. And the arrows merely denote the passing of *control* from one logical activity to the next. Unlike in state diagrams, where arrows denote operations or processes that can be either classical or quantum, in activity diagrams, they denote the flow of control. It would be a category error to even attempt to classify these as either classical or quantum.

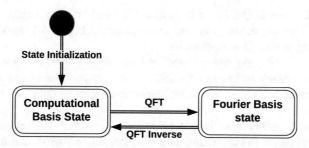

Fig. 6.4 Q-UML state diagram of an object of class **QFT_n**. One can tell immediately that both represented states are quantum states, and the transitions between them are mediated via quantum operators, due to the use of bold text and double lines

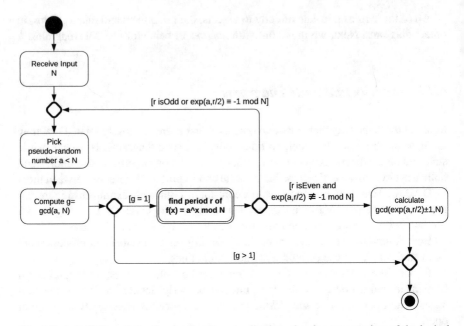

Fig. 6.5 A Q-UML activity diagram for Shor Application, showing an overview of the logical control flow of the program. The sole quantum operation is displayed using a double-lined border and bold text

This relates back to the discussion in Sect. 6.2. While algorithms may operate on classical and/or quantum information, the algorithms themselves—the logical flow-control of a program—are always classical objects.

Next, we discuss sequence diagrams in Q-UML.

6.4.4   Sequence Diagrams

Sequence diagrams in Q-UML, like in base UML, allow us to portray the *dynamic* relationship between modules in a software program. Figure 6.6 shows a Q-UML sequence diagram for Shor Application.

Like before, we make use of **bold** text and double lines to portray quantum information textually and pictorially. Names of quantum classes and the labels of quantum messages are typeset in bold. The arrows depicting quantum messages use double lines.

In another departure from the original version of Q-UML [5], we now also have the borders of quantum classes and their lifelines, active objects, and threads using double lines. Once again, this change was made for consistency and readability.

Note that although the *relationship* between **ShorFactor** and **ShorOrder** is quantum, the messaging between them is *not*. A module is marked as quantum if

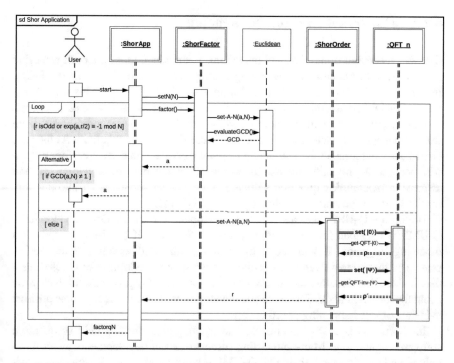

Fig. 6.6 Q-UML sequence diagram for Shor Application. Once again, bold text and double lines are used to represent quantum classes/objects, their lifelines and threads, and quantum communication between them

it uses quantum resources in any form, either directly as part of its internal implementation or as part of an aggregated module. If an aggregated sub-class is quantum, then the encompassing class must also be marked as quantum. In a class diagram, the quantum composition relationships inform us—especially in the case of a seemingly classical module that does not *in itself* use quantum resources—which composed modules are using quantum resources.

Also, note the communication between the objects **ShorOrder** and **QFT_n**. The module **QFT_n** operates on a quantum state. Hence, both "set" messages are quantum. Likewise, the return messages ρ and ρ' are quantum states. However, the request to perform a quantum Fourier transform (QFT) or a QFT inverse operation can (and therefore must) be communicated classically. This diagram showcases the level of granularity available to us using these diagrams with the proposed extensions.

6.4.5 Discussion and Further Reading

Q-UML, its design principles, and the axioms upon which those are built were first introduced at the Quantum Software Engineering Workshop of the IEEE/ACM 42nd International Conference on Software Engineering, in 2020 [5, 8]. This was among the first major international events centered around quantum software engineering.

QSE is still a very young field. Q-UML—and the work surrounding—has been from its inception an attempt to shape the future direction of this field. At its core, Q-UML is what it says it is: a modeling language for quantum software. Hopefully, it will become a pragmatically useful one: used in the design, development, and discussion of complex quantum software. This chapter serves as an introduction, for the working quantum software engineer, to Q-UML.

Hopefully, Q-UML will also serve as a template for further QSE development. Q-UML is a testbed for the axiom put forth in Sect. 6.2. If Q-UML succeeds as a modeling language, it will prove the utility of the said axiom and the design principles that spawn from it. Regardless of the speed of adoption of Q-UML as a practical tool, its development serves one other purpose: to spark a useful discussion about the direction of QSE research and development. There is already some positive evidence of this happening [8–10].

In short, this is a very interesting and exciting time for the field of quantum software engineering. Many interesting discoveries and developments await those willing and able to search them out. Q-UML is work in *one* possible direction in this field. But it is also an attempt to argue how work in *any* direction in this new field should be conducted. For example, the development of a formal specification language for quantum software (something that Q-UML is certainly *not*) could also be based on the same axiom/principles as Q-UML. And so, hopefully, the contents of this chapter are useful to any researcher doing work in this field, regardless of the direction they wish to take.

Acknowledgments The author would like to acknowledge funding through the EPSRC Quantum Communications Hub (EP/T001011/1). The author would like to thank Hector Perez-Gonzalez for his valuable work, knowledge, and insight, during the collaboration that gave birth to Q-UML, and would also like to thank Joanna I. Ziembicka for useful comments during the preparation on this manuscript.

References

1. Jackendoff R (1996) How language helps us think. Pragmatics Cognition 4(1):1–34
2. Mercer N (2002) Words and minds: how we use language to think together. Routledge
3. Ryder BG, Soffa ML, Burnett M (2005) The impact of software engineering research on modern programming languages. ACM Trans Softw Eng Methodol 14(4):431–477. https://doi.org/10.1145/1101815.1101818
4. Nielsen MA, Chuang I (2002) Quantum computation and quantum information

5. Pérez-Delgado CA, Perez-Gonzalez HG (2020) Towards a quantum software modeling language. In: Proceedings of the IEEE/ACM 42nd International Conference on Software Engineering Workshops, pp 442–444
6. Seidl M, Scholz M, Huemer C, Kappel G (2015) UML@ classroom: an introduction to object-oriented modeling. Springer
7. Shor PW (1994) Algorithms for quantum computation: discrete logarithms and factoring. In: Proceedings 35th annual symposium on foundations of computer science. IEEE, pp 124–134
8. Abreu R, Ali S, Yue T (2021) First international workshop on quantum software engineering (q-se 2020). ACM SIGSOFT Softw Eng Notes 46(2):30–32
9. Moguel E, Berrocal J, García-Alonso J, Murillo JM (2020) A roadmap for quantum software engineering: applying the lessons learned from the classics. In: Q-SET@ QCE. pp 5–13
10. Sánchez P, Alonso D (2021) On the definition of quantum programming modules. Appl Sci 11(13):5843

Chapter 7
Quantum Software Models: Density Matrix for Universal Software Design

Iaakov Exman and Alon Tsalik Shmilovich

7.1 Introduction

Quantum Software Models [1] have been inspired by *Linear Software Models* [2, 3] which represent software System Under Design (SUD) by linear algebraic structures such as the modularity matrix and the Laplacian matrix [4]. The common motivation behind the *Linear* and *Quantum* kinds of Software Models consists of three arguments:

- *Linear algebra*—is both the basis of Linear Software Models' entities and the basis of Quantum Computation objects (see, e.g., Nielsen and Chuang [5]).
- *Density matrix as a scaled Laplacian*—a density matrix is easily obtained by scaling a Laplacian matrix, as explained in Sect. 7.1.2.
- *Modularization as the Models' goal*—the purpose of both Software Models is to design modular software systems for the sake of human understanding.

This Introduction overviews Quantum Software Models' concepts and purpose.

7.1.1 *Bipartite Graph and Its Laplacian Matrix*

A Laplacian matrix L [6] is generated from a graph, according to the equation

$$L = D - A \tag{7.1}$$

I. Exman (✉) · A. T. Shmilovich
Software Engineering Department, The Jerusalem College of Engineering – Azrieli, Jerusalem, Israel
e-mail: iaakov@jce.ac.il

© The Author(s), under exclusive license to Springer Nature Switzerland AG 2022
M. A. Serrano et al. (eds.), *Quantum Software Engineering*,
https://doi.org/10.1007/978-3-031-05324-5_7

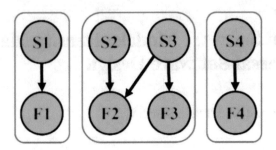

Fig. 7.1 Abstract bipartite graph—Its eight vertices form a Structors set {S1,S2,S3,S4} and a Functionals set {F1,F2,F3,F4}. For instance, the Structor S3 provides two Functionals F2 and F3. This graph shows three modules, *connected components*, surrounded by (blue) round rectangles: one 2-by-2 module {S2,S3,F2,F3} and two 1-by-1 modules {S1,F1} and {S4,F4}. (Figures in color online)

Column Labels	F1	F2	F3	F4	S1	S2	S3	S4
Row Labels F1	1	0	0	0	−1	0	0	0
F2	0	2	0	0	0	−1	−1	0
F3	0	0	1	0	0	0	−1	0
F4	0	0	0	1	0	0	0	−1
S1	−1	0	0	0	1	0	0	0
S2	0	−1	0	0	0	1	0	0
S3	0	−1	−1	0	0	0	2	0
S4	0	0	0	−1	0	0	0	1

$L =$

Fig. 7.2 Laplacian matrix fitting the bipartite graph in Fig. 7.1.—As the graph has eight vertices, the matrix has eight columns and eight rows, each labeled either by a Functional **F***i* or a Structor **S***k* (yellow background). Columns and rows are labeled in the same vertex order. The Degree diagonal matrix has eight elements (green background). The Adjacency matrix elements, in the upper-right quadrant and reflected around the diagonal in the lower-left quadrant, are either zero-valued or negative by Eq. (7.1). The three system modules are also marked in (blue) color

where D is a diagonal **D**egree matrix showing graph vertex degrees and A is the **A**djacency matrix showing for vertex pairs, whether they are linked neighbors, in which case the respective matrix element is 1-valued; otherwise, it is 0-valued.

We represent software systems by bipartite graphs, with two distinct vertex sets, where each vertex is only linked to vertices in the other set. The *Structors* **S***i* vertex set generalizes object-oriented design (OOD) classes. The *Functionals* **F***k* vertex set generalizes class methods. A Structor providing a Functional, e.g., a class containing a method definition/declaration, is linked by an arrow to the respective Functional. A sample abstract software system bipartite graph is seen in Fig. 7.1.

The bipartite graph in Fig. 7.1 generates the Laplacian matrix seen in Fig. 7.2.

7.1.2 From Laplacian to Density Matrix

The Laplacian matrix of a graph is symmetric, as can be observed in Fig. 7.2, and is easily verified to be positive semidefinite [7]. On the other hand, the state of a quantum system, in von Neumann's density operator picture of the Hilbert formulation of quantum mechanics, is identified with a density matrix [8], which is a positive semidefinite trace one, Hermitian matrix.

Braunstein and co-authors [9] observed that the Laplacian matrix $L(G)$ of a graph G, scaled by the degree-sum $d(G)$, has trace one. Thus, they defined the scaled Laplacian as the density matrix ρ of the graph G:

$$\rho = L(G)/d(G). \tag{7.2}$$

As we represent any software system by a bipartite graph and by its corresponding Laplacian matrix, we re-define the density matrix ρ in Eq. (7.2) as the *design* **density matrix** of the given software system.

For instance, the degree-sum for the Laplacian matrix in Fig. 7.2 is $d(G) = 10$. Thus, the scaling factor to obtain the density matrix ρ of the graph G in Fig. 7.1 is $1/d(G) = 0.1$.

7.1.3 Density Matrix for Universal Software Design

An important claim of this chapter: it does not make sense to have distinct design procedures for quantum, classical, and hybrid software systems.

We take into account the success of Laplacian-based design procedure [4] for classical software systems in *Linear Software Models* and the simple relation of the density matrix ρ to the Laplacian in Eq. (7.2). Thus, ρ is a *plausible* proposal for a Universal Software Design procedure: for classical systems, the Laplacian is similar to the density matrix; for quantum systems, the density matrix is a basic quantum notion; hybrid systems are composed of classical and quantum sub-systems.

This chapter demonstrates formally and illustrates by case studies that:

- Any software system—quantum, classical, or hybrid—can be designed from the information in the *design* density matrix of the system.

The *design* density matrix is a density matrix for all purposes. Thus, we shall generally omit the *design* qualifier, unless when in need to emphasize this feature.

7.1.4 Chapter Organization

This chapter is organized as follows: Sect. 7.2 provides the Universal Software Design theory. Section 7.3 describes the Quantum Software Design and illustrates it with two case studies. Section 7.4 does the same for Classical Software Design. Section 7.5 describes typical hybrid software architecture and its Hybrid Software Design. Section 7.6 cites related work. A discussion in Sect. 7.7 concludes the chapter.

7.2 Quantum-Wise Universal Software Design Theory

Justified by the prevalent view in physics—classical systems are a classical limit of quantum systems—we state the Universal Software Design theory in quantum terms. Hybrid systems are a combination of quantum and classical sub-systems.

Specifically, this section re-defines software modules as sub-spaces of the software system state space and states how to obtain modules' number and their components. Then, it formulates the Quantum Modularization Procedure, arguing that it is a Universal Software Design procedure.

7.2.1 Modules as Sub-spaces of the Software System State Space

A projection operator, in short, a *projector*, operates on its argument projecting it into a sub-space of the relevant Hilbert state space.

Strictly speaking, a density matrix is the matrix representation of von Neumann's density operator [8], itself a projector. In the scientific literature, one freely interchanges the matrix for its operator. Using Dirac's bra-ket notation [10], a density operator ρ is a kind of ket-bra, as seen in Eq. (7.3):

$$\rho = /\psi\rangle\langle\psi/ \tag{7.3}$$

where ψ is a generic symbol of a quantum state [5].

The density matrix ρ operates on the system state space. A set of orthonormal basis vectors—a set of kets—spans the system state space. For instance, by scaling the Laplacian matrix in Fig. 7.2, one obtains a density matrix according to Eq. (7.2). The eight corresponding kets in the computational basis set are $|000\rangle$, $|001\rangle$, $|010\rangle$, $|011\rangle$, $|100\rangle$, $|101\rangle$, $|110\rangle$, and $|111\rangle$.

Modules are re-defined next as software sub-systems with internal interactions.

Definition 1: Module of a Software System
A module is a sub-system of a given software system, spanning a sub-space of the whole software system state space. Each module sub-space is orthogonal to all other module sub-spaces of the software system.

7.2.2 Number and Components of Software Modules

A projector can be associated with each ket in the computational basis set. For instance, the ket $|111\rangle = (0\ 0\ 0\ 0\ 0\ 0\ 0\ 1)^T$. Applying the density matrix ρ fitting the Laplacian in Fig. 7.2 on the ket $|111\rangle$ obtains the rightmost density matrix column, labeled **S4,** i.e., $0.1* (0\ 0\ 0\ -1\ 0\ 0\ 0\ 1)^T$. The resulting projector, adding the respective bra $\langle 111|$ at the ket's r.h.s., is $\rho\ |111\rangle = 0.1* (-|011\rangle + |111\rangle)\langle 111|$. The relevant density matrix as a whole may be expressed as a sum of the basis set projectors, with appropriate coefficients.

The number of software system modules is obtained from its density matrix:

Theorem 1: Number of Modules of a Software System
The number of modules in a software system represented by its density matrix is the number of partition classes of the basis kets' projectors corresponding to the density matrix of the software system.

Proof:
By linear algebra arguments (see, e.g., [4]), software modules are obtained from the software system Laplacian matrix eigenvectors, fitting the zero-valued eigenvalues. The proof (see, e.g., [1]) should show that projectors applied to the lowest Laplacian eigenvectors also obtain zero-valued eigenvalues. □

The components—i.e., Structors and Functionals—in a given module are obtained according to Theorem 2.

Theorem 2: Components of Modules of a Software System
The module components in a software system represented by its density matrix are given by the Structors and Functionals fitting the respective basis kets/bras in the projectors of the module partition class of the software system density matrix.

Proof:
As the projectors partition classes are also partition classes of the kets/bras in the density matrix, there is a one-to-one correspondence with the respective module Structors and Functionals. □

7.2.3 Quantum Modularization Procedure

Given the above definition of software system modules, we formulate the Modularization Procedure in quantum terms in the next textbox.

> **Procedure 1: Quantum Modularization of Software Systems**
> 1. *Structors and Functionals*—extract Structors and Functionals lists and their relationships, from a quantum and/or classical source diagram.
> 2. *Bipartite Graph*—transform the Structors and Functionals lists and relationships into a bipartite graph.
> 3. *Laplacian Matrix*—generate a Laplacian matrix from the bipartite graph.
> 4. *Density Matrix*—obtain the density matrix by scaling the Laplacian.
> 5. *Projectors*—apply the density matrix on the basis kets, obtaining the projectors for each ket.
> 6. *Projectors' Sum*—express the density matrix as a sum of projectors.
> 7. *Partition Projectors' Sum*—partition projectors into disjoint sets, each partition fitting a different module.
> 8. *Module Numbers*—is the number of disjoint projector sets by Theorem 1.
> 9. *Module Composition*—given by the labelled basis kets subset of projectors, by Theorem 2.

Some clarifications are necessary for this procedure:

- <u>Source Diagrams</u>—typical Structors and Functionals sources are class diagrams for classical systems and high-level quantum circuits for quantum systems, as illustrated in the next sections of this chapter.
- <u>Module Composition</u>—basis kets columns are labelled by Fi and Sk.

7.2.4 Universality of Software Design

To assure universality of software system design, we first need to state two definitions

- Allowed sub-system types—a minimal number
- Allowed transition types in hybrid sub-systems—a minimal number

The allowed sub-system types are defined next.

Definition 2: Allowed Sub-system Types in a Software System Involving Quantum Computation

In a software system involving quantum computation, there may be any number of sub-systems of only the following allowed types:

Type 1: *Classical sub-system*—an object-oriented system containing classical functions whose data are only composed of classical bits

Type 2: *Quantum sub-system*—a system containing quantum gates, which can be aggregated into boxes, whose data are only composed of qubits (or equivalently composed of qutrits or qudits in general).

Type 3: *Hybrid sub-system*—a system containing only a restricted number of transition types from classical to quantum sub-systems or vice versa.

For non-object-oriented classical systems, such as functional-oriented programming, see "Future Work" in Sect. 7.7. Aggregation of quantum gates into boxes is assumed to be a trivial action, to be illustrated in the next section.

The allowed transition types for hybrid software sub-systems are defined next.

Definition 3: Allowed Transition Types in a Hybrid Sub-system
In a hybrid software sub-system, there may be any number of transitions of only the following types:

Classical to Quantum Transition

• Translation of a number into qubit labels
• Insertion of numbers into a function applicable to qubits

Quantum to Classical Transition

• A measurement

Next, we formulate the Universality Thesis of Software Design.

Universality Thesis of Software Design
The Quantum Modularization Procedure is applicable to any software system involving quantum computation, containing any number of only the allowed sub-systems and any number of only the allowed transitions within hybrid sub-systems.

The plausibility of this Thesis relies upon two aspects:

• Any software system falls in the above types—for all known practical purposes.
• The Quantum Modularization Procedure is applicable—to systems in the above types. In other words, one needs to show—in Lemma 1—that for the allowed sub-system types and transitions, one is able to make the first step of the Quantum Modularization Procedure 1, viz., to extract Structors and Functionals lists and their relationships. Once the first step has been done, all the subsequent steps of the procedure are enabled.

Lemma 1: Applicability of the Quantum Modularization Procedure
Extraction of Structors and Functionals for the above software sub-system and transition types is done as follows:

(a) For *classical sub-systems*—the source diagram is a UML class diagram; Structors are classes in the diagram; Functionals are the class methods in the diagram.

(b) For *quantum sub-systems*—the source diagram is a high-level quantum circuit; Structors are "boxes," i.e., small-size collections of gates; Functionals are the gates/functions in the diagram.

(c) For *hybrid sub-systems*—the transitions must be precisely specified, obtaining clear-cut Structors and Functionals.

Proof:

(a) *Classical sub-systems*—applicability is self-evident.

(b) *Quantum sub*-systems—quantum circuits are usually described in terms of gates; thus, it suffices to add boxes where needed and suitable, each box with at least one gate inside.

(c) *Hybrid sub-systems*—applicability follows from conversions inside transitions whose final outcomes—by convention or by strict algebraic rules—are Structors and/or Functionals:

- In *quantum to classical transitions*—the Structor, i.e., the "box," is a measurement device, and the corresponding Functional, by convention, is "measuring," although not an actual logical gate.
- In *classical to quantum transition*—addition of Structors ("boxes") is not mandatory—but qubits and/or functions may be added to existing gates. Qubits are initialized with labels, e.g., binary numbers standing for "input" classical bits. Functions of gates may have classical bits in any legitimate role of conventional functions, such as coefficients or exponents. This is formalized by higher-order functions [11] (explained in Sect. 7.5.1). □

7.3 Quantum Software Design

This section deals with the specifics of Quantum Software Design. Then it analyzes two slightly different case studies, emphasizing diverse points of interest: the elementary Deutsch algorithm and the Grover search algorithm.

7.3.1 From Quantum Circuit to Density Matrix

A high-level quantum circuit is the source diagram from which one extracts Structors and Functionals from a quantum software sub-system. Here, we define quantum circuits rather informally. Quantum circuits have the double character of a sequential diagram and a structure diagram.

A quantum circuit has horizontal parallel qubit lines, upon which there are quantum gates. A quantum gate may cover a single qubit line (e.g., the Hadamard gate), two qubit lines (e.g., the CNot gate), three qubit lines (e.g., the Toffoli gate), or more qubit lines. In a quantum circuit as a sequential diagram, "time" increases from left (the input qubits) to right (the outputs, typically a measurement).

Quantum gates can be aggregated inside "boxes," the hierarchical software structure building blocks. These are boxed subcircuits—cf. the Quipper quantum programming language [12]. When subcircuits are repeatedly used within a larger system circuit, they are boxed and labeled by a generic name, meaningful for the software engineer. There may be boxes executed in parallel—displayed vertically on different qubit line subsets. Quantum circuits are coined "high-level" since the exact number of gates of the same type inside a box may be left unspecified.

Given a quantum circuit, the Structors are the circuit boxes. The Functionals are gates inside the boxes. Following the Modularization Procedure, one obtains a bipartite graph, generates the Laplacian matrix, and scales it to obtain the design density matrix. Modules are density matrix partitions into disjoint projector sets.

7.3.2   First Quantum Case Study: Deutsch Algorithm

The Deutsch algorithm is a very simple example found in the quantum computing literature (e.g., [5, 13]). Given are four possible Boolean functions whose domain and range are both $\{0, 1\}$. These functions can be either *constant*—e.g., $f(0)=f(1)=0$—or so-to-speak *balanced*, e.g., $g(0)=0$ and $g(1)=1$.

The problem solved by the Deutsch algorithm—given an unknown Boolean function h—decides with minimal function evaluations whether h is constant or balanced. A classical system needs two h evaluations: $h(0)$ and $h(1)$. The Deutsch algorithm needs only one evaluation, due to the quantum circuit in Fig. 7.3.

Structors and Functionals (Fig. 7.4) are extracted from the quantum circuit (Fig. 7.3), by the Quantum Modularization Procedure. Through the Structors and

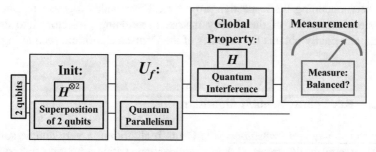

Fig. 7.3 Deutsch algorithm quantum circuit—One sees two qubit lines. There are four boxes: (1) Init applies one Hadamard gate per input yielding qubits superposition. (2) Unitary function U_f causes quantum parallelism, saving one unknown function evaluation. (3) Global Property avoids extra measurements. (4) Single qubit Measurement asks whether the unknown function is "Balanced?"

I. Exman and A. T. Shmilovich

Structors		Functionals	
S1	Init	F1	$H^{\otimes 2}$ Superposition
S2	U_f	F2	Quantum Parallelism
S3	Global Property	F3	Quantum Interference
S4	Measurement	F4	Measure: Balanced?

Fig. 7.4 Deutsch algorithm Structors and Functionals—Extracted from the quantum circuit in Fig. 7.3

	$|000\rangle$	$|001\rangle$	$|010\rangle$	$|011\rangle$	$|100\rangle$	$|101\rangle$	$|110\rangle$	$|111\rangle$
Column Labels	F1	F2	F3	F4	S1	S2	S3	S4
$\langle 000|$ F1	1	0	0	0	−1	0	0	0
$\langle 001|$ F2	0	1	0	0	0	−1	0	0
$\langle 010|$ F3	0	0	1	0	0	0	−1	0
$\langle 011|$ F4	0	0	0	1	0	0	0	−1
$\langle 100|$ S1	−1	0	0	0	1	0	0	0
$\langle 101|$ S2	0	−1	0	0	0	1	0	0
$\langle 110|$ S3	0	0	−1	0	0	0	1	0
$\langle 111|$ S4	0	0	0	−1	0	0	0	1

$\rho = 0.125*$

Fig. 7.5 Deutsch algorithm density matrix—Obtained from the Laplacian, scaled by the sum of degrees in the main diagonal. For this matrix, the scaling factor is $1/8 = 0.125$

Functionals bipartite graph, one obtains a density matrix (Fig. 7.5), i.e., a scaled Laplacian. The column and row labels are Structors and Functionals {F1,...,F4 S1,....S4}. K*ets* above the columns, in Fig. 7.5, are *not* alternative labels. One applies the density matrix on a basis set ket to obtain its fitting column. For example, applying the density matrix on the ket $|\mathbf{101}\rangle$ obtains the column labelled **S2**.

Performing the last steps of the Quantum Modularization Procedure 1, one applies the Deutsch algorithm density matrix in Fig. 7.5, upon the computational basis kets, obtaining the respective projectors. These added together results in an equivalent expression of the density matrix. Partitioning projectors into disjoint classes, one finally obtains the modules of the Deutsch algorithm, seen in Fig. 7.6.

7.3.2.1 Key Points: Deutsch Algorithm

- *Hybrid sub-system transitions*—the Deutsch algorithm, a very simple software system, already illustrates all the three transitions within a hybrid sub-system, in Definition 3, even though the transitions are not explicit. The first transition is in the input to the Init Structor: one inserts classical bits as labels of the input qubits, which is a quite common action to initiate a quantum circuit. The second somewhat subtle transition (see higher-order functions in Sect. 7.5.1) occurs in

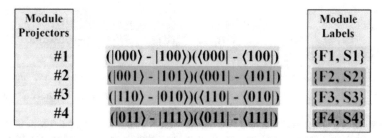

Module Projectors		Module Labels
#1	$(\lvert 000 \rangle - \lvert 100 \rangle)(\langle 000 \rvert - \langle 100 \rvert)$	{F1, S1}
#2	$(\lvert 001 \rangle - \lvert 101 \rangle)(\langle 001 \rvert - \langle 101 \rvert)$	{F2, S2}
#3	$(\lvert 110 \rangle - \lvert 010 \rangle)(\langle 110 \rvert - \langle 010 \rvert)$	{F3, S3}
#4	$(\lvert 011 \rangle - \lvert 111 \rangle)(\langle 011 \rvert - \langle 111 \rvert)$	{F4, S4}

Fig. 7.6 Deutsch algorithm modules from projectors—There are four modules, obtained from the density matrix in Fig. 7.5. The scaling factor was omitted for clarity in each module

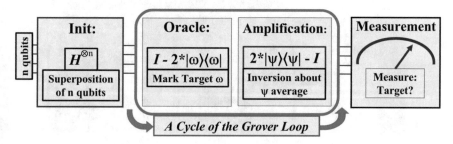

Fig. 7.7 Grover search quantum circuit—There are four boxes (light blue background), each one with the respective gates, and three modules

the function $f(x)$—the Boolean function whose domain and range are both classical bits—used inside the U_f box. The third transition is the measurement generating the classical output from the qubit being measured.

7.3.3 Second Quantum Case Study: Grover Search

Grover search (e.g., [14]) is a quantum algorithm useful to search unstructured databases. It displays a quadratic speedup on the number of queries, relative to a classical computation. It is done in four steps, seen in the quantum circuit in Fig. 7.7:

1. Transform the input into an *equal superposition* state by means of the nth tensor power of the *Hadamard gate* H.
2. An *oracle* recognizes and *marks the target* item.
3. Target *amplification* cycles are performed by "*inversion about the average.*"
4. *Measure* the amplified target.

Structors and Functionals from the quantum circuit in Fig. 7.7 are listed in Fig. 7.8.

Modules	Structors		Functionals	
F1, S1	S1	Init	F1	$H^{\otimes n}$ Superposition
The Grover Loop	S2	Oracle	F2	Mark Target ω
	S3	Amplification	F3	Inversion about ψ Average
F4, S4	S4	Measurement	F4	Measure: Target?

Fig. 7.8 Grover search Structors and Functionals—The Structors fit to the four boxes in Fig. 7.7. Oracle and Amplification composing the Grover Loop module are surrounded by a (dark blue) frame

			$|000\rangle$	$|001\rangle$	$|010\rangle$	$|011\rangle$	$|100\rangle$	$|101\rangle$	$|110\rangle$	$|111\rangle$
		Column Labels	F1	F2	F3	F4	S1	S2	S3	S4
$\langle000|$	Row	F1	1	0	0	0	−1	0	0	0
$\langle001|$	Labels	F2	0	2	0	0	0	−1	−1	0
$\langle010|$		F3	0	0	1	0	0	0	−1	0
$\langle011|$	$\rho = 0.1*$	F4	0	0	0	1	0	0	0	−1
$\langle100|$		S1	−1	0	0	0	1	0	0	0
$\langle101|$		S2	0	−1	0	0	0	1	0	0
$\langle110|$		S3	0	−1	−1	0	0	0	2	0
$\langle111|$		S4	0	0	0	−1	0	0	0	1

Fig. 7.9 Grover search density matrix—Now we may reveal that the bipartite graph in Fig. 7.1 and the Laplacian matrix in Fig. 7.2 fit the Grover search algorithm. For this matrix, the scaling factor is $1/10 = 0.1$

Module Projectors		Module Labels
#1	$(|000\rangle - |100\rangle)(\langle000| - \langle100|)$	{F1, S1}
#2	$(|001\rangle - |110\rangle)(\langle001| - \langle110|) +$	{F2, F3, S2, S3}
	$(|001\rangle - |101\rangle)(\langle001| - \langle101|) +$	
	$(|010\rangle - |110\rangle)(\langle010| - \langle110|)$	
#3	$(|011\rangle - |111\rangle)(\langle011| - \langle111|)$	{F4, S4}

Fig. 7.10 Grover search modules from projectors—There are three modules, obtained from the density matrix in Fig. 7.9. The scaling factor was omitted for clarity in each module

The Grover search density matrix from the above Structors and Functionals, through the bipartite graph and the scaled Laplacian matrix, is seen in Fig. 7.9.

The last steps of the Quantum Modularization Procedure 1, apply the Grover search density matrix in Fig. 7.9, upon the computational basis kets, obtaining the respective projectors. Partitioning projectors into disjoint classes, one finally obtains the three modules of Grover search, seen in Fig. 7.10.

7.3.3.1 Key Points: Grover Search

- *Grover Iteration 2-by-2 Module*—Two possible facts justify the Grover Loop Cycle Structors pair (*Oracle* and *Amplification*) as a single module. First fact: in contrast to the Init and Measurement Structors whose Functionals are invoked just once, the Grover Loop is invoked together in repeated cycles until the Amplification is high enough to measure the target item with high probability. Second fact: the Amplification Functional is written as $2*|\psi\rangle\langle\psi| - I$ where I is the identity operator and ψ is any of the items being searched, while the Oracle can be written as $I - 2*|\omega\rangle\langle\omega|$ where ω stands for the marked target [15]. The Oracle and Amplification Functionals are the same function, except for its argument and the multiplication by -1 which is related to the "inversion" about the average. This situation is similar to class "inheritance" in classical software systems.
- *Alternative Design*—The Grover search design shown in the density matrix in Fig. 7.8—with a 2-by-2 module—is not the only conceivable design. One may decide to keep separate the Structors pair in the Grover Loop Cycle, to enable independent optimization of the Oracle and Amplification in terms of actual gates (see, e.g., Figgatt et al. [16]). Then, Grover search, instead of a 2-by-2 module, would have only 1-by-1 modules, similar to the Deutsch algorithm in Fig. 7.5.

7.4 Classical Software Design

This section deals with the specifics of Classical Software Design, illustrating that a design procedure anchored in a quantum notion, viz., a density matrix, is efficient as well for classical software systems. Two case studies are then analyzed, stressing diverse key points: the Command Design Pattern and the Firefox for iOS.

7.4.1 *From Class Diagram to Density Matrix*

A UML class diagram is the information source of Structors and Functionals from a classical software sub-system. Class diagrams are exclusively structural diagrams, not displaying behavior features, as a time axis or system states. This in contrast to the double character quantum circuits with both structure and time sequence.

UML classes are basic structure units—whose generalization are Structors. Classes contain methods (i.e., functions) that can be, but are not necessarily, invoked. Functionals are the generalization of class methods.

There are a few kinds of relationships among classes: inheritance, composition, and association. The only kind of relationship directly appearing in design bipartite graphs is inheritance, i.e., two or more Structors offering the same Functional, which is a common source of modules within a software system.

7.4.2 First Classical Case Study: Command Design Pattern

The Command Design Pattern is a behavioral pattern described in the well-known book on Design Patterns (popularized as GoF—"Gang of Four" authors [17]). The design pattern purpose is to abstract typical application commands—copy, paste, delete, and save—to enable different requests and support "undo" and "redo" operations. The Structors and Functionals from a class diagram ([17], page 236) are in Fig. 7.11.

ICommand is an abstract interface. The Concrete Command is the implementation of a command. Invoker is a device asking the command to carry out the request, such as a menu item or button. Receiver is a document or file that receives the action of the command.

The Command density matrix obtained from the above Structors and Functionals, by means of a bipartite graph and the scaled Laplacian matrix, is seen in Fig. 7.12.

The last steps of the Quantum Modularization Procedure 1, apply the Command Design Pattern density matrix in Fig. 7.12, upon the computational basis kets, getting the respective projectors. Partitioning projectors into disjoint classes yields the three modules of the Command Design Pattern, seen in Fig. 7.13.

Structors		Functionals	
S1	*I*Command	F1	Execute *Command*
S2	Concrete Command	F2	Specify *Command*
S3	Action Invoker	F3	Invoke
S4	*I*File Receiver	F4	*Receiver* Action
S5	Concrete Receiver	F5	Specify *Receiver*

Fig. 7.11 Command Design Pattern, Structors and Functionals—It has two inheritance cases: {S1, S2} *I*Command and Concrete Command (light blue) and {S4, S5} *I*File Receiver and Concrete File Receiver (light green). *I* means interface

Row Labels	Column Labels	$\lvert 0000\rangle$	$\lvert 0001\rangle$	$\lvert 0010\rangle$	$\lvert 0011\rangle$	$\lvert 0100\rangle$	$\lvert 0101\rangle$	$\lvert 0110\rangle$	$\lvert 0111\rangle$	$\lvert 1000\rangle$	$\lvert 1001\rangle$
		F1	F2	F3	F4	F5	S1	S2	S3	S4	S5
$\langle 0000\rvert$ F1		2	0	0	0	0	-1	-1	0	0	0
$\langle 0001\rvert$ F2		0	1	0	0	0	0	-1	0	0	0
$\langle 0010\rvert$ F3		0	0	1	0	0	0	0	-1	0	0
$\langle 0011\rvert$ F4		0	0	0	2	0	0	0	0	-1	-1
$\langle 0100\rvert$ F5	$\rho = 1/14*$	0	0	0	0	1	0	0	0	0	-1
$\langle 0101\rvert$ S1		-1	0	0	0	0	1	0	0	0	0
$\langle 0110\rvert$ S2		-1	-1	0	0	0	0	2	0	0	0
$\langle 0111\rvert$ S3		0	0	-1	0	0	0	0	1	0	0
$\langle 1000\rvert$ S4		0	0	0	-1	0	0	0	0	1	0
$\langle 1001\rvert$ S5		0	0	0	-1	-1	0	0	0	0	2

Fig. 7.12 Command Design Pattern density matrix—The diagonal degree matrix has 10 elements (green) and the sum of degrees = 14. The Adjacency matrix has modules (blue) corresponding to the Structors and Functionals in Fig. 7.12, showing the two inheritance cases

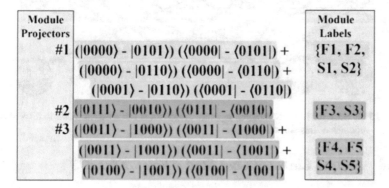

Module Projectors		Module Labels
#1	$(\lvert 0000\rangle - \lvert 0101\rangle)\,(\langle 0000\rvert - \langle 0101\rvert) +$ $(\lvert 0000\rangle - \lvert 0110\rangle)\,(\langle 0000\rvert - \langle 0110\rvert) +$ $(\lvert 0001\rangle - \lvert 0110\rangle)\,(\langle 0001\rvert - \langle 0110\rvert)$	{F1, F2, S1, S2}
#2	$(\lvert 0111\rangle - \lvert 0010\rangle)\,(\langle 0111\rvert - \langle 0010\rvert)$	{F3, S3}
#3	$(\lvert 0011\rangle - \lvert 1000\rangle)\,(\langle 0011\rvert - \langle 1000\rvert) +$ $(\lvert 0011\rangle - \lvert 1001\rangle)\,(\langle 0011\rvert - \langle 1001\rvert) +$ $(\lvert 0100\rangle - \lvert 1001\rangle)\,(\langle 0100\rvert - \langle 1001\rvert)$	{F4, F5 S4, S5}

Fig. 7.13 Command Design Pattern modules—Obtained by partitioning projectors into three disjoint sets (in different colors), in the figure middle. Structors and Functionals are seen in the figure r.h.s.

7.4.2.1 Key Points: Command Design Pattern

- *Basis kets are even, but not necessarily powers of 2*—basis kets are *even* due to Structors and Functionals being in equal numbers. Look at the upper-right quadrant of the Laplacian matrix or equivalently at its density matrix.[1] But, basis kets used to generate the relevant projectors are not necessarily powers of 2, as seen for the Command Design Pattern Fig. 7.12.

---

[1] This is a linear algebra theorem first proved within software design in the context of the modularity matrix [3]. It is true when Structor vectors are all mutually linear independent and Functionals vectors also are all mutually linear independent.

	Structors		Functionals
S1	TextInputAlert/ConfirmPanelAlert	F1	Init
S2	MsgAlert/JSAlertInfo	F2	AlertControl
S3	ChangePassCodeViewControl	F3	Scrollers
S4	PagingPassCodeViewControl	F4	PasscodeInputView
S5	BasePassCodeViewControl	F5	ViewDidLoad
S6	BaseCollectSynch	F6	ReasonToNotSync
S7	ResetTableSynch	F7	ResetSyncWithStorage

Fig. 7.14 Firefox for iOS—Structors and Functionals—Obtained from the GitHub source, listed without revealing the software modules

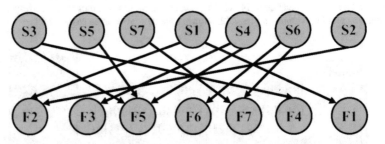

Fig. 7.15 Firefox for iOS—Scrambled bipartite graph—It is obviously difficult to discern at first sight the modules of this software system

7.4.3 Second Classical Case Study: Firefox for iOS

The second classical case study is a subset of the widely used Firefox browser, specifically its version for the iOS Apple operating system. The software system was extracted from and is publicly available in GitHub [18].

The chosen subset contains three modules: Input alert, AuthenticationManager, and a Synchronizer. The purpose of this case study is to show that, after scrambling the modules, the Universal Modularization Procedure, based upon the density matrix, blindly restores the correct modularity. The system's Structors and Functionals are in Fig. 7.14.

The Firefox iOS software system scrambled bipartite graph is shown in Fig. 7.15.

The corresponding density matrix obtained from the scrambled bipartite graph in Fig. 7.15, through its Laplacian, is shown in Fig. 7.16.

This system's modules, obtained from disjoint sets of projectors, are seen in Fig. 7.17. The corresponding corrected bipartite graph is shown in Fig. 7.18. Compare these results with our previous analysis within Linear Software Models [4].

Row Labels	Column Labels	$\lvert0010\rangle$ F2	$\lvert0011\rangle$ F3	$\lvert0101\rangle$ F5	$\lvert0110\rangle$ F6	$\lvert0111\rangle$ F7	$\lvert0100\rangle$ F4	$\lvert0001\rangle$ F1	$\lvert1010\rangle$ S3	$\lvert1100\rangle$ S5	$\lvert1110\rangle$ S7	$\lvert1000\rangle$ S1	$\lvert1011\rangle$ S4	$\lvert1101\rangle$ S6	$\lvert1001\rangle$ S2
$\langle0010\rvert$	F2	2	0	0	0	0	0	0	0	0	0	-1	0	0	-1
$\langle0011\rvert$	F3	0	1	0	0	0	0	0	0	0	0	0	-1	0	0
$\langle0101\rvert$	F5	0	0	3	0	0	0	0	-1	-1	0	0	-1	0	0
$\langle0110\rvert$	F6	0	0	0	1	0	0	0	0	0	0	0	0	-1	0
$\langle0111\rvert$	F7	0	0	0	0	2	0	0	0	0	-1	0	0	-1	0
$\langle0100\rvert$	F4	0	0	0	0	0	1	0	-1	0	0	0	0	0	0
$\langle0001\rvert$	F1 $\rho = 1/22*$	0	0	0	0	0	0	1	0	0	0	-1	0	0	0
$\langle1010\rvert$	S3	0	0	-1	0	0	-1	0	2	0	0	0	0	0	0
$\langle1100\rvert$	S5	0	0	-1	0	0	0	0	0	1	0	0	0	0	0
$\langle1110\rvert$	S7	0	0	0	0	-1	0	0	0	0	1	0	0	0	0
$\langle1000\rvert$	S1	-1	0	0	0	0	0	-1	0	0	0	2	0	0	0
$\langle1011\rvert$	S4	0	-1	-1	0	0	0	0	0	0	0	0	2	0	0
$\langle1101\rvert$	S6	0	0	0	-1	-1	0	0	0	0	0	0	0	2	0
$\langle1001\rvert$	S2	-1	0	0	0	0	0	0	0	0	0	0	0	0	1

Fig. 7.16 Firefox for iOS—Scrambled density matrix—It is obtained from the scrambled bipartite graph in Fig. 7.15. The degree matrix is in the diagonal (green). The sum of degrees is 22; thus, the Laplacian scaling factor is 1/22

Module Projectors	Firefox Correct Modules	Module Labels
#1	$(\lvert0001\rangle - \lvert1000\rangle)\,((\langle0001\rvert - \langle1000\rvert) +$ $(\lvert0010\rangle - \lvert1000\rangle)\,((\langle0010\rvert - \langle1000\rvert) +$ $(\lvert0010\rangle - \lvert1001\rangle)\,((\langle0010\rvert - \langle1001\rvert) +$	{F1, F2, S1, S2}
#2	$(\lvert0011\rangle - \lvert1011\rangle)\,((\langle0011\rvert - \langle1011\rvert) +$ $(\lvert0100\rangle - \lvert1010\rangle)\,((\langle0100\rvert - \langle1010\rvert) +$ $(\lvert0101\rangle - \lvert1010\rangle)\,((\langle0101\rvert - \langle1010\rvert) +$ $(\lvert0101\rangle - \lvert1100\rangle)\,((\langle0101\rvert - \langle1100\rvert) +$ $(\lvert0101\rangle - \lvert1011\rangle)\,((\langle0101\rvert - \langle1011\rvert) +$	{F3, F4, F5, S3, S4, S5}
#3	$(\lvert0110\rangle - \lvert1101\rangle)\,((\langle0110\rvert - \langle1101\rvert) +$ $(\lvert0111\rangle - \lvert1110\rangle)\,((\langle0111\rvert - \langle1110\rvert) +$ $(\lvert0111\rangle - \lvert1101\rangle)\,((\langle0111\rvert - \langle1101\rvert)$	{F6, F7 S6, S7}

Fig. 7.17 Firefox for iOS correct modules—They are obtained from the disjoint sets of projectors, fitting the density matrix in Fig. 7.16. The Modularization Procedure automatically corrects the information obtained from the scrambled bipartite graph and its density matrix

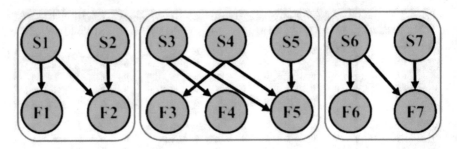

Fig. 7.18 Firefox for iOS corrected bipartite graph—Redrawn based upon the modules in Fig. 7.17

7.5   Hybrid Software System Design

Hybrid software systems have a classical software sub-system and at least one quantum software sub-system, linked by hybrid transitions between these sub-systems. This section reduces design of hybrid software systems to its classical and its quantum sub-systems, based upon the quantum notion of a density matrix and their relevant transitions. Two case studies illustrate hybrid systems: the teleportation protocol and a classical sub-system with a quantum co-processor.

7.5.1   Hybrid Architecture: "Quantum Data, Classical Control"

The "Quantum Data, Classical Control" (Fu et al. [19]) paradigm is reflected by respective diagrams for quantum software and for classical software. For quantum software, we adopted the quantum circuit as the source of information. Quantum circuits, besides the quantum gates acting as Functionals within Structors, display "data flow," from a Structor to the next one, along the time axis. For classical software, besides the class diagram as a source of Structors and Functionals, classical UML behavior diagrams, e.g., statechart and sequence diagrams, display "control flow" performing selection (e.g., if-then-else), loops, and procedures.

Hybrid software systems need both *data flow* and *control flow*, and the natural division of responsibility between quantum sub-systems and classical sub-systems at the design level is "Quantum Data, Classical Control." Indeed, hybrid transitions, as qubit measurement results, can serve as classical control, e.g., to decide whether a quantum gate should be applied or not.

An open problem in hybrid software design is how to convert classical number types into quantum qubits, back and forth. An interesting partial solution (Selinger and Valiron [11]) is to formulate hybrid transitions between classical and quantum objects as higher-order functions (also called operators[2]). The latter are defined as functions that either get functions as input or return a function as output.

Two examples of higher-order functions serving as transitions from quantum to classical entities—and vice versa—are as follows:

• **Quantum to Classical Transition**—as a higher-order function can be an expression of the form shown in Eq. (7.4):

$$(qubit \otimes qubit \rightarrow qubit \otimes qubit) \rightarrow bit \qquad (7.4)$$

Equation (7.4) has two functions, each denoted by an arrow. The first function within parentheses is a quantum function—whose domain is a tensor product of a pair of qubits and whose range also is a tensor product of a pair of qubits; the second function has as domain the first quantum function, and its range is a classical bit.

• **Classical to Quantum Transition**—as a higher-order function can be an expression of the form shown in Eq. (7.5):

$$(bit \rightarrow bit) \rightarrow (qubit \otimes qubit \rightarrow qubit \otimes qubit) \qquad (7.5)$$

Equation (7.5) has three functions, each denoted by an arrow. The first function within parentheses is a classical function with classical bits in both domain and range; the other function also within parentheses is a quantum function as explained for Eq. (7.4); the middle function has as domain (the input) the classical function and its range as the quantum function.

Equation (7.4) is a higher-order function, as it gets the quantum function (within parentheses) as an input. Equation (7.5) is a higher-order function, as both its input and output are themselves functions.

The examples above illustrate transitions in the Deutsch algorithm, seen in Fig. 7.3. The expression in Eq. (7.4) is a higher-order function characterizing the whole Deutsch algorithm. U_f gets a pair of qubits as input and outputs a pair of qubits. The overall Deutsch algorithm outputs a classical bit (after measurement).

The expression in Eq. (7.5) reflects the encoding from the classical Boolean function h—unknown whether it is constant or balanced—into U_f a quantum function, also in the Deutsch algorithm depicted in Fig. 7.3.

---

[2] A higher-order functions' special case is also called functional. It is not used in this chapter, avoiding confusion with Functional as class method generalization.

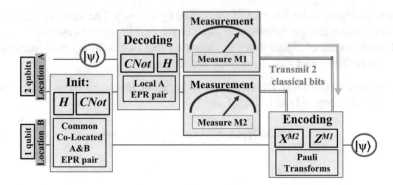

Fig. 7.19 Teleportation Protocol—quantum circuit—It involves three qubits, two in location A and one in location B. The goal is to move the quantum state $|\psi\rangle$ from location A to location B, by transmitting two classical bits, obtained by measurement of a decoding of the quantum state. Qubits are shown by single lines. Classical bits are denoted by double lines (green arrow)

7.5.2   First Hybrid Case Study: Teleportation Protocol

The Teleportation Protocol ([5] and references therein) is a well-known hybrid software system. Its purpose is to move a quantum state $|\psi\rangle$ from location A (Alice's location) to location B (Bob's location) by transmitting two classical bits.

A teleportation quantum circuit is seen in Fig. 7.19.

Initially, co-located Alice and Bob get a common EPR pair applying Hadamard (*H*) and Controlled-NOT (*CNot*) gates to a starting qubit pair. Then, they travel to their locations A and B. Alice decodes the $|\psi\rangle$ state into another local EPR pair.

This system is ***hybrid*** because Alice's two qubits are measured into *two classical bits*, transmitted to location B, where they serve to select which of the Pauli operators (X and Z) will encode the finally moved $|\psi\rangle$ quantum state. These transitions can be expressed as higher-order functions as in Eq. (7.6):

$$(qubit \otimes qubit \rightarrow bit \otimes bit\,) \rightarrow qubit \tag{7.6}$$

where the function within parentheses stands for measurements of the qubits pair into a pair of classical bits and the external function outputs the teleported qubit.

The Structors and Functionals extracted from the high-level quantum circuit in Fig. 7.19 are shown in Fig. 7.20.

Three explanations are needed for the Structors and Functionals in Fig. 7.20:

- ***Systematic dealing with qubit pairs***—In both boxes, *Init* and *Decoding*, there is no sense to separate the Hadamard and CNot gates, in distinct Structors, since their goal is to generate EPR pairs.
- ***Systematic dealing with classical bit pair***—In the *Measurements* and *Encoding* boxes, there is no sense to separate the resulting classical bit pair or their effect in

Structors		Functionals	
S1	Init	**F1**	**Co-Located EPR Pair**
S2	Decoding	**F2**	**Local EPR Pair**
S3	Measurements	**F3**	**Measure 2 qubits**
S4	Encoding	**F4**	**Pauli Transforms**

Fig. 7.20 Teleportation Protocol—Structors and Functionals—These follow the quantum circuit of Fig. 7.19, with four boxes, the four Structors, and the Functionals inside the boxes

the Pauli transform. The measurements are made in parallel because this is possible, but the classical bits have no independent meaning; they are used together to restore the $|\psi\rangle$ quantum state in the different location, at the end of the teleportation.

- *Classical transmission of the classical bits is not a Structor by itself*—Classical transmission here is not a computation; it rather is a plain communication action that should not affect the classical bit values.

The density matrix generated from the above Structors and Functionals has only 1-by-1 modules in a strictly diagonal fashion, similar to the Deutsch algorithm density matrix in Fig. 7.5, so it is not repeated here.

7.5.2.1   Key Points: Teleportation Protocol

- *Boxes in Parallel*—this case study shows, for the first time in this chapter, boxes in parallel. In this case, the number of Structors extracted is just one and not the number of parallel boxes. This should be taken as a generic rule.

7.5.3   Second Hybrid Case Study: Quantum Co-processor

A classical CPU (central processing unit) with one or more quantum co-processors, serving as accelerators of specific computations, is a common architecture for hybrid software systems. This is illustrated by the simplified high-level quantum circuit seen in Fig. 7.21 (see Fu et al. [20, 21]).

The quantum co-processor circuit in Fig. 7.21 has several differences from the standard quantum circuits shown in previous case studies:

- *The quantum device is an even higher-level abstraction*—it does not display specific gates such as *CNot* or *H*.
- *Some boxes are rather lower-level abstractions*—for instance, the register file and the codeword generator are much closer to hardware.

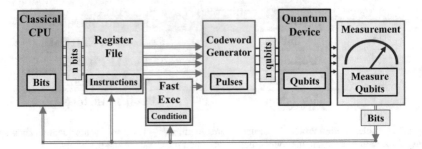

Fig. 7.21 Quantum co-processor attached to a classical CPU—high-level quantum circuit—The classical CPU (green), the left-most box, is the source of instructions for the quantum co-processor. These instructions, stored in a register file, are then used to generate pulse codewords to activate the quantum co-processor device (blue) upon its qubits. The latter are measured to obtain classical bits. These bits can be used for fast conditional execution, or for inclusion in the instructions of the register file, or as final results returned to the classical CPU

- *It displays measurement results recycled back to previous boxes*—this is part of classical control mechanisms. For instance, fast conditional execution enables execution of a *CNot*.

  From the quantum co-processor case study, one learns a few interesting lessons.

7.5.3.1 Key Points: Quantum Co-processor

- *Control mechanisms*—in order to deal with Structors consuming (instead of providing) Functionals, one needs to use a density matrix containing consumers in addition to provider Structors (see, e.g., Exman & Wallach [22]). This will be done elsewhere in a different paper.
- *Modularization to optimize implementation*—throughout this chapter, we referred to modularization to optimize design, in particular for quantum systems, the optimization in terms of gates. In the case of hybrid systems, in which the quantum sub-system is a co-processor, there is an additional motivation of optimizing implementation, as discussed by Shi et al. in their paper "Optimized Compilation of Aggregated Instructions" [23]. This explains the motivation for a quantum circuit with lower-level abstraction boxes.

7.6 Related Work

This "Related Work" section is neither extensive nor comprehensive, due to space limitations. It focuses on the most important concepts relevant to the topics dealt with in this chapter: modularity, hybrid software systems, and universality.

7.6.1 Modularity: Laplacian and Density Matrix

Linear Software Models, developed by Exman and co-authors, to modularize classical software systems, are based upon algebraic structures. Examples are the modularity matrix [3], the modularity lattice, and the Laplacian matrix (e.g., [6]). Exman and Sakhnini [4] used bipartite graphs to get the Laplacian from modularity matrices. Exman and Wallach [22] applied these models to software consumers.

Braunstein and co-authors [9] made the transition from graphs' Laplacian matrices to quantum computing density matrices, investigating separability issues. They were followed by Wu [24] working in the same area.

In the quantum software system context, modularity is relevant to clustering quantum gates into modules—as in the work by Exman and Shmilovich [1]—and also to optimal compilation of aggregated instructions, as dealt with by Shi et al. [23] (see also Sects. 7.6.3 and 7.7.1 of this chapter, on design universality).

Other approaches to classical modularity design are the economics-based Design Rules by Baldwin and Clark [25] and DSM (Design Structure Matrix) (see, e.g., [26]). These have been applied to many engineering fields, but less so to software. We are not aware of such applications to quantum software systems.

7.6.2 Hybrid Software Systems: Architecture and Formalization

A standard architecture for hybrid software systems consists of a classical CPU and one or more quantum co-processors. Fu et al. (e.g., [19–21]) proposed a quantum micro-architecture—called **QuMA**—for such hybrid software systems, to enable a fully programmable quantum computer.

A similar goal for a hybrid quantum-classical architecture—coined XACC (e**X**treme-scale **ACC**elerator)—was proposed by McCaskey and co-authors [27]. It is based upon a co-processor model, independent of the underlying quantum hardware, enabling programs to be executed on various QPUs (quantum processing unit) types though a unified API (Application Programming Interface). An extensible compiler frontend enables language-independent quantum programming.

Hornibrook et al. [28] focus on other hybrid architecture aspects. The *cryogenic* aspect distributes sub-systems across various temperature stages of the refrigeration tower, starting from a classical CPU at room temperature at the top, an FPGA controller at 4 Kelvin, down to the quantum co-processor at 20 milli-Kelvin at the bottom. Another aspect refers to the essential error-correcting code.

Finally, the approach of Selinger and Valiron (e.g., [11]) formalizes transitions between classical numbers and quantum qubits, and vice versa, by means of *higher-order functions*, introduced within the context of quantum lambda calculus.

7.6.3 Design Universality

Here, we point out to different universality meanings relevant to software. A deeper consideration of these issues is given in Sect. 7.7.1 of the "Discussion."

The first issue is a minimal number of quantum gates, from which any combination of other gates can be designed. Two papers published in 1995 deal with this issue. The paper by Deutsch, Barenco, and Ekert (DBE-1995) [29] entitled "Universality in Quantum Computing" states: "almost every gate operating on two or more qubits is a universal gate."

The DBE-1995 paper is recommended for anyone dealing with quantum computing, stating many foundational ideas: "quantum computer properties are not postulated *in abstracto*, but are deduced entirely from the laws of physics" [31]. DBE-1995 also conjectures that *non-universal gates* are precisely (a) the 1-qubit gates and collections of 1-qubit gates and (b) the classical gates. If this conjecture is true, it reveals the existence of classical computation as a closed and stable "approximation" to quantum computation.

The second paper telling us that "Almost any quantum logic gate with two or more inputs is computationally universal" was published by Seth Lloyd [32] in July 1995. It proves a similar result to the DBE-1995 paper and refers to previous papers dealing with the notion of quantum gates' universality.

Another universality issue appears in the already referred paper by Shi et al. [23] proposing a *universal quantum compilation* methodology to aggregate quantum gates into clusters manipulating up to 10 qubits at a time. Its motivation is to optimize performance when implementing the design into a specific quantum computer architecture. It is universal in the sense that its compilation is independent of the specific architecture.

7.7 Discussion

This section focuses on deep ideas in this chapter: universality, classical software systems as classical limit of quantum systems, and software duality as state and operator. It concludes with future work items.

7.7.1 Universality of Quantum, Classical, and Hybrid Design

Here, we frame universality of software design in a wider and deeper context while critically inquiring what has been achieved and how it has been achieved and what is still lacking.

The universality of software systems design means that we shall use the same technical approach to the design of quantum, classical, and hybrid software systems and there are deep reasons for doing software design in this way.

We rely on ideas of the already mentioned (DBE-1995) [29] paper for the deep arguments in favor of universality of software design:

- *The idea of sub-systems (in other words modularity)*—DBE-1995 cautiously states that "it is not so clear that computational systems must in turn be composed of well-defined, albeit interacting, subsystems"; on the other hand, "it is hard to conceive of a technology to manufacture complex computing machines, other than from simple sub-systems which are themselves computing machines."
- *Classical computation as a good approximation (a limit of) quantum computation*—DBE-1995 cautiously states the *conjecture* of classical gates as non-universal gates, inferring "the existence of classical computation as a closed and stable regime within quantum computation."

In practice, the easy conversion of a Laplacian matrix into a density matrix (by Braunstein et al. [9]) tells us that classical and quantum software systems can equally be designed by the same approach, as explained along this chapter.

It remains the issue of hybrid software systems design. Apparently, internal transitions between classical and quantum sub-systems within hybrid systems are a tough nut to crack. In formalization terms, the higher-order functions seem to be a promising solution. In terms of implementation of design into actual computers, the problem deserves further considerations.

7.7.2   Classical Software Systems as Classical Limit of Quantum Systems

In Sect. 7.7.1, the argument was already made that classical software systems are classical limits of quantum software systems, as general classical physics is a limit of quantum physics, given certain conditions.

The issue considered here is why preferring to describe classical software systems by quantum notions, such as von Neumann's density matrix, instead of adapting classical UML to quantum systems, by suitable additions to UML diagrams, as it has been done recently (see Perez-Castillo et al. [30]).

The merits of UML extensions are as follows: (a) Model abstractions are more flexible than concrete specific implementations; (b) there are a huge literature and large experience with UML; and (c) one could combine classical representation with the UML quantum extensions to deal with hybrid systems. On the other hand, von Neumann's density matrix is anchored in the solid mathematical basis of quantum theory.

7.7.3   Software Duality as State and Operator

Two arguments for von Neumann's density matrix as the software design procedure starting point and for using of higher-order functions to express classical/quantum transitions within hybrid software systems are given here.

Software has a dual character of state and operator. Software static code is a *readable* description of a ***state***. Software is also *runnable* on a given input, i.e., an operator applied to an input state, producing an output state—thus, it is an ***operator***.

The density matrix describes a ***state*** of the quantum system and is itself an ***operator***—a kind of projector—applicable to states.

Concerning higher-order functions, Selinger and Valiron [11] state: "the heart of high-order computation paradigm is the idea that *functions are data.*" Higher-order functions have the dual character of being a function, i.e., an ***operator***, and data, i.e., a ***state***, as they are inputs/outputs of other functions or stored in data structures.

7.7.4   Future Work

Important theoretical issues for future work are to rigorously fill in the gaps in hybrid software systems and the question of applicability to functional programming. In practical terms, one needs an extensive investigation of a variety of case studies of different kinds of application and a multiplicity of sizes.

7.7.5   Main Contribution

The main contribution of this chapter is to explicitly formulate the idea that there is a universal procedure for software system design for quantum, classical, and hybrid software systems, based upon the density matrix and complemented by higher-order functions in the hybrid cases.

References

1. Exman I, Shmilovich AT (2021) Quantum software models: the density matrix for classical and quantum software systems design. http://arxiv.org/abs/2103.13755
2. Exman I (2012) Linear software models. In: Jacobson I, Goedicke M, Johnson P (eds) GTSE 2012, SEMAT Workshop on General Theory of Software Engineering, KTH, Stockholm, Sweden, pp 23–24. Video: http://www.youtube.com/watch?v=EJfzArH8-ls
3. Exman I (2014) Linear software models: standard modularity highlights residual coupling. Int J Softw Eng Knowl Eng 24:183–210. https://doi.org/10.1142/S0218194014500089

4. Exman I, Sakhnini R (2018) Linear software models: bipartite isomorphism between laplacian eigenvectors and modularity matrix eigenvectors. Int J Softw Eng Knowl Eng 28(7):897–935. https://doi.org/10.1142/S0218194018400107
5. Nielsen MA, Chuang IL (2000) Quantum computation and quantum information. Cambridge University Press, Cambridge
6. Merris R (1994) Laplacian matrices of graphs: a survey. Linear Algebr Appl 197–198:143–176
7. Weisstein EW (2021) Positive definite matrix. https://mathworld.wolfram.com/PositiveDefiniteMatrix.html
8. von Neumann J (1927) Wahrscheinlichkeitstheoretischer Aufbau der Quantenmechnik. Nachrichten von der Gesellschaft der Wissenschaften zu Gottingen, Mathematisch-Physikalische Klasse:245–272. https://eudml.org/doc/59230
9. Braunstein SL, Ghosh S, Severini S (2006) The Laplacian of a graph as a density matrix: a basic combinatorial approach to separability of mixed states. arXiv:quant-ph/0406165v2
10. Paul AM (1974) Dirac, the principles of quantum mechanics, 4th edn. Oxford University Press, Oxford
11. Selinger P, Valiron B (2009) Quantum lambda calculus. In: Gay S, Mackie I (eds) Semantic techniques in quantum computation. Cambridge University Press, Cambridge, pp 135–172
12. Green AS, Lumsdaine PL, Ross NJ, Selinger P, Valiron B (2013) Quipper: a scalable quantum programming language. arXiv:1304.3390
13. Deutsch D (1985) Quantum theory, the Church-Turing Principle and the universal quantum computer. Proc R Soc Lond A 400:97
14. Grover LK (1997) Quantum Computers can search arbitrarily large databases by a single query. Phys Rev Lett 79(23):4709–4712
15. Arikan E (2002) An information-theoretic analysis of Grover's algorithm. arXiv:quant-ph/0210068v2
16. Figgatt C, Maslov D, Landsman KA, Linke NM, Debnath S, Monroe C (2018) Complete 3-Qubit Grover Search on a programmable quantum computer. Nat Commun 8:1918. https://doi.org/10.1038/s41467-017-01904-7
17. Gamma E, Helm R, Johnson R, Vlissides J (1995) Design patterns: elements of reusable object-oriented software. Addison-Wesley, Boston, MA. {the GoF book}
18. GitHub, Firefox iOS mobile browser (2021) https://github.com/mozilla-mobile/firefox-ios
19. Fu X et al. eQASM: an executable quantum instruction set architecture. In: Proceedings of the 25th International Symposium on High-Performance Computer Architecture (HPCA'19). arXiv:1808.02449
20. Fu X et al (2017) An experimental microarchitecture for a superconducting quantum processor. http://arxiv.org/abs/1708.07677 [quant-ph]
21. Fu X, Rol MA, Bultink CC, van Someren J, Khammassi N, Ashraf I, Vermeulen RFL, de Sterke JC, Vlothuizen WJ, Schouten RN, Almudéver CG, DiCarlo L, Bertels K (2018) A microarchitecture for a superconducting quantum processor. IEEE Micro:40–47
22. Exman I, Wallach H (2020) Linear software models: an Occam's razor set of algebraic connectors integrates modules into a whole software system. Int J Softw Eng Knowl Eng 30(10):1375–1413. https://doi.org/10.1142/S0218194020400185
23. Shi Y, Leung N, Gokhale P, Rossi Z, Schuster DI, Hoffmann H, Chong FT (2019) Optimized compilation of aggregated instructions for realistic quantum computers. In: Proceedings of the Asplos'19. pp 1031–1044
24. Wu CW (2009) Multipartite separability of Laplacian matrices of graphs. Electr J Combinat 16: #R61
25. Baldwin CY, Clark KB (2000) Design rules, vol I. The power of modularity. MIT Press, MA
26. Cai Y, Sullivan KJ (2006) Modularity analysis of logical design models. In: Proc. 21st IEEE/ACM Int. Conf. Automated Software Eng. ASE'06, Tokyo, Japan, pp 91–102
27. McCaskey J, Dumitrescu EF, Liakh D, Chen M, Feng W, Humble TS (2018) A language and hardware independent approach to quantum–classical computing. SoftwareX 7:245–254. https://doi.org/10.1016/j.softx.2018.07.007

28. Hornibrook JM et al (2014) Cryogenic control architecture for large-scale quantum computing. arXiv:1409.2202
29. Deutsch D, Barenco A, Ekert A (1995) Universality in quantum computation. Proc R Soc Lond A. Also: arXiv:quant-ph/9505018 – May 1995
30. Perez-Castillo R, Jimenez-Navajas L, Piattini M. Modelling quantum circuits with UML. In: Proceedings of the QSE'2021 Quantum Software Engineering Workshop. arXiv:2103.16169
31. Feynman RP (1982) Simulating physics with computers. Int J Theor Phys 21:467
32. Lloyd S (1995) Almost any quantum logic gate is universal. Phys Rev Let 75(2):346–349

Chapter 8
Quantum Service-Oriented Architectures: From Hybrid Classical Approaches to Future Stand-Alone Solutions

David Valencia, Enrique Moguel, Javier Rojo, Javier Berrocal, Jose Garcia-Alonso, and Juan M. Murillo

8.1 Introduction

During the last decades, quantum computing [1] has been a very promising and relevant research field, which encompasses not only computer science but also other scientific fields such as information theory or quantum physics. In later years, one can say that the development of quantum computers has reached a turning point with the advent of noisy intermediate-scale quantum (NISQ) computers [2], with tens of qubits, which allow to tap on tasks that outperform capabilities of classical computers.

The latter, along with confluence of other socioeconomic circumstances, are producing an ever-growing interest on quantum computing from commercial companies [3]. An example of the actual situation and possible future quantum commercial landscape can be found on the fact that several major computing corporations, such as IBM,[1] are starting to build their own quantum computers with the idea of offering them to end users on a pay-per-use model. Each of the particular solutions proposed by enterprises is accompanied by their own quantum programming languages which are laying the basis of future development of quantum services and software engineering.

Although a promising quantum computing era leading the future of computing engineering is more clearly devised each day, the current state of art of quantum computing is more focused on the integration of quantum computers with classical ones, which has been coined as hybrid classical-quantum computing [4, 5]. With this outlook in mind, a natural way of exploiting the collaborative coexistence and

---

[1] https://www.ibm.com/quantum-computing

D. Valencia · E. Moguel (✉) · J. Rojo · J. Berrocal · J. Garcia-Alonso · J. M. Murillo
University of Extremadura, Cáceres, Spain
e-mail: davaleco@unex.es; enrique@unex.es; javirojo@unex.es; jberolm@unex.es;
jgaralo@unex.es; juanmamu@unex.es

© The Author(s), under exclusive license to Springer Nature Switzerland AG 2022   149
M. A. Serrano et al. (eds.), *Quantum Software Engineering*,
https://doi.org/10.1007/978-3-031-05324-5_8

pay-per-use perspective lies in the principles of service computing and engineering; in fact, many of the research done and efforts of companies lean on the usage of quantum infrastructures to allow consumption of quantum infrastructure as a service with an approximation similar of usage of classical computing resources, i.e., IBM Quantum Computing or Amazon Braket[2] in what can be coined as a Quantum Service-Oriented Computing (QSOC) strategy. The underlying idea of the solutions proposed by companies is based on the facts that quantum computers are still very hard to operate and very expensive to own.

Again, all the aforementioned architectures are extremely aligned with another interesting and successful approach during the last decades, the microservices architectural pattern [6], in which complex systems are devised as distributed microservices, each of them being an independent process that interacts with the rest through consumption of services, appearing to the end users as a whole virtual computer. In this way, incorporating quantum computers to this paradigm will allow to tackle on both classical and quantum problems from a microservices point of view. Thus, the first step on this line of work must focus on the conversion from quantum software to microservices to be integrated on existing architectures.

From a microservice standpoint, the integration of quantum software should not be very different from classical microservices, in a way that it can be considered an independent process with the ability to interact with the rest of the system through consumption of services, and the underlying hardware is irrelevant. Nonetheless, current state of the art of quantum computing proves the latter to be a false assumption, forcing the necessity of specific approaches to generate hybrid microservices architectures. In particular, executing a quantum algorithm as a microservice is feasible with it being wrapped by a classical service, by means of quantum software development kits, although with some limitations imposed by current state of the art of quantum computing. First and foremost, quantum algorithms invocation and execution are extremely coupled with underlying hardware, leading to vendor locking. Secondly, results produced, mainly due to the probability distribution over possible quantum states [7], by quantum algorithms differ from classical solutions, further increasing the coupling with the quantum processor used. This also exposes another problem associated with NISQ computers, which is related to existing noise, leading to results subject to errors usually dependent on the specific quantum computer and qubit topology. Last but not least, related with quantum system collapse, one finds that it is not possible to obtain intermediate verification of results, further affecting and reducing service orchestration.

From all of the above, it is clear that integration of classical-quantum services is a very interesting and promising approach which continues the road laid down by cloud computing, but invoking a quantum microservice in an agnostic way is not possible, which violates all principles of service-oriented computing, producing that all of the advantages of this paradigm are lost, specifically those related to software quality x-abilities, i.e., composability, maintainability, reusability, and so on. To

---

[2] http://aws.amazon.com/braket

cope with this problem, some of the techniques and methodologies of classical service engineering must be translated to quantum service engineering domain, and several new ones must be researched and proposed.

The chapter is organized as follows: first, traditional microservices and their characteristics are explored; in the next section, an actual commercial proposal for development and execution of quantum software similarly to cloud computing is explored using two well-known problems solved with different quantum computing approaches; in Sect. 8.4, a proposal of a quantum service architecture is shown to try to cope with problems detected in the previous section; finally, in the last sections, the conclusion and related and future works are showcased.

8.2 Background

In order to address the integration of quantum and classical microservices under a single architecture, it is necessary to understand how current classical microservices work. This section does not pretend to be an exhaustive review of microservices, as there is a wealth of literature on this topic [8, 9]. It is simply intended to present an overview of how microservices work and to discuss those architectural and design patterns that will need to be adapted to support quantum microservices.

Microservices architecture is an application architectural style in which an application is composed of many discrete, network-connected components. These components are called microservices [10]. The microservices architectural style can be considered an evolution of the SOA (services-oriented architecture) architectural style [11]. The main differences between the two of them lie on the fact that while applications built with SOA services tended to focus on technical integration issues, and the level of services implemented were often very larger-grained technical APIs, the microservices approach remains focused on implementing clear business capabilities through fine-grained business APIs.

But aside from service design issues, perhaps the biggest difference is the deployment style. For many years, applications have been packaged monolithically, that is, a team of developers would build a large application that did everything needed for a business need. Once built, that application was deployed multiple times to an application server. In contrast, in the microservices architectural style, several smaller applications are built and packaged independently, each implementing only part of the whole.

In general, SOA and microservices architecture do not compete. Both approaches can coexist, each bringing its own advantages. In particular, those that make microservices architecture desirable are the following:

- The services are not integrated into the main system (loosely coupled), so they are easier to develop and deploy. They can have independent scalability, and failures can be isolated to a particular microservice, rather than a section or operation of the application.

- Radical changes in the technology stack are not necessary, but the most appropriate technology can be used for each service independently of the technologies used in the rest of microservices.
- Microservices are, in general, easier to maintain and test since they are small pieces of software doing only one specific thing.
- From the development point of view, it is easier to get in and start being productive, as the developers deal with the operation of several small services instead of a complex one. In this way, the integration of microservices development with DevOps and Agile methodologies is easier.

On the other side, relaying on a microservices architecture has the following disadvantages associated with it:

- The complexity of microservices systems tends to be higher than their monolithic counterparts. Additional to the systems functionalities, the coordination between the different microservices has to be addressed. This usually involves different communications protocol and synchronization mechanisms that increase the overall system complexity.
- Similarly, deploying and operating a microservices system is much more complicated than deploying a monolith system. The management and maintenance of the different microservices requires greater coordination and effort from the operations team.
- A microservices system tends to require higher computing capabilities than a monolith. Although each microservice can be optimized for its tasks, its deployment requires its own container, dependencies, etc. that are replicated for each service. The aggregated needs of the microservices are usually greater than that of an alternative monolith.

In any case, the development of microservices, like any other software artefact, is based on software engineering development processes. Due to the microservices architecture success, in the software development industry as well as in academia, there are a great number of techniques, methodologies, and tools to help developers create this type of system.

Some of the most relevant are the decomposition patterns that help determine which parts of the system are assigned to each microservice. Also, specifications like Open API [12] help developers standardize their endpoints and provide code generation tools that facilitate the work of developers.

Once a microservice application has been developed, it also has to be deployed and maintained. These tasks are covered under the DevOps term [13, 14] and include aspects related to the integration, testing, administration, monitoring, etc. of microservices.

For traditional systems, the first step in operating a microservices system is the deployment. Many of the advantages provided by this architecture, such as the scalability, are possible, thanks to the deployment strategy followed. Therefore, when deploying microservices, it is necessary to take into account aspects such as where each service is going to be deployed (several services on the same host machine or each service in a different machine), the type of deployment (serverless, containers, VMS, etc.), orchestration, activity logging, etc.

To hide this complexity for the microservices consumers, the API Gateway integration pattern is used. An API Gateway is the single-entry point for any microservice call. It can work as a proxy service to route a request to the microservice in question. It can also aggregate the results to send back to the consumer or even create a fine-grained API for each specific type of client. It also can take care of additional aspects like authentication/authorization. All this allows developers of microservices systems to handle multiple calls to multiple microservices from different channels, to handle different protocols, and to provide response in different formats to different clients.

Once the services are deployed, all the issues related to management and maintenance must also be considered. Considering communications between the different services, transaction management, maintaining data consistency, monitoring of running services, security, testing and many other aspects.

As mentioned above, all these aspects have been studied for researchers and practitioners, and good practices have been proposed and adopted to improve the development of microservices. However, as far as the authors know, there are no studies on which of these practices can be adapted to the creation of quantum microservices or which need to be replaced by more specific alternatives.

8.3 Current Status of Quantum Microservices: The Amazon Braket Case Study

In the present section, a brief review of the current leading technology solutions is presented in order to ease understanding and evaluation of underlying hardware supporting quantum microservices, along with their strengths and drawbacks.

8.3.1 Main Quantum Computing Approaches

As indicated before, we are facing a new era of quantum computing, led mainly by the noisy intermediate-scale quantum (NISQ) computers, in whose one may find reminiscences of beginning of the transistor era of classical computing, when the evolution started to grow exponentially, finally leading to the great breakthrough that enabled the current development of information systems. This evolution has been a challenging process that, among other advances, has motivated the development of software engineering as it is today. Researchers and industry must prepare to face a similar process in the coming years, now facing the development of quantum computing.

Current commercial quantum computing hardware and computers can be roughly classified in two categories: quantum gate arrays and adiabatic quantum computers. In the first category, we can find proposals of commercial quantum computers of companies such as IBM's with their Quantum System One[3] with more than 20 qubits and Rigetti's Aspen-9[4] with more than 30 qubits. On the other category, their main exponent is D-Wave's Advantage[5] architecture, with more than 5000 qubits.

Most current information systems are supported by cloud computing at any level (IaaS, PaaS, or SaaS). Today's quantum computers are no different in this regard and are already available in the cloud under pay per use. One example of this can be found on Amazon's bracket. Amazon defines Braket as a fully managed quantum computing service. Specifically, Braket provides a development environment to build quantum algorithms, test them on quantum circuit simulators, and run them on different quantum hardware technologies; it is a strategy allowing Amazon to further expand their position, as the global leader regarding cloud computing and services technologies through AWS, into the quantum computing area. Braket offers both adiabatic and gate array-based quantum computers as underlying hardware to execute the codes developed in their platform. At the moment of writing this chapter, Braket supports three different quantum computer simulators and real quantum computers from three different hardware vendors: Rigetti and IonQ (gate-based) and D-Wave (quantum annealing).

The approach followed by Amazon Braket tries to cope with the first choice a developer must make when faced with building a quantum program, that is: *Should we exploit both mainstream quantum possibilities (adiabatic and gate-based) or work only with one type of architecture? In that case, which one?* The aim of Braket is to provide a higher abstraction level so users (potentially developers) are agnostic of the underlying hardware and focused on the problem requirements. Additionally, flexibility and scalability are also benefited. Nonetheless, due to the relative novelty of the quantum proposals along with the particularities of quantum computing, getting all the advantages of the new abstraction level is still more of a wish than a reality. To illustrate this, this chapter will evaluate the complexity and shortcomings of developing two quantum algorithms as services in Amazon Braket, one especially suitable for quantum gate-based architectures (prime factoring) and a second one suitable for quantum annealing (traveling salesperson problem).

8.3.1.1 Prime Factoring

Prime factorization is a particular application of integer factorization, a fundamental problem in number theory that is computationally hard, but it is not believed to belong to the NP-hard class of problems [15]. Nonetheless, it is a problem that has

---

[3] https://www.research.ibm.com/quantum-computing/system-one/

[4] https://www.rigetti.com/

[5] https://www.dwavesys.com/quantum-computing

been used as a basic hardness assumption for cryptographic algorithms, such as the famous RSA algorithm. Thus, integer factorization and identification of new methods to address this task acquire an important role in information security.

The problem proposed is basically to try to decompose a non-prime integer number in nontrivial divisors, as indicated in Eq. (8.1), where N denotes the non-prime integer and p and q are the nontrivial (prime) divisors:

$$N = pq \qquad (8.1)$$

There are multiple proposals and algorithms for the solution of this problem, being the most famous Shor's algorithm [7]. This algorithm is normally described in terms of quantum gates and circuits, suitable for development and execution on machines such as IBM's Q computing chip [16], but when considering other approaches on quantum computing, such as Adiabatic Quantum Computing based on concepts such as quantum annealing, Shor's algorithm implementation is not direct. Nonetheless, other algorithms have been proposed for prime factoring, such is the case of the algorithm proposed by Wang et al. in [17]. In particular, in the studies conducted on this paper, these will be the algorithms proposed for integer factorization: Shor's algorithms for quantum machines programmed with quantum circuits and gates, such as Rigetti's [18] and IonQ's [19], and integer factorization based on quantum annealing for adiabatic quantum machines such as D-Wave's [20]. The selection of these algorithms is done without losing generality, in fact as Shor's algorithm is a very well-known study example for gate-based quantum computers, whereas the algorithm proposed for quantum annealing is selected because clearly shows the intricacies of specifying a problem in a QUBO form. Particularly, in Fig. 8.1, a part of the code generated for the factorization of number 21 is shown.

However, when working with quantum annealing, the problem must be reformulated to take the form of a QUBO or Ising, defining it by means of graphs with valued vertex and valued links between these vertices where vertex represents variables and links represent dual relationships between variables. Any higher-order relationship such as those found on terms involving three or more variables must be mathematically transformed to simpler two-variable-related terms. This task can be of great complexity due to the necessity of ample and profound comprehension of the problem and dexterity on mathematical knowledge and tools. To illustrate this, in Fig. 8.2 are shown the values of the weights of the nodes along with the edges between nodes for the factorization of 21. The steps to call the execution on D-Wave's quantum computer using Amazon Braket are also included.

8.3.1.2 Traveling Salesperson Problem (TSP)

Contrary to prime factoring, this is a recognized example in the class of NP-Class problems [21], which can be categorized as an optimization problem. In the traditional definition of the problem, there exists a traveling salesperson that must visit all cities inside a route, minimizing the traveled distance. Thus, in the classical

```
1    def period(a,N, device="LocalSimulator"):
2        global Ran_Quantum_period_finding
3        Ran_Quantum_period_finding = 1
4        num_qubits = 5
5        C_reg = [0,0,0]
6        quantum_circuit = Circuit()
7
8        quantum_circuit.x(0)
9        quantum_circuit.h(4)
10       quantum_circuit.h(4)
11   #   quantum_circuit.measure(4,C_reg[0])
12   #   # Reinitialize to |0>
13   #   quantum_circuit.reset(4)
14
15       quantum_circuit.h(4)
16       for k in range(2):
17           cmod(quantum_circuit,a)
18       if C_reg[0] == 1:
19           quantum_circuit.rz(4,pi/2.0)
20       quantum_circuit.h(4)
21
22       quantum_circuit.h(4)
23       cmod(quantum_circuit,a)
24       if C_reg[1] == 1 :
25           quantum_circuit.rz(4,pi/2.0)
26       if C_reg[0] == 1 :
27           quantum_circuit.rz(4,pi/2.0)
28       quantum_circuit.h(4)
29
30       result = run(quantum_circuit, device)
31       counts = result.measurement_counts
```

Fig. 8.1 Circuit for Shor's algorithm

```
1    dwave_sampler = BraketDWaveSampler(s3_folder,'arn:aws:braket:::device/qpu/d-wave/DW_2000Q_6')
2    dw_sampler_embedding=EmbeddingComposite(dwave_sampler)
3    h={'s1': 580, 's2': 420, 's3': 144, 's4': 128}
4    J={('s1','s2'): 152, ('s1','s3'): -144, ('s1','s4'): -512, ('s2','s3'): 16,('s2','s4'): -512, ('s3','s4'): 128}
5    sampleset=dw_sampler_embedding.sample_ising(h,J,num_reads=100)
```

Fig. 8.2 D-Wave's invocation for the factoring of 21

definition of the problem, there exist cities, usually described as nodes, and roads connecting those cities, which can be considered as links between these nodes, each with a weight indicating the distance. An example of this problem is shown in Fig. 8.3.

The main difficulty of these kinds of problems relates to the increment of possible solutions with the increase of the problem size, i.e., with 5 cities, there exist 12 possible routes, whereas for 25 cities, the number of routes grows to 3.1×10^{23}. Furthermore, this particular problem has been expanded into more realistic and complex formulations, usually in the forms of restrictions, such as the case of the (Capacitated) Vehicle Routing Problem [22] or the case of TSP with Time Windows [23].

Resolving this problem by classical computing methods is not always optimal, and several methods, with their limitations, have been developed over the years as replacement to brute force solutions on these optimization problems. In recent years,

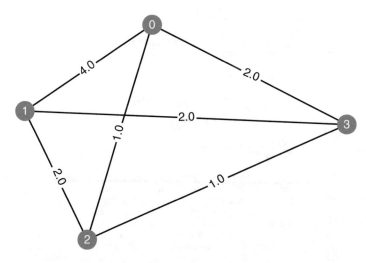

Fig. 8.3 Example of a graph defining a TSP with four cities and the roads interconnecting them

due to the expansion of quantum computing, researchers began to develop quantum algorithms that solve these problems: both for the perspective of adiabatic quantum computing [24] and for the perspective of gate-based quantum computing [25, 26].

To solve the problem in Amazon Braket, the code described in Fig. 8.4 has been developed to work with quantum gate-based computers.

On the other hand, using quantum annealing to solve this problem is quite straightforward, only needing to invoke a call to function, which is shown in Fig. 8.5.

8.3.2   Limitations of Getting Service-Oriented Computing Benefits in Quantum Computing Environments

Taking as a starting point the problems described in the previous section and the description of their solutions in each quantum computational model, the aim of this section is to highlight the difficulties encountered when trying to provide agnostic implementations of the underlying computational model using Amazon Braket.

More specifically, the experiments carried out allow us to conclude that there is some roughness, limitations, and problems that arise when a quantum piece of software is expected to be provided as a service. They are mainly related to the fact that, using current proposals to integrate quantum technologies such as Amazon Braket, the benefits of service-oriented computing are lost.

First and foremost is the impossibility of abstracting the service from the underlying quantum computational model. The consequence is that both the service developer and the users of the service are left with the problem of vendor locking.

```
1    def circuit(eigenstate):
2
3        if len(eigenstate)!=n_eigenvector:
4            return None
5
6        circuit = Circuit()
7
8        for i in range(0, n_eigenvector):
9            if eigenstate[i]=="1":
10               circuit.x(n_anc+i)
11
12       for i in range(n_anc):
13           circuit.h(i)
14
15       cont_U(circuit,0,math.pi/2,math.pi/8,math.pi/4,0,1)
16       cont_U(circuit,math.pi/2,0,math.pi/4,math.pi/4,2,1)
17       cont_U(circuit,math.pi/8,math.pi/4,0,math.pi/8,4,1)
18       cont_U(circuit,math.pi/4,math.pi/4,math.pi/8,0,6,1)
19       for i in range(2):
20           cont_U(circuit,0,math.pi/2,math.pi/8,math.pi/4,0,2)
21           cont_U(circuit,math.pi/2,0,math.pi/4,math.pi/4,2,2)
22           cont_U(circuit,math.pi/8,math.pi/4,0,math.pi/8,4,2)
23           cont_U(circuit,math.pi/4,math.pi/4,math.pi/8,0,6,2)
24       for i in range(4):
25           cont_U(circuit,0,math.pi/2,math.pi/8,math.pi/4,0,3)
26           cont_U(circuit,math.pi/2,0,math.pi/4,math.pi/4,2,3)
27           cont_U(circuit,math.pi/8,math.pi/4,0,math.pi/8,4,3)
28           cont_U(circuit,math.pi/4,math.pi/4,math.pi/8,0,6,3)
29       for i in range(8):
30           cont_U(circuit,0,math.pi/2,math.pi/8,math.pi/4,0,4)
31           cont_U(circuit,math.pi/2,0,math.pi/4,math.pi/4,2,4)
32           cont_U(circuit,math.pi/8,math.pi/4,0,math.pi/8,4,4)
33           cont_U(circuit,math.pi/4,math.pi/4,math.pi/8,0,6,4)
34       for i in range(16):
35           cont_U(circuit,0,math.pi/2,math.pi/8,math.pi/4,0,5)
36           cont_U(circuit,math.pi/2,0,math.pi/4,math.pi/4,2,5)
37           cont_U(circuit,math.pi/8,math.pi/4,0,math.pi/8,4,5)
38           cont_U(circuit,math.pi/4,math.pi/4,math.pi/8,0,6,5)
39       for i in range(32):
40           cont_U(circuit,0,math.pi/2,math.pi/8,math.pi/4,0,6)
41           cont_U(circuit,math.pi/2,0,math.pi/4,math.pi/4,2,6)
42           cont_U(circuit,math.pi/8,math.pi/4,0,math.pi/8,4,6)
43           cont_U(circuit,math.pi/4,math.pi/4,math.pi/8,0,6,6)
44
45       qft_dagger(circuit,6)
46
47       machine = LocalSimulator()
48       result = machine.run(circuit, shots=10000).result()
49       counts = result.measurement_counts
50
51       return counts
```

Fig. 8.4 Solution of the traveling salesperson problem implemented for gate-based quantum computers

In particular, because the formulation of the solution for a given problem is completely different depending on the underlying quantum computational model, each implementation for a given solution requires different number and type of parameters depending on the underlying quantum machine. The difficulties are even

```
 1    def TSP_annealing(G):
 2
 3        dw_sampler = BraketDWaveSampler(s3_folder,
 4                              'arn:aws:braket:::device/qpu/d-wave/DW_2000Q_6')
 5        dw_sampler = EmbeddingComposite(dw_sampler)
 6
 7        n_shots = 1000
 8        start_point = 0
 9        best_distance = sum(weights.values())
10        best_route = [None]*len(G)
11
12        for l in lagrange_list:
13            print('Running quantum annealing for TSP with Lagrange parameter=', l)
14            route = traveling_salesperson(G, dw_sampler, lagrange=1,
15                                  start=start_point, num_reads=n_shots,
16                                  answer_mode="histogram")
17
18            total_distance, distance_with_return = get_distance(route, data)
19
20            if distance_with_return < best_distance:
21                best_distance = distance_with_return
22                best_route = route
23
24        return best_route, best_distance
```

Fig. 8.5 Solution of the traveling salesperson problem using quantum annealing

greater when facing solutions to problems whose formulation depends on factors such as the size of the problem. This is the case of the solution provided for prime factorization on an adiabatic architecture. As mentioned, that solution is formulated using a QUBO or Ising (Fig. 8.2). Transforming the formulation to a two-variable term formulation is a task whose complexity increases with the size of the number to be factorized, mainly due to the introduction of auxiliary terms to simplify high-order terms. The resulting number of parameters (two-variable terms) also depends on this size.

Another limitation lies in the number of qubits available especially in the case of gate-based systems. This fact directly limits the ability to run the solutions. For example, in the case of the TSP shown in Fig. 8.3, when considering the Gate-based solution, the number of qubits amounts to 14 (8 for eigenstates + 6 for phase), so this small problem exceeds the number of qubits available (11 qubits) executed on the IonQ hardware. This shows not only the limited power of the current hardware but also the need for mechanisms to be included in quantum service computing to determine the number of qubits needed so the executions can be launched in appropriated powerful enough quantum computers. Due to the nature of quantum algorithms for the different architectures, there is no trivial way obtain this number. This will be a key question in developing quantum services execution schedulers. However, this is not the only feature to have into account. There are many others with implications in several other aspects of the service, such as the case of response and awaiting time. Due to the nature of quantum computations making use of quantum entanglement to explore all solutions at the same time, it is not possible to query the system because it will be forced to collapse. Thus, it is not possible to initially estimate response times without affecting the outcome of the algorithm and can only base it on statistical calculations from previous execution times.

Finally, one of the biggest hurdles is related to the inherent nature of quantum computing and their underlying physical phenomena that serve as base for the quantum architecture. It is the case of ion traps or quantum chips. Due to the problems that arise due to the characteristics of current quantum computers, mainly noise in the qubits state, the experiments must be conducted several times to be statistically consistent. Along with the latter, depending on the architecture executing the quantum code, one must work with a panoply of solutions ranging from energy levels of solutions to "simple" probabilities and cases. This goes directly against the agnostic nature of services, in which the underlying technology should be irrelevant for the service consumer. For a real quantum service technology, the responsibility of performing the different executions to get a consistent result cannot be delegated in the client nor the customer who only wants to use a technology to get a correct result, at least within a given margin of error, and with an economic cost known in advance. How the number of shots required is estimated will have a direct impact in the cost of the service executions. This reveals some issues, related with service quality and costs, which still have to be addressed by quantum services engineering.

8.4   Directions for a Future QSOC

Taking into account the examples depicted in the previous section, it is clear that using classical SOC and microservices principles to develop hybrid quantum-classical information systems is still far from being possible. Thus, some methodologies and techniques may have to be imported directly from the classical world to the quantum world, while many others will need to be adapted, and some new ones will have to be introduced.

A good starting point is to define a set of good practices that provides support to the development and operation of quantum microservices. This is just the purpose of Fig. 8.6. It proposes several steps that should be taken into account to create quantum software that can be consumed as a microservice. The proposed steps are based on current microservices and quantum technologies and try to exploit the benefits of both worlds.

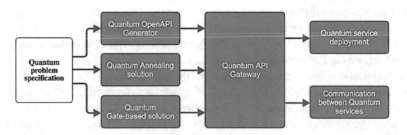

Fig. 8.6 Quantum services recommended practices

The first step to create a quantum microservice is the specification of the quantum problem to be addressed. This step is very tightly related with the abovementioned decomposition patterns of classical microservices. A microservice should focus on implementing a single business capability. In the specific case of quantum services, and given the current state of quantum hardware, any part of the problem that can be solved by traditional services should be implemented as such. Only specific problems that benefit from running on a quantum computer should be implemented as quantum algorithms.

Once this decomposition is done, the quantum services functionality should be defined abstracting as many details as possible from the underlying quantum hardware. For traditional services, one of the most extended mechanisms to perform this task is the OpenAPI Specification. It defines a standard, language-agnostic interface to RESTful APIs which allows both humans and computers to discover and understand the capabilities of services without access to source code or documentation. The same standard can be used for quantum services, although some modifications may be needed to included specific quantum aspects such as the number of qubits needed to run the service given a certain input or the number or shots to be executed.

From the OpenAPI specification of traditional services, a code generation tool is able to generate API client libraries, server stubs, documentation, and configuration automatically for dozens of programming languages. This tool can be extended to support code generation for quantum services. This would abstract quantum microservices developers from most of the specific details of the supported quantum hardware and gain the support of the classical service community that are already used to the OpenAPI ecosystem.

Although such quantum code generation tools can abstract many implementation details, a quantum algorithm still needs to be developed to perform the microservice computation. A quantum annealing solution, or a quantum gate-based solution (or both), should be provided as the body of the generated quantum service.

Another interesting area to explore is related to the deployment of services. From this point of view, the situation is very different to traditional services. To the authors' knowledge, actually, it is not possible to deploy services on quantum machines; thus, the quantum software to be executed is deployed upon execution, leading to a redeployment with each invocation. This implies an increase in the computational resources needed to execute quantum microservices. Each time a quantum microservice is consumed, it has to be deployed first. However, this disadvantage can be turned into an advantage. A Quantum API Gateway should be able to perform all the task that a traditional API Gateway performs and, at the same time, apply a heuristic to decide the best quantum hardware in which to deploy the service at each time. This heuristic could take into account the available quantum computers in which the service can be run, the number of qubits needed, the cost of running the service on each quantum computers, and other similar aspects. From this information, the optimal hardware can be chosen for each user on real time, providing a greater flexibility than traditional services where the deployment is only performed one time.

Another necessary step is involved in the communication between traditional microservices and quantum microservices. For this particular problem, one approximation could be following an approach similar to how many traditional microservices manage communications, using queues for the messages. However, the collapse of the quantum systems should be taken into account. Once the quantum algorithm that runs as the body of a quantum microservice has started is execution, it will not be possible to consult its state without collapsing the system and, almost certainly, invalidating the execution. Therefore, communications between quantum services should be managed before or after the quantum core of the service is executing and communication systems should be adapted to this behavior. The Quantum API Gateway can also help coordinate these aspects each time a quantum service is deployed.

From all the above, it is clear that there are two key elements needed in order to be able to efficiently integrate hybrid quantum computing services, the specification of the problem and the Quantum API Gateway. Both allow developers to mitigate the problems of vendor lock-in and impossibility of deployment on quantum computers. Additionally, a code generation tool can also help bridge the gap between them in a way that is familiar to most services developers. Thus, we feel that the focus of quantum microservices engineering should be in designing and developing these set of proposed good practices in order to translate the benefits of traditional microservices to hybrid quantum microservices.

8.5 Related Works

To date, works that focus on quantum microservices or hybrid microservices architectures are still sparse, and this is because quantum software engineering is a young discipline. However, some researchers are starting to focus on this and related topics.

Already there are works that begin to explore the research opportunities of quantum services and the potential of quantum services in the cloud [27]. In this paper, researchers from different studies emphasize the problems encountered during their research in this area. In particular, it includes the problems caused by the need for different implementations of the same quantum algorithms for different hardware vendors or the problems in deploying quantum services on quantum computers.

As previously mentioned, in [28], the researchers further explore the deployment of quantum services through an extension of TOSCA for quantum software deployment. This proposal shares some similarities with the work proposed in this book chapter. Because quantum applications must be deployed again for each invocation, a classical computer is needed to host and deploy these applications. Therefore, we propose the use of a classical web service to wrap quantum algorithms and expose them as endpoints.

In the same way, in [29], the researchers propose a procedure for the deployment of algorithms in cloud-based quantum computers. This procedure is only valid for circuit-based quantum algorithms because their proposal is based on starting from a generic quantum circuit and then compiling that circuit in a specific quantum computer.

The fact that quantum algorithms are highly dependent on the hardware on which they will be executed generates vendor lock-in problems. Therefore, there are already works that aim to minimize these problems by parameterizing quantum circuits [25, 30]. This technique allows the development of quantum circuits that can be modified by means of input parameters, thus being able to be used to adapt the algorithms to different computers or depending on the problem to be covered. However, this technique cannot be applied to quantum annealing-based hardware.

From a commercial technological perspective, along with Amazon Braket, there are different technological proposals related to the homogenization and simplification of quantum access to computers and services. A clear example is Azure Quantum [31], one of the main alternatives to Amazon Braket. Azure Quantum offers a quantum software development kit that attempts to unify a heterogeneous set of hardware and software solutions.

Other technology companies, software developers, and researchers are creating high-level development environments, toolkits, APIs, and other technologies to increase the level of abstraction of quantum software. For example, the IBM Company proposes the IBM Quantum environment [32], while other developers are focusing on specific areas such as quantum machine learning [20]. However, to the authors' knowledge, they do not provide any specific advantage over Amazon Braket for the development of quantum microservices or hybrid solutions.

Additionally, for the development of quantum microservices with a similar quality as that of classical services, it is not enough to simplify the development and deployment of quantum algorithms. For this, other aspects of service engineering [33] need to be taken into account.

Some researchers are focusing on the orchestration aspects of quantum complex algorithms. In [34] the authors propose a hardware-based orchestrator to control the flow of complex quantum and hybrid applications. However, for quantum microservices to be used with the same ease than classical services, software orchestration solutions are still needed.

In this sense, once microservices are deployed and orchestrated, they need to be managed. To this end, work lines around quantum DevOps practices are starting to emerge. In [35], the author proposes a methodology to test the reliability of quantum computers on a periodic manner. This reliability is used to estimate whether a given hardware will provide results of sufficient quality and to select the most suitable hardware available to run a quantum service.

Finally, in [36], the authors focus on trust and security issues in quantum services. The current model in which quantum services are managed introduces some trust issues regarding the specific hardware in which a given quantum task is run and other related issues.

All the papers presented in this section reveal that further research is needed to develop an effective quantum services engineering discipline.

8.6 Conclusion

In this chapter, we have presented an analysis of current quantum software from a service-oriented computing point of view. We have used Amazon Braket to deploy quantum services by wrapping them in a classical service and used prime factoring and traveling salesman problems as examples to hint the differences and intricacies of running the same service on a different quantum hardware, even when done under a common development umbrella and platform such as Braket.

This research and the derived work have allowed us to clearly present the current limitations in the construction and use of quantum services. To this end, we have organized these limitations and argued the intensive research efforts needed to bring the benefits of service-oriented computing to the quantum world.

Due to the young nature of quantum software engineering, most areas of this discipline, including service-oriented computing, are still in their first steps. However, the paradigm shift underlying quantum computing implies that there can be no direct translation of proposals and techniques. Running quantum algorithms as traditional services is not enough to fully explode their advantages; on the contrary, it will only degrade the solution.

Therefore, we believe that an effort is needed to generate new techniques, methodologies, and tools to fully expose all the perks and benefits, already demonstrated by cloud and service computing, into quantum software and services.

Acknowledgments This work was supported by the projects 0499_4IE_PLUS_4_E (Interreg V-A España-Portugal 2014-2020) and RTI2018-094591-B-I00 (MCIU/AEI/FEDER, UE), by the FPU19/03965 grant, by the Department of Economy and Infrastructure of the Government of Extremadura (GR18112, IB18030), and by the European Regional Development Fund.

References

1. Steane A (1998) Quantum computing. Rep Prog Phys 61(2):117
2. Preskill J (2018) Quantum computing in the nisq era and beyond. Quantum 2:79
3. MacQuarrie ER, Simon C, Simmons S, Maine E (2020) The emerging commercial landscape of quantum computing. Nat Rev Phys 2(11):596–598
4. McCaskey A, Dumitrescu E, Liakh D, Humble T (2018) Hybrid programming for near-term quantum computing systems. In: 2018 IEEE International Conference on Rebooting Computing (ICRC). IEEE, pp 1–12
5. Sodhi B (2018) Quality attributes on quantum computing platforms. arXiv preprint. arXiv:1803.07407
6. Dragoni N, Giallorenzo S, Lafuente AL, Mazzara M, Montesi F, Mustafin R, Safina L (eds) (2017) Microservices: yesterday, today, and tomorrow. Present Ulterior Softw Eng:195–216
7. Nielsen MA, Chuang I (2002) Quantum computation and quantum information
8. Newman S (2015) Building microservices: designing fine-grained systems. O'Reilly Media
9. Richardson C (2018) Microservices patterns: with examples in Java. Manning Publications
10. Martin Fowler and James Lewis. Microservices, a definition of this new architectural term. 2014.

11. Brown K, Woolf B (2016) Implementation patterns of microservices architectures. HILLSIDE Proc Conf Pattern Lang Prog 22:1–35
12. Schwichtenberg S, Gerth C, Engels G (2017) From open API to semantic specifications and code adapters. In: Proceedings – 2017 IEEE 24th International Conference on Web Services, ICWS 2017. Institute of Electrical and Electronics Engineers, pp 484–491
13. Balalaie A, Heydarnoori A, Jamshidi P (2016) Microservices architecture enables DevOps: migration to a cloud-native architecture. IEEE Software 33(3):42–52
14. Fitzgerald B, Stol KJ (2017) Continuous software engineering: a roadmap and agenda. J Syst Softw 123:176–189
15. Jiang S, Britt KA, McCaskey AJ, Humble TS, Kais S (2018) Quantum annealing for prime factorization. Scientific Rep 8(1):1–9
16. Haring R, Ohmacht M, Fox T, Gschwind M, Satterfield D, Sugavanam K, Coteus P, Heidelberger P, Blumrich M, Wisniewski R et al (2011) The ibm blue gene/q compute chip. IEEE Micro 32(2):48–60
17. Wang B, Feng H, Yao H, Wang C (2020) Prime factorization algorithm based on parameter optimization of Ising model. Scientific Rep 10(1):1–10
18. Motta M, Sun C, Tan ATK, O'Rourke MJ, Ye E, Minnich AJ, Brandao FGSL, Chan GK-L (2020) Determining eigenstates and thermal states on a quantum computer using quantum imaginary time evolution. Nat Phys 16(2):205–210
19. Kielpinski D, Monroe C, Wineland DJ (2002) Architecture for a large-scale ion-trap quantum computer. Nature 417(6890):709–711
20. Feng H, Wang B-N, Wang N, Wang C (2019) Quantum machine learning with d-wave quantum computer. Quantum Eng 1(2):e12
21. Warren RH (2013) Adapting the traveling salesman problem to an adiabatic quantum computer. Quantum Inf Proc 12(4):1781–1785
22. Irie H, Wongpaisarnsin G, Terabe M, Miki A, Taguchi S (2019) Quantum annealing of vehicle routing problem with time, state and capacity. In: International Workshop on Quantum Technology and Optimization Problems. Springer, pp 145–156
23. Papalitsas C, Andronikos T, Giannakis K, Theocharopoulou G, Fanarioti S (2019) A qubo model for the traveling salesman problem with time windows. Algorithms 12(11):224
24. Warren RH (2020) Solving the traveling salesman problem on a quantum annealer. SN Appl Sci 2(1):1–5
25. Matsuo A, Suzuki Y, Yamashita S (2020) Problem-specific parameterized quantum circuits of the VQE algorithm for optimization problems. arXiv
26. Srinivasan K, Satyajit S, Behera BK, Panigrahi PK (2018) Efficient quantum algorithm for solving travelling salesman problem: an IBM quantum experience. arXiv
27. Leymann F, Barzen J, Falkenthal M, Vietz D, Weder B, Wild K (2020) Quantum in the cloud: application potentials and research opportunities. In: Proceedings of the 10th International Conference on Cloud Computing and Service Science (CLOSER 2020). SciTePress, pp 9–24
28. Wild K, Breitenbücher U, Harzenetter L, Leymann F, Vietz D, Zimmermann M (2020) TOSCA4QC: two modeling styles for TOSCA to automate the deployment and orchestration of quantum applications. In: 24th IEEE International Enterprise Distributed Object Computing Conference, EDOC 2020, Eindhoven, The Netherlands, October 5–8, 2020. IEEE, pp 125–134
29. Sim S, Cao Y, Romero J, Johnson PD, Aspuru-Guzik A (2018) A framework for algorithm deployment on cloud-based quantum computers. arXiv preprint. arXiv:1810.10576
30. Adelomou AP, Ribe EG, Cardona XV (2020) Using the Parameterized Quantum Circuit combined with Variational-Quantum-Eigensolver (VQE) to create an Intelligent social workers' schedule problem solver. arXiv
31. Cuomo D, Caleffi M, Cacciapuoti AS (2020) Towards a distributed quantum computing ecosystem. IET Quantum Commun 1(1):3–8
32. Cross A (2018) The ibm q experience and qiskit open-source quantum computing software. APS March Meeting Abstracts 2018:L58–003

33. Li S, He Z, Jia Z, Zhong C, Cheng Z, Shan Z, Shen J, Babar MA (2021) Understanding and addressing quality attributes of microservices architecture: a systematic literature review. Inf Softw Technol 131:106449
34. Cohen Y, Sivan I, Ofek N, Ella L, Drucker N, Shani T, Weber O, Grinberg H, Greenbaum M (2020) Quantum orchestration platform integrated hardware and software for design and execution of complex quantum control protocols. Bull Am Phys Soc 65
35. Gheorghe-Pop I-D, Tcholtchev N, Ritter T, Hauswirth M (2020) Quantum devops: towards reliable and applicable nisq quantum computing. In: 2020 IEEE Globecom Workshops (GC Wkshps). IEEE, pp 1–6
36. Phalak K, Ash-Saki A, Alam M, Topaloglu RO, Ghosh S (2021) Quantum puf for security and trust in quantum computing. arXiv preprint. arXiv:2104.06244

Chapter 9
Quantum Software Testing: Current Trends and Emerging Proposals

Antonio García de la Barrera, Ignacio García-Rodríguez de Guzmán, Macario Polo, and José A. Cruz-Lemus

9.1 Introduction

In 1982, Nobel Laureate Richard Feynman asked: "What kind of computer are we going to use to simulate physics?", thereby inaugurating the "second quantum revolution." In fact, from this point, the very idea for a quantum computer was born, and quantum computer science began in earnest. Over the last three decades, our understanding of "quantum computers" has expanded drastically, as the efforts to make real such an "exotic" computer have made steady yet remarkable progress [1]. Using various "counterintuitive" principles such as superposition and entanglement, quantum computers now yield faster computing speeds, providing high value in many different and important applications. In fact, there are thousands of very interesting applications for this new paradigm, covering several areas [2]: economics and financial services, chemistry, medicine and health, supply chain logistics, energy, agriculture, etc.

The prospects for quantum computing are indeed exciting, and extraordinary expectations are now fueling a global effort to perfect quantum computing [3]. The most important companies (Google, IBM, Microsoft, Intel, Atos, Alibaba, etc.) are investigating how to take the most advantage of this new technology in their businesses. Also, many countries (China, the USA, Japan, Russia, the UK, etc.) are investing huge quantities of money in quantum technology. The involvement of

A. G. de la Barrera · I. G.-R. de Guzmán (✉)
aQuantum, Alarcos Research Group, Department of Technologies and Information Systems, Escuela Superior de Informática, University of Castilla-La Mancha, Ciudad Real, Spain
e-mail: Antonio.GAmo@uclm.es; Ignacio.GRodriguez@uclm.es

M. Polo · J. A. Cruz-Lemus
aQuantum, Alarcos Research Group, Institute of Technologies and Information Systems, University of Castilla-La Mancha, Ciudad Real, Spain
e-mail: Macario.Polo@uclm.es; JoseAntonio.Cruz@uclm.es

governments is of great importance, as has been evidenced by the introduction of the National Quantum Initiative Act in the USA, the funding of the Institute for Quantum Computing by the Canadian government, or the European Union's "Quantum Manifesto and Quantum Technologies Flagship" initiative.

A variety of quantum computers is already available, such as IBM Q, IonQ, Rigetti, D-Wave, Microsoft Quantum, and Google Quantum. Tens of quantum programming languages exist (e.g., qGCL, Q Language, QML, Quipper, OpenQASM, Qiskit, Q#) [4], as well as software development kits (e.g., Forest, Qiskit, Cirq, QDK, Orquestra) [4]. A comprehensive review of quantum computing literature, and a detailed overview of quantum software tools and technologies, plus quantum computer hardware development, can be found in [5].

As the Quantum Software Manifesto[1] states: "Given the recent rapid advances in quantum hardware, it is urgent that we step up our efforts in quantum software," stressing the importance of quantum software. It is necessary to go a step further and raise awareness of the need for quantum software engineering (QSE) that can enable us to produce quantum software with the necessary quality and productivity [6].

The main current design for quantum computers is the so-called gate-based quantum computing, very similar to today's classical approaches, which consist in dividing an algorithm into a sequence of a few very basic "primitive operations" or gates. In this kind of quantum computer, one of the tools most used for creating quantum programs is the quantum circuit. In fact, there exist several quantum circuit simulators (Quirk,[2] QCEngine,[3] etc.), and some quantum vendors such as IBM use the circuit as the main element for Qiskit programming.[4] Quantum circuits are a very good artefact with which to design quantum programs, since the transformation from quantum circuits to quantum code is quite direct and furthermore entails a more agnostic representation of a quantum algorithm (viewed from the point of view of programming language).

So, given the current state of quantum software development, the promising present and future of quantum computing, and the challenges posed by the Quantum Software Manifesto, we would like to focus in this chapter on the strengthening of quantum software engineering. Therefore, and with the aim of contributing to the development of the quantum software testing process (focusing on quantum circuit level), (1) we firstly present a review of the state of the art of the current proposals about quantum software testing, followed with (2) the proposal of the adaptation of the classical software mutation testing technique to the quantum software testing context.

The chapter is organized as follows: the second section summarizes the review of the state of the art of the last years regarding quantum software testing; the third section presents the adaptation of the mutation technique to quantum software; the

---

[1] https://www.qusoft.org/quantum-software-manifesto/
[2] https://algassert.com/quirk
[3] http://machinelevel.com/qc/
[4] https://qiskit.org/

fourth section presents a prototype to automate the application of the technique; and finally, the fifth section outlines some conclusions of our work.

9.2   Current Trends on Quantum Software Testing

This section presents a general view of the current state of the art of quantum software testing, classified in (1) overviews, (2) frameworks, (3) probabilistic testing and verification, (4) Hoare logic applications, and (5) reversible circuits testing.

9.2.1   Overview Proposals

Some publications present overviews, challenges, and predictions about the current state of the art and the future of software engineering concerning quantum computing. They offer different perspectives about testing and verification, from state-of-the-art surveys to bug taxonomies.

In [7], Zhao presents a comprehensive literature review on quantum software engineering. The term "quantum software engineering" is defined in the paper as "the use of sound engineering principles for the development, operation, and maintenance of quantum software and the associated document to obtain economically quantum software that is reliable and works efficiently on quantum computers." A quantum software cascade-based lifecycle is also presented. Then, a quantum software engineering state-of-the-art survey is conducted, summarizing the available technology with a focus on analysis, design, implementation, testing, and maintenance.

In [8], Miranskyy et al. discuss current classic software debugging tactics, showing which ones can be directly adopted for quantum software testing. They also list novel techniques suited for the quantum-computer-specific debugging issues, such as superposition or entanglement verification, or the possibility of test probability distributions employing approximate copies of the algorithm's output.

Polo [9] introduces some challenges and ideas regarding the testing of quantum programs, providing a brief overview of the existing approaches to the subject. The work focuses on functional testing, discussing the place of the test suite in hybrid classic/quantum systems, white box testing (particularly mutation), and, finally, the applicability of classic model-based testing in model representation of quantum circuits.

In [10], Huang and Martonosi survey a range of QC programs, performing debugging on small-scale simulations using different languages and technologies. Based on this experience, they conduct a comparative study assessing how the quantum environment can support testing and debugging. They also state that a quantum algorithm consists of three main conceptual parts, inputs, operations, and outputs, and they point out that bugs can result from a mistake in any of these stages.

Finally, a bug taxonomy is presented, giving examples of each kind of bug together with how to prevent them.

In [11], Sodhi considers state-of-the-art quantum computing platforms (QCPs) to identify all relevant characteristics from a software architecture perspective. By this means, the general architecture and typical programming model of a QCP are specified. Then, the significant characteristics of QCPs—from an architectural point of view—are listed and traced to the quality attributes, including testability, briefly evaluating the impact on these.

Finally, in [12], Miranskyy et al. discuss several use cases for quantum algorithms. Based on this, they address the use of quantum components as black-box artifacts in solution libraries and compare two approaches to the testing of quantum components: a unitary test perspective and a system of systems (SoS) approach. As a result, they offer some tricks to analyze quantum programs during runtime.

9.2.2   Frameworks

Some of the selected publications present technological environments or methodologic-level approaches aiming to provide—or including—a frame or context for the testing activities.

In [13], Dey et al. addressed the need for systematic techniques for cost-effective quantum software development, remarking how the different behavior of quantum systems causes a barrier in the adoption of classic Software Development Life Cycles (SDLCs). To this end, they propose a Quantum Development Life Cycle (QDLC) model based on classical waterfall models. For the testing stage, they propose a state reconstruction technique named quantum-state tomography. It is based on repeated preparation and measurement in which the preparation and measurement are repeated $22*n$ times for an n-qubit system.

In [14], Campos and Souto establish the need for a benchmark to ease the reproducibility of quantum software engineering research. To this end, they propose the development of a framework named QBugs, which includes a catalog of quantum algorithms, a catalog of reproducible bugs, and supporting infrastructure to enable empirical and controlled experimenting. In addition, they plan to—with the use of GIT—automatically map each bug report labeled as "bug" or "issue" to the commits introducing and solving the bug, automatically adding the identified problem-solution tuple to the bug catalog.

In [15], Gomes et al. establish the need for pre-developed quantum software components to increase the community of developers and their effectiveness and efficiency. To this end, they propose the creation of quantum algorithm and data structure libraries, both for the development and testing of quantum programs.

In [16], Reutter and Vicary introduce a knot-based language to design and verify quantum algorithms. They offer a scheme for interpreting knot diagrams, called shaded tangles, as quantum programs, allowing to yield substantial new insight about how the program works along with a fully topological verification. Furthermore, it is observed that isotopic tangles yield equivalent programs.

Property-based testing is a structured method for automated testing using program specifications. In [17], Honarvar et al. introduce a property-based framework for quantum programs in Q#, concerning property specification, test case generation, and analysis of test results. The authors provide an overview of the framework's architecture and mode of use, a prototype, and some examples of its application results.

In [18], Steiger et al. introduce a framework, named ProjectQ, for quantum algorithm development. It transforms high-level domain-specific language (DSL) code to several low-level instruction sets, enabling developers to test quantum algorithms on efficient simulations or through the IBM Quantum Experience cloud service. For this purpose, it uses a Python-embedded DSL and a set of compilers. The framework includes tools for circuit drawing and resource estimation and allows extension mechanisms such as plug-ins.

Fuzz testing, colloquially known as "fuzzing," is a set of software testing techniques implying the generation of a set of inputs aiming to finding errors and identifying security flaws. Greybox fuzzing, the most deployed fuzzing strategy, combines light program instrumentation with the new input data generation. In [19], Wang et al. present QuanFuzz, a search-based test input generation tool for quantum software. It analyses the system under test by instrumenting the source code and identifying which parts of the source code are associated to the measurement results and then mutates the initial input matrix, selecting those mutations which improve the probability weight for a value of the quantum register to trigger sensitive branches. Benchmark results shows QuanFuzz achieves 20–60% higher coverage compared to traditional test input generation.

In [20], Betanzo introduces QuTAF, a test automation framework based on the robot framework [21], for quantum applications testing on real quantum machines. While focused on identifying hardware-related errors, it is proven that QuTAF can identify software bugs as failing test cases.

Quipper is a functional language that enables a high-level approach for the definition of quantum circuits. QPMC is a model checker developed for the verification of quantum protocols specified as quantum Markov chains. In [22], Anticoli et al. present Entangλe, a framework for translating Quipper-like programs into the QPMC model checker, allowing to perform automatic formal verification of quantum protocols.

In [23], Smelyanskiy et al. present a high-performance distributed quantum simulator for classic computers named qHiPSTER, which can simulate single-qubit gates and controlled two-qubit gates for testing purposes. It has been performance-checked for up to 40-qubit algorithms, achieving high performance and hardware efficiency limited by memory and bandwidth.

9.2.3 Probabilistic Testing and Verification

While classic computing shows a deterministic behavior, quantum physics properties as superposition mean that quantum computers deliver probabilistic measures
when classical observations are made on qubits; that is, when a qubit in a superposition state is collapsed into a classical value, it takes a given value with a given
probability. Some selected publications address quantum computing validation from
a probabilistic perspective from circuit and software levels.

Krishnaswamy et al. [24] propose a general fault modeling method to capture
both probabilistic and deterministic faults. The authors discuss how the behavior of
quantum circuits is inherently probabilistic, and they state that, while the goal of
traditional testing has always been to detect the presence of faults, probabilistic
testing aims to estimate fault probability—what the authors call "track uncertainty."
This work presents a technology-agnostic, probabilistic equivalent called the "probabilistic transfer matrix" (PTM) method. It is inspired by traditional fault models
representing faults and deriving test vectors that propagate fault effects to outputs.

In [25], Huang and Martonosi address the problem of quantum software validation. They particularly highlight the need for new tools to write quantum algorithms
as program code, citing the difficulty of probing the internal states of programs and
interpreting such states even with existing observations. They also mention the lack
of testing guidelines for quantum testing. Based on statistical tests over classical
observations, they present quantum program assertions that allow programmers to
determine whether a quantum program state matches the expected value in one of
either classical, superposition, or entangled types of states. They use such assertions
to test three benchmark quantum programs and to lay out a strategy for using
quantum programming patterns to place assertions and prevent bugs.

In [26], Li et al. propose Proq, a runtime assertion scheme based on projections
(closed subspaces of the state space), and checked on projective measurement that
reduces the number of assertions significantly compared to repeated executions.
They prove that projection-based assertions can statistically assure that a quantum
function is close to its expected behavior.

The standard weakest precondition calculus, introduced by Dijkstra [27] and
extended to probabilistic programs by Morgan et al. [28], has been successfully
employed to reason about the correctness of classic software. In [29], Feng et al.
extend the proof rules presented by Morgan et al. for classic probabilistic loops so
that they can be used to prove any correct assertion about quantum loops.

In [30], Baltag et al. present a decidable logic for reasoning about the correctness
of quantum programs. It captures system properties through probabilistic predication
formulas, stating that a given quantum state will collapse to a state which satisfies a
given condition with a given probability. They propose first-order quantifiers ranging over quantum states and two second-order quantifiers, one ranging over
quantum-testable properties, the other over quantum "actions." This technique is
used to describe the correctness of quantum teleportation, quantum search algorithm,
and the Deutsch-Jozsa algorithm.

9.2.4 Hoare Logic Applications

Formal verification involves proving the correctness of an algorithm against a formal specification. Hoare provided in [31] a set of logical rules allowing to reason about the correctness of software, which has been the basis for a wide variety of testing research, including some approximations for Hoare-like logic for verifying quantum programs.

In [32], Barthe et al. propose a relational program logic based on a quantum analogue of probabilistic couplings in order to perform a verification of the properties of quantum programs, such as reliability of quantum teleportation against noise and uniformity for samples generated by the quantum Bernoulli factory.

Liu et al. [33] formalize the theory of quantum Hoare logic (QHL), particularly the syntax and semantics of quantum programs; they establish rules for QHL and verify the soundness and completeness of the deduction system for partial correctness of quantum programs.

In [34], Zhou et al. derive a variant of QHL, named *applied quantum Hoare logic* (aQHL), which significantly simplifies verification of quantum programs. It is developed by restricting QHL to projections, a class of preconditions, and post-conditions and adding several rules for reasoning about the robustness of quantum programs.

Ying et al. [35] study the definition of invariants in quantum programs (an invariant of a software at a given location is an assertion that is always true when the location is reached, allowing to check partial correctness of a program). They also address the problem of generating additive invariants for quantum software by reducing it to a semidefinite programming (SDP) problem and applying an SDP solver.

In [36], Kakutani presents a Hoare-style logic for the verification of quantum, probabilistic programs. Hartog's probabilistic Hoare logic [37] is extended in this work, and the QPL language [38] is taken as the target.

Finally, Sun and He present the basic idea of *categorical logic for quantum programs* (CLQP) [39]. CLPQ combines the logic of quantum programming (LQP)—an extension of quantum Hoare logic—with categorical quantum mechanics (CQM). They present its syntax, semantics, and proof system along with a proof-of-concept over Deutsch's algorithm's correctness.

9.2.5 Reversible Circuits Testing

From the point of view of circuit verification, reversibility provides some interesting properties, such as the conservation of energy and, thus, of information [40]. In the current state of the art, the most used "high-level" models and languages in quantum algorithm definition are still representations of circuits, thus keeping some of the circuits' properties that are interesting for unitary testing of quantum algorithms.

This is the reason why this topic has been considered relevant for this work. Some of the selected publications focus on reversible quantum circuit verification and the applicability of the classical reversible circuit existing techniques and approaches to their quantum equivalents.

In Patel et al. [41], the test-set generation problem is considered, focusing on how it is affected by the reversibility of circuits. It is demonstrated that reversibility simplifies the problem in a significant way. An algorithm for finding complete test sets is presented and compared to conventional automatic test pattern generation (ATPG, hereinafter), obtaining test sets approximately half the size of the ATPG ones. The authors also discuss how this work may be extended to reversible quantum circuits, considering the inherent differences between the deterministic fault-free classical circuits and the probabilistic fault-free quantum circuits.

In [42], Mondal et al. propose a fault detection scheme for any type of reversible circuits consisting of entirely positive, negative, or mixed controlled Toffoli gates. It is suitable for large circuits and has been tested on several benchmark circuits, detecting faults, and identifying the faulty zone. After presenting the results, a comparative analysis with other works is performed.

Finally, Zamani et al. [43] present a test generation method for reversible circuits, adoptable by built-in self-test (BIST) implementations, which achieves a high fault coverage. In the proposed approach, each test pattern is the output of the circuit to the previous test pattern. A test generation algorithm to minimize test time is also presented, achieving 100% fault coverage. Encouraging results were found in the application of the benchmark simulation experiments of the proposed method.

9.2.6   Analysis of the Current State of the Art

According to the state of the art presented in the previous sections, a brief analysis of the different findings will be presented, in order to outline in what extent the current proposals support the emerging quantum software testing process of quantum software engineering.

One of the main identified strengths is that experience with classic software engineering has enabled the community to become aware of the need for a quantum software engineering—and more specifically a quantum software testing engineering—in a very incipient state of quantum computing. This has enabled the development of elements such as lifecycles [13], bug taxonomies [10, 14], or testing frameworks [20] significantly earlier than their classic counterparts. On the other hand, the low abstraction level of the models and languages used for quantum algorithm definition implies that some techniques developed for quantum circuit testing may be possibly applied to the unitary testing of quantum software. Another point that derives from the low abstraction level is that the graphical platform-independent models (PIM) are—with some exceptions [16]—based on a broadly accepted meta-model, favoring standardization, abstraction, reuse, and independence from technological providers.

On the other hand, the main weakness found is the lack of a settled and well-proven body of knowledge on quantum software engineering, as the state-of-the-art testing of quantum algorithms and protocols is still rudimentary [17]. Even though the tendency in SE is to raise the level of abstraction, the artifacts used for quantum algorithm specification are still mainly circuit representations, lacking the advantages of higher-level versions. Moreover, the life cycles proposed so far [7, 13] are cascade-based approaches. While state-of-the-art classic SE lifecycles have transformed testing processes into a set of transversal and iterative tasks, waterfall models offer a more isolated and sequential vision of testing and verification. Besides, there is still a lack of off-the-shelf components [15], such as testing libraries, and technological environments that support verification and testing activities [17, 22] are still reduced in number, matureness, and integration.

However, there is a vast body of knowledge on classic testing engineering. Although some techniques, processes, and activities have been assessed and adapted, there are still others that are yet to be addressed, for example, the integration of quantum processes and artifacts on classical platforms like KDM [44] or UML [45] is an emerging field of study. Furthermore, the quantum as a service approach that is expected to prevail in the near future [46] will make it possible to approach integration testing and verification management through already established "as a Service" practices, such as component integration techniques, provider service-level agreements, or continuous integration processes [47]. Finally, from the perspective of Model-Driven Architectures (MDA) [48], the low abstraction level of current platform-independent and specific models (PIMs/PSMs) eases the mapping effort between different models and languages significantly. This favors MDA's practices such as reuse and automatic transformation and testing of high-level executable models.

Finally, it is crucial to point out the different threats that must be considered concerning quantum software testing. Firstly, quantum programming is less intuitive and more complex, and thus more error-prone due to quantum mechanics [49, 50]. The fact that a significant proportion of practitioners have a background in physics or mathematics rather than computer science can also be a source for reluctance about the introduction of SE practices such as higher-abstraction-level artifacts or the adoption of novel development/testing processes [51]. Secondly, the QaaS predictable future combined with the low abstraction level of artifacts can derive in low portability of models and code and solid dependency of the hardware providers.

9.3 From Classic to Quantum Software Testing: Redefining the Mutation Technique

9.3.1 Introduction

Considering the previous analysis of the state of the art, it is obvious the lack of techniques and tools to implement a quantum software engineering-based quantum software testing process. In order to start tackling with such situation, the current section presents a redefinition of one of the most powerful techniques to perform software testing in classic software development: software mutation.

Mutation testing has been widely used to improve the quality of test suites ever since the inception of structure programming [52] to optimized applications in object-oriented development [53, 54]. Also, mutation testing has been applied to different software domains [55]. Mutants are usually generated by automated tools that, through mutation operators, introduce syntactic changes in the programs. Most of the time, these changes can be interpreted as small mistakes that a *competent programmer* [56] might commit and that, under given circumstances, could lead to the program showing an unexpected behavior. This situation is more common for programmers who come from the field of classical computing [57].

Thus, mutation tools can imitate simple human errors and are premised on the *coupling effect* (i.e., if a test suite is sensitive enough to detect simple faults, it will be also able to detect more complex faults [58]). Each mutation operator is specialized in introducing one particular type of change that may cause an error.

To the best of our knowledge, mutation is a technique that to date has not been exploited in quantum circuit development, except for two proposals which do mention the concept of mutation. The first of these is [59], where the authors apply metamorphic testing to quantum software (written in Q#). In this approach, the concept of "mutant" is only mentioned as a part of the validation of the approach and as a method to modify the original source code. Although this approach is focused on Q# programs, mutants proposed in this paper are just possible examples of modifications that could be carried out on quantum software. The second such proposal is [60], in which the authors present a novel quantum mutant-based fault injection technique, based on the replacement of certain gates by other ones.

9.3.2 Quantum Specific Errors and Operators

Quantum computing is a young discipline, and as yet there are few fault models. Two of the most significant are those produced by Lukac et al. [61] and by Biamonte et al. [61], who, respectively, collect (1) faults due to *quantum noise* or gate-building construction and (2) *programmer faults*.

We are concerned here with the second type, which we have grouped into the following categories: *missing gates*, *wrong gates*, *bridging faults* (a multi-qubit gate which connects wrong qubits), and *initialization errors*. We have included an additional category for representing *entanglement faults*.

The proposed, designed, and implemented mutation operators appear in Table 9.1. Each operator includes its description and one example of its application. Note that each operator can be applied several times to the same circuit, producing one mutant circuit per application.

The *wrong gate* operators swap X, Y, Z, and H gates with the others, thus showing a similar behavior. As a result, we give only three examples of its application.

9.4   Quantum Mutation Support Tool

9.4.1   Description of the Prototype

QuMu is a tool for the mutation testing of quantum circuits. It is based on the circuit representation given by the Quirk quantum circuit simulator.[5] In Quirk, a circuit is represented by an ordered set of columns, and on each column, there is an ordered set of gates. Quirk exports the circuits as a JSON object, and from this, QuMu creates a circuit representation. In Fig. 9.1, the diagram shows the most meaningful operations in each class. Note that *Gate* is an abstract class that has as many concrete specializations (Fig. 9.6) as types of gates that we want to mutate.

Mutation operators are specializations of the abstract Operator class (Fig. 9.2), which declare two abstract operations:

- *isApplicableTo* returns *true* whether this operator is applicable to a quantum circuit passed as a parameter. If it is, then the operation saves in the *mutablePositions* map whichever rows are mutable in each column.
- If it was determined that the operator was applicable to the circuit, *apply* goes through all the columns and rows saved in *mutablePositions* and generates a mutant for each mutable position. Every mutant is then saved in a database.

The operators are organized in a hierarchical structure (Fig. 9.3) like that shown in Table 9.1, which allows for operations which are common to several operators to be reused: for example, the *isApplicableTo* method in the abstract *EntanglementOperator* class is valid for all three of its specializations.

The determination of the applicability of an operator to a given circuit relies on reflective programming: for example, the isApplicableTo method in

---

[5] https://algassert.com/quirk

Table 9.1 Quantum mutation operators

Family	Operator	Description	Examples	
			Original circuit	Mutant circuit
Initialization	Change initial value	Changes the initial value of a qubit		
	First gate duplication	Duplicates a one-qubit gate placed in the first column of the circuit		
	Further gate duplication	Duplicates a one-qubit gate placed in the second and next columns		
Wrong gate	Swap X-Y	These operators swap one Pauli or Hadamard gate with a different Pauli or Hadamard gate		
	Swap X-Z			Swap H-Y
	Swap X-H			
	Swap Y-X			
	Swap Y-Z			Swap X-Y
	Swap Y-H			

	Swap Z-Y		
	Swap Z-H		
	Swap H-X		
	Swap H-Y		
	Swap H-Z		Swap Y-X
Missing gate	One-qubit gate removal	Removes a one-qubit gate at any location of the circuit	Removed the fourth qubit
	Multi-qubit gate removal	Removes a multi-qubit gate at any location of the circuit	
	Control gate removal	Removes one control gate in a multi-qubit gate	Removed the second column
Bridging faults	Swap controls and controlled qubits	Swaps the control gate with one of the controlled gates	
Entanglement faults	Wrong entanglement initialization	Moves the H gate to the X row	

(continued)

Table 9.1 (continued)

Family	Operator	Description	Examples	
			Original circuit	Mutant circuit
	Entanglement corruption	Shifts the H gate to the right of the control column		
	Force unentanglement	Removes the H gate in the first column		
	Force entanglement	Detects inverse situations to an entanglement and converts them into entanglements		

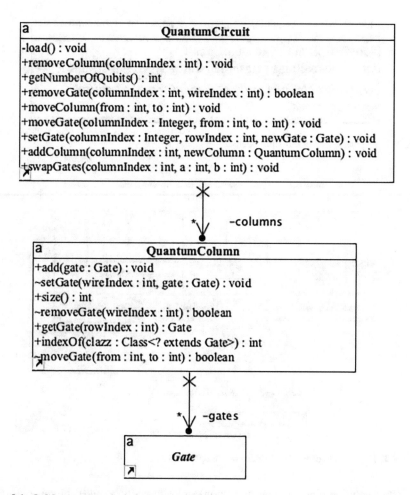

Fig. 9.1 QuMu representation of a quantum circuit

OneQubitGateRemoval looks for gates implementing the IOneQubitGate interface (Fig. 9.4). Currently, the only gates implementing this interface are X, Y, Z, and H— and so the operator would not be applicable to the Square of Z gate. If we want to apply this operator to this gate, we only need to ensure that SquareOfZ implements the IOneQubitGate.

Once the two subsystems (i.e., the circuit with its columns and gates and the operators) have been defined, the generation and execution of mutants is performed by two engines:

- The first engine (mutant generation) iterates over the selected mutation operators and over the columns and gates of the circuit.

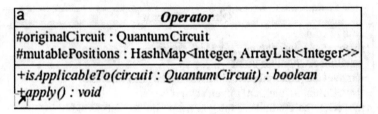

Fig. 9.2 A generic QuMu mutation operator

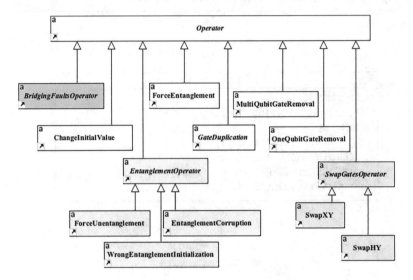

Fig. 9.3 Partial view of the architecture of the operators

- The second engine (mutant execution) uploads every mutated circuit onto the Quirk website, performs the execution simulation of the mutant, downloads the results, and saves them in the database.

9.4.2 Quantum Software Mutation Example

Figure 9.5 shows the top side of QuMu, which is implemented as a web application. The tester may either load one of circuits saved in the database (shown in the dropdown list of the section "Original circuit") or may paste its Quirk's JSON specification into the "Your circuit" section.

The circuit is drawn in the third section ("Loaded circuit"), which is an iframe element containing the Quirk web page.

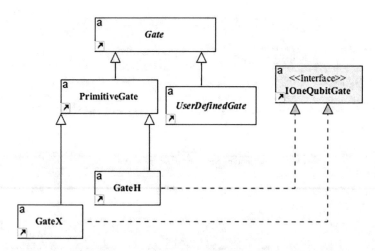

Fig. 9.4 isApplicableTo uses reflection to decide the applicability of an operator

In Sect. 9.4 (Fig. 9.5), the tester selects the operators they want to apply to the circuit and presses the Generate mutant's button. When the server receives the request, it generates the mutants, saves them in the database, and returns the results to the user-agent.

For the circuit shown in Fig. 9.5, QuMu generates 58 mutants. Figure 9.6 shows the 15th mutant, generated by the Control Gate Removal operator to the control gate at the CNOT gate, in the fifth column.

According to the distribution matrixes obtained from the execution of mutants, they are classified into three different states: alive mutants, killed mutants, and injured mutants.

9.4.2.1   Killed Mutants

In Quirk, all the circuits include a matrix of $n \times n$ (with n being the number of qubits) on the right side, which shows the distribution of probabilities of each pair of qubits. Each cell is represented by a complex number (r, i) that represents the amplitude matrixes.

Figure 9.7 details the matrixes which correspond to the original and to the 18th mutant. Since the distribution of the results is different, this mutant can be clearly marked as killed.

1) Original circuit (select from the list or paste it):

Either select or paste a circuit below:
Available circuits: [Adder with Hadamard ▾]

2) Your circuit:

JSON code:

{"cols":[["H","H","H"],["•","•",1,"X"],["•","X"],[1,"•","•","X"],[1,"•","X"],["•","X"]]}

If you want to save the above circuit, enter a name and press the button
[Name of the pasted circuit]
[Save as new circuit]

[Draw the circuit]

3) Loaded circuit:

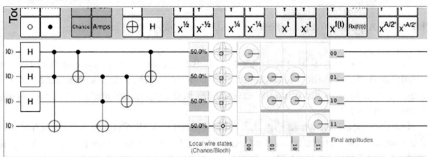

4) Mutations operators:

Initialization errors	Missing gate	Bridging faults	Wrong gate
Select/Unselect	Select/Unselect	Select/Unselect	Select/Unselect
☐ Change Initial Value	☐ Control Gate Removal	☐ Entanglement Corruption	☐ Swap H Y
☐ First Gate Duplication	☐ Multi Qubit Gate Removal	☐ Force Entanglement	☐ Swap X H
☐ Further Gate Duplication	☐ One Qubit Gate Removal	☐ Force Unentanglement	☐ Swap X Y
		☐ Swap Control And Controlled Qubits	☐ Swap X Z
		☐ Wrong Entanglement Initialization	☐ Swap Y X
			☐ Swap Y Z
			☐ Swap Z H
			☐ Swap Z X
			☐ Swap Z Y

[Generate mutants]

Fig. 9.5 Top side of QuMu

9.4.2.2 Alive Mutants

The circuits in Fig. 9.8 are the original adder circuit (top row) and its 15th mutant, whose change has also been generated by the *Control Gate Removal* operator (i.e., the control gate at the second column has been removed). Both distribution matrixes are exactly equal, and, hence, this mutant is *alive*.

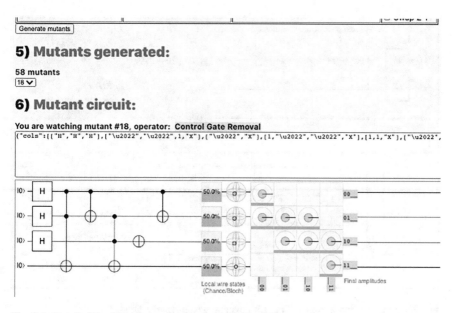

Fig. 9.6 Detail of the 18th mutant for the circuit in Fig. 9.5

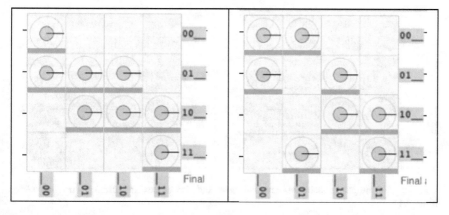

Fig. 9.7 Probabilities in the original (left) and in the 18th mutant, which is killed

9.4.2.3   Injured Mutants

There are other mutants that offer the same result as the original but leave the qubits with a different phase. The *Change Initial Value* operator has produced the Mutant 1, the first qubit input value of which has been changed from 0 to 1.

As is seen in Fig. 9.9, the original and the mutant distribution matrixes are almost identical, but there is a difference in the final phase of the first qubit: the quantum particle points outside the paper in the original circuit and inside the paper in the

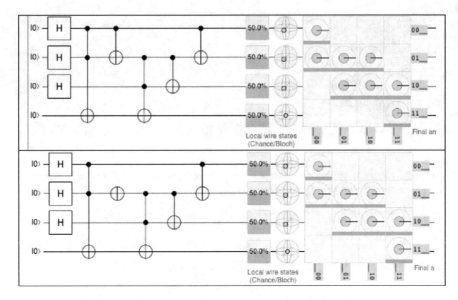

Fig. 9.8 Original circuit (top) and the 15th mutant, which remains alive

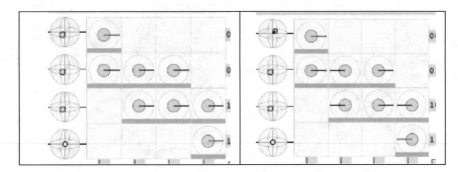

Fig. 9.9 The output probabilities are the same, but the phases are different (original versus Mutant 1)

mutant. However, the absolute values of the complex numbers representing each cell in the matrix are the same, and, thus, both outputs are indistinguishable when the qubits are measured.

We refer to this type of mutant as "injured."

7) Result analysis:

Analyze results

Killing matrix			
58 mutants	53 killed mutants Score (in [0, 1]): 0.9137	56 injured mutants Score (in [0, 1]): 0.9656	Operator
Mutant	Killed	Injured	
m1	Alive	Injured	Change Initial Value
m2	Alive	Injured	Change Initial Value
m3	Alive	Injured	Change Initial Value
m4	Killed	Injured	Change Initial Value
m5	Killed	Injured	First Gate Duplication
m6	Killed	Injured	First Gate Duplication
m7	Killed	Injured	First Gate Duplication

Fig. 9.10 First rows of the killing and injured matrixes for the Hadamard adder

9.4.2.4 Showing the Analysis Results in QuMu

QuMu includes a mutant execution engine and a mutant results analyzer. Once the mutants have been generated, the first one iterates over each successive mutant, reads the output produced by Quirk, extracts the probability distribution matrix, and saves it onto a database. Then, the results analyzer compares the distribution matrixes of the original circuit with every mutant, showing, respectively, either a killing or an injured matrix (Fig. 9.10).

9.5 Conclusions and Future Work

Quantum computing is no longer a promise, but a reality, and its impact in current and future society trends has been proven and recognized by academy and governments (which play crucial responsibilities on the success of quantum software engineering [62]) since "quantum computers have the potential to solve tasks that we don't even dare dream of today and that classical computers can never solve" [63]. However, quantum software (as a new and substantially different paradigm) lacks a methodological background to ensure a quality development process and quality products, as it has been claimed in different studies. A quantum software engineering study field is emerging to avoid a potential quantum software crisis, and many areas must be developed. That means that we must commence quantum software engineering right now, thus seeking to be prepared, and endeavoring to avoid low-quality quantum software plagued with errors and productivity problems.

To achieve all the benefits that quantum computing offers, though, this new paradigm will need to be developed in an appropriate way. Testing processes and tools are of particular importance—as is evident from classic software engineering. As a first step in our walkthrough to the statement of a standardized quantum software testing process, we present in this chapter (1) an analysis of the current state of the art about quantum software testing, and aligned to our aim of contributing to create a body of knowledge for quantum software testing (and, in turn, contribute to quantum software engineering), and (2) we propose the redefinition of the quantum software mutation-based testing technique, together with a prototype to make feasible the application of the proposal.

The analysis of the state-of-the-art reveals that quantum physics characteristics have an important impact on the verification and validation of quantum software, as well as superposition, which turn the deterministic nature of (classic) software into a stochastic one for quantum software. Other quantum characteristics, such as the inability to clone/copy the exact state of a qubit, make impossible to check the intermediate state of a particular qubit. Despite these physical barriers to perform testing on quantum programs, several trends have been identified: (1) proposals dealing with the stochastic nature of quantum software, (2) adaptations of the Hoare logic, and (3) the use of quantum circuits' reversibility property.

Finally, a redefinition of the software testing based on mutation technique has been proposed for quantum software testing. An initial set of errors has been identified, and the corresponding mutant operators has been designed to simulate the errors in "quantum circuits under tests." To demonstrate the feasibility of the technique, a prototype has been developed, and initial experiments show the possibility to identify not only "killed and alive" quantum mutants but also a new type of quantum mutant, the "injured" one. More research must be carried out in order to find new errors and determine the most common ones and for refinements in the redefinition on the technique.

Acknowledgments The research work presented in this chapter is framed within the following projects: TESTIMO (Consejería de Educación, Cultura y Deportes de la Junta de Comunidades de Castilla La Mancha y Fondo Europeo de Desarrollo Regional FEDER, SBPLY/17/180501/000503) and "QHealth: Quantum Pharmacogenomics Applied to Aging," 2020 CDTI Missions Program (Center for the Development of Industrial Technology of the Ministry of Science and Innovation of Spain). We would like to thank all the aQuantum members, especially Guido Peterssen and Pepe Hevia, for their help and support.

References

1. Maslov D, Nam Y, Kim J (2019) An outlook for quantum computing [point of view]. Proc IEEE 107(1):5–10
2. López, M.A. and Silva, M.M.D., Quantum technologies: digital transformation, social impact, and cross-sector disruption. 2019.
3. Humble TS, DeBenedictis EP (2019) Quantum realism. Computer 52(06):13–17
4. LaRose R (2019) Overview and comparison of gate level quantum software platforms. Quantum 3:130
5. Gill SS (2020) Quantum computing: a taxonomy, systematic review and future directions. 2010(15559). ArXiv

6. Piattini M, Peterssen G, Pérez-Castillo R, Hevia JL, Serrano MA, Hernández G, García-Rodríguez de Guzmán I, Paradela CA, Polo M, Murina E, Jiménez L, Marqueño JC, Gallego R, Tura J, Phillipson F, Murillo JM, Niño A, Rodríguez M (2020) The Talavera Manifesto for Quantum Software Engineering and Programming. In: QANSWER
7. Zhao J (2020) Quantum software engineering: landscapes and horizons. arXiv preprint arXiv:2007.07047
8. Miranskyy A, Zhang L, Doliskani J (2020) Is your quantum program bug-free? In: Proceedings – 2020 ACM/IEEE 42nd International Conference on Software Engineering: New Ideas and Emerging Results, ICSE-NIER 2020
9. Usaola MP (2020) Quantum software testing. In: QANSWER
10. Huang Y, Martonosi M (2019) QDB: from quantum algorithms towards correct quantum programs. In: OpenAccess Series in Informatics
11. Sodhi B (2018) Quality attributes on quantum computing platforms. arXiv preprint arXiv:1803.07407
12. Miranskyy A, Zhang L, Doliskani J (2021) On testing and debugging quantum software. arXiv preprint arXiv:2103.09172
13. Dey N, Ghosh M, Chakrabarti A (2020) QDLC–the quantum development life cycle. arXiv preprint arXiv:2010.08053
14. Campos J, Souto A (2021) QBugs: a collection of reproducible bugs in quantum algorithms and a supporting infrastructure to enable controlled quantum software testing and debugging experiments. arXiv preprint arXiv:2103.16968
15. Gomes C, Fortunato D, Fernandes JP, Abreu R (2020) Off-the-shelf components for quantum programming and testing. In: CEUR Workshop Proceedings
16. Reutter D, Vicary J (2018) Shaded tangles for the design and verification of quantum programs (extended abstract). In: Electronic Proceedings in Theoretical Computer Science, EPTCS
17. Honarvar S, Mousavi MR, Nagarajan R (2020) Property-based testing of quantum programs in Q#. In: Proceedings – 2020 IEEE/ACM 42nd International Conference on Software Engineering Workshops, ICSEW 2020
18. Steiger DS, Häner T, Troyer M (2018) ProjectQ: an open source software framework for quantum computing. Quantum 2:49
19. Wang J, Gao M, Jiang Y, Lou J, Gao Y, Zhang D, Sun J (2018) QuanFuzz: Fuzz testing of quantum program. arXiv preprint arXiv:1810.10310
20. Betanzo Sanchez F (2020) QuTAF: a test automation framework for quantum applications
21. Bisht S (2013) Robot framework test automation. Packt Publishing
22. Anticoli L, Piazza C, Taglialegne L, Zuliani P (2018) Entangλe: A translation framework from quipper programs to quantum markov chains. In: Communications in computer and information science, pp 113–126
23. Smelyanskiy M, Sawaya N, Aspuru-Guzik A (2016) qHiPSTER: the quantum high performance software testing environment. arXiv preprint arXiv:1601.07195
24. Krishnaswamy S, Markov IL, Hayes JP (2007) Tracking uncertainty with probabilistic logic circuit testing. IEEE Des Test Comput 24(4):312–321
25. Huang Y, Martonosi M (2019) Statistical assertions for validating patterns and finding bugs in quantum programs. In: Proceedings – International Symposium on Computer Architecture
26. Li G, Zhou L, Yu N, Ding Y, Ying M, Xie Y (2020) Projection-based runtime assertions for testing and debugging Quantum programs. In: Proceedings of the ACM on Programming Languages. 4(OOPSLA)
27. Dijkstra EW, Dijkstra EW, Dijkstra EW, Dijkstra EW (1976) A discipline of programming, vol 613924118. Prentice-Hall, Englewood Cliffs
28. Morgan C, McIver A, Seidel K (1996) Probabilistic predicate transformers. ACM Trans Program Lang Syst (TOPLAS) 18(3):325–353
29. Feng Y, Duan R, Ji Z, Ying M (2007) Proof rules for the correctness of quantum programs. Theoretical Comput Sci 386(1–2):151–166

30. Baltag A, Bergfeld JM, Kishida K, Sack J, Smets SJL, Zhong S (2013) Quantum probabilistic dyadic second-order logic. Lecture Notes in Computer Science (including subseries Lecture Notes in Artificial Intelligence and Lecture Notes in Bioinformatics).:64–80
31. Hoare CAR (1969) An axiomatic basis for computer programming. Commun ACM 12(10): 576–580
32. Barthe G, Hsu J, Ying M, Yu N, Zhou L (2020) Relational proofs for quantum programs. In: Proceedings of the ACM on Programming Languages. 4(POPL)
33. Liu J, Zhan B, Wang S, Ying S, Liu T, Li Y, Ying M, Zhan N (2019) Formal verification of quantum algorithms using quantum hoare logic. In: Lecture Notes in Computer Science (including subseries Lecture Notes in Artificial Intelligence and Lecture Notes in Bioinformatics), pp 187–207
34. Zhou L, Yu N, Ying M (2019) An applied quantum hoare logic. In: Proceedings of the ACM SIGPLAN Conference on Programming Language Design and Implementation (PLDI)
35. Ying M, Ying S, Wu X (2017) Invariants of quantum programs: characterisations and generation. In: Conference Record of the Annual ACM Symposium on Principles of Programming Languages
36. Kakutani Y (2009) A logic for formal verification of quantum programs. In: Lecture Notes in Computer Science (including subseries Lecture Notes in Artificial Intelligence and Lecture Notes in Bioinformatics), pp 79–93
37. den Hartog J (1999) Verifying probabilistic programs using a hoare like logic. In: Annual Asian Computing Science Conference. Springer
38. Selinger P (2004) Towards a quantum programming language. Mathematical Struct Comput Sci 14(4):527–586
39. Sun X, He F (2020) A first step to the categorical logic of quantum programs. Entropy 22(2)
40. Fredkin E, Toffoli T (1982) Conservative logic. Int J Theoretical Phys 21(3):219–253
41. Patel KN, Hayes JP, Markov IL (2004) Fault testing for reversible circuits. IEEE Trans Computer-Aided Des Integr Circ Syst 23(8):1220–1230
42. Mondal B, Bandyopadhyay C, Rahaman H (2016) A testing scheme for mixed-control based reversible circuits. In: 2016 Sixth International Symposium on Embedded Computing and System Design (ISED). IEEE
43. Zamani M, Tahoori MB, Chakrabarty K (2012) Ping-pong test: compact test vector generation for reversible circuits. In: 2012 IEEE 30th VLSI Test Symposium (VTS). IEEE
44. Jiménez-Navajas L, Pérez-Castillo R, Piattini M (2020) Reverse engineering of quantum programs toward KDM models. In: International Conference on the Quality of Information and Communications Technology. Springer
45. Pérez-Castillo R, Jiménez-Navajas L, Piattini M (2021) Modelling quantum circuits with UML. arXiv preprint arXiv:2103.16169
46. Leymann F, Barzen J, Falkenthal M, Vietz D, Weder B, Wild K (2020) Quantum in the cloud: application potentials and research opportunities. arXiv preprint arXiv:2003.06256
47. Bratman H, Court T (1975) The software factory. Computer 8(5):28–37
48. OMG (2003) MDA Guide v1.0. Business Process Integration chapter
49. Ying M (2011) Floyd-hoare logic for quantum programs. ACM Trans Program Lang Syst 33(6)
50. Piattini M, Serrano M, Perez-Castillo R, Petersen G, Hevia JL (2021) Toward a quantum software engineering. IT Prof 23(1):62–66
51. Theocharis G, Kuhrmann M, Münch J, Diebold P (2015) Is water-scrum-fall reality? On the use of agile and traditional development practices. In: International Conference on Product-Focused Software Process Improvement. Springer
52. Agrawal H (1989) Design of mutant operators for the C programming language. Software Engineering Research Center, Purdue University, West Lafayette.
53. Polo M, Piattini M, García-Rodríguez I (2009) Decreasing the cost of mutation testing with second-order mutants. Softw Test Verif Reliab 19(2):111–131
54. Deng L, Offutt AJ (2018) Reducing the cost of android mutation testing

55. Deng L, Offutt J, Ammann P, Mirzaei N (2017) Mutation operators for testing android apps. Inf Softw Technol 81(C):154–168
56. DeMillo RA, Lipton RJ, Sayward FG (1978) Hints on test data selection: help for the practicing programmer. Computer 11(4):34–41
57. Li G, Zhou L, Yu N, Ding Y, Ying M, Xie Y (2020) Projection-based runtime assertions for testing and debugging quantum programs. Proc ACM Program Lang 4
58. Offutt AJ (1992) Investigations of the software testing coupling effect. ACM Trans Softw Eng Methodol 1(1):5–20
59. Honarvar S, Mousavi MR, and Nagarajan R. Property-based testing of quantum programs in Q#. 2020.
60. Boncalo O, Udrescu M, Prodan L, Vladutiu M, Amaricai A (2007) Assessing quantum circuits reliability with mutant-based simulated fault injection'. In: 2007 18th European Conference on Circuit Theory and Design, pp 942–945
61. Lukac M, Kameyama M, Perkowski M, Kerntopf P, Moraga C (2017) Fault models in reversible and quantum circuits. In: Adamatzky A (ed) Advances in Unconventional Computing, Theory, vol 1. Springer International, Cham, pp 475–493
62. Piattini M, Peterssen G, Pérez-Castillo R (2020) Quantum computing: a new software engineering golden age. SIGSOFT Softw Eng Notes 45(3):12–14
63. EQF (2020) Strategic research agenda. European Quantum Flagship. European Commission

Chapter 10
Quantum Software Measurement

Miguel-Angel Sicilia, Marçal Mora-Cantallops, Salvador Sánchez-Alonso, and Elena García-Barriocanal

10.1   Introduction

Software measurement plays an important role in software engineering. As software engineering activities are diverse (including managing, costing, planning, modeling, analyzing, specifying, designing, implementing, testing, and maintaining), so are the possible metrics for processes and artifacts. Measurement is critical to the management of the software process, and practitioners and researchers count with a relatively mature body of knowledge for that purpose in the form of metrics, process frameworks, and even maturity models. All of these are built on the experience of decades of inquiry about development practice and provide the empirical and theoretical foundations for the discipline [1]. Consequently, they are regularly included as part of the educational path for software engineers [2]. However, the progressive availability of practical quantum computers raises the question of the extent to which those foundations can be transferred to the activity of developing programs based on these new devices, provided that their computational models depart rather radically from classical computers.

The programming of quantum computers (or quantum computer simulators) can be done with low-level primitives, but a relatively coherent set of higher-level abstractions have appeared in the last years [3]. Together with these abstractions, a considerable number of "quantum-specific" programming languages have been proposed and developed, together with their associated tooling (compilers, graphical programming languages, and middleware abstracting real quantum computers and simulators, among others). Further, there are known algorithms as the *quantum Fourier transform* (QTF) or *quantum phase estimation* that appear to be used as

M.-A. Sicilia (✉) · M. Mora-Cantallops · S. Sánchez-Alonso · E. García-Barriocanal
Computer Science Department, University of Alcalá, Alcalá de Henares, Spain
e-mail: msicilia@uah.es; marcal.mora@uah.es; sal-vador.sanchez@uah.es;
elena.garciab@uah.es

© The Author(s), under exclusive license to Springer Nature Switzerland AG 2022   193
M. A. Serrano et al. (eds.), *Quantum Software Engineering*,
https://doi.org/10.1007/978-3-031-05324-5_10

building blocks or library components and that might be considered in some sense as higher-level primitives. All these achievements might make software engineering for quantum computers appear as a maturing field of practice.

However, if we consider quantum software development activity nowadays in terms of volume of effort spent, it becomes obvious that the situation cannot be compared with that of classical software. This is due to its youth and relative lack of maturity, but also since quantum software is in general aimed only at solving some problems for which classical computers are deemed less efficient. This entails that empirical studies are limited by the availability of actual quantum source code, but also and more importantly by the general lack of studies related to resources or processes used in producing that software.

The above-described situation portrays quantum software metrics and measurement as an almost completely uncharted territory. For its exploration today, we can only resort to our knowledge of classical software measurement, which may to some extent be reused, reformulated, or maybe repurposed. It is even unclear if the nature of quantum software and its specificity may render inadequate some ideas that are applicable to developing traditional application or business software, since quantum programs might with time become reusable libraries written by specialized developers, in a situation completely different to that of the current profession of software engineer.

This chapter approaches the topic in its title from the just presented perspective, to look ahead in a future in which quantum software development becomes widespread at least for a class of problems in which effective and affordable quantum computers are available. In that direction, it should be noted that the chapter speculates with ideas that may become obsolete or inadequate as quantum hardware evolves or innovations in that hardware or its programming interfaces depart significantly from current practice.

The rest of this chapter is structured as follows. Section 10.2 provides a brief overview of the landscape of programming languages and software tools available for quantum development and reviews the scarce literature in the topic of software metrics. Then, Sect. 10.3 approaches the idea of software quantum metrics in contrast with "classical" software metrics, pointing to some differences. Then, Sect. 10.4 proposes some tentative research directions in quantum software metrics. Finally, conclusions and outlook are provided in Sect. 10.5.

10.2 Background

10.2.1 Quantum Instruction Sets

As with classical computers, programming quantum computers are expected to be predominantly done using some form of high-level programming language for the expression of quantum algorithms. However, it is important to understand that there are several different "quantum instruction sets" that mediate the translation of algorithms to physical instructions and that provide a programming experience close to assembly or virtual machine programming.

In some cases, those assembly-like languages are targeted mainly to a concrete hardware platform. This could be the case, for example, the case of Jaqual [4], designed for the *Quantum Scientific Computing Open User Testbed* (QSCOUT) trapped-ion quantum computer testbed. Another example, Quil [5]—developed for Rigetti's uperconducting quantum processors—assumes a shared-memory architecture. However, there are also notable examples of hardware-agnostic instruction sets, for example, common QASM (cQASM) [6] and the Open Quantum Assembly Language (OpenQASM), the latter now in its third version [7].

There is relevant research activity in compilers and optimizers for those languages. Häner et al. [8] argue that the toolchain for quantum computers is substantially different from its classical counterpart, including the specificity of optimizing steps, which may include gate rewriting or synthesis strategies, and also the choice of *quantum error correction* (QEC) strategies. The extent to which those quantum toolchains will be able to abstract the underlying constraints and features of devices is still unclear. Today, languages and libraries still expose developers with the devices themselves. As an example, Google Cirq Python-based language[1] explicitly exposes the hardware (e.g., via a Device class) but at the same time is prepared for optimizing circuits, which brings a level of device independence. In this direction, another interesting recent proposal is that of automating the selection of quantum hardware [9]. That selection is today based on the constraints and capacity of available hardware devices but may in the future be extended to more advanced features, eventually that of automating program to device matching.

10.2.2 High-Level Quantum Programming Languages

A number of quantum programming languages have been proposed in recent years, ranging from imperative to functional and also low level to high level. Most of them are based on the quantum gate model paradigm, but some use other paradigms as the continuous gate model or quantum annealing. In the case of open-source projects, their degree of maturity and maintenance is heterogeneous, as discussed by Fingerhuth et al. [10]. In the category of functional languages, there have been several approaches to establish the theoretical foundations based on the lambda calculus. For example, funQ is a language based on the syntax and type system described by Selinger and Valinor [11].

There are many imperative languages or libraries available. The Quantum Computation Language (QCL) [12] was one of the first languages, with quantum types and quantum functions as counterparts of the classical ones. The Q language [13] is a C++ embedded language. The $Q \mid SI\rangle$ language [14] is a .Net embedded language

---

[1] https://quantumai.google/cirq

that supports quantum programming using a quantum extension of the while-language. Some of these languages are explicitly designed to be familiar to developers of classical software by creating analogies of data types, data structures, and control flow. As an example, the Scaffold language [15] follows a syntax resembling the C/C++ languages and has as explicit goals "familiarity and ease of use" for "users familiar with basic quantum computing and classical computer programming." It also features the interesting concept of *classical code to quantum gates sequence* (C2QG) modules which "allow programmers to describe the functionality of some parts of the algorithm from a higher perspective," similar to existing hardware description languages (HDLs) that translate those into gate constructs [16]. In a similar direction to higher-level abstraction and programmer friendliness, the *Silq* language [17] incorporates novel constructs and annotations explicitly addressing conciseness and readability of quantum programs.

While some of the languages mentioned are actually libraries or domain-specific languages built on top of an existing classical programming language, there are some that are specific to quantum programming. Notably, Q# is a domain-specific language explicitly designed to express quantum algorithms. Q# provides a type system, constructs to safely interleave classical and quantum computations, and other features as functional constructs which aid composition [18].

Quantum programming languages are often used inside software development kits (SDKs) that are usually packaged with local simulators and libraries to access simulators or real quantum computers. For example, Qiskit,[2] founded by IBM Research, provides a range of tools for accessing quantum computing platforms following the gate model, including tools for quantum hardware verification and specialized software frameworks for machine learning, finance, and ground state energy computations. Ocean[3] is a suite of tools D-Wave Systems provide for solving problems with quantum computers using the binary quadratic model (BQM).

Arguably, software practitioners today are faced with a variety of language, tool, and framework options, albeit the actual quantum devices are still in general limited for many applications. The predominant option is the gate model, and there is notable activity in language design, with an emphasis on developer adoption in some cases. This at first glance appears as a promising landscape for studies focused on programming language productivity, a concept that has been characterized in terms of time to implementation and efficiency [19].

10.2.3 Quantum Software Practices

The literature on actual software development practices for quantum computing is scarce and fragmentary. Dey et al. [20] have proposed a *Quantum Development Life*

---

[2]https://qiskit.org
[3]https://docs.ocean.dwavesys.com/

Cycle (QDLC). QDLC includes a "waterfall-like" process encompassing quantum feasibility study, quantum requirement specification, quantum system design, quantum software coding and implementation, quantum testing, and quantum software quality management. While the proposal has not gone through any kind of empirical assessment and there are no studies on its use, QDLC provides an interesting point of departure to software process design and measurement in future work.

Weder et al. [21] discuss a proposal for a quantum software life cycle consisting of ten phases, a gate-based quantum software application. Their proposal is more specific and detailed than the one of Dey et al., as it starts with the design task of splitting the application in quantum and classical parts and then going to phases that start from a hardware-agnostic version of the programs to lower-level concerns as optimization, hardware selection, and finally deployment and testing. However, the life cycle departs from assumptions on the programming model and the current limitations of quantum computers that may change in the future.

In a different direction, Gheorghe-Pop et al. [22] discuss the concept of "Quantum DevOps." Their proposal revolves around the idea of a cycle of activities: release, evaluate, deploy, monitor, and feedback. This resembles widespread notions of the DevOps concept, i.e., integrating some management and engineering perspectives on the continuous delivery of software updates while guaranteeing their correctness and reliability [23]. However, the proposal is preliminary and only mentions some quantum computer-specific tasks.

As a summary, the emerging literature on quantum software practices not surprisingly attempts to tailor existing processes and practices to the particularities of quantum computing, incorporating specificities of the devices and the fact that quantum computers are used as co-processors. Arguably, it is still early to assess how effective these practices are at a significant scale, but still some initial potential directions will be provided in Sect. 10.4.

10.2.4   Quantum Software Metrics

The literature specific to quantum software measurement in general is to the best of our knowledge also scarce. Sicilia et al. [24] discussed a small-scale study on measuring some aspects of the codebase of the Q# language available in open-source repositories, including size measured as appearance of gates and some initial insights on modular structure. However, that study is limited since it addresses only a single SDK, which may not be generalizable, and the coded analyzed is mainly libraries and test cases, which may not be representative of the practice of quantum programming for particular business cases. The work of Cruz-Lemus et al. [25] proposes specific metrics for *understandability* specific to the gate model, which can be subject to future empirical examination.

Zhao [26] proposes some basic metrics for quantum software, which mainly focus on measuring the size and structure of quantum programs. Regarding lines of code (LOC), the proposal is discriminating gates and measurement primitives, and counting the size of qubit registers used, or the number of distinct gates. Following the idea of Halstead's software science, they also propose measures that revolve around counting combining counts of total and distinct occurrences of operators and operands. For design metrics, there is a proposal of some sort of quantum architectural description language (qADL) from which metrics counting lines, components, and connections could be derived. For detailed design, the proposal is using the number of "quantum design patterns" and, for specification type, some measures using the recently proposed Unified Modeling Language (UML) extension called Q-UML [27]. None of these proposals are validated or empirically tested in the paper.

Zhao [26] also proposes adapting McCabe's cyclomatic complexity metric based on quantum control flow graphs (QCFGs) and Henry and Kafura's information flow metric based on the concepts of *fan-in* and *fan-out* between modules, but the proposed metric does not detail what modules are in software and how they can be identified; neither discusses if this should be applicable separately to classical-to-quantum coupling or quantum-to-quantum coupling in some way.

There are also proposed metrics estimating attributes of quantum hardware. For example, the Total Quantum Factor (TQF) [28] gives a rough estimate of the size of the quantum circuit (circuit width times circuit depth) that can be run before the processor's performance decoheres. While these are not strictly software metrics, they are useful for the connection of software to hardware relevant to the current limitations of quantum computers.

As a summary, we can find some initial explorations of potential metrics that may be reused or repurposed from classical software metrics. There is ample room for initial empirical studies on those, especially those staying at module, code fragment, or programming construct level, for which it is easier to find samples or devise experiments.

10.3   Some Similarities and Differences

A quantum computer is a device that exploits the properties of quantum mechanics to solve certain computational problems more efficiently than allowed by conventional computers. Since measurement is related to some attribute of an entity, when considering quantum software metrics, it is important to first grasp how quantum software development is different from software engineering in general. Fenton and Bieman [29] classify software entities in three categories: processes, products, and resources. In what follows, we discuss potential differences and similarities for each of these categories.

10.3.1   Software Artifacts in Quantum Software Engineering

Everything produced by the software processes are artifacts. Code is the artifact that receives more attention since it is the core product in software engineering. However, there are other elements that may deserve attention, as design or specification documents.

There exist a large body of literature on the measurement of internal and external classical software attributes, notably on metrics on size and structure (internal) and quality (external). Some of them may be reformulated including constructs of quantum software as done in [26]. However, those simple reinterpretations do not come without controversial issues, as it is not clear that the constructs used for classical software may be assimilated to their quantum counterparts. For example, metrics of complexity as McCabe's are deemed useful due to some apparent correlation with number of defects. It is still to be demonstrated that this still holds in the case of quantum software. We have identified a number of topics in which classical and quantum software fundamentally appear to diverge and need to be accounted for.

10.3.2   Diverging Programming Models

The gate model is the most common but not the unique computational paradigm. For example, quantum annealers as D-Wave's quantum computers focus on the specifics of optimization problems. Concretely, programming into that paradigm is methodically done as the expression of a binary quadratic model (BQM). The BQM class of problems consists of Ising models and quadratic unconstrained binary optimization (QUBO) models and has the general form in (10.1).

$$\min \left(\sum_a a_i v_i \sum_i \sum_j b_{i,j}, v_i v_j + c \right) \tag{10.1}$$

In principle, it seems that metrics addressing different of these models may be developed separately and measurement in general would more likely require different resorting to different elements. For example, in the Gate model, the idea of gates as transformations gives some uniformity to the structuring of programs, which can be used as a foundation to propose metrics, for example, based on understandability, as a proxy for software quality attributes as maintainability [25]. It should be noted that these will be specific to the gate model, and, for example, a QUBO model might require a separate set of metrics that deal with its specifics.

Regarding the gate model, previous work on metrics in HDL gate-based languages as VHDL may also provide useful insights. Protheroe and Pessolano [30] described a set of metrics for a range of VHDL specifications that correlated with circuit metrics and proposed their use as a measure of design quality. However, it is not clear that such results may be directly translated to the quantum gate model, as this is a generalization of its classical counterpart and includes gates that have not a direct correlation with classical logic gates, as for example, rotations.

10.3.3 Interpretations of Modularity and Separation of Concerns

Modularity is arguably the key internal property of software design. It becomes a key property for large software systems.

Also, in principle, there is not a concept of dependencies between subsystems or high-level modules if we consider these to be pure quantum software, as these dependencies become mediated by classical software, which typically commands the quantum computer as a co-processor and then takes the results back from measurement, possibly connecting those results to other computation stage, which may or may not as well use quantum programs. This idea suggests that from the viewpoint of higher-level design, there is no need for additional concepts or metrics other than those already existing. This hypothesis revolves around the idea of quantum program as specialized "black boxes" that carry some special task on demand and that are governed by classical software for which dependency-based or other metrics may still be adequate.

In the case of detailed design, Exman and Shmilovich [31] propose the use of *linear software model* (LSM) for both classical and quantum software design represent classical software systems by a bipartite graph with two sets of vertices, one set standing for *structors*—a generalization of classes—and another for *functionals*, a generalization of class methods. However, LSM is a formal approach based on linear algebra for a theory of software rather than of software engineering [32], so it is not addressing the practice of development itself but rather fundamentals of software composition.

10.3.4 Specificities of Hardware Constraints and Error Correction

As mentioned, hardware constraints of quantum computers are still first-class citizens in high-level languages of libraries for quantum development. Also, developers in some cases are exposed to the specifics of QEC and non-determinism are in some cases. However, progress in optimization and tooling together with more powerful and reliable future quantum computers may completely abstract out these or relegate them to some form of low-level or "system programming" paradigm in the future.

10.3.5   Software Processes in Quantum Software Engineering

A process is usually associated with some time scale. Process activities have duration—they occur over time, and they may be ordered or related in some way that depends on time, so that one activity must be completed before another can begin. Examples of direct process measurements are duration, effort, or number of incidents.

In QDLC [20], we highlight the following as the most relevant differences that relate too process issues:

- In the feasibility study, there is a need for a sort of *operational feasibility* which for classical applications is often not done, as it is taken for granted that hardware and software will pose no restrictions other than cost.
- Architectural design as a split process of the quantum and classical parts, with the former requiring eventually a selection of the most adequate quantum computing paradigm.
- The inclusion of hardware-specific considerations in testing and quality management.

However, some of these differences may respond nowadays to limitations related to the lack of maturity of quantum hardware, which might become less an issue in the next years. And of course, there are other differences in requirements, design, and coding, but they are dependent more on the knowledge of the underlying technologies and frameworks that actual changes in process.

10.3.6   Software Resources in Quantum Software Engineering

The resources that we are likely to measure include any input for software production. Thus, personnel (individual or teams), materials, tools (both software and hardware), and methods are candidates for measurement.

Evidence on human resources needs and productivity is still lacking data, and it would be difficult to get that data in the short term, since that would require the widespread adoption of quantum computers, which is still an uncertain future event. However, there are a considerable number of tools that go beyond programming language support, which include frameworks and libraries together with simulators. These could make a difference in future software estimation models, which can be expected since the role of tools in the software process has been recognized and studied in the past [33].

Further, the complexity and characteristics of the domain have also been considered a cost driver in classical software development [34]. Since the problems addressed by quantum computers are in nature specific, i.e., improving the computational cost of particular algorithms, they render existing estimation models inadequate. It is unclear if the emerging application domains of quantum computing (e.g., chemistry, finance) or their algorithmic subfields (e.g., machine learning) would require different estimation models.

In a different direction, it is still to be discerned if the paradigm of agile development can be applied to quantum development, again due to it being targeted to particular algorithmic problems.

10.4 Research Directions

In this section, we propose a tentative collection of research directions for quantum software measurement, in an attempt to provide an agenda for the future. This list stems from the previous discussion and takes into account the specificities of quantum computing. Nonetheless, it is important to understand that these can only be provisional and incomplete since it is expected that the field of quantum software will rapidly evolve in the coming years.

10.4.1 Software Size

One of the key elements in software metrics is size, which is a well-known cost driver in software estimation and can be considered to be related to complexity, a key topic in software development. There are roughly two approaches to size, the consideration of functional requirements and the measurement of some software product (code or other artifacts).

Software size in quantum programs is an open area of research and is dependent on the programming paradigm and possibly on the programming language. Empirical studies on the number of constructs of quantum programs can be done by comparing programs in different languages and libraries and studying their relations. This would eventually lead to useful platform-invariant measures of size.

Research direction (RD_SIZ_1) Propose and validate constructs and metrics of actual or projected quantum code size. □

If we approach size from the functional viewpoint, it is unclear if quantum software requires new concepts or models, since, in principle, the use of quantum computing or classical computing is a decision based on nonfunctional requirements. Concretely, that decision stems for the need of reducing computational complexity. In consequence, there is a need to examine if functional approaches to size require adaptation.

Research direction (RD_SIZ_2) Evaluate the impact of quantum software development in functional approaches to software size. □

The impact of quantum computing may be related to the correlation of functional size to actual artifact size or complexity. For example, architectures that are designed to deal with hard computational problems may be no longer necessary if quantum computers are used. There is some previous evidence in comparing function points and formal specifications to code size for embedded software, which points to the latter as more adequate [35]. This might be a point of departure for the estimation of quantum functional size from specifications.

10.4.2   Software Structure

In classical development, *coupling* is used to capture the degree of interdependence between different modules, determined in some way by their interface complexity. A highly coupled system is in general considered result of poor design. However, these considerations require research before reusing them to the case of quantum programs, including the impact of the interface of classical to quantum parts of a software system.

Research direction (RD_STR_1) Empirically study the dependency and interface structure of quantum programs at different levels of abstraction and contrast the findings with classical software. □

From that understanding, it would be possible to propose metrics of quantum code structure or transpose the ones from classical software that have been found adequate.

Research direction (RD_STR_2) Propose and validate constructs and metrics of quantum code structure. □

It should be noted that it is possible that empirical findings suggest a different approach to software structure size in quantum software, because quantum computers are coprocessors that are delegated some particular parts of the computation. It is possible that there would be a need to devise completely new metrics and study structure separating the quantum and classical parts of the system.

10.4.3   Software Quality

Software quality as defined in the ISO/IEC 9126 standard is related to a number of aspects or characteristics that are to some extent difficult to disentangle and measure [36]. While some of these aspects as those related to *accuracy* can be addressed and measured by concrete practices as testing, others are more difficult to characterize, as those concerning *maintainability*. The motivation of quantum computers lies in one of these factors, *efficiency*, which is assumed to be the justification of using quantum computers a priori.

The complexity of software in its different phases and artifacts (specification, design, code, and others) is considered a driver of quality since complexity is associated with more difficulty in attaining quality. In consequence, complexity is a key ingredient to understand and measure quantum software.

Research direction (RD_QUA_1) Study the relative complexity of quantum code, design, and other related elements. □

From an empirical standpoint, quality is directly related to testing in its different forms (unitary, integration, system), and thus the testing of quantum software is of importance. This is also due to the fact that quantum software is subject to some error stemming from the implementation layer, and the approach to testing is different.

Research direction (RD_QUA_2) Study quantum software testing concepts and metrics and its differences with classical software. □

Beyond complexity and correctness, there are other elements in the collection of factors concerning quality that may be impacted by quantum computing. Some appear to be solved by tooling, as *portability*, but there are others as *reliability* that may deserve separate consideration for quantum software, at least given the current state of quantum computing technology.

Research direction (RD_QUA_3) Explore the differences of classical versus quantum internal quality attributes of software and its specificities. □

10.4.4   Resources

Since data about real-world quantum developer teams would be available only after the widespread adoption of quantum computers, the most promising current research directions are in the examination of *potential cost drivers*. Tentative lists of those can be obtained from the broad literature on cost estimation, maturity, and productivity regarding the classical software process. The low hanging fruit in this direction is studying language and tool impact, which leads us to a first potential direction.

Research direction (RD_RES_1) Study the effect of quantum programming languages and associated tooling in developer productivity or its drivers. □

It should be noted that evidence of programming language impact in productivity points to divergent results in new developments and in evolution projects [37], and this difference would be difficult to discern in quantum computing due to the current lack of empirical data. Experiments comparing cognitive properties of quantum programming languages or libraries may shed light on its potential impact on productivity. In this direction, an important milestone would be that of the writing fixed sets of benchmarks in each language and measuring the implementation effort and running time incurred, following the proposal in [19].

Research direction (RD_RES_2) Study the relative complexity of quantum programming in diverse application fields or domains and its impact. □

Productivity in one of its dimensions is driven by the effort needed by developers, which is related to understandability [25], among other factors. This aspect of productivity can be approached via experimental methods with developers, and studies related to metrics that predict such understandability may be used as a departure point, e.g., [38].

10.4.5 Processes

Research on the process aspects of quantum software development is arguably the most difficult aspect for research, since there are not many organizations that currently use quantum software, and they are typically enterprises specialized in a concrete domain. Thus, potential models for estimating cost and effort could hardly generalize to a future scenario in which a large portion of the IT industry regularly uses quantum software.

However, there is room for small-scale experiments in cost estimation, and there, the topic of cost estimation based on actual hardware usage can be approached since there are vendors that yet provide actual quantum computation services hosted in the cloud. Another potential topic for future research is the fit of particular process paradigms, as agile development, with the development of applications that include quantum software. These can be approached initially using case study research designs or other approaches that may benefit from the close observation of existing mature quantum development teams, as was done for agile methods in its early phases [39].

10.5 Conclusions and Outlook

Quantum computing is an emerging new paradigm that demands a change in how software development is approached, including at a very fundamental level the mental models required for the task of programming, but also a different approach to software processes in general. Further, quantum computers play the role of coprocessors in current systems and are still subject to limitations in computational capacity and other practical aspects. Despite those differences, quantum programming language design has been an active area in the last years, which provides a fertile ground for software measurement at levels of understandability or developer productivity. Nonetheless, the understanding of the specificities or processes or human resources needed in quantum development face limitations in the availability of data or the lack of studies and may be more difficult to approach in the short term.

As a general conclusion, software measurement in quantum development is today a largely unexplored topic, despite the variety, heterogeneity, and effort spent in building programming languages and software tooling for quantum computers. We have discussed the current scattered literature on the topic and discussed tentative directions for further research in the short term, guided by an identification of differences and commonalities of classical and quantum software from the viewpoint of artifact, processes, and resources.

References

1. Abran A, April A, Buglione L (2010) Software measurement body of knowledge. Encyclopedia of software engineering 1(1):1
2. Villavicencio M, Abran A (2010) Software measurement in software engineering education: a comparative analysis. In: International Conferences on Software Measurement IWSM/MetriKon/Mensura. pp 633–644
3. Miszczak JA (2012) High-level structures for quantum computing. Synthesis Lect Quantum Comput 4(1):1–129
4. Morrison BC, Landahl AJ, Lobser DS, Rudinger KM, Russo AE, Van Der Wall JW, Maunz P (2020) Just another quantum assembly language (Jaqal). In: 2020 IEEE International Conference on Quantum Computing and Engineering (QCE). IEEE, pp 402–408
5. Smith RS, Curtis MJ, Zeng WJ (2016) A practical quantum instruction set architecture. arXiv preprint arXiv:1608.03355
6. Khammassi N, Guerreschi GG, Ashraf I, Hogaboam JW, Almudever CG, Bertels K (2018) cQASM v1.0: towards a common quantum assembly language. arXiv preprint arXiv:1805.09607
7. Cross AW, Javadi-Abhari A, Alexander T, de Beaudrap N, Bishop LS, Heidel S et al (2021) OpenQASM 3: a broader and deeper quantum assembly language. arXiv preprint arXiv:2104.14722
8. Häner T, Steiger DS, Svore K, Troyer M (2018) A software methodology for compiling quantum programs. Quantum Sci Technol 3(2):020501
9. Weder B, Barzen J, Leymann F, Salm M (2021) Automated quantum hardware selection for quantum workflows. Electronics 10(8):984
10. Fingerhuth M, Babej T, Wittek P (2018) Open source software in quantum computing. PLoS One 13(12):e0208561
11. Selinger P, Valiron B (2006) A lambda calculus for quantum computation with classical control. Math Struct Comput Sci 16(3):527–552
12. Ömer B (2005) Classical concepts in quantum programming. Int J Theoretical Phys 44(7):943–955
13. Bettelli S, Calarco T, Serafini L (2003) Toward an architecture for quantum programming. Eur Phys J D-Atom Mol Optical Plasma Phys 25(2):181–200
14. Liu S, Wang X, Zhou L, Guan J, Li Y, He Y et al (2018) $Q S$: a quantum programming environment. In: Symposium on real-time and hybrid systems. Springer, Cham, pp 133–164
15. Abhari AJ, Faruque A, Dousti MJ, Svec L, Catu O, Chakrabati A et al (2012) Scaffold: quantum programming language. Princeton University, NJ
16. Abhari AJ, Patil S, Kudrow D, Heckey J, Lvov A, Chong FT, Martonosi M (2015) ScaffCC: scalable compilation and analysis of quantum programs. Parallel Comput 45:2–17
17. Bichsel B, Baader M, Gehr T, Vechev M (2020) Silq: a high-level quantum language with safe uncomputation and intuitive semantics. In: Proceedings of the 41st ACM SIGPLAN Conference on Programming Language Design and Implementation, pp 286–300

18. Svore K, Geller A, Troyer M, Azariah J, Granade C et al (2018) Q#, enabling scalable quantum computing and development with a high-level DSL. In: Proceedings of the Real World Domain Specific Languages Workshop 2018, pp 1–10
19. Kennedy K, Koelbel C, Schreiber R (2004) Defining and measuring the productivity of programming languages. Int J High Performance Comput Applications 18(4):441–448
20. Dey N, Ghosh M, Chakrabarti A (2020) QDLC–the quantum development life cycle. arXiv preprint arXiv:2010.08053
21. Weder B, Barzen J, Leymann F, Salm M, Vietz D (2020) The quantum software lifecycle. In: Proceedings of the 1st ACM SIGSOFT International Workshop on Architectures and Paradigms for Engineering Quantum Software, pp 2–9
22. Gheorghe-Pop ID, Tcholtchev N, Ritter T, Hauswirth M (2020) Quantum DevOps: towards reliable and applicable NISQ quantum computing. In: 2020 IEEE Globecom Workshops (GC Wkshps). IEEE, pp 1–6
23. Leite L, Rocha C, Kon F, Milojicic D, Meirelles P (2019) A survey of DevOps concepts and challenges. ACM Computing Surv (CSUR) 52(6):1–35
24. Sicilia MA, Sánchez-Alonso S, Mora-Cantallops M, García-Barriocanal E (2020) On the source code structure of quantum code: insights from Q# and QDK. In: International Conference on the Quality of Information and Communications Technology. Springer, Cham, pp 292–299
25. Cruz-Lemus JA, Marcelo LA, Piattini M (2021) Towards a set of metrics for quantum circuits understandability. In: International Conference on the Quality of Information and Communications Technology. Springer, Cham, pp 239–249
26. Zhao J (2021) Some size and structure metrics for quantum software. arXiv preprint arXiv:2103.08815
27. Pérez-Delgado CA, Pérez-González HG (2020) Towards a quantum software modeling language. In: Proceedings of the IEEE/ACM 42nd International Conference on Software Engineering Workshops, pp 442–444
28. Sete EA, Zeng WJ, Rigetti CT (2016) A functional architecture for scalable quantum computing. In: 2016 IEEE International Conference on Rebooting Computing (ICRC). IEEE, pp 1–6
29. Fenton N, Bieman J (2014) Software metrics: a rigorous and practical approach. CRC Press
30. Protheroe D, Pessolano F (2000) An objective measure of digital system design quality. In: Proceedings IEEE 2000 First International Symposium on Quality Electronic Design (Cat. No. PR00525). IEEE, pp 227–233
31. Exman I, Shmilovich AT (2021) Quantum software models: the density matrix for classical and quantum software systems design. arXiv preprint arXiv:2103.13755
32. Exman I (2015) Linear software models: key ideas. arXiv preprint arXiv:1510.04652
33. Baik J, Boehm B, Steece BM (2002) Disaggregating and calibrating the CASE tool variable in COCOMO II. IEEE Trans Softw Eng 28(11):1009–1022
34. Abdukalykov R, Hussain I, Kassab M, Ormandjieva O (2011) Quantifying the impact of different non-functional requirements and problem domains on software effort estimation. In: 2011 Ninth International Conference on Software Engineering Research, Management and Applications. IEEE, pp 158–165
35. Staples M, Kolanski R, Klein G, Lewis C, Andronick J, Murray T et al (2013) Formal specifications better than function points for code sizing. In: 2013 International Conference on Software Engineering (ICSE). IEEE, pp 1257–1260

36. Jung HW, Kim SG, Chung CS (2004) Measuring software product quality: a survey of ISO/IEC 9126. IEEE Softw 21(5):88–92
37. Delorey DP, Knutson CD, Chun S (2007) Do programming languages affect productivity? A case study using data from open source projects. In: First International Workshop on Emerging Trends in FLOSS Research and Development (FLOSS'07: ICSE Workshops 2007). IEEE, p 8
38. Scalabrino S, Bavota G, Vendome C, Linares-Vásquez M, Poshyvanyk D, Oliveto R (2017) Automatically assessing code understandability: how far are we? In: 2017 32nd IEEE/ACM International Conference on Automated Software Engineering (ASE). IEEE, pp 417–427
39. Dyba T, Dingsoyr T (2009) What do we know about agile software development? IEEE Softw 26(5):6–9

Chapter 11
Quantum Software Modernization

Luis Jiménez-Navajas, Ricardo Pérez-Castillo, and Mario Piattini

11.1 Introduction

Thanks to the efforts of researchers and organizations around the world, there exist supercomputers capable of performing millions of operations per second, such as Fugaku [1] or Summit [2]. Even with the computational power of these classical supercomputers, there are operations that we cannot perform, as introduced in previous chapters.

For those kinds of problems, quantum computing allows us to carry out operations in a reasonable time, whereas on some of today's supercomputers, it would take years to complete. This is because some of the most demanding operations (e.g., the simulation of molecule structures or number factorization) are, at least, approachable. This has implied that the interest of companies in quantum computing has dramatically increased in the last few years. More and more organizations have become aware of the benefits that this new computing paradigm can bring to the society [3].

Researchers around the world are providing evidence, albeit still theoretical, of the benefits and challenges of quantum computing. This means that companies around the world must be prepared for this new technological leap, which may leverage a new "golden age" in the software engineering field [4]. The advances in quantum computing have taken place simultaneously with the development of quantum programming languages and their respective compilers [5]. Which implies a direct and necessary evolution of software engineering toward quantum computing. The combination of quantum physics and computer science changes the way in which programs are designed, developed, and executed. Nevertheless, this

L. Jiménez-Navajas (✉) · R. Pérez-Castillo · M. Piattini
aQuantum, Alarcos Research Group, Institute of Technologies and Information Systems,
University of Castilla-La Mancha (UCLM), Ciudad Real, Spain
e-mail: luis.jimeneznavajas@uclm.es; ricardo.pdelcastillo@uclm.es; mario.piattini@uclm.es

© The Author(s), under exclusive license to Springer Nature Switzerland AG 2022   209
M. A. Serrano et al. (eds.), *Quantum Software Engineering*,
https://doi.org/10.1007/978-3-031-05324-5_11

technological leap from classical computing to quantum cannot be made by discarding everything that has been built up to now and starting from scratch [6]. There are several reasons for this, one of them being that, possibly, there are certain operations in the systems of the companies that are so simple that it does not make sense to implement them using quantum computing because of the cost versus the potential gain [7]. Another reason is that companies have based strategic decisions on the business rules embedded in their classical information systems overtime (which is not available anywhere else) and its full replacement becomes too risky.

The solution to that problem should not be the whole replacement of the current information systems (henceforth called classical systems), but to modernize those information systems that could benefit from the computational power of the quantum computing paradigm. This means migrate toward classical-quantum information systems, also known as hybrid information systems. The challenge of software modernization of hybrid information systems is actually claimed by the Talavera Manifesto on Quantum Software Engineering and Programming [8], and indeed, there is some works in the literature about how to decide whether the applications of the organizations will truly benefit from investment into quantum computing early on or should wait before it is mature enough [9].

ADM (architecture-driven modernization) [10] may be the right path to accomplish the evolution of classical systems toward hybrid ones, as it has been proved to be effective in the evolution of legacy information systems. ADM is the evolution of traditional software reengineering that follows the MDE (model-driven engineering) principles.

The remaining of this chapter is structured as follows. First, it discusses the challenge that quantum computing brings to our information systems and the transformation that it entails. Then, it is followed with the process of quantum software modernization for evolving toward hybrid information systems. After this is a running example of such process. The last section draws some conclusions.

11.2   Hybrid Information Systems

This section first introduces the notion of classical-quantum information systems (cf. Sect. 11.2.1), and then it discusses the challenges of such hybrid information systems (cf. Sect. 11.2.2).

11.2.1   Classical-Quantum Information Systems

In recent years, it has been theoretically demonstrated that quantum computing could bring benefits to different fields of science, like in finances [11], chemistry [12], or

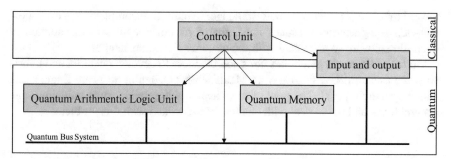

Fig. 11.1 Quantum von Neumann Architecture (Adapted from [15])

machine learning [13]. Although those benefits are only theoretical, the expectations for implementing some of those promising quantum applications are huge.

This is why it is expected that in the future, companies or organizations will employ quantum algorithms to perform functions that could be benefited from the enhanced performance, for example, using Grover's algorithm to perform searches where massive amounts of data are found [14].

For this to become a reality, it does not necessarily imply a complete replacement of current information systems toward quantum software systems. There are several reasons for this. Firstly, not all companies will need to evolve to the new computing paradigm, as (until now) quantum algorithms help us solve very specific tasks and the business model of some companies may not allow them to employ these algorithms. Another reason might be that the implementation of their information systems with quantum software would not make a great difference in performance since the functions that these information systems accomplish are simplistic regarding quantum computing, while the cost of its implementation would skyrocket.

Furthermore, the requests needed to ask a quantum computer to perform certain operations would require from classical information systems. Classical software is also responsible for receiving the replies, as well as translating them into end-user answers. Most of today's quantum programs are remotely executed on cloud quantum computers, and the results they return are then interpreted by classical programs.

Even more, at hardware level, hybrid systems have been also studied. For example, Fig. 11.1 shows the architecture of quantum computer employing the quantum von Neumann architecture [15], where the overall system is divided into two components, a classical part which contains a control unit which controls the quantum computer and a quantum component, which contains the quantum arithmetic logic unit (QALU) which is in charge of manipulating the quantum information transported through the quantum bus system and saved in the quantum memory which should rely on multiplexing technology for large storage capability. Between the two main components, an input and output region have the role of interface to the "classical world" in order to initialize and/or measure the qubit.

Therefore, is believed that in the near future, organizations and companies will develop (and/or migrate toward) hybrid information systems, which combine classical and quantum software [6, 16]. The evolution of classical information systems toward hybrid ones implies a great challenge. In order to accomplish such evolution, software reengineering practices must, therefore, be brought into the domain of quantum software so as to deal with the aforementioned challenges.

So far, there are no guidelines nor good practices to develop quantum and hybrid software as claimed by the Talavera Manifesto for Quantum Software Engineering and Programming [17]. The goal of this chapter is to provide some guidelines and general ideas on how to deal with challenges associated with this problem.

11.2.2 Challenges of Hybrid Information Systems

Once it is understood that companies will not completely replace their current information systems to start from scratch with quantum systems, it is time to discuss what kind of companies or organizations could benefit from the evolution of their current information systems.

As mentioned above, if we evolve all current information systems to the quantum software (imagine running such quantum information systems on computers with a reasonable number of qubits), perhaps, only a small fraction of them will speed up, while others will stay the same at best.

However, companies that will be able to take advantage of quantum computing and will consider evolving their information systems will have to face a number of challenges and will have to study in depth which components or functions to evolve. In the vast majority of cases, this evolution would consist of carrying out the most demanding operations in a provider's cloud [18]. This would be one of the scenarios to be faced, figuring out which functions to evolve and which algorithms that are isolated in third-party systems should be used while communications with cloud providers would be done through classical computing, i.e., the classical information system would evolve into an information system with quantum cloud components.

Another scenario could occur if organizations want to take advantage of the quantum computing hype and start to move their business models toward the new paradigm. This would imply a direct evolution of their information systems toward hybrid information systems, as they will still have certain business processes that remain implemented by classical computing.

Since today's computational power for NISQ (noisy intermediate-scale quantum) devices is still limited to a degree, several NISQ devices could be used in a distributed quantum computing architecture [19]. This will entail another important challenge for the mentioned evolution toward hybrid information systems.

According to [20], hybrid information systems will also face obstacles in code portability, tool integration, program validation, and the orchestration of workflow development. These problems together with the low maturity of the quantum solutions market will lead to other important challenges. Today, there exist a huge volatility in quantum technology (quantum computers, programming languages, development tools, etc.). Thus, today's companies that bet to a specific technology could find tomorrow that such technology become obsolete soon.

11.3 Quantum Software Modernization

In this section, the overall quantum software modernization will be explained. For a better understanding, as the process presented is based on ADM, one section is aimed to explain the traditional software reengineering and its evolution to architecture-driven modernization. Then, how the evolution toward hybrid information systems may be achieved is finally explained.

11.3.1 Traditional Reengineering

Almost all technologies evolve over time, and so information systems should evolve consequently. This evolution can have negative effects on those systems that were developed in the past, like degradation or aging, making those information systems *legacy*, which means that the source code that was developed could be technologically obsolete [21]. Reengineering allows "the preservation of the business knowledge, making possible to carry out evolutionary maintenance of the legacy information systems assuming low risks and low costs" [22]. The overall reengineering process is typically presented as a "horseshoe" model [23] (see Fig. 11.2) where reengineering consists of three main stages:

Reverse engineering The system is analyzed to identify its components and inter-relationships and create abstract representations of the system in another form or at a higher level of abstraction.

Restructuring The transformation from one representation form to another at the same relative abstraction level. This stage can consist of refactoring, i.e., the internal structure is improved while preserving the subject system's external behavior (functionality and semantics). Or additionally, it can add new functionality at this abstraction level.

Forward engineering The final stage consists of the renovation by generating the new source code and other software artefacts at lower abstraction level.

Software reengineering projects have traditionally failed when dealing with specific challenges like the standardization and automation of the reengineering process [25]. First, standardization constitutes a challenge since the reengineering processes have been typically carried out in many different ad hoc manners. Reengineering projects must, therefore, focus their efforts on a better definition of the process. Furthermore, the code cannot be the only software asset that the

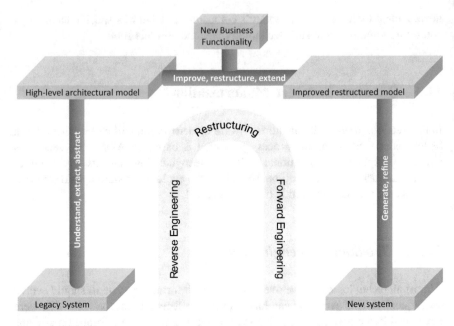

Fig. 11.2 Horseshoe software reengineering model (Adapted from [24])

standardization covers, since "the code does not contain all the information that is needed" [26].

The reengineering process must be formalized to ensure an integrated management of all the knowledge involved in the process, such as source code, data, business rules, and so on. Second, automation is also a very important problem. In order to prevent failure in large complex legacy systems, the reengineering process must be mature and repeatable [27]. In addition, the reengineering process needs to be aided by automated tools in order to enable companies to handle the maintenance costs [25].

11.3.2 Architecture-Driven Modernization

In order to address the mentioned challenges, traditional reengineering evolved toward architecture-driven modernization (ADM) [28]. ADM consists of the use of tools that facilitate the analysis, refactoring, and transformation of existing system toward a modernization for supporting new requirements, migration of systems, or even their interoperability. To accomplish this, ADM makes use of reengineering and model-driven engineering (MDE) principles [29], i.e., software artefacts are represented and managed as models, and automatic model transformation are defined between them. Thus, ADM attempts to address the mentioned flaws of traditional reengineering.

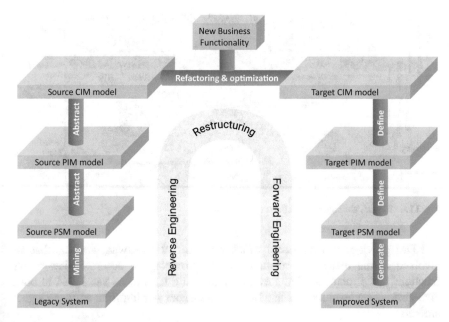

Fig. 11.3 Horseshoe modernization model

The horseshoe reengineering model has been adapted to ADM, and it is known as the horseshoe modernization model (see Fig. 11.3). There are three kinds of models in the horseshoe model [30].

Computation Independent Model (CIM) is a view of the system from the computation independent viewpoint at a high abstraction level. A CIM does not show details of the system's structure. CIM models are sometimes called domain models and play the role of bridging the gap between the domain experts and experts in the system design and construction.

Platform Independent Model (PIM) is a view of a system from the platform independent viewpoint at an intermediate abstraction level. A PIM has a specific degree of technological independence to be suitable for use with a number of different platforms of a similar type.

Platform Specific Model (PSM) is a view of a system from the platform specific viewpoint at a low abstraction level. A PSM combines the specifications in the PIM with the details that specify how that system uses a particular type of platform or technology.

As a part of ADM initiative, the OMG released the Knowledge Discovery Metamodel (KDM) within a broad set of proposed standards [31]. KDM addresses the main challenges that appear in the modernization of legacy information systems, and it is the cornerstone of the set of proposed standards, since the other standards are defined around KDM [32]. KDM uses the OMG's standards for representing the models through XMI.

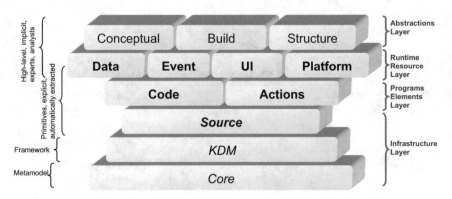

Fig. 11.4 Layers, packages, and concerns in KDM

KDM provides a meta-model which represents the software artifacts that are involved in the legacy information system, providing an accurate view of the functions and structures of it. Reverse engineering techniques use KDM to build high-abstraction level models in a bottom-up manner starting from software legacy artifacts.

The KDM specification has different perspectives [32], and in order to simplify the managing of its structure, four layers were designed. Each layer is, therefore, based on the previous one, and each of them contains several packages representing different concerns related to legacy information systems. Different KDM packages and layers could be used depending on the artefacts analyzed (cf. Fig. 11.4).

According to the horseshoe modernization model, the ADM-based process can be categorized into three kinds of modernization processes [33]. These depend on the abstraction level reached in the reverse engineering stage. The reverse engineering stage is probably the most important stage in the horseshoe modernization model. This is because this activity conditions the abstraction level achieved in each kind of modernization process and, therefore, the resources provided and possibilities to restructure LISs. A higher abstraction level usually implies a greater amount of knowledge and rich information which provide the modernization process with more restructuring possibilities.

Figure 11.5 shows the three kinds of modernization processes depending on the maximum abstraction level reached during the reverse engineering stage.

Technical Modernization This kind of modernization considers the lowest abstraction level and is historically that which is most commonly applied to legacy systems. A company carries out a technical modernization project when it wishes to deal with platform or language obsolescence, new technical opportunities, conformance to standards, system efficiency, system usability, or other similar modernization factors. This is sometimes not strictly considered to be a modernization process since it focuses solely on corrective and preventive modifications, but in any case, it addresses adaptive or perfective modifications according to the modernization definition.

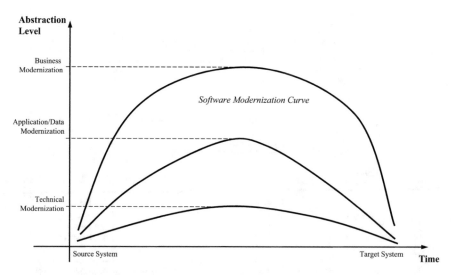

Fig. 11.5 Three kinds of horseshoe modernization models (Adapted from [33])

Application/Data Modernization This kind of modernization considers an intermediate abstraction level since it focuses on restructuring a legacy system at the level of application and data design to obtain the target system. This kind of modernization is driven by several modernization factors such as improving system reusability, reducing the delocalized system logic or system complexity, and applying design patterns. There is a fine line between this kind of modernization and the previous one, but that line is crossed when there is some impact on the system design level.

Business Modernization This kind of modernization increases the abstraction level to the maximum. The restructuring stage therefore takes place at the level of business architecture, i.e., the business rules and processes that govern a legacy system in the company. Apart from technical models and application/data models, this kind of modernization also incorporates business semantic models which are a key asset in (1) preserving the business knowledge embedded in legacy systems and (2) aligning the company's business requirements with the future target systems.

11.3.3   *Software Modernization of Hybrid Information Systems*

Software engineering has evolved as new (or adapted) technologies and methodologies are emerging to deal with the mentioned challenges of hybrid information systems. Now, as a result of the new quantum paradigm, new difficulties have emerged as explained before.

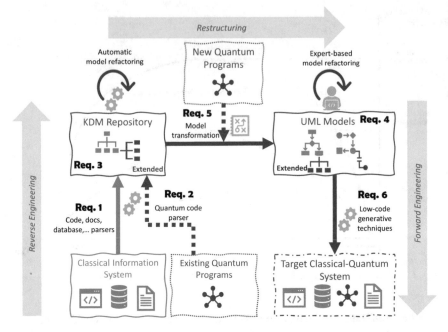

Fig. 11.6 Quantum software modernization approach

A solution based on reengineering, and more specifically on ADM [34], was already proposed in [16] to achieve the evolution of classical information systems toward hybrid ones. That solution introduced "quantum software reengineering" and ensured that it might be used in three complementary scenarios:

- Migrate existing, isolated quantum algorithms, and integrate them into the hybrid information systems.
- Migrate classical legacy information systems toward hybrid architectures that support the integration of classical-quantum information systems.
- Transform or add new business operations supported by quantum software that will be integrated into the target hybrid systems.

Figure 11.6 shows the overall quantum reengineering process. Pérez-Castillo et al. [6] proposed a software modernization based on existing standards such as UML and KDM. This chapter addresses the quantum software modernization by using KDM and UML, which does not mean that the process is limited to those standards. In fact, alternative standards may be used during the quantum software modernization process.

The reverse engineering stage consists of analyzing existing information systems artefacts such as the source code, database schemas, etc. It could analyze classical systems plus quantum programs if these exist. The output of the reverse engineering phase is a set of KDM models that comprise a KDM repository. As previously explained, this KDM repository represents, in a technology-agnostic way, all the different perspectives and concerns of the legacy information systems in a holistic way. In this way, previous knowledge and business rules might be preserved, and the impact of the integration of quantum programs is reduced. Of course, KDM must be extended (through their ordinary extensions mechanisms) to support the representation of quantum software aspects.

During the restructuring stage (see Fig. 11.6), KDM models are (semi)-automatically transformed into high-abstraction level models representing analysis and design aspects of the target hybrid systems. To achieve this, the meta-model employed in this case might be UML. Like the KDM extension, UML should be extended to support the new systems' analysis and design elements concerning quantum computing. In this point, software engineers can use this UML extension to manually model quantum aspects for new, target systems which are integrated with the existing elements previously gathered by reverse engineering.

Finally, the forward engineering stage (see Fig. 11.6) consists of a set of techniques that are able to generate many parts of the source code for the target hybrid systems. Today, there exist many well-proven generators for different classical programming languages to produce code from UML models. However, there is no generators for quantum programming languages from high abstraction models. In our concern, this must be provided and integrated with other existing generative techniques.

In order to carry out the quantum software modernization process, a number of requirements can be identified (as labelled with Req. in Fig. 11.6).

- *Requirement 1*: This indicates that as much information as possible from classic information systems (e.g., source code, database schemas, or documentation) must be extracted by means of a series of efficient and well-designed techniques to be represented by means of KDM models. The KDM models of each component shall be stored in a repository.
- *Requirement 2*: This requirement is almost the same as requirement 1, except that instead of analyzing elements of classical information systems, it analyses elements of quantum programs.
- *Requirement 3*: In order for KDM to be able to handle the different quantum elements that appear on quantum programs (i.e., quantum gates or qubits), it is necessary to extend KDM by means of its standard extension mechanisms, which in the case of KDM would be by using the "Extension Family."
- *Requirement 4*: As happens with KDM, this requirement is due to the fact that it is necessary to extend the UML meta-model to be able to work with the different quantum elements. However, to accomplish this, an "UML Profile" will be employed.
- *Requirement 5*: Once the two chosen standards in the quantum software modernization process have been extended, a model transformation will be carried out automatically. This transformation will take into account the extension mechanisms of both standards.

- *Requirement 6*: By means of automatic code generation techniques, it will show the low-level implementation with quantum gates and the integration of these in the target hybrid system.

11.4   Running/Application Example

This section shows an example of the application of the quantum software modernization process. For this purpose, it has been divided into three subsections, one for each phase of the software modernization process (reverse engineering, restructuring, and forward engineering). However, since there is already literature on the generation of KDM models from code extracted from classical information systems, the reverse engineering phase focuses on the generation a KDM model from Q# [6], the restructuring phase performs the transformation of KDM models to UML, and the forward engineering phase superficially explains the automatic quantum code generation.

11.4.1   Reverse Engineering

The KDM standard was not created with the aim to evolve classical information systems toward hybrid ones. Therefore, it was necessary to extend it through its built-in extension mechanism to support the representation of the different quantum entities, to accomplish the third requirement of the quantum software modernization process. The full headway of the adaptation of KDM to quantum programs was proposed in [16], which is briefly summarized in the next lines.

The default extension mechanism provided by KDM is the extension family. In this extension family, the different components that can be found in a quantum programming language are represented in this group, shown in Fig. 11.7. This mechanism collects a set of stereotypes that are then used in the ordinary elements provided by KDM.

```
<extensionFamily>
    <stereotype name="quantum programming language" />
    <stereotype name="quantum program" />
    <stereotype name="quantum operation" />
    <stereotype name="quantum gate" />
    <stereotype name="qubit" />
    <stereotype name="qubit measure" />
    <stereotype name="control qubit" />
    <stereotype name="qubit array" />
</extensionFamily>
```

Fig. 11.7 Extension family of KDM for quantum components

Table 11.1 Matching KDM
elements with the defined one
of the extension family

KDM element	Extension family element
CodeModel	Quantum program
CallableUnit	Quantum operation
ActionElement	Quantum gate
StorableUnit and ParameterUnit	Qubit
ActionElement	Qubit measure
ActionRelation	Control qubit
StorableUnit	Qubit array

```
1  namespace Quantum.QSharpApplication1 {
2    open Microsoft.Quantum.Canon;
3    open Microsoft.Quantum.Intrinsic;
4
5      operation HelloQ () : (Result) {
6        using (var qubit = Qubit()){
7            H(qubit);
8            let r = M(qubit);
9            return r;
10       }
11     }
12  }
```

Fig. 11.8 Example of a Q# program

Table 11.1 shows the KDM elements in which each stereotype is applied to represent all the different quantum entities (shown in Fig. 11.7). In KDM, the *CodeModel* are those elements which collect the facts of the same program, so as it will appear once in every program, it was assigned the stereotype *Quantum Program*. The *Quantum Operations* are the typical methods of any usual programming language that we already know, but these ones use quantum components. Nevertheless, because the different *Quantum Operations* can be called between them, they were assigned the *CallableUnit* element. The *ActionElement* element is assigned to those elements which describe a basic unit of behavior, just like the *Quantum Gate* and *Qubit measure* (this last stereotype is assigned to the Measure gate) do.

The *Qubit* and *Qubit Array* stereotype are mapped in KDM to *StorableUnit* since in the different quantum programming languages, a qubit is nothing more than a variable with a stored value (in this case a 0 or 1). Further details about the usage of the KDM extension are in the previous work [16].

This extension, as presented in [7], makes it possible to generate KDM models by analyzing programs developed in Q#. Figure 11.8 shows an example of a short program developed in Q#. In such program, an operation (which is equivalent to methods or functions in traditional programming) is defined in line 5; in line 6, a qubit variable is declared. Then, a Hadamard's gate is applied in line 7 to the qubit declared on the previous line. In line 8, the result of the appliance of the gate is measured and returned in line 9.

```
1    <?xml version="1.0" encoding="UTF-8"?>
2    <kdm:Segment xmlns:kdm="http://www.omg.org/spec/KDM/20160201/kdm"
3    xmlns:action="http://www.omg.org/spec/KDM/20160201/action"
4    xmlns:code="http://www.omg.org/spec/KDM/20160201/code"
5    xmlns:xmi="http://www.omg.org/XMI"xmlns:xsi="http://www.w3.org/2001/XMLSchema-
6    instance" xmi:version="2.0" name="Program_160250587.xml">
7      <extensionFamily xmi:id="id.0">
8        <stereotype name="quantum programming language" xmi:id="id.1" />
9        <stereotype name="quantum program" xmi:id="id.2" />
10       <stereotype name="quantum operation" xmi:id="id.3" />
11       <stereotype name="quantum gate" xmi:id="id.4" />
12       <stereotype name="qubit" xmi:id="id.5" />
13       <stereotype name="qubit measure" xmi:id="id.6" />
14       <stereotype name="control qubit" xmi:id="id.7" />
15       <stereotype name="qubit array" xmi:id="id.8">
16         <tag tag="array index" id="id.9" />
17       </stereotype>
18    </extensionFamily>
19    <model xmi:id="id.10" xmi:type="code:CodeModel" name="Program_160250587.xml">
20      <codeElement xsi:type="code:CompilationUnit" name="Program.qs"
21      xmi:id="id.11">
22        <codeElement xmi:type="code:CodeModel" name="Q# Common definitions"
23        xmi:id="id.12">
24          <codeElement xmi:id="id.13" xmi:type="code:DataType" name="Data"
25          stereotype="id.8" />
26          <codeElement xmi:id="id.14"xmi:type="code:IntegerType"name="Integer" />
27          <codeElement xmi:id="id.15"xmi:type="code:BooleanType"name="Boolean" />
28        </codeElement>
29        <codeElement xsi:id="id.16" xsi:type="code:IncludeDirective"
30        name="openMicrosoft.Quantum.Canon;" />
31        <codeElement xsi:id="id.17" xsi:type="code:IncludeDirective"
32        name="openMicrosoft.Quantum.Intrinsic;" />
33        <codeElement xmi:type="code:CallableUnit" name="HelloQ" xmi:id="id.18"
34        stereotype="id.3">
35          <codeElement xmi:type="code:StorableUnit" xmi:id="id.19" name="qubit"
36          stereotype="id.5" />
37          <codeElement xmi:type="action:ActionElement" xmi:id="id.20"
38          kind="operator" name="Hadamard" stereotype="id.4" >
39            <source language="Q#" snippet="H(qubit)" />
40            <actionRelation xsi:type="action:Addresses" from="id.20" to="id.19"/>
41            <actionRelation xsi:type="action:Flow" from="id.20" to="id.21" />
42          </codeElement>
43          <codeElement xmi:type="action:ActionElement" xmi:id="id.21"
44          kind="operator" name="Measure" stereotype="id.4">
45            <source language="Q#" snippet="M(qubit)" />
46            <actionRelation xsi:type="action:Addresses" from="id.21" to="id.19"/>
47          </codeElement>
48        </codeElement>
49      </codeElement>
50    </model>
51    </kdm:Segment>
```

Fig. 11.9 Resulting KDM file of the previous Q# program

Figure 11.9 depicts the resulting KDM model from the Q# program shown in Fig. 11.8. The extension family defined on Fig. 11.7 can be seen from lines 7 to 17 of Fig. 11.9. From line 33 to 48, the operation of the algorithm is defined. As said previously, Q#'s operations (traditional methods) are defined as "CallableUnits"; also those operations can receive qubits as parameters. In line 35, a qubit is declared as a "StorableUnit" as a qubit, on reflection, is just a variable which stores a result (the qubit's state). Finally, from line 37 to 47 are described the action and the data flow of the different quantum gates that appear in the algorithm. For example, from line 37 to 42, it is described the Hamard's gate, which inside it, in line 39 is found the textual representation (in this case, "H(register)"), in line 40 the qubit in which is applied (by means of the id's), and in line 41, the next quantum gate which acts (with the "actionRelation" of type "Flow").

11.4.2   Restructuring

In a similar way to KDM, it is necessary to extend the UML meta-model in order to manage all the different quantum entities in UML and to accomplish the fourth requirement. There are several ways to do this, but we proposed in [6] an extension by creating an UML Profile. UML profiles are created as a set of stereotypes, tagged values, and constraints defined for some of the existing UML elements. A key aspect of this extension mechanism is that the defined profile would remain fully compliant with UML. This is an advantage since researchers and practitioners can use our proposal and integrate it with the existing modelling tools without further training.

Figure 11.10 shows the preliminary UML profile to graphically represent quantum programs by means of activity diagrams. On the right side of the image, the stereotypes that have been added to be able to work with the different quantum entities are grouped together: *quantum circuit*, *qubit*, *quantum gate*, *controlled qubit*, *measure*, and *reset*. The left side of Fig. 11.10 shows the UML meta-model excerpt for representing UML Activity Diagrams. Leftward arrows from stereotypes to

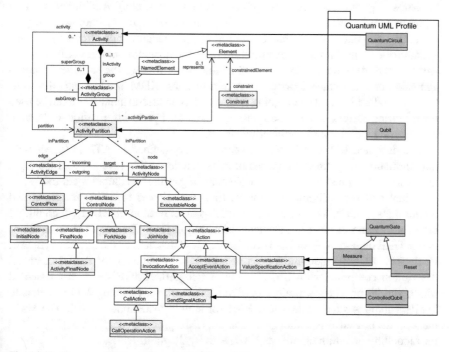

Fig. 11.10 Quantum UML profile extracted from [35]

meta-class elements are extension elements that are used to indicate that the properties of a meta-class are extended through the respective stereotype.

The ≪*QuantumCircuit*≫ stereotype points directly to the *Activity* meta-class because, to represent a quantum algorithm, a single activity diagram with the ≪*QuantumCircuit*≫ stereotype will be used. Within this activity diagram, qubits will be represented as *ActivityPartition* with the ≪*Qubit*≫ stereotype. Graphically, the qubits can be seen as horizontal lines where the different quantum gates can be placed. This way of representing qubits is similar to the way IBM Quantum Experience [36] does it. All the quantum gates are *action* elements, but depending on the way they act or behave on a qubit, they will have one stereotype or another. The gates that affect the state of the qubit without any control qubit (such as the Hadamard gate or the Pauli's family) are represented as *call operation actions* plus the stereotype ≪*QuantumGate*≫. However, those quantum gates employing a control qubit are represented by multiple *action* elements. The control qubit of the gate is represented as *send signal action* with the stereotype ≪*controlled qubit*≫ and the other part of the gate as *accept event action* with the ≪*quantum gate*≫ stereotype. In order to keep the relationship between both parts, *constraints* have been used between the involved elements. Additionally, special operations like qubit measuring and qubit resetting are represented with value specification action elements and the respective stereotypes ≪*measure*≫ and ≪*reset*≫.

KDM models, represented according to the quantum extension family [4], are able to manage all the different quantum programs' components and their interrelationships (e.g., quantum circuits, qubits, quantum gates, etc.). Additionally, KDM represents such components independently on the quantum technology and programming languages. Such standardization of the quantum code allows to manage quantum elements without a specific concern on the quantum platform or framework where it was developed. The proposal of this paper follows the same technology-agnostic approach since it focuses on transforming KDM models into the well-known standard UML. The outgoing UML models are useful since these can be used for capturing further analysis and design details for hybrid information systems in restructuring and forward engineering stages.

The designed KDM-to-UML has been formally defined in ATL [37]. An ATL transformation program is composed of rules that define what elements of the input meta-model are transformed in other elements regarding the output meta-model.

A key part for designing the model transformation is to define the input and output meta-models. The input meta-model is an extension of KDM which allows the identification of quantum elements proposed in [16]. The output meta-model is the ECORE meta-model for UML version 2.5.1, which defines the abstract syntax of UML. This ECORE meta-model can be seen in [38] and contains the UML model description compliant with EMOF meta-model [39]. EMOF stands for Essential MOF, and "it provides a straightforward framework for mapping MOF models to implementations such as JMI and XMI for simple metamodels" [40]. The UML meta-model is used as is, although a quantum UML profile as depicted in [35] is used for modelling quantum circuits as UML activity diagram.

Table 11.2 Summary of the transformations accomplished

Q# element	Input KDM	Output UML
Quantum program	CompilationUnit	Interaction
Quantum operation	CallableUnit	Activity
Qubit declaration	StorableUnit	ActivityPartition
Quantum gate	ActionElement	CallOperationAction/ AcceptEventAction/ SendSignalAction
Data flow between gates	Flow	ControlFlow

Having defined the meta-models, the design of the ATL transformation attempts to identify which quantum entities could match with elements of the UML metamodel.

The KDM-to-UML transformation followed a top-down order. Thus, the first KDM elements that were transformed to UML are those that group the remaining nested elements, i.e., the *Segment* element as the KDM model's root element (which may contain from different perspectives the description of a whole system, including its components and interrelationships) [41], while the last, and more atomic, KDM element is the *actionRelation*, which specifies on which qubit a quantum gate acted and its flow control.

Table 11.2 shows a short summary of the transformations that have been carried out, where on the left side is the Q# element that has been analyzed, on the middle of the table its KDM modelling, and on the right side its UML transformation.

11.4.3   Forward Engineering

As mentioned before, the phase of forward engineering consists of generating the new source code of the target system and other software artefacts at lower abstraction level from the previous models. Generative and *low-code* methods for automatically generating source code from abstract models have been widely addressed in the literature.

Usually when creating a tool which generates code from models, first, it is necessary to define the type of models from which to generate the source code. The kind of concerns represented in the model (static or dynamic perspective of the system) directly impact on the type of code to be generated. As in the previous section, we focused on generating activity diagrams, some examples of code generation from dynamic models are shown.

Dominik Gessenharter et al. [42] presented an approach for code generation for activities preceded by model transformation. Such approach generates Java code from UML activity diagrams. It handles classes with their own attributes and associations, considering the control nodes that the model may have. Sunitha Edacheril et al. [43] approach associates activity diagrams with sequence diagram, allowing the generation of code from both type of models. The aim of making an association between those diagrams is because the control and data flow are better defined in UML activity diagrams, while the method invocations (so, the communication among the different objects) are better gathered from sequence diagrams.

Alexander Knapp et al. [44] presented a Java code generator from UML state machines diagrams called HUGO, which generates the different Java classes from each of the classes defined in the UML model. Such classes contain the method bodies of the specific operations and signal receptions which reproduce. It also runs a method to set up and initialize the associated state machine.

Regarding quantum computing, there are frameworks and projects which generate quantum programs from quantum circuits. IBM Quantum Experience [36] allows designing quantum circuits and export those circuits in the open-source Quantum Assembly Language (OpenQASM) [45], which is a widely employed language in the industry. Quantum Programming Studio [46] is a web application which allows users to develop quantum circuits, run them on multiple quantum computers, and export them in multiple quantum programming languages.

Finally, other proposal like Quantum Intermediate Representation (QIR) [47] from Microsoft intends to serve as a common interface between the different quantum programming languages and the target quantum computation platforms. For this, any gate-based quantum platform may be represented in QIR as it does not specify any specific quantum instruction, allowing to the computing environment chosen to perform specific transformations. QIR follows the same pattern as compilers, which compile source language into an intermediate representation where it can be optimized and transformed.

11.5   Conclusions

Every day we are coming closer to a world where organizations can have access to quantum computers or be able to run quantum algorithms that benefit their business models. Moreover, the estimated predictions point to a large increase in the value of services developed in this new paradigm.

However, the organizations which could benefit from quantum computing are not yet ready for this paradigm leap. It has always been said that it is not the strongest that survives, but the one that adapts the best. This phrase can be applied to our context since, in a not-too-distant future, the organizations that best adapt their business models (hence, their information systems) or create new strategies considering the new paradigm will be able to survive to the competence.

In this context, quantum software modernization has been introduced in this chapter as a solution to carry out the evolution of classical information systems toward hybrid information systems. This process makes it easier the combination of both computing paradigms, quantum and classical. This process consists of three phases, reverse engineering, restructuring, and forward engineering.

The main implication of this kind of solutions is that it deals with the challenges of hybrid information systems. Thus, software modernization helps the companies identify which components from their business models could be evolved or even start new businesses following this new paradigm through the use of techniques and standards which have been proved to be effective solving such problems.

References

1. Dongarra JJUoT-KICL (2020) Technical Report. ICLUT-20-06, Report on the Fujitsu Fugaku system
2. Wells J et al (2016) Announcing supercomputer summit. Oak Ridge National Lab. (ORNL), Oak Ridge, TN
3. Haroche S, Raimond J-MJPT (1996) Quantum computing: dream or nightmare? 49(8):51–54
4. Piattini M, Peterssen G, Pérez-Castillo R (2020) Quantum computing: a new software engineering golden age. SIGSOFT Softw Eng Notes 45:12–14
5. Mueck L (2017) Quantum software. Nature Publishing Group
6. Pérez-Castillo R, Serrano MA, Piattini M (2021) Software modernization to embrace quantum technology. Adv Eng Softw 151:102933
7. Jiménez-Navajas L, Pérez-Castillo R, Piattini M (2020) Reverse engineering of quantum programs toward KDM models. In: International Conference on the Quality of Information and Communications Technology. Springer
8. Piattini M et al (2020) The Talavera manifesto for quantum software engineering and programming. In: QANSWER
9. Misra J et al (2021) When to build quantum software?
10. OMG. Architecture driven modernization task force. https://www.omg.org/adm/
11. Egger DJ et al (2020) Quantum computing for Finance: state of the art and future prospects
12. Cao Y et al (2019) Quantum chemistry in the age of quantum computing. 119(19): 10856–10915
13. Ristè D et al (2017) Demonstration of quantum advantage in machine learning. 3(1):1–5
14. Chuang IL, Gershenfeld N, Kubinec M (1998) Experimental implementation of fast quantum searching. Phys Rev Lett 80(15):3408–3411
15. Brandl MFJapa (2017) A quantum von Neumann architecture for large-scale quantum computing
16. Jiménez-Navajas L, Pérez-Castillo R, Piattini M (2020) Reverse Engineering of Quantum Programs Toward KDM Models. In: 13th International Conference on the Quality of Information and Communications Technology (QUATIC) (Online Conference). Springer International, Faro, Portugal, pp 249–262
17. Piattini M et al (2020) The Talavera manifesto for quantum software engineering and programming. CEUR Workshop Proc 2561:1–5
18. MacQuarrie ER et al (2020) The emerging commercial landscape of quantum computing. Nat Rev Phys 2(11):596–598
19. Ferrari D et al (2021) Compiler design for distributed quantum computing. IEEE Trans Quantum Eng 2:1–20
20. McCaskey A et al (2018) Hybrid programming for near-term quantum computing systems. In: 2018 IEEE International Conference on Rebooting Computing (ICRC)
21. Ulrich WM (2002) Legacy systems: transformation strategies
22. De Lucia A et al (2007) Emerging methods, technologies, and process management in software engineering, pp 1–276

23. Kazman R, Woods SG, Carriere SJ (1998) Requirements for integrating software architecture and reengineering models: CORUM II. In: Reverse Engineering – Working Conference Proceedings, pp 154–163
24. OMG (2016) Architecture-Driven Modernization (ADM): Knowledge Discovery Meta-Model (KDM), v1.4. OMG, p 372. https://www.omg.org/spec/KDM/1.4/PDF
25. Sneed HM (2005) Estimating the costs of a reengineering project. In: Proceedings of the 12th Working Conference on Reverse Engineering. IEEE Computer Society, pp 111–119
26. Müller HA et al (2000) Reverse engineering: a roadmap. In: Proceedings of the Conference on The Future of Software Engineering. ACM, Limerick, Ireland
27. Canfora G, Penta MD (2007) New frontiers of reverse engineering. In: 2007 Future of Software Engineering. IEEE Computer Society
28. Ulrich WM, Newcomb PH (2010) Information systems transformation
29. Schmidt DC (2006) Developing applications using model-driven design environments. IEEE Comput Soc 39(2):25–32
30. Miller J, Mukerji J (2003) MDA Guide Version 1.0.1. OMG, p 62. www.omg.org/docs/omg/03-06-01.pdf
31. OMG (2009) Architecture-driven modernization standards roadmap. https://www.omg.org/adm/ADMTF%20Roadmap.pdf
32. Pérez-Castillo R, De Guzmán IGR, Piattini M (2011) Knowledge Discovery Metamodel-ISO/IEC 19506: a standard to modernize legacy systems. Comput Standards Interf 33:519–532
33. Khusidman V, Ulrich W (2007) Architecture-driven modernization: transforming the enterprise. DRAFT V.5. OMG, p 7. http://www.omg.org/docs/admtf/07-12-01.pdf
34. Pérez-Castillo R, de Guzmán IGR, Piattini M (2011) Architecture-driven modernization. In: Modern software engineering concepts and practices: advanced approaches. IGI Global, p 75–103
35. Pérez-Castillo R, Jiménez-Navajas L, Piattini M (2021) Modelling quantum circuits with UML. In: 43rd ACM/IEEE International Conference on Software Engineering Workshops. 2021 IEEE/ACM 2nd International Workshop on Quantum Software Engineering (Q-SE). IEEE Computer Society, Virtual (originally in Madrid), p 7–12
36. IBM. IBM quantum experience webpage. https://quantum-computing.ibm.com/
37. Foundation E. ATL – a model transformation technology. https://www.eclipse.org/atl/
38. UML ECORE. https://github.com/ricpdc/qrev-api/blob/main/qrev-api/resources/metamodels/uml.ecore
39. Eclipse (2021) EMF, ECore & Meta Model. https://www.eclipse.org/modeling/emft/search/concepts/subtopic.html
40. OMG (2006) The Essential MOF (EMOF) model. https://it-dev.mpiwg-berlin.mpg.de/svn/JET/trunk/doc/latex/Diplomarbeit/websources/OMG/06-01-01.pdf
41. OMG (2016) Architecture-Driven Modernization: Knowledge Discovery Meta-Model (KDM). https://www.omg.org/spec/KDM/1.4/PDF
42. Gessenharter D, Rauscher M (2011) Code generation for UML 2 activity diagrams. In: European Conference on Modelling Foundations and Applications. Springer
43. Viswanathan SE, Samuel PJIS (2016) Automatic code generation using unified modeling language activity and sequence models. 10(6):164–172
44. Knapp A, SJPtWTfSD Merz, Verification (2002) Model checking and code generation for UML state machines and collaborations. p 59–64
45. Cross AW et al (2017) Open quantum assembly language
46. (2019) Quantum Programming Studio webpage. https://quantum-circuit.com/
47. Microsoft (2020) Quantum immediate representation. https://devblogs.microsoft.com/qsharp/introducing-quantum-intermediate-representation-qir/

Chapter 12
Quantum Software Tools Overview

José A. Cruz-Lemus and Manuel A. Serrano

12.1 Quantum Software

Quantum software development is a complex process that not only has the drawbacks of classical software development but also has several characteristics that make it a difficult process, such as the emergence of concepts like qubit superposition or entanglement [1].

But quantum software development is not only a complex task, in general, software development, quantum or classical, is a difficult enterprise prone to failure [2]. For this reason, building software has long been supported by various tools that help avoid errors and automate many of the repetitive tasks that must be performed during the development cycle. This trend has reached a high level of utilization in current trends such as continuous software engineering [3] and DevOps [4].

Because of this complexity, if we want quantum computing to advance properly, producing quality software at large scale and in an industrial way, we will need to rely on the principles of software engineering, such as those proposed in the Talavera Manifesto [5], propose and use life cycles [6], and use tools that simplify and automate the stages of the creation process[1] and even help in the reengineering and migration of legacy systems to new quantum or hybrid systems [7].

Although we are at an early stage of quantum computing, manufacturers of quantum computers are providing environments, tools, libraries, and APIs to facilitate the programming of such computers (e.g., IBM Qiskit[2] or D-Wave Leap[3]). In

---

[1] https://aquantum.uclm.es/lang/en/indexEn.php
[2] https://qiskit.org/
[3] https://www.dwavesys.com/build/getting-started/

J. A. Cruz-Lemus (✉) · M. A. Serrano
aQuantum, Alarcos Research Group, Escuela Superior de Informática & Instituto de Tecnologías y Sistemas de Información, University of Castilla-La Mancha, Ciudad Real, Spain
e-mail: JoseAntonio.Cruz@uclm.es; Manuel.Serrano@uclm.es

© The Author(s), under exclusive license to Springer Nature Switzerland AG 2022 229
M. A. Serrano et al. (eds.), *Quantum Software Engineering*,
https://doi.org/10.1007/978-3-031-05324-5_12

addition, there are other players that provide environments that can work with various platforms, such as Microsoft Q#,[4] Zapata Computing's Orquestra,[5] or QuantumPath.[6] Finally, there are academic and independent proposals that have created tools and languages oriented to the agnostic construction of quantum software; a collection of such tools can be found in the aQuantum fundamentals portal.[7]

Throughout this section, the different quantum software layers and the existent quantum software tools and platforms will be presented.

12.1.1 Quantum Software Layers

Quantum computers are systems too complex to handle and program directly. At the same time, they are powerful devices which can deal with problems which had been really difficult in classical programming. That is why the usual implementation of a quantum computer is a stack of layers, although this stack is not a standard, quantum platforms follow a similar approach.

Quantum software development is performed by designing the quantum circuits using drag-and-drop controls or directly coding them in user-friendly environments. Later, with the aim of becoming a proper quantum application, the quantum circuits are converted to an equivalent, intermediate representation in a quantum programming language such as OpenQASM [8, 9] or pyQuil [10]. These quantum applications must be compiled, adapted, and optimized to be run on quantum devices, taking into account the quantum processor architecture and its sets of quantum gates and operators.

Once the quantum algorithm has been compiled for the target platform, another step, known as "Quantum Error Correction" (QEC), is performed. The quantum algorithm is enriched with instructions for preventing quantum errors due to decoherence and quantum noise.

After the QEC, the quantum algorithm is compiled at a hardware level and brought closer to the target quantum machine by specifying it in the quantum firmware of the quantum computer, which represents the lowest layer of the quantum computer stack.

The physical qubits of the quantum processor are adapted to the requirements specified in the quantum algorithm by using technology-dependent optimizations. All this process is graphically presented in Fig. 12.1.

All commercial environments and existing quantum computer adapt this stack, including the compilation, error correction, and optimization in the bottom layers, which are closer to the physical device. At the same time, some intermediate layers

---

[4] https://docs.microsoft.com/en-us/azure/quantum/

[5] https://www.zapatacomputing.com/orquestra/

[6] https://quantumpath.es/

[7] https://aquantum.uclm.es/lang/en/IfnCuanticaEn.php

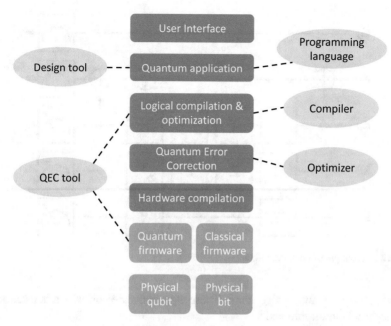

Fig. 12.1 Full quantum computer stack

adding libraries and optimized algorithms for various applications (e.g., chemistry, optimization, artificial intelligence, etc.) are included for facilitating the developers' tasks.

12.2 Quantum Software Technologies

This section reviews several software technologies by listing and classifying them, including the following subsections: programming languages, simulators and design environments, tools and libraries, main vendors full-stacks, and development and run platforms.

12.2.1 Quantum Programming Languages

Programming quantum computers usually imply the definition of a quantum circuit (see Fig. 12.2) so that it represents the operations being applied to each of the qubits in the quantum computer. This graphical notation is useful for small examples and for building prototypes, but as circuits get bigger, it stops being practical. As a result, several quantum programming languages have been proposed to ease the

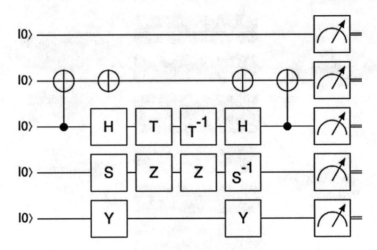

Fig. 12.2 Example of quantum circuit

specification of quantum algorithms. These algorithms are normally a translation of the quantum circuit into code.

Several quantum programming languages have been proposed in recent years. Some of them are quantum circuit-oriented, while others are closer to high-level languages. Again, some of these new arrivals cannot really be considered as autonomous languages, but libraries built over classical or embedded languages. These libraries can be invoked from general-purpose, classical programming languages such as C# or Python.

As an example, Fig. 12.3 provides a translation to OpenQASM of the quantum circuit shown in Fig. 12.2.

Although most of the quantum programming languages follow the imperative and functional paradigms, there are also some other languages which are based on object-orientation, circuits, or even multi-paradigm approaches.

12.2.1.1 Quantum Imperative Programming Languages

Most of the quantum computing languages are imperative. While some of the proposals provide a language of their own (usually assembler-based proposals), most of them are extensions to other classical programming language, Python in most cases.

Tables 12.1 and 12.2 (based on [35]) provide information on the imperative quantum programming languages, including their year of invention, name, the language on which it is based on, and bibliographical references.

```
1   OPENQASM 2.0;
2   include "qelib1.inc";
3
4   qreg q[5];
5   creg c[5];
6
7   cx q[2], q[1];
8   s q[3];
9   y q[4];
10  x q[1];
11  h q[2];
12  z q[3];
13  y q[4];
14  x q[1];
15  t q[2];
16  z q[3];
17  tdg q[2];
18  sdg q[3];
19  h q[2];
20  cx q[2], q[1];
21  measure q[0] -> c[0];
22  measure q[1] -> c[1];
23  measure q[2] -> c[2];
24  measure q[3] -> c[3];
25  measure q[4] -> c[4];
```

Fig. 12.3 Algorithm example in OpenQASM

Table 12.1 Low abstraction quantum imperative programming languages

Year	Name	Language	Reference(s)
1998	QCL	C	[11]
2006	LanQ	C	[12, 13]
2012	Scaffold	C (C++)	[14, 15]
2016	QASM	Assembly language	[16]
2017	OpenQASM	Assembly language	[8, 9]
2017	cQASM	Assembly language	[17]
2020	Jaqual	Assembly language	[18]

As previously commented, most low-level imperative languages (see Table 12.1) are assembler-based proposals, as an evolution or adaptation of OpenQASM, while high-level quantum languages proposals (see Table 12.2) are more varied, although the prevalence of Python is clear.

Nevertheless, there are multiple proposals associated with other programming languages and platforms, such as Julia, Scala, C++, or .Net framework languages.

Table 12.2 High abstraction quantum imperative programming languages

Year	Name	Language	Reference(s)
2000	qGCL	Pascal	[19, 20]
2003	Q language	C++	[21]
2008	NDQJava	Java	[22]
2009	Cove	C#	[23]
2012	Scaffold	C (C++)	[14, 15]
2013	Chisel-Q	Scala	[24]
2016	FJQuantum	Feather-weight Java	[25]
2016	ProjectQ	Python	[26]
2016	pyQuil (Quil)	Python	[10]
2017	Quiskit	Python	[27]
2018	IQu	Idealized Algol	[28]
2018	Strawberry Fields	Python	[29]
2018	Balckbird	Python	[29]
2018	QuantumOptics.jl	Julia	[30]
2018	Cirq	Python	[31]
2018	Q#	C#	[32]
2018	Q|SI>	.Net language	[33]
2020	Silq	Python	[34]

12.2.1.2 Quantum Functional Programming Languages

Although mainstream quantum programming languages are generally imperative, there are several proposals which are based on functional programming. Some of these proposals are new languages, usually based on lambda calculus, but many others are designed as extensions of functional programming languages, such as F# or Haskell. However, there are also proposals based on Python, which have been gradually expanded to include extensions that make it a multi-paradigm language, allowing functional quantum extensions.

Table 12.3 presents the information of the main functional quantum programming languages, using the same format than the tables in the previous subsection. Some programming languages support both imperative and functional programming.

12.2.1.3 Other Quantum Programming Languages

Following the same format as previous tables, Table 12.4 presents information about other quantum programming languages, including circuit-based, declarative, and other types, which were not included in any other table in this section.

Table 12.3 Quantum functional programming languages

Year	Name	Language	Reference(s)
1996	Quantum Lambda Calculi	Lambda calculus	[36]
2000	λq	Lambda calculus	[37]
2004	QFC (QPL)	Flowchart	[38–40]
2005	QML	Similar to Haskell	[41]
2005	cQPL	Denotational	[42]
2013	QuaFL	Haskell	[43]
2013	Quipper	Haskell	[44, 45]
2013	Chisel-Q	Scala	[24]
2014	LIQUi|>	F#	[46]
2015	Proto-Quipper	Haskell	[47]
2016	ProjectQ	Python	[26]
2016	qPCF	Lambda calculus	[28, 48]
2017	Quiskit	Python	[27]
2018	Strawberry Fields	Python	[29]
2018	Balckbird	Python	[29]
2018	Cirq	Python	[31]
2020	Silq	Python	[34]

Table 12.4 Other quantum programming languages

Year	Name	Language	Reference(s)
2004	CQP	Process calculus	[49–51]
2005	QPAlg	Process calculus	[52, 53]
2011	QuECT	Java	[54]
2017	Forest	Python	[10]
2017	QWIRE	Coq proof assistant	[55]

12.2.2   *Quantum Software Simulators and Design Environments*

Building quantum computers is difficult. Besides, there is a limited access to the few actual quantum computers currently available. Thus, a set of different quantum simulators[8] has emerged to assist in designing and planning quantum circuits and algorithms. This way, when a new quantum algorithm is developed, the initial proof-of-concept validation is normally conducted with a simulator.

Quantum simulators are mostly based on the management of arrays, and only a few of them are also based on graphs. The following list (based on [56]) presents some well-known quantum simulators:

---

[8]https://www.quantiki.org/wiki/list-qc-simulators

- Atom QASM Quantum Circuit Previewer[9] is an Atom[10] editor package that converts QASM (Quantum Assembly) code into a graphical representation of the quantum circuit in real time and provides additional information about the circuit, such as its depth, number of instructions, and state vector visualizations.
- cuQuantum SDK[11] is a development platform for simulating quantum circuits on GPU-accelerated systems provided by Nvidia.
- DDSIM [57] is part of the JKQ tools and provides a decision diagram-based quantum circuit simulator which allows the simulation of quantum circuits defined in a REAL or OpenQASM format.
- Intel-QS (Quantum Simulator) or QHIPSTER (The Quantum High Performance Software Testing Environment) [58] is a high-performance environment using parallel algorithms.
- LIQUi|>[12] from Microsoft is an integrated language for quantum simulation. The simulations can be run on multiple platforms, but they can be integrated on other applications or executed stand-alone scripts.
- ProjectQ [59] is an open-source array-based simulator which can easily be extended by domain experts. It allows the simulation of up to approximately 30 qubits on a desktop machine. It also contains an emulator capable of determining the results for some algorithms (e.g., Shor's algorithm) faster than an average simulator.
- QCEC [60] is part of the JKQ toolset for quantum computing [57] which can be used for quantum circuit equivalence checking. It also includes some quantum mapping tools (QMAP).
- QDENSITY/QCWAVE [61] is a Mathematica package for simulating a quantum computer.
- Qibo [62] is an open-source software for fast evaluation of quantum circuits and adiabatic evolution which uses hardware accelerators.
- QuCirDET [63] is a design and simulation tool for quantum circuits.
- Quirk[13] is an open-source web-based simulator built upon JavaScript that can be executed inside the web browser. An example of this system can be seen in Fig. 12.4.
- Qulacs [64] is a fast simulator for quantum circuits intended for research purposes.
- QuIDDPro [65] is a graph-based simulator, specialized in the simulation of Grover's algorithm.

---

[9] https://atom.io/packages/qasm-circuit-preview

[10] https://atom.io/

[11] https://www.hpcwire.com/2021/04/13/gtc21-nvidia-launches-cuquantum-dips-a-toe-in-quantum-computing/

[12] http://stationq.github.io/Liquid/

[13] https://algassert.com/quirk

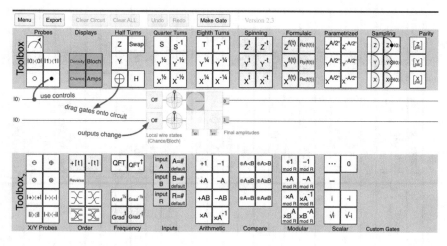

Fig. 12.4 Quirk simulator overview

- QuTe[14] is a Quantum Testbed which provides a high-performance quantum computing simulation platform open to research teams worldwide.
- QX [66] is a simulation platform based on arrays which parallelizes quantum gates for performance improvement.

12.2.3   Quantum Tools and Libraries

Table 12.5 (based on [102, 103]) shows the most important quantum software tools and libraries, including information about their type of distribution license, whether it allows the use of quantum gates, their main capabilities, the programming language(s) they rely on, and some bibliographical references.

12.2.4   Quantum Annealing Environments

The main advantage of quantum computing is reducing the execution time of time-consuming algorithms, and due to this, a new type of quantum platforms has emerged in recent times that implements one or several circuits solely oriented to solving combinational optimization problems, known as Quantum Approximate Optimization Algorithm (QAOA) [104].

---

[14] https://qute.ctic.es/

Table 12.5 Quantum software tools and technologies

Name	License	Q Gates	Other capabilities	Language	Reference(s)
BackupBrain[a]	Open source	Yes	Algorithms, Diagrams	JavaScript	
Bloch Sphere	Open source	Yes	Algorithms, Diagrams	Java	[67]
CHP[b]	Open source	Yes	Algorithms	C	
Cirq	Open source	Yes	All	Python	[68]
Drqubit[c]	Open source, freeware	Yes	Parallelism	MATLAB	
Eqcs	Open source	Yes	None	C	[69]
Feynman	Open source	Yes	Algorithms, Parallelism	Maple	[70]
HOQST	Open source	Yes	Diagrams	Julia	[71]
Jsquis	Open source	Yes	None	Javascript	[72]
LanQ	Open source	Yes	Algorithms, Parallelism	LanQ	[12]
libquantum	Open source	Yes	Algorithms, Parallelism	C, C++	[73, 74]
Linerar AI[d]	Freeware	Yes	Algorithms, Diagrams	Mathematica	
M-fun	Open source	Yes	None	MATLAB/Octave	[75]
Mukai[e]	Commercial	No	Accelerators, Diagrams	Python	
Open Qubit	Open source	Yes	Algorithms	C++	[76]
OpenQASM	Open source	Yes	Diagrams	QASM	[8, 9, 77]
OpenQUACS	Open source	Yes	Algorithms, Parallelism	Maple	[78]
ProjectQ	Open source	Yes	All	Python	[59]
Q-gol	Open source	Yes	Algorithms	CaML	[79]
Q-Kit[f]	Freeware	Yes	All		
Q++[g]	Open source	Yes	Algorithms, Diagrams	C++	
QCAD	Freeware	Yes	Diagrams		[80]
QCGPU	Open source	Yes	Parallelism	Rust & OpenCL	[81]
Qchas[h]	Open source	Yes	Diagrams	Haskell	
QCircuits	Open source	Yes	All	Python	[82]
QDENSITY	Open source	Yes	Diagrams	Mathematica	[83]

Name	License	Standalone	Features	Language	Ref.
Qi[i]	Open source	Yes	None	Mathematica	[84]
Qinf	Open source	Yes	Diagrams	Maxima	[85]
QIO	Open source	Yes	Diagrams	Qio + Haskell	[86]
Qiskit	Open source	Yes	All	Python	[87]
QMDD	Open source	No	Diagrams	C++	
QOCS[j]	Open source	Yes	Algorithms	OCaML	[88]
Qrack	Open source	No	None	C++	[89]
Qsims	Open source, commercial	Yes	Algorithms, Parallelism	C++	[90]
QSWalk.jl	Open source	Yes	None	Julia	
QUA[k]	Commercial	No	Optimization	QUA	
Quantavo	Open source	Yes	Algorithms, Parallelism	Maple	[91]
Quantencomputer	None	Yes	Algorithms	MATLAB	[92]
Quantum[l]	Freeware	Yes	All	Mathematica	[65]
Quantum Circuit	Open source	Yes	Algorithms, Diagrams	Javascript	[93]
Quantum Fog	Open source	Yes	All		[94]
Quantum Programming Studio	Open source	Yes	Algorithms, Parallelism, Diagrams	Javascript	
Quantum User Interface[m]	Open source	Yes	None	Protobuf	
Quantum.NET[n]	Open source	Yes	None	.NET	[95]
Quantum++	Open source	No	None	C++	[30]
QuantumOptics.jl	Open source	No	Algorithms, Diagrams	Julia	[96]
QuantumUtils	Open source	Yes	Parallelism, Diagrams	Mathematica	
QuantumWalk.jl[o]	Open source	Yes	Algorithms	Julia	
Qubit Workbench[p]	Commercial	Yes	Algorithms, Diagrams		[97]
Qubit Workbench[q]	Freeware	Yes	None		[98]
Qubit4Matlab	Open source	Yes	All	MATLAB	[99]
QuEST	Open source	Yes	None	C	
QuIDE	Open source	Yes	All	.NET	

(continued)

Name	License	Q Gates	Other capabilities	Language	Reference(s)
QX Simulator[r]	Open source	No	Parallelism	Quantum Code	
Scaffold/ScaffCC	Open source	No	Algorithms	Scaffold	[15]
SimQubit	Open source	Yes	Algorithms, Diagrams	C++	[100]
Staq	Open source	Yes	None	C	[95]
Tequila	Open source	Yes	None	Python	[101]

[a] https://backupbrain.github.io/quantum-compiler-simulator/
[b] https://www.scottaaronson.com/chp/
[c] http://www.dr-qubit.org/
[d] http://linearal.sourceforge.net
[e] https://quantumcomputinginc.com/products.php
[f] https://sites.google.com/view/quantum-kit/home
[g] https://sourceforge.net/projects/qplusplus/
[h] https://hackage.haskell.org/package/qchas
[i] https://github.com/iitis/qi
[j] https://github.com/dillanchang/QOCS
[k] https://www.quantum-machines.co/
[l] http://homepage.cem.itesm.mx/lgomez/quantum/index.htm
[m] https://qui.research.unimelb.edu.au/
[n] https://github.com/phbaudin/quantum-computing
[o] https://github.com/iitis/QuantumWalk.jl
[p] https://elyah.io/product
[q] https://elyah.io/product
[r] http://quantum-studio.net

This paradigm consists in the construction of a mathematical model that represents the objective and a set of constraints existing in an optimization problem. One of the main vendors of this second type of quantum computers is D-Wave Systems,[15] which propose to solve several optimization problems by constructing a binary quadratic model (BQM), consisting of a collection of binary-valued variables, i.e., variables that can have only two possible values (e.g., 0 or 1) and are affected by biases and interactions between them.

Apart from D-Wave, there are some other less known platforms such as the Fujitsu digital annealer[16] which has a similar behavior to D-Wave computers. On the other hand, this type of algorithm can be simulated on IBM quantum computers through QAOA circuits[17] and on Microsoft's Q# environment and its cloud platform, Azure Quantum,[18] as well as on the Amazon Braket computing service.[19]

These types of algorithms and environments are largely specialized in solving a specific type of optimization problem, for which they are highly efficient, although they do not have, at the moment, the capacity to solve those problems that do not fit the paradigm.

12.2.5   Full-Stack Software of Main Quantum Computing Vendors

The most important characteristics of each of the main full-stack quantum software platforms sold by the main vendors (see Fig. 12.5) are discussed in this section.

- D-Wave[20] is a Canadian firm offering an adiabatic quantum computer, specialized in the performance of optimization. They use "QMASM" as a machine language. This language is below the open-source qbsolv library, which can solve optimization problems by decompiling QUBO (Quadratic Unconstrained Binary Optimization) problems.
- Google's platform is called Quantum AI.[21] It works with quantum circuits on near-term quantum computers. This platform is based on Cirq, a Python library "for writing, manipulating and optimizing quantum circuits and running them against quantum computers and simulators" [105]. Some other Python library can be run on top of Cirq, for instance, OpenFermion, which focuses on simulating fermionic systems.

---

[15] https://www.dwavesys.com/solutions-and-products/cloud-platform/

[16] https://www.fujitsu.com/global/services/business-services/digital-annealer/

[17] https://qiskit.org/textbook/ch-applications/qaoa.html

[18] https://azure.microsoft.com/es-es/services/quantum/

[19] https://aws.amazon.com/braket/

[20] https://dwavesys.com/

[21] https://quantumai.google/

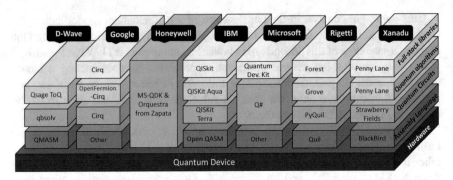

Fig. 12.5 Main quantum full stack platforms

- Honeywell[22] is a US company based in North Carolina. They are focused on quantum computing based on Trapped-ion technology. Their quantum computers do not have open access yet, but they are thought to be compatible, in the future, with quantum algorithms that can run on other companies' computers.
- IBM[23] provides several quantum computers on a cloud-based service. These are programmed through quantum circuits using a web quantum composer or by defining them in Open QASM language. These circuits are supplied to the quantum computer through the Qiskit Terra library as a platform provider. Several libraries focused on specific domains, such as Qiskit Aqua, can be found on top of them.
- Microsoft's stack is based on the use of the Q# language programming. It provides a set of libraries, API, and simulators using the Quantum Development Kit (QDK). The access to the quantum computers has been migrated to its use on the cloud via Azure services.
- Rigetti[24] is a US company based in California. They provide access to its quantum processors via their ASPEN-8 processors. Several software components make their software stack up, among others, the PyQuil programming language (a Python library) and Quil, an optimizing compiler for gate-based quantum programs.
- Xanadu[25] use photonic technology for quantum computing. This technology provides robustness and scalability and can operate at room temperature. Its devices are accessed through the Xanadu quantum cloud and feature the Strawberry Fields programming language provided as another Python library. Several libraries, such as TensorFlow, can be used on top of this stack to carry out domain-oriented applications. In addition, Xanadu provides a Python library called "Penny Lane" for programming a quantum computer the same way a

---

[22] https://www.honeywell.com/us/en/company/quantum

[23] https://quantum-computing.ibm.com/

[24] https://www.rigetti.com/

[25] https://www.xanadu.ai/

neural network is trained. This library can also be used on other quantum platforms such as Google, IBM, or Rigetti.

12.2.6 Quantum Software Development and Run Platforms

In addition to the previously discussed full-stack environments, there are also some other suites for designing and running quantum applications and workflows. Normally, these platforms interact with different quantum computers, tools, and simulators:

- 1QBit[26] provides a hardware-agnostic platform to solve intractable industry problems, including 1Qloud which is a powerful optimization platform enabled by quantum and classical computers.
- Aliro[27] is a quantum platform oriented to creating and optimizing quantum networks and quantum-secure communications, using Entanglement as a Service (EaaS) so that it can be used by applications.
- Braket[28] is the proposal from Amazon for quantum computing. It provides access to different quantum computers and simulators hosted on the AWS platform. An SDK is also provided for creating quantum algorithms which can be run on any compatible quantum hardware (such as Rigetti or D-Wave). It can also be used on hybrid approaches such as Penny Lane or Jupyter notebooks. It includes a repository with pre-designed algorithms and tutorials and a machine and user administration environment. Although Braket does not specifically support hybrid software, it offers a Platform as a Service (PaaS) for an easy with classical software.
- Classiq Technologies[29] is a platform for designing quantum algorithms through automation and synthesis. It creates such quantum algorithms from ideas without needing to code at a quantum gate level by using a programming environment that organizes the entire quantum software stack and creates algorithms compatible with the main quantum programming environments (such as Q#, Cirq, or Qiskit). The algorithms are also portable to different types of quantum hardware.
- Orquestra from Zapata[30] is a quantum programming environment based on the construction of quantum workflows. These workflows allow working at the appropriate level of abstraction, but, at the same time, the programmer can get closer to the hardware if needed. Deployment, scaling, and parallelization of workflows can be performed by submitting them to Orquesta Quantum Engine

---

[26] https://1qbit.com/
[27] https://www.aliroquantum.com/
[28] https://aws.amazon.com/braket
[29] https://www.classiq.io/
[30] https://www.zapatacomputing.com/orquestra/

servers via REST API and can be executed both on classical and quantum devices.

- QPath[31] is a quantum software development and life cycle application platform which implements a complete life cycle pipeline to create professional quantum software solutions. It allows using different quantum programming languages and platforms for coding new quantum algorithms, using a quantum software engineering approach. It provides several connections to the main quantum platforms, such as D-Wave, Rigetti, or IBM. Finally, it can be used to integrate classical and quantum software to build hybrid systems.
- Strangeworks QC[32] is a platform designed to serve as the central hub for all quantum hardware and software vendors, enterprises, academia, and other entities, by facilitating the application of quantum computing to a broad range of problems.
- t|ket⟩ from CQC (Cambridge Quantum Computing)[33] is an architecture-agnostic quantum software stack with its own compiler. It allows translating machine-independent algorithms into optimized executable circuits.

12.3   Current Limitations and Future Trends

Today, the main limitations of quantum computing can be mainly grouped into two categories, the lack of knowledge and experience in the construction of quantum algorithms and the availability of quantum computers.

Regarding the first problem, apart from training, the emergence of new programming methods, as well as advances in quantum software engineering, as supported by the Talavera Manifesto [5] will probably be supportive in this new paradigm. On the other hand, the problems associated with the technology lead to low availability of quantum computers, as the low number of qubits available, the quantum noise problems, qubits decoherence, and general availability of these computers. These limitations can be alleviated in the future as the technology advanced.

Regarding tools and platforms, the main existing problems are related to the current lack of software engineering culture; nowadays, we have a low level of abstraction in the construction of quantum software, the absence of standards that allow the reuse of code through components, or the lack of tools like the ones we use in the construction of classic software such as project management or testing tools.

In the future, tools for testing, quality, etc. that do not exist today will be of paramount importance. If we really want quantum software to become a reality, the emergence of quantum software engineering is inevitable [106], which will give rise to a new golden age of computing [107].

---

[31] https://www.quantumpath.es/eng/

[32] https://strangeworks.com/

[33] https://cambridgequantum.com/

Acknowledgments We would like to thank all the aQuantum members, especially Guido Peterssen and Pepe Hevia, for their invaluable help and support. This work was partially funded by the "QHealth: Quantum Pharmacogenomics Applied to Aging" project, the 2020 CDTI Missions Program [Center for the Development of Industrial Technology of the Ministry of Science and Innovation of Spain and the AETHER-UCLM: A smart data holistic approach for context-aware data analytics focused on Quality and Security project (Ministry of Science and Innovation of Spain, PID2020-112540RB-C42)].

References

1. Mueck L (2017) Quantum software. Nature 549(7671):171–171
2. Dijkstra EW (1972) The humble programmer. Commun ACM 15(10):859–866
3. Humble J, Farley D (2010) Continuous delivery: reliable software releases through build, test, and deployment automation. Pearson Education
4. Kim G, Humble J, Debois P, Willis J, Forsgren N (2021) The DevOps handbook: how to create world-class agility, reliability, & security in technology organizations. IT Revolution
5. Piattini M, Peterssen G, Pérez-Castillo R, Hevia JL et al (2020) The Talavera Manifesto for Quantum Software Engineering and Programming. QANSWER 2020 QuANtum SoftWare Engineering & pRogramming. Proceedings of the 1st International Workshop on the QuANtum SoftWare Engineering & pRogramming, Talavera de la Reina, Spain, February 11–12, 2020. http://ceur-ws.org/Vol-2561/paper0.pdf
6. Weder B, Barzen J, Leymann F, Salm M, Vietz D (2020) The quantum software lifecycle. In: Proceedings of the 1st ACM SIGSOFT International Workshop on Architectures and Paradigms for Engineering Quantum Software, pp 2–9
7. Pérez-Castillo R, Serrano MA, Piattini M (2021) Software modernization to embrace quantum technology. Adv Eng Softw 151:102933
8. Cross AW, Bishop LS, Smolin JA, Gambetta JM (2017) Open quantum assembly language. arXiv preprint arXiv:1707.03429
9. Cross AW, Javadi-Abhari A, Alexander T, de Beaudrap N, Bishop LS, Heidel S, Ryan C, Smolin J, Gambetta JM, Johson BR (2021) OpenQASM 3: a broader and deeper quantum assembly language. arXiv:2104.14722v1
10. Smith RS, Curtis MJ, Zeng WJ (2016) A practical quantum instruction set architecture. arXiv:1608.03355
11. Ömer B (2005) Classical concepts in quantum programming. Int J Theoretical Phys 44(7): 943–955
12. Mlnarik H (2007) Operational semantics and type soundness of quantum programming language LanQ. arXiv preprint arXiv:0708.0890
13. Mlnarik H (2008) Semantics of quantum programming language LanQ. Int J Quant Inf 6 (Suppl 01):733–738
14. Abhari AJ, Faruque A, Dousti MJ, Svec L, Catu O, Chakrabati A, Chiang C-F, Vanderwilt S, Black J, Chong F (2012) Scaffold: Quantum programming language. Princeton University, NJ
15. Abhari AJ, Patil S, Kudrow D, Heckey J, Lvov A, Chong FT, Martonosi M (2015) Scaffcc: Scalable compilation and analysis of quantum programs. Parallel Comput 45:2–17
16. Pakin S (2016) A quantum macro assembler. In: 2016 IEEE High Performance Extreme Computing Conference (HPEC). IEEE, pp 1–8
17. Khammassi N, Guerreschi GG, Ashraf I, Hogaboam JW, Almudever CG, Bertels K (2018) cQASM v1.0: towards a common quantum assembly language. arXiv:1805.09607v1
18. Morrison BC, Landahl AJ, Lobser DS, Rudinger KM, Russo AE, Van Der Wall JW, Maunz P (2020) Just another quantum assembly language (Jaqal). In: 2020 IEEE International Conference on Quantum Computing and Engineering (QCE). IEEE, pp 402–408

19. Sanders JW, Zuliani P (2000) Quantum programming. In: International Conference on Mathematics of Program Construction. Springer, pp 80–99
20. Zuliani P (2004) Non-deterministic quantum programming. In: Proceeding QPL 2004. Facoltà di Scienze e Tecnologie Informatiche Libera Università di Bolzano Italy. pp 179–195
21. Bettelli S, Calarco T, Serafini L (2003) Toward an architecture for quantum programming. Eur Phys J D-Atom Mol Optical Plasma Phys 25(2):181–200
22. Jia-Fu X, Song F-M, Qian S-J, Dai J-A, Zhang Y-J (2008) Quantum programming language NDQJava. J Softw 19(1):1–8
23. Purkeypile M (2009) Cove: a practical quantum computer programming framework. PhD Dissertation. Colorado Technical University. https://arxiv.org/abs/0911.2423
24. Liu X, Kubiatowicz J (2013) Chisel-Q: designing quantum circuits with a scala embedded language. In: 2013 IEEE 31st International Conference on Computer Design (ICCD). IEEE, pp 427–434
25. Feitosa SS, Vizzotto JK, Piveta EK, Du Bois AR (2016) FJQuantum–a quantum object oriented language. Electron Notes Theoretical Comput Sci 324:67–77
26. Häner T, Steiger DS, Smelyanskiy M, Troyer M (2016) High performance emulation of quantum circuits. In: SC'16: Proceedings of the International Conference for High Performance Computing, Networking, Storage and Analysis. IEEE, pp 866–874
27. Aleksandrowicz G, Alexander T, Barkoutsos P, Bello L, Ben-Haim Y, Bucher D, Cabrera-Hernández FJ, Carballo-Franquis J, Chen A, Chen C-F, Chow JM, Córcoles-Gonzales AD, Cross AJ, Cross A, Cruz-Benito J, Culver C, González SDLP, Torre EDL, Ding D, Dumitrescu E, Duran I, Eendebak P, Everitt M, Sertage IF, Frisch A, Fuhrer A, Gambetta J, Gago BG, Gomez-Mosquera J, Greenberg D, Hamamura I, Havlicek V, Hellmers J, Herok Ł, Horii H, Hu S, Imamichi T, Itoko T, Javadi-Abhari A, Kanazawa N, Karazeev A, Krsulich K, Liu P, Luh Y, Maeng Y, Marques M, Martín-Fernández FJ, McClure DT, McKay D, Meesala S, Mezzacapo A, Moll N, Rodríguez DM, Nannicini G, Nation P, Ollitrault P, O'Riordan LJ, Paik H, Pérez J, Phan A, Pistoia M, Prutyanov V, Reuter M, Rice J, Davila AR, Rudy RHP, Ryu M, Sathaye N, Schnabel C, Schoute E, Setia K, Shi Y, Silva A, Siraichi Y, Sivarajah S, Smolin JA, Soeken M, Takahashi H, Tavernelli I, Taylor C, Taylour P, Trabing K, Treinish M, Turner W, Vogt-Lee D, Vuillot C, Wildstrom JA, Wilson J, Winston E, Wood C, Wood S, Wörner S, Akhalwaya IY, Zoufal C (2019) Qiskit: an open-source framework for quantum computing. Scott Aaronson and B. Toth. 2003. Simulation and synthesis of stabilizer quantum circuits
28. Paolini L, Piccolo M, Zorzi M (2019) QPCF: higher-order languages and quantum circuits. J Autom Reason 63(4):941–966
29. Killoran N, Izaac J, Quesada N, Bergholm V, Amy M, Weedbrook C (2019) Strawberry fields: a software platform for photonic quantum computing. Quantum 3:129
30. Krämer S, Plankensteiner D, Ostermann L, Ritsch H (2018) QuantumOptics. jl: a Julia framework for simulating open quantum systems. Comput Phys Commun 227:109–116
31. Google AI Quantum team (2018) Cirq. https://github.com/quantumlib/Cirq
32. Svore K, Geller A, Troyer M, Azariah J, Granade C, Heim B, Kliuchnikov V, Mykhailova M, Paz A, Roetteler M (2018) Q# enabling scalable quantum computing and development with a high-level dsl. In: Proceedings of the Real World Domain Specific Languages Workshop 2018, pp 1–10
33. Liu S, Wang X, Zhou L, Guan J, Li Y, He Y, Duan R, Ying M (2018) Q |SI ⟩: a quantum programming environment. In: Symposium on Real-Time and Hybrid Systems. Springer, pp 133–164
34. Bichsel B, Baader M, Gehr T, Vechev M (2020) Silq: A high-level quantum language with safe uncomputation and intuitive semantics. In: Proceedings of the 41st ACM SIGPLAN Conference on Programming Language Design and Implementation, pp 286–300
35. Zhao J (2020) Quantum software engineering: landscapes and horizons. arXiv preprint arXiv:2007.07047

36. Maymin P (1996) Extending the lambda calculus to express randomized and quantumized algorithms. arXiv preprint quant-ph/9612052
37. Van Tonder A (2004) A lambda calculus for quantum computation. SIAM J Comput 33(5): 1109–1135
38. Selinger P (2004) Towards a quantum programming language. Math Struct Comput Sci 14(4): 527–586
39. Selinger P (2004) Towards a semantics for higher-order quantum computation. In: Proceedings of the 2nd International Workshop on Quantum Programming Languages, TUCS General Publication No, vol 33, pp 127–143
40. Selinger P, Valiron B (2006) A lambda calculus for quantum computation with classical control. Math Struct Comput Sci 16(3):527
41. Altenkirch T, Grattage J (2005) A functional quantum programming language. In: 20th Annual IEEE Symposium on Logic in Computer Science (LICS'05). IEEE, pp 249–258
42. Mauerer W (2005) Semantics and simulation of communication in quantum programming. arXiv preprint quant-ph/0511145
43. Lapets A, da Silva MP, Thome M, Adler A, Beal J, Roetteler M (2013) QuaFL: a typed DSL for quantum programming. In: Proceedings of 1st annual workshop on functional programming concepts in domain-specific language (FPCDS'13), pp 19–26
44. Green AS, Lumsdaine PL, Ross NJ, Selinger P, Valiron B (2013) An introduction to quantum programming in quipper. In: International Conference on Reversible Computation. Springer, Berlin, pp 110–124
45. Green AS, Lumsdaine PL, Ross NJ, Selinger P, Valiron B (2013) Quipper: a scalable quantum programming language. In: ACM SIGPLAN Conference on Programming Language Design and Implementation, PLDI '13, Seattle, WA, June 16–19. pp 333–342
46. Wecker D, Svore KM (2014) LIQUi|>: a software design architecture and domain-specific language for quantum computing. arXiv:1402.4467
47. Rios F, Selinger P (2017) A categorical model for a quantum circuit description language. In: Proceedings 14th International Conference on Quantum Physics and Logic (QPL 2017), pp 164–178
48. Paolini L, Zorzi M (2017) qPCF: a language for quantum circuit computations. In: International Conference on Theory and Applications of Models of Computation. Springer, Cham, pp 455–469
49. Gay SJ, Nagarajan R (2004) Communicating quantum processes. In: Proceedings of the 2nd International Workshop on Quantum Programming Languages, pp 91–107
50. Gay SJ, Nagarajan R (2005) Communicating quantum processes. In: Proceedings of the 32nd ACM SIGPLAN-SIGACT Symposium on Principles of Programming Languages, pp 145–157
51. Gay SJ (2006) Quantum programming languages: survey and bibliography. Math Struct Comput Sci 16(4):581–600
52. Jorrand P, Lalire M (2004) From quantum physics to programming languages: a process algebraic approach. In: International Workshop on Unconventional Programming Paradigms. Springer, Berlin, pp 1–16
53. Lalire M, Jorrand P (2004) A process algebraic approach to concurrent and distributed quantum computation: operational semantics. arXiv preprint quant-ph/0407005
54. Chakraborty A (2011) QuECT: a new quantum programming paradigm. arXiv preprint arXiv:1104.0497
55. Paykin J, Rand R, Zdancewic S (2017) QWIRE: a core language for quantum circuits. In: Proceedings of the 44th ACM SIGPLAN Symposium on Principles of Programming Languages, POPL 2017, Paris, France, January 18–20. ACM, pp 846–858
56. Zulehner A, Wille R (2019) Advanced simulation of quantum computations. IEEE Trans Comput-Aided Des Integr Circuits Syst 38(5):848–863
57. Wille R, Hillmich S, Burgholzer L (2020) JKQ: JKU tools for quantum computing. In: 2020 IEEE/ACM International Conference On Computer Aided Design (ICCAD). IEEE, pp 1–5

58. Smelyanskiy M, Sawaya NP, Aspuru-Guzik A (2016) qHiPSTER: the quantum high performance software testing environment. arXiv preprint arXiv:1601.07195
59. Steiger DS, Häner T, Troyer M (2018) ProjectQ: an open source software framework for quantum computing. Quantum 2:49
60. Burgholzer L, Wille R (2021) QCEC: A JKQ tool for quantum circuit equivalence checking. Softw Impacts 7:100051
61. Tabakin F, Juliá-Díaz B (2011) QCWAVE–a Mathematica quantum computer simulation update. Comput Phys Commun 182(8):1693–1707
62. Efthymiou S, Ramos-Calderer S, Bravo-Prieto C, Pérez-Salinas A, García-Martín D, Garcia-Saez A, Latorre JI, Carrazza S (2020) Qibo: a framework for quantum simulation with hardware acceleration. arXiv preprint arXiv:2009.01845
63. Prousalis K, Konofaos N (2016) QuCirDET: a design and simulation tool for quantum circuits. In: 2016 5th International Conference on Modern Circuits and Systems Technologies (MOCAST). IEEE, pp 1–4
64. Suzuki Y, Kawase Y, Masumura Y, Hiraga Y, Nakadai M, Chen J, Nakanishi KM, Mitarai K, Imai R, Tamiya S, Yamamoto T, Yan T, Kawakubo T, Nakagawa YO, Ibe Y, Zhang Y, Yamashita H, Yoshimura H, Hayashi A, Fujii K (2020) Qulacs: a fast and versatile quantum circuit simulator for research purpose. arXiv:2011.13524v1
65. Viamontes GF, Markov IL, Hayes JP (2009) Quantum circuit simulation. Springer
66. Khammassi N, Ashraf I, Xiang F, Almudever CG, Bertels K (2017) QX: a high-performance quantum computer simulation platform. Proc Design Autom Test Europe 2017:464–469
67. Huo C (2009) A Bloch sphere animation software using a three dimensional Java simulator. Doctoral dissertation, University of Cincinnati
68. Omole V, Tyagi A, Carey C, Hanus AJ, Hancock A, Garcia A, Shedenhelm J (2020) Cirq: a python framework for creating, editing, and invoking Quantum circuits. http://sdmay20-08.sd.ece.iastate.edu/docs/Design-Document-v2.pdf
69. Johan A. Brandhorst-Satzkorn. 2012. A review of freely available quantum computer simulation software.
70. Radtke T, Fritzsche S (2005) Simulation of n-qubit quantum systems. I. Quantum registers and quantum gates. Comput Phys Commun 173(1–2):91–113
71. Chen H, Lidar DA (2020). HOQST: Hamiltonian Open Quantum System Toolkit. arXiv preprint arXiv:2011.14046
72. Srivastava R, Choi I, Cook T, NQIT User Engagement Team (2016) The commercial prospects for quantum computing. Networked Quantum Information Technologies
73. Glendinning I, Ömer B (2003) Parallelization of the QC-lib quantum computer simulator library. In: International Conference on Parallel Processing and Applied Mathematics. Springer, Berlin, pp 461–468
74. da Silva Feitosa S, da Silva Bueno JA (2016) Simulating quantum parallelism in CPU and GPU using the LibQuantum library. Communications and Innovations Gazette Magazine 1(2): 26–36
75. Tolba S, Rashad MZ, El-Dosuky MA (2013) Q#, a quantum computation package for the . NET platform. arXiv preprint arXiv:1302.5133
76. Schneider SD (2000) Quantum systems simulator. Doctoral dissertation, Massachusetts Institute of Technology
77. McKay DC, Alexander T, Bello L, Biercuk MJ, Bishop L, Chen J, Chow JM, Córcoles AD, Egger D, Filipp S, Gomez J, Hush M, Javadi-Abhari A, Moreda D, Nation P, Paulovicks B, Winston E, Wood CJ, Wootton J, Gambetta JM (2018) Qiskit backend specifications for OpenQASM and OpenPulse experiments. arXiv preprint arXiv:1809.03452
78. McCubbin CB (2000). Openquacs, an open-source quantum computation simulator in maple. Doctoral dissertation, University of Maryland, Baltimore County
79. Caraiman S, Archip A, Manta V (2009) A grid enabled quantum computer simulator. In: 2009 11th International Symposium on Symbolic and Numeric Algorithms for Scientific Computing. IEEE, pp 189–196

80. Nielsen E, Gao X, Kalashnikova I, Muller RP, Salinger AG, Young RW (2013) QCAD simulation and optimization of semiconductor double quantum dots. Technical report. Sandia National Laboratories
81. Kelly A (2018) Simulating quantum computers using OpenCL. arXiv preprint arXiv:1805.00988
82. Zagorodko PV (2020) Research of possibilities of quantum programming for realization of tasks of machine learning. Doctoral dissertation
83. Juliá-Díaz B, Burdis JM, Tabakin F (2006) QDENSITY—a Mathematica quantum computer simulation. Comput Phys Commun 174(11):914–934
84. Moran CC (2016). Quintuple: a python 5-qubit quantum computer simulator to facilitate cloud quantum computing. arXiv preprint arXiv:1606.09225
85. Altenkirch T, Green AS (2010) The quantum IO monad. Semantic Tech Quantum Computation:173–205
86. Cross AW (2018) The IBM Q experience and QISKit open-source quantum computing software. In: APS March Meeting Abstracts, vol 2018. pp L58-003
87. Miller MD, Thornton MA (2006) QMDD: a decision diagram structure for reversible and quantum circuits. In: 36th International Symposium on Multiple-Valued Logic (ISMVL'06). IEEE, pp 30–30
88. Naeem W, Chuhdhry Y (2019) Q-Studio. Doctoral dissertation, Department of Computer Science, COMSATS University Islamabad, Lahore campus
89. Beals TR (2008) Quantum communication and information processing. University of California, Berkeley
90. Glos A, Miszczak JA, Ostaszweski M. QSWalk.jl: Julia package for quantum stochastic walks analysis. arXiv preprint arXiv:1801.01294
91. Feito A (2008) Quantavo: a maple toolbox for linear quantum optics. arXiv preprint arXiv:0806.2171
92. Terörde M (2019) Registry-Spuren verursacht durch die Quantenprogrammiersprache Q
93. Dekant H, Tregillus H, Tucci R, Yin T (2019). artiste-qb-net/quantum-fog: Python tools for analyzing both classical 29 and quantum Bayesian Networks [Electronic resource]. https://github.com/artiste-qb-net/quantum-fog
94. Ivancova O, Korenkov V, Tyatyushkina O, Ulyanov S, Fukuda T (2020) Quantum supremacy in end-to-end intelligent IT. Pt. I: Quantum software engineering-quantum gate level applied models simulators. Syst Anal Sci Educ 1:52–84
95. Amy M, Gheorghiu V (2020) staq-a full-stack quantum processing toolkit. Quantum Sci Technol
96. Hincks N, Granade CE, Borneman T, Cory DG (2015) Controlling quantum devices with nonlinear hardware. Physical Rev Appl 4(2):024012
97. Tóth G (2008) QUBIT4MATLAB V3.0: a program package for quantum information science and quantum optics for MATLAB. Comput Phys Commun 179(6):430–437
98. Jones T, Brown A, Bush I, Benjamin SC (2019) QuEST and high performance simulation of quantum computers. Scientific Rep 9(1):1–11
99. Patrzyk J (2014) Graphical and programming support for simulations of quantum computations. Master of Science Thesis supervised by Katarzyna Rycerz
100. Patrzyk J, Patrzyk B, Rycerz K, Bubak M (2015) Towards a novel environment for simulation of quantum computing. Comput Sci 16(1):103–129
101. Kottmann JS, Alperin-Lea S, Tamayo-Mendoza T, Cervera-Lierta A, Lavigne C, Yen T-C, Verteletskyi V, Schleich P, Anand A, Degroote M, Chaney S, Kesibi M, Curnow NG, Solo B, Tsilimigkounakis G, Zendejas-Morales C, Izmaylov AF, Aspuru-Guzik A (2020) TEQUILA: a platform for rapid development of quantum algorithms. arXiv:2011.03057v1
102. Gill SS, Kumar A, Singh H, Singh M, Kaur K, Usman M, Buyya R (2020) Quantum computing: a taxonomy, systematic review and future directions. arXiv preprint arXiv:2010.15559

103. Hevia JL, Peterssen G, Ebert C, Piattini M (2021) Quantum computing. IEEE Softw 38(5): 7–15
104. Farhi E, Goldstone J, Gutmann S (2014) A quantum approximate optimization algorithm. arXiv preprint arXiv:1411.4028
105. LaRose R (2019) Overview and comparison of gate level quantum software platforms. Quantum 3:130
106. Piattini M, Serrano M, Pérez-Castillo R, Peterssen G, Hevia JL (2021) Towards a quantum software engineering. IT Professional, IEEE 23(1):62–66. https://doi.org/10.1109/MITP.2020. 3019522
107. Piattini M, Peterssen G, Pérez-Castillo R (2020) Quantum computing: a new software engineering golden age. ACM SIGSOFT Softw Eng Newsl 45(3):12–14

Chapter 13
Quantum Software Development with QuantumPath®

Guido Peterssen, Jose Luis Hevia, and Mario Piattini

13.1 Introduction

As David Deutsch states: "Quantum theory is the most profound explanation known to science. It violates many of the assumptions of common sense and all previous science ... And yet this seemingly strange territory is the reality of which we and all that we experience are a part. There is no other" [1]. This new, astonishing physics theory describes the behavior of matter at subatomic levels (photons, electrons, etc.). Quantum computers are based on the principles of this theory, such as superposition and entanglement, and they seek to boost computational power exponentially. In fact, many problems that have until now been impossible to solve, in practical terms, might very well be able to be addressed by means of quantum computing [2]. Therefore, interesting developments are taking place in cryptography, artificial intelligence, communications, optimization, pharmacology, medicine, chemistry, materials development, etc. [3].

As several experts point out, if the nineteenth century can be considered the machine age, and the twentieth century the information age, the twenty-first century will be the quantum age. For our part, we are confident that quantum computing may become the main driver of a new "golden age" of software engineering [4]. However, developing quantum software today is difficult, because software engineers have to do with a new technological and programming paradigm. There is also a wide variety of quantum programming languages [5], many quantum development

G. Peterssen · J. L. Hevia (✉)
aQuantum, Alhambra IT, Madrid, Spain
e-mail: guido.peterssen@alhambrait.com; jluis.hevia@alhambrait.com

M. Piattini
aQuantum, Alarcos Research Group, Institute of Technologies and Information Systems, University of Castilla-La Mancha, Ciudad Real, Spain
e-mail: mario.piattini@uclm.es

© The Author(s), under exclusive license to Springer Nature Switzerland AG 2022   251
M. A. Serrano et al. (eds.), *Quantum Software Engineering*,
https://doi.org/10.1007/978-3-031-05324-5_13

environments [6], a wide variety of types of quantum simulators and hardware, and there is still no methodology for developing high-quality quantum software. In this context, it is easy to understand the enormous difficulties to overcome in the creation of "universal" competencies for the development of quantum software.

For those (like us) for whom the future of quantum computing is already here, the challenge to contribute to the acceleration of the development of commercial quantum software is to overcome, as soon as possible and in multiple ways, these enormous obstacles which, by their complexity, they will hardly have an immediate social and cultural solution.

In this chapter, we present QuantumPath® (QPath®), which is a quantum software development platform to support the design, implementation, and execution of quantum software applications.[1]

The rest of the chapter is organized as follows: Sect. 13.2 provides an overview of the QPath® platform principles and functionalities. Section 13.3 summarizes offers some of the advantages of QPath®. An example of QPath® use is shown in Sect. 13.4. Section 13.5 presents the conclusions and future work.

13.2   QPath® Principles and Functionalities

When creating QPath®, we set out to follow the following principles:

- Agnosticism, in the sense that the platform shall support both quantum gate-based and annealing technology.
- Extensibility. Since quantum technologies are in the process of continuous research and evolution, it is necessary that the system can adapt to change through a complete and well-designed model of extensions.
- Integration, an environment that will enable the integration of quantum/classical (hybrid) information systems.
- Independency, i.e., an environment that shall make programmers independent of the specific details of each platform and language, following the principle of "write once, run everywhere." Therefore, it masks the complexities of the different environments by supporting the necessary transformations and automating the whole process through efficient tools.
- Optimization, because the environment shall collect and analyze all the stored telemetry.
- Scalability, the environment shall be scalable. It shall be deployed in as many servers as necessary to guarantee a growth according to the number of users and processes generated.

---

[1] https://www.quantumpath.es/

- Security. The system shall be designed to be secure. It shall provide secure accesses to the service layers, as well as guarantees the protection of the system assets.
- Software engineering because the platform shall support the quantum software life cycle and its engineering.
- Usability, i.e., the platform shall help visually design the quantum assets of the application and define the environment's requirements and explore the results using a unified scheme, without worrying about the language of quantum computers.

QPath® is an ecosystem of tools, services, and processes—gathered on a platform—that offers a complete and complex hybrid information system that allows and execute quantum processing units regardless of the environment in which they run, abstracting the classic application from the complexities that characterize them.

To fully comply with your accommodation, QPath® is composed of two large functional units:

- CORE Modules, the core of the QuantumPath platform, capable of managing solutions independent of quantum technology assisted by general purpose tools
- The APPs platform, which integrates with the CORE modules of the QPath® system and makes it easier for development teams to manage the life cycle of hybrid software projects

The QPath® Core offers different functionalities, which we summarize in the next sections.

13.2.1   Management of Solutions and Their Assets

QPath® includes all the elements necessary to compose a "quantum application": (application) solution and its relationships to the quantum execution context in which it will unfold; quantum circuits and their different approaches depending on the type of technology used; direct code units, when more direct contact with a particular machine is required; intermediate language treatment of the assets of a quantum application; and main flows for the coordination of the all necessary elements that make up an algorithm and organizes its execution control. All the data elements stored in the cloud system are stored encrypted from origin to storage, to fulfil the privacy of knowledge premise of the product at all levels.

13.2.2   Tools for the Design of Quantum Assets

QPath® consists of several tools both from the context of agnostic and platform-specific solutions.

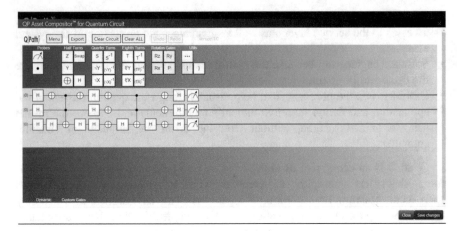

Fig. 13.1 Circuit editor of QPath®

13.2.2.1 Circuit Editor

The circuit editor allows the graphical design (Fig. 13.1) of quantum gate circuits through a web user interface (UI) built upon the Quirk Quantum Circuit Simulator,[2] with drag and drop support to compose the circuit.

This editor will generate an intermediate QpIL language that will make it possible to launch algorithms based on quantum gate circuits on any quantum gate hardware.

13.2.2.2 Annealer Compositor

Annealer Compositor is a high-level tool that allows you to model optimization problems in a fully graphical and visual way (Fig. 13.2), without the need to use any programming language. The design of the optimization problem is simplified to the definition of four elements: parameters, auxiliary data, classes of variables, and rules. Once the editing is finished with the Annealer Compositor, the system compiles the circuit and generates the corresponding code in annealing metalanguage.

Once defined the basic metadata of an "annealing circuit" (name, description, etc.), which is how in QPath® these assets are called, the application allows us to edit the circuit with the Annealer Compositor.

This editor helps enormously in the modeling of an optimization problem, whose design is simplified to the definition of these four elements:

---

[2] https://algassert.com/quirk

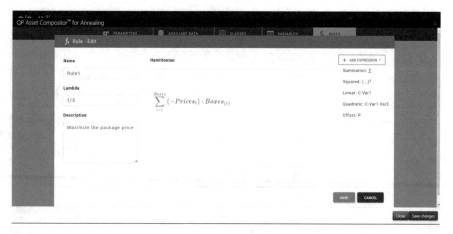

Fig. 13.2 Annealer compositor of QPath®

- Parameters. Variables with constant values that allow to parameterize some of the properties of the problem and that can be used in the Hamiltonians of the different rules or constraints of the problem
- Auxiliary data. Arrays of data, with values that can also be used in the Hamiltonians of the different rules of the problem
- Classes. Defines the different types of real variables involved in the problem
- Rules. Set of rules that model the objective function and constraints of the problem

Especially useful is the mathematical formula editor (Fig. 13.3) that simplifies the task of defining the Hamiltonians associated with the constraints of the problem.

Once the editing is finished with the Annealer Compositor, the system compiles the circuit and generates the corresponding code in annealing meta-language, a proprietary meta-language, which allows the definition of optimization problems, using the same logical structure as the Annealer Compositor.

13.2.2.3   Flow Editor

As with a classical solution, we can take circuits as components that need to be orchestrated in an application where there can be multiple steps. So, to have an application in which to launch the circuits, we will need to define a flow using the editor shown. The flow has the responsibility of coordinating the way in which the circuits and all the elements that QPath® will be executed and coordinating (see Fig. 13.4).

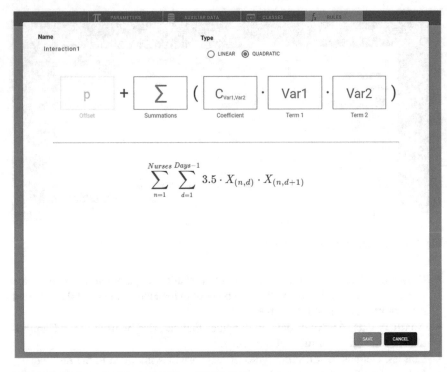

Fig. 13.3 Mathematical formula editor of QPath®

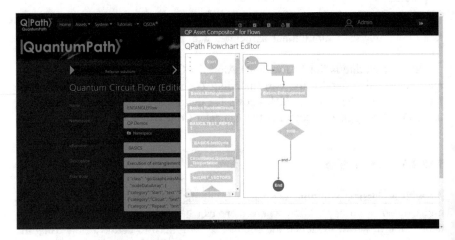

Fig. 13.4 Flow editor of QPath®

Fig. 13.5   DirectCode Asset editor

13.2.2.4   Direct Code Editor

QPath®'s DirectCode editor (Fig. 13.5) allows to create pieces of code for a specific hardware, taking advantage of all the potential of the hardware provider. Using this tool, a user can write the circuit in the same language understood by a specific technology (e.g., QASM for Qiskit, OCEAN for D-Wave, etc.). To simplify this process, and make the code "semi-agnostic," the DirectCode editor will let the user to write the code inside a module abstraction and provide managed items that will be integrated into the pipeline of QPath®. Fulfilling a small set of requisites, the defined code will be independent of the final provider target.

The DirectCode, finally, will encapsulate the defined code as a standard circuit to be used into the main pipeline of QPath®.

13.2.3   Connection Points and qSOA

QPath® makes possible the interconnection of quantum applications in an ecosystem of classic solutions. Using a clear publishing service (Fig. 13.6), a concise layer of REST API services is provided that allows any classic application to consume quantum algorithms stored in the system with minimal effort or create new ones using and injecting the QPath® IL.

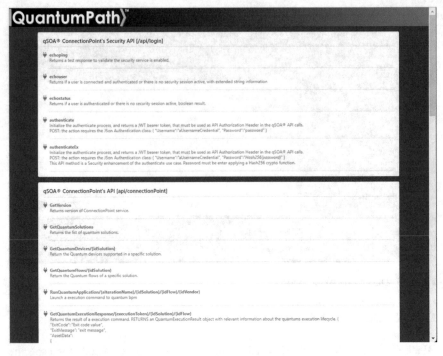

Fig. 13.6 QSOA API REST Fast Help

For example, the following Connection Point probes whether the job token of the identified solution and application has been completed and its outcome: (/api/connectionPoint/GetQuantumExecutionResponse/jobtoken/idSolution/idFlow)

```
HTTP GET HEADERS
content-type: application/json
Authorization: Bearer tokenJWT
RESPONSE
{
"ExitCode": "OK",
"ExitMessage": null,
"ExecutionData": {
"Solution": "WEBINARAnneal",
     "Flow": "BoxFlows",
"Device": "dwave_ExactSolver_simulator",
     "Histogram": histogram struct ",
     "Duration": 157226789
}
}
```

QPath® supports the qSOA (Quantum Service Oriented Architecture) based on connection points, which facilitates the creation of new layers of quantum services

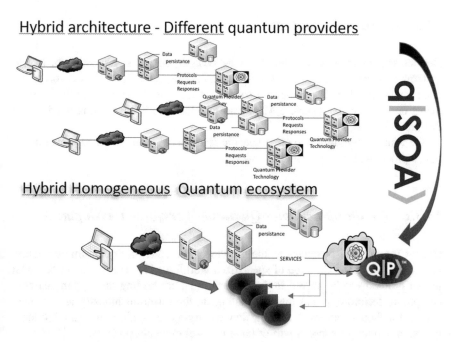

Fig. 13.7   qSOA of QPath®

and their integration into classical systems using a clear homogeneous and secure API based on well-known open protocols and data format. This qSOA (Fig. 13.7) therefore avoids to design, build, and test new integrations with the cloud API of every quantum provider. Some examples of the operation of this architecture can be found in https://www.aquantum.es/resources/webinars/.

13.2.4   Enterprise Backend

The backend is responsible for the complete operation of the platform, a backend that—by design—contemplates security, high availability, load balancing, and asynchronous customer processing. Fully scalable and reliable, it provides the necessary components for all work to be processed in a decoupled way to the customer and able to launch the execution units in the best possible context. This backend manages the approved connections to suppliers of quantum simulators and quantum computers, and that will collect all the telemetry from the process, providing knowledge and automatic assistance wherever needed.

QPath® allows the user to work with different quantum technologies such as those from IBM, Microsoft, Rigetti, D-Wave, AWS Braket, and Fujitsu, as well as with third-party quantum computing simulators such as QuTech or CTIC.

13.3 QPath® Advantages

Besides the advantages derived from its design principles, agnosticism, hybrid systems support, integration of third-party solutions, etc., QPath® also solves the main challenges faced by quantum software platforms [7] and fulfils the requirements derived for the Talavera Manifesto for Quantum Software Engineering and Programming [8].

We want to highlight two other specific features of QPath® related to workforce development and quality issues.

13.3.1 QPath® Facilitates Quantum Workforce Development

One of the greatest obstacles to the growth of the emerging quantum computing industry today is the shortage of specialized workforce [9]. This is one of the most urgent problems to be solved in the countries that are leading the race in quantum computing technology and that are betting on the quantum industry as a growth engine for their economies. In fact, they are trying, designing, and running large quantum literacy projects as part of huge national quantum projects.

Bearing in mind, among other issues, this situation regarding the lack of workforce required for the development of commercial quantum software, QPath® facilitates the work of engineers and programmers in the development of quantum software that does not demand "universal" skills for the development of high-quality quantum software since it enables the quantum software life cycle and engineering and the integration of quantum/classical information systems with its ecosystem of tools, services, and processes that makes it possible to execute quantum process units in a transparent way with respect to the quantum environment in which they are executed. So, QPath® supports multidisciplinary teams, allowing them to focus only on the functional knowledge required for the quantum solution in any field of activity: Chemistry, Economy, Financial Services, Energy, Agriculture, Medicine and Health, Privacy and Cryptography, Logistics, Defense and National Security, etc.

All existing quantum providers add extensive repositories of information, code, algorithms, training materials, and a long list of other types of resources that greatly facilitate access to their quantum technologies. But they are only valid for working in their environments, so if you must change the environment, you will need to learn how to work in the new one and re-develop quantum algorithms and applications from scratch. Something similar happens in the acquisition of the knowledge required to develop with these toolkits.

QPath® contributes effectively to the rapid incorporation of a specialized workforce to the deficient market of quantum developers, thanks to its truly agnostic architecture, designed to simplify the work of quantum software developers and, through their activity in the life cycles of the projects, actively contribute to ongoing global quantum literacy in a direct and practical way.

Besides this, QPath® developers have at their disposal aQuantum Knowledge,[3] a portal with contents, materials, technical support, user forums, etc. focused on institutions, companies, and professionals to initiate and accelerate the adoption of the development of quality quantum algorithms and software for the real world.

13.3.2   QPath® Solves the Quality Problems of Quantum Computing Platforms

QPath® further solves most of the quality problems of quantum computing platforms [10]:

- Lower level of the programming abstractions, which increases code complexity impacting in maintainability, testability, reliability, and availability
- Platform heterogeneity, which deteriorates software cohesion, affecting maintainability, reliability, robustness, reusability, and the manageability and testability of the system
- Remote software development and deployment, which make programming, testing, and debugging quantum programs slower affecting maintainability and testability
- Dependency on the known quantum algorithms, affecting the ability to perform enhancement and corrective maintenance, and testability and interoperability (with classical software)
- Limited portability of software, which provokes the lack of standardization in several areas, affecting availability, interoperability, maintainability, and scalability
- Lack of native quantum operating system, decreasing performance, manageability, reliability, scalability, and security
- Fundamentally different programming model, which can increase code complexity affecting maintainability, interoperability, security, and testability

QPath® solves most of the previous mention quality problems of quantum computing platforms, since:

- Lower level of the programming abstractions: QPath® is agnostic about quantum programming languages and technologies, supporting visual designers of gates-based circuits and the Annealer Compositor.
- Platform heterogeneity: QPath® provides the necessary tools for the development team to focus on the development of the solution without having to worry about the specificities of quantum platforms and their necessary requirement.

---

[3] aQuantum Knowledge.

- Remote software development and deployment: QPath® offers a complete set of tools for the design, construction, testing, and execution of quantum assets both from the context of agnostic and platform-specific solutions.
- Dependency on the known quantum algorithms: QPath® supports the creation of new quantum algorithms through its development, testing, and implementation, to their deployment and the reuse of the existing ones. Extensibility capacity in the main and critical modules of the platform. So that it is possible to attach to the platform new connectors supported by partner and third-party technologies, which expand the value added of the product.
- Limited portability of software: QPath® allows you to create your quantum application assets and set the environment's requirements, let the underground details to the system, from model to results, the lifecycle path is automatic). QPath® follows the principle of "write once, run everywhere."
- Lack of native quantum operating system: QPath®'s enterprise backend contemplates—by design—the security, high availability, load balancing, and asynchronous customer processing.
- Fundamentally different programming model: QPath® is a platform designed to support the integration of hybrid classical/quantum software and therefore contains the necessary tools to facilitate the integration of classical software with quantum computing. Moreover, QPath® makes it easy for classic development teams to manage hybrid software projects life cycle.

For all these reasons, QPath® is an excellent platform for the development of quality practical quantum software, which integrates transparently with the main quantum computers solving most of the quality problems of quantum computing platforms.

13.4   Example of Quantum Development with QPath®

Imagine we want to add a simple QRNG (Quantum Random Number Generator) into a Navision data form, using a preconfigured quantum provider into NAV environment. To do that, we start defining the solution and the assets into QPath® (Fig. 13.8).

After that, we define the QNRG using the circuit editor (Fig. 13.9).

And we must compose the corresponding flow (Fig. 13.10).

And then we can execute it and, selecting different quantum machines, explore the results (Fig. 13.11).

On the other side, we have to extend Navision using the qSOA REST API (Fig. 13.12). After that, we use the Navision QPath Setup Dialog (custom NAV

Fig. 13.8 Example in QPath®: defining the solution and the assets

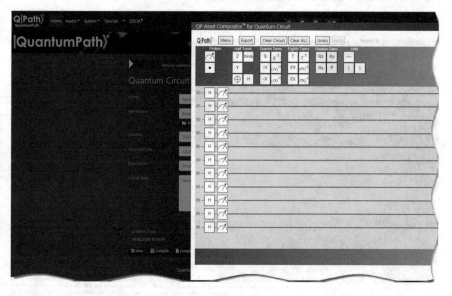

Fig. 13.9 Example in QPath®: defining the QNRG

extensions developed), as shown in Fig. 13.13. In Fig. 13.14, customer pending data to validate and seal with hash is shown with the QRNG numbers obtained dialog. Finally, the customers that have been validated and sealed have a hash generated with the QRNG returned using a developed protocol (Fig. 13.15).

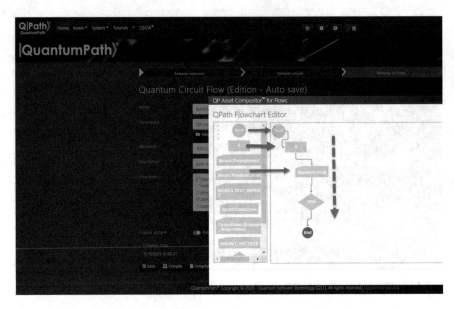

Fig. 13.10 Example in QPath®: composing the flow

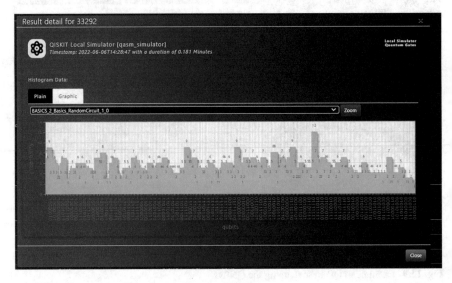

Fig. 13.11 Example in QPath®: executing the QNRG

In this example, all the executions have been recorded with telemetry, and the results have been applied into the NAV data with a really known software architecture. It should be noted that if the QRNG will improve over time, Navision could execute the call more accurately and better without modifying any code.

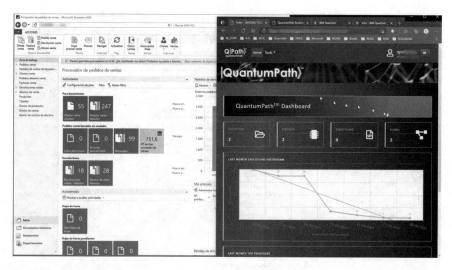

Fig. 13.12 Example in QPath®: main Navision dashboard

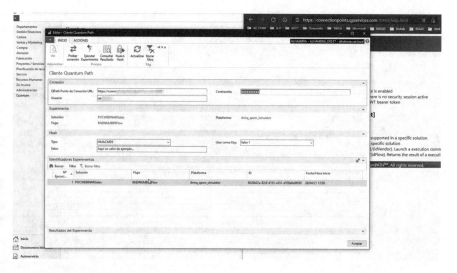

Fig. 13.13 Example in QPath®: Navision QPath® setup dialog

13.5   Conclusions and Future Work

We are convinced that the development of the quantum industry will not have a
future at a social scale if it only depends on the essential quantum scientists,
mathematicians, and physicists, as in its time the classical computing industry

Fig. 13.14 Example in QPath®: QRNG numbers obtained dialog

Fig. 13.15 Example in QPath®: customers with a hash generated by the QRNG

would not have had the current success if it had only depended on cybernetic engineers.

As with classical computing, it will be software engineers and programmers, in interaction with users and the market, who will end up defining how and for what quantum computing will be used when developing practical commercial applications that will contribute to it, first, its usefulness and, progressively, its universality.

In recent years, quantum computing has experienced a breakthrough. More and more companies are taking up the challenge of designing and manufacturing quantum computers, and the supply of tools for quantum software development is growing all the time.

The problem that arises, and more in these moments of rapid evolution and lack of standardization in quantum programming, is the fear of betting on a platform that does not continue in the future. All this leads companies to slow the adoption of quantum applications, which is dangerous because the use of quantum technologies can lead to a relatively important period of learning and experimentation. In addition to not being able to take advantage of all the benefits offered by this new paradigm in a timely manner.

But we are already in the fourth era of software development, and so we must prepare ourselves to take full advantage of it. The "Talavera Manifesto" urges to take care of producing quantum software by applying knowledge and lessons learned from the software engineering field. This implies to apply or adapt the existing software engineering processes, methods, techniques, practices, and principles for the development of quantum software (or it may imply creating new ones). Precisely, one of the great advantages that quantum computing offers us is the opportunity to experience what the pioneers of software engineering did in the 1960s of the last century [11].

This has been one of the main challenges we faced when creating QPath®, as a Quantum Software Development and Application Lifecycle Platform. QPath® proposes an environment that makes programmers independent of the specific details of each platform and language, following the principle of "write once, run everywhere." In this way, QPath® supports the execution of quantum process units transparently from the environment in which they are executed. Therefore, it masks the complexities of the different environments by supporting the necessary transformations and automating the whole process through efficient tools.

This allows to accelerate the construction and deployment of quantum applications, abstracting their technical complexities, since programmers can focus on the domain of the problem or business model, needing only the functional knowledge required for the solution.

As future work, we are working in the APP platform, which integrates with the CORE modules of the QPath® system and makes it easier for development teams to manage the life cycle of hybrid software project.

We believe that in this way, QPath® can significantly contribute to the adoption of quantum technologies and specifically enable companies to develop and deploy applications based on these technologies, safeguarding their investments. As Latorre [12] already warned: "The future quantum business will grow, whether we like it or not, because the future of our technology is quantum."

Acknowledgments This work is part of "QHealth: Quantum Pharmacogenomics Applied to Aging," 2020 CDTI Missions Programme (Center for the Development of Industrial Technology of the Ministry of Science and Innovation of Spain) and FEDER. We would like to thank all the aQuantum members for their help and support.

References

1. Deutsch D (2012) Beginning of infinity: explanations that transform the world. Penguin Books, London
2. Aaronson S (2018) The limits of quantum computers. Sci Am March:62–69
3. IDB (2019) Quantum technologies. Digital transformation, social impact, and cross-sector disruption. Interamerican Development Bank
4. Piattini M, Peterssen G, Pérez-Castillo R (2020) Quantum computing: a new software engineering golden age. ACM SIGSOFT Softw Eng Notes 45(3)
5. Piattini M, Serrano M, Pérez-Castillo R, Peterssen G, Hevia JL (2021) Towards a quantum software engineering. IT Prof 23(1):62–66. https://doi.org/10.1109/MITP.2020.3019522
6. Hevia JL, Peterssen G, Ebert C, Piattini M (2021) Quantum Software Development toolkits. Submitted to IEEE Software
7. Hevia JL (2020) Requirements for quantum software platforms. Q-SET'20: 1st Quantum Software Engineering and Technology Workshop, Denver—Broomfield, CO, 13 Oct 2020. CEDUR-Ws.org/Vol-2705/short3.pdf
8. Piattini M, Peterssen G, Pérez-Castillo R, Hevia JL et al (2020) The Talavera manifesto for quantum software engineering and programming. QANSWER 2020 QuANtum SoftWare Engineering & pRogramming. Proceedings of the 1st International Workshop on the QuANtum SoftWare Engineering & pRogramming, Talavera de la Reina, Spain, 11–12 Feb 2020. http://ceur-ws.org/Vol-2561/paper0.pdf
9. Peterssen G (2020) Quantum technology impact: the necessary workforce for developing quantum software. Proceedings of the 1st International Workshop on the QuANtum SoftWare Engineering & pRogramming (QANSWER), Talavera de la Reina, Spain, 11–12 Feb 2020
10. Sodhi B, Kapur R (2021) Quantum computing platforms: assessing impact on quality attributes and SDLC activities (Accepted in ICSA 2021). https://doi.org/10.13140/RG.2.2.20190.66886/1
11. Cusumano M (2018) Technology strategy and management. The business of quantum computing. Commun ACM 61(10):20–22
12. Latorre JI (2017) Cuántica. Tu futuro en juego. Ariel. (In Spanish), Barcelona

Chapter 14
Quantum Software Development with Classiq

Nir Minerbi

14.1 The Hardware Race Is On, But What About Software?

The quantum hardware race has started: companies such as IBM, Intel, Google, Honeywell, Xanadu, IonQ, Rigetti, and Alibaba are racing to build ever-more-powerful quantum computers. IBM, for instance, is promising[1] over 400 qubits in 2022 and over 1000 qubits in 2023.

As important as the hardware is, the software is also critical in powering a quantum revolution. Without powerful software, quantum computing will fail to deliver on its promise, just like classical computers are practically useless without a robust operating system and software infrastructure.

14.2 The Limitations of Today's Software Development Tools

Today, however, the process of developing quantum software is in its infancy. Quantum programming languages like Q# from Microsoft, Qiskit from IBM, or Cirq from Google primarily operate at the gate level. The programmer essentially specifies which qubit is connected to what quantum gate, almost like connecting a giant switchboard. Such languages also offer certain building blocks, but if a required building block is not yet implemented, the user needs to specify the exact sequence of interconnections between qubits and quantum gates. Even if a building

---

[1] https://research.ibm.com/blog/quantum-development-roadmap

N. Minerbi (✉)
Classiq Technologies, Tel Aviv, Israel
e-mail: nir@classiq.io

© The Author(s), under exclusive license to Springer Nature Switzerland AG 2022   269
M. A. Serrano et al. (eds.), *Quantum Software Engineering*,
https://doi.org/10.1007/978-3-031-05324-5_14

block is available—such as a Grover search—the user still needs to build custom code. In the case of a Grover search, the user needs to build the oracle, and that is done at the gate level. If the user wishes to design a completely new algorithm, that new algorithm also has to be coded at the gate level.

This process is similar to creating a digital circuit by laboriously placing AND, OR, and NOT logical gates. It is a useful tool to educate newcomers on the inner workings of gates, but it fails to scale: such a process works when there are a few dozen logical gates, but it is practically impossible to scale to thousands of gates or beyond.

14.3   The Unfortunate Side Effect of Gate-Level Development Tools

When it is difficult to create sophisticated quantum software, it becomes difficult to find quantum software engineers. To use today's methods, quantum software engineers need to be experts in quantum information theory and have a working understanding of quantum physics as well as a proficiency in linear algebra.

Such resumes are hard to find and are typically PhD-level graduates of major universities. As talented as these folks are, they typically lack domain expertise in molecular biology, option pricing, supply-chain optimization, or any other domain-specific field. Because writing new algorithms at the gate level is difficult, it is also challenging to integrate non-quantum experts into quantum teams.

14.4   Finding a Historical Analogy

Earlier, we compared quantum programming to the process of designing of digital circuits. The evolution of digital circuit design served as inspiration to the Classiq team in formulating our approach to software development.

An Intel 8086 processor has about 29,000 transistors, whereas a modern i7 has over 4 billion transistors.[2] These processors and many other complex chips were not designed at the gate level. While an electronic engineer can undoubtedly put together a working circuit with 20–30 logical gates, creating the Netlist even for an 8086 chip by hand is simply impossible.

However, providing a high-level functional model to a computer and asking the computer to convert this into a working circuit is most certainly possible. Design languages like VHDL came to the rescue. With VHDL, Verilog, and similar hardware description languages, a human designer describes the desired high-level

---

[2] https://en.wikipedia.org/wiki/Transistor_count

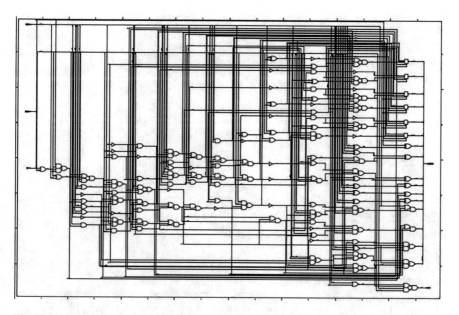

Fig. 14.1 Example of a transistor circuit

functionality, and a computer synthesizes this high-level description into detailed gate interconnections.

Such languages have made it possible to design truly complex circuits and to effectively debug and maintain them. High-level languages also promote code reuse so that the figurative wheel does not need to be reinvented every time.

For instance, consider the following circuit[3] (Fig. 14.1):

Such a circuit might look difficult to understand, debug, and maintain, but when exploring the VHDL code that described this circuit (and was used to generate it), these tasks seem much less daunting (Fig. 14.2):

At Classiq, we believe in applying a VHDL-like approach to quantum computing. While the particular elements of the language will be very different from the electronic design equivalent, we believe users will achieve the same benefits: being able to design sophisticated quantum circuits, which perhaps could not be designed otherwise.

We call this concept "quantum algorithm design."

---

[3] Source: Bob Reese, Mississippi State University http://esd.cs.ucr.edu/labs/tutorial/

```
Library IEEE;
use IEEE.std_logic_1164.all;
use work.iscas.all;
entity adder_cs is
port (
  signal a,b: in std_logic_vector (15 downto 0);
  signal cin: in std_logic;
  signal sum: out std_logic_vector(15 downto 0);
  signal cout: out std_logic
);
 end adder_cs;
architecture behavior of adder_cs is
 begin
   process (a,b,cin)
   variable temp_sum: std_logic_vector (sum'range);
   variable temp_cout: std_logic;
   constant groups: iarray(0 to 2) := (4,5,7);
   begin
    carry_select_adder(groups,a,b,cin,temp_sum, temp_cout);
    sum <= temp_sum;
    cout <= temp_cout;
   end process;
 end behavior;
```

Fig. 14.2 VHDL code of the previous circuit

14.5   What Is Quantum Algorithm Design?

Quantum algorithm design (QAD) is the quantum version of computer-aided design (CAD). With QAD, quantum software engineers and scientists innovate and produce much faster than ever before. Like in traditional computer-aided design, QAD users achieve extraordinary results by letting computers handle the things that computers are good at, freeing users to think, invent, and innovate.

14.6   What Does Classiq Do?

Classiq's quantum algorithm design platform automatically synthesizes complete quantum circuits from high-level functional models. What does this mean? It means that within seconds, an engineer can transform a high-level functional description into a working quantum circuit. For instance, here is a code fragment that implements quantum arithmetic (Fig. 14.3):

Fig. 14.3 Quantum
arithmetic code fragment

```
{
    "qubits_count": 12,
    "min_depth": 1,
    "max_depth": 10,
    "segments": [
        {
            "function": "ArithmeticExpression",
            "qubits_count": 12,
            "symbolic_statement": "(a+b) * (a-b)",
            "register_sizes": {"a": 2, "b": 2},
            "optimization_criteria": "depth",
            "add_as_single_gate": false
        }
    ]
}
```

Quantum algorithm design synthesizes a quantum circuit from this high-level functionality while meeting the designer-specified constraints (more on constraints later). Such a circuit is shown below.

Such a circuit would be very difficult to generate by hand but is much easier to generate using the quantum algorithm design approach (Fig. 14.4).

14.7 Where Does Quantum Algorithm Design Fit in the Quantum Software Stack?

The Classiq QAD engine ingests a high-level functional model of the desired quantum circuit and a constraints file. It can output code in various quantum languages, including Qiskit, Q#, Cirq, and more. Furthermore, it includes pre-configured integrations into most major quantum cloud providers, including IBM, Amazon Braket, and Azure Quantum (Fig. 14.5).

The output of the Classiq engine is an agnostic quantum circuit, described in any gate-level programming language. Compilers and transpilers ingest that output and adapt it to the hardware of choice.

The ability to output code in various formats and be compatible with a variety of cloud providers means that it is very easy to port code from one hardware target to another. These days, when the industry is still in development, some companies are

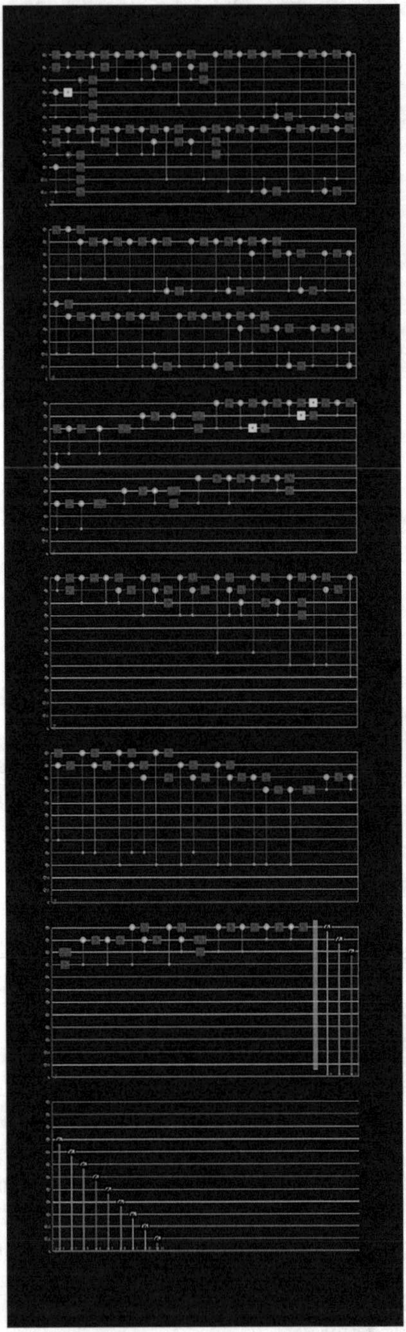

Fig. 14.4 Generated quantum circuit

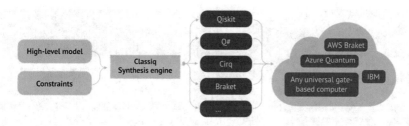

Fig. 14.5 QAD in a quantum software stack

hesitant to commit to any particular hardware architecture. Thus, the ability to deploy quantum circuits across a wide range of hardware backends is essential.

14.8   How Is QAD Different from a Compiler?

The Classiq quantum algorithm design platform does not replace quantum compilers or transpilers. Compilers ingest the output of the Classiq platform and have an important role to perform, adapting the code to the particular hardware-specific connectivity and available gates.

Where QAD adds significant value is in system-level optimization and in satisfying the constraints dictated by the designer.

A compiler can perform specific optimizations because it understands the connectivity and properties of the target hardware. A compiler can also perform local optimizations such as eliminating two back-to-back Hadamard gates.

QAD, in contrasts, provides system-level optimizations. For instance, when creating a circuit for quantum arithmetic, QAD can preserve intermediate values if they are used downstream or recover the qubits that hold them and use them for some other purposes. QAD can do that because it understands the intent of the algorithm designer. A compiler that looks at a concrete gate-level quantum circuit (in QASM or another format) cannot.

QAD platforms analyze thousands upon thousands of options to come up with the optimal solution. This level of analysis and optimization simply does not exist in compilers.

14.9   What Are Constraints in the QAD Context?

Just like different people consider different constraints and wishes when they buy a home, different quantum designers have different constraints that they want to impose on the output circuit. These could be driven by hardware constraints, personal preference, or a host of other reasons.

Here are some of the constraints that the QAD platform can handle:

```
{} load-probs.clsq  ×

examples  >  {} load-probs.clsq  >  ...
   1    {
   2        "qubits_count": 4,
   3        "max_depth": 100,
   4        "segments": [{
   5            "function": "StatePreparation",
   6            "function_params": {
   7                "probabilities": {"pmf":[0.05, 0.11, 0.13, 0.23, 0.27, 0.12, 0.03, 0.06]},
   8                "error_metric": {"KL": {"upper_bound": 0.001}}
   9            }
  10        }]
  11    }
```

Fig. 14.6 State preparation code loading probability mass functions

- The width and depth of the circuit. How many qubits can you use? How deep can the circuit be before errors creep in? A designer might want, for instance, to add qubits (increase the width) as a way of reducing the depth.
- The usage of particular types of gates or preferred gate sets. Suggestions from the target hardware vendor might drive this gate set.
- The desired accuracy. As can be seen later in this document, functional blocks such as state preparation can be built in a variety of ways depending on the desired accuracy.
- The connectivity of particular qubits, allowing to minimize the use of swap gates.

One of the unique capabilities of the Classiq platform is that it analyzes many thousands of options to find the best one that satisfies these constraints. The designer can change the constraints and regenerate the circuit to explore various options. Doing this by hand might take days, but with Classiq, it takes seconds.

For instance, the following state preparation code (loading probability mass functions) (Fig. 14.6):

Generates the following circuit (Fig. 14.7):

But since this circuit might be too deep, the designer might try to change the accuracy of the loaded states from 0.01 to 0.05 (Fig. 14.8):

Resulting in a simpler circuit (Fig. 14.9):

This demonstrates the division of labor that is so important in QAD: the designer defines the high-level functional model and the constraints and then lets the computer analyze thousands of options to find a circuit that implements this while meeting the constraints.

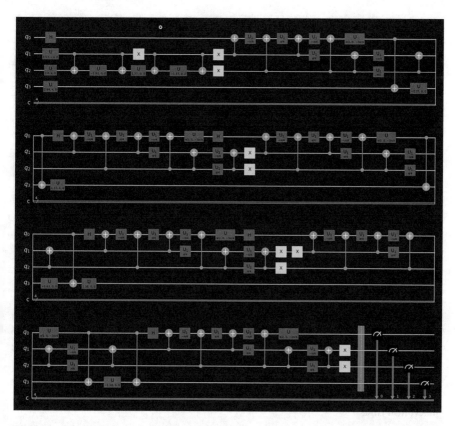

Fig. 14.7 Generated circuit from preparation code

```
{} load-probs.clsq  ●

examples > {} load-probs.clsq > [ ] segments > {} 0 > {} function_params > {} error_metric > {} KL > # upper_bound
 1   {
 2       "qubits_count": 4,
 3       "max_depth": 100,          I
 4       "segments": [{
 5           "function": "StatePreparation",
 6           "function_params": {
 7               "probabilities": {"pmf":[0.05, 0.11, 0.13, 0.23, 0.27, 0.12, 0.03, 0.06]},
 8               "error_metric": {"KL": {"upper_bound": 0.05}}
 9           }
10       }]
11   }
```

Fig. 14.8 Updated preparation code

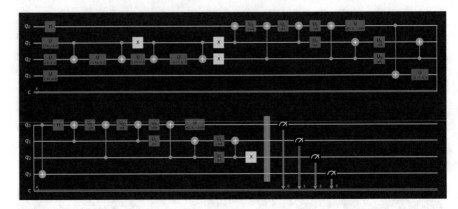

Fig. 14.9 New version of the circuit

14.10   Can the Constraints Always Be Met?

Of course not. It may be that the QAD platform cannot find a solution in a reasonable amount of time. This can happen when the platform indicates that the constraints are unsatisfactory, meaning that the engine proved mathematically that the requirements couldn't be met. Perhaps the number of qubits or depth of the circuit is too small, or other constraints make it impossible. In other cases, the synthesis may just take too long, and the user could elect to relax some of the constraints and shorten the circuit generation time.

14.11   What Are the Advantages of Quantum Algorithm Design?

Quantum algorithm design lets the designer focus on the algorithm's functionality instead of on the low-level implementation. This translates to substantial advantages both today and tomorrow:

"Today," when the quantum computers have a few or at most dozens of qubits, this approach provides dramatic time-saving. It also allows estimating the resources required to run a particular algorithm before spending too much time building it. It may be that some algorithms are just too complex for today's machines, and a quick way to determine this is beneficial.

"Tomorrow," when there will be hundreds or thousands of qubits, we believe that this approach will make the impossible possible. The complexity of these machines will be too much for even highly skilled quantum information scientists. The ability to generate sophisticated algorithms from high-level functional models will be paramount.

Both today and tomorrow, there is a significant advantage to be gained by making quantum more accessible. Just like a Web designer does not need to understand how a CMOS gate works, a quantum software engineer should not need to understand the intricacies of the hardware. By focusing on the functional requirements, teams can integrate experts from other fields. For instance, a financial option pricing expert might join a team using quantum computers for sophisticated pricing models. Similarly, supply-chain experts or chemists can join their company's quantum teams.

14.12 If QAD Is an Abstraction Layer, Are We Losing Optimization Capabilities?

It is true that if you are an expert in "to the metal" code, you could theoretically squeeze the last bit of optimization from your software. Still, QAD provides you with other critically important advantages, as well as optimizations that couldn't be reached otherwise. The synthesis engine also examines many possible solutions—more than a person could realistically examine—and chooses the optimal circuit.

One advantage is the ability to move your code between various hardware providers quickly. It is unclear which platforms will win, and organizations seek to mitigate risks by writing portable code.

Another advantage is that programming "to the metal" quickly becomes unfeasible with the growing complexity of quantum computers. Last, high-level functional code is much easier to debug and maintain than the equivalent of "quantum assembly language."

14.13 Don't Some Existing Tools Already Provide Building Blocks?

Existing development tools indeed provide some templates, for instance, for VQE. However, customizing those templates requires a lot of work. Search algorithms, for example, require an oracle function, and creating such functions is very easy with QAD yet impossible with any other current methods. A Monte Carlo option pricing circuit, for instance, might require a sophisticated payoff function which will be very difficult to create, debug, and maintain with standard development tools. But such a payoff function will be much easier to create with QAD.

Additionally, if one wishes to create an entirely new algorithm, QAD will make this process much easier.

14.14   The Quantum Future Is Bright

Progress in quantum computing hardware will not deliver the desired benefits without significant matching progress in software. Quantum algorithm design software makes it possible to implement more sophisticated algorithms on more advanced machines while also widening the available labor pool and allow domain-specific experts to work together with PhD-level quantum engineers.

If you have captured a beautiful photo but want to improve and clean it up, you probably don't want to do so pixel by pixel. Most would prefer using Photoshop or other photo editing software that allows users to specify *what* you want to be done and then automatically implement it at the pixel level.

Similarly, if your team members developed a new quantum algorithm, they don't want to code, debug, and maintain it gate by gate. The ability to synthesize quantum circuits from high-level functional models, while satisfying the constraints that are important to the designer, makes such a task both feasible and enjoyable. This is the vision that unites us at Classiq and the one we are working to bring to life.

Chapter 15
Quantum Software Frameworks for Deep Learning

Filipa Ramos Ferreira, João Paulo Fernandes, and Rui Abreu

15.1 Introduction

The exploration of the quantum mechanics phenomena for computational purposes promises to revolutionize the technological world we live in [1]. This is even more impressive as several areas are expected to benefit from the expansion of the limits that classical computing is known to impose.

Quantum computers have the power of providing solutions for some of the problems of practical interest for which a classical computer cannot, at least in a timely manner. Problems in this category range from multidisciplinary domains such as Chemistry, Medicine, Routing, or Finance [2]. As a matter of example, quantum computing is expected to take molecular modelling to an entirely new level of accuracy, as modelling energetic reactions using classical computers requires the use of approximations which reduce the value of a model and increase the amount of lab work that chemists need to do to validate it.[1]

---

[1] https://www.scientificamerican.com/article/how-quantum-computing-couldremake-chemistry/

F. Ramos Ferreira
Faculty of Engineering, University of Porto, Porto, Portugal
e-mail: filiparamos@fe.up.pt

J. P. Fernandes (✉)
Artificial Intelligence and Computer Science Laboratory, Faculty of Engineering, University of Porto, Porto, Portugal
e-mail: jpaulo@fe.up.pt

R. Abreu
Faculty of Engineering, University of Porto, Porto, Portugal

Instituto de Engenharia de Sistemas e Computadores: Investigacão e Desenvolvimento em Lisboa, Porto, Portugal
e-mail: rui@computer.org

© The Author(s), under exclusive license to Springer Nature Switzerland AG 2022 281
M. A. Serrano et al. (eds.), *Quantum Software Engineering*,
https://doi.org/10.1007/978-3-031-05324-5_15

For fairness, we should actually clarify that besides the theoretical advantages generally associated with quantum computing, we have already seen in practice concrete evidence of quantum computers largely outperforming classical computers. This is known as *quantum supremacy*, whose evidence have been reported before [3, 4].

In this chapter, we focus on the exploration of quantum computing in the context of deep learning. This is certainly a promising context as the properties of the Hilbert Space that can be used to mathematically formulate quantum mechanics ensure a theoretical advantage which allows performing computations in highly dimensional data. This is precisely the current bottleneck of the classical approach, and the potential of quantum-inspired approaches has led to an explosion of hybrid deep learning models being proposed in literature, such as [5, 6].

Even so, we must denote that several proposals of machine and deep learning algorithms are still purely grounded on a theoretical basis since they would require a full-scale quantum computer to be validated. For example, [7] develop a quantum neural network that performs MNIST classification. The training procedure is achieved through the down sampling of the images to 16 data bits still run on simulation due to the inaccessibility to a physical quantum computer with the required characteristics. Even more, classification is kept binary, filtering only two classes from the original dataset. Nevertheless, on such small-scaled experiments, there have been indications that some models can already present similar or even superior performance on simple tasks, when compared to their classical counterparts [8, 9].

The widespread use of quantum computing, however, still faces some significant hurdles, regardless of the application domain. For once, quantum physicists and computer engineers still face the challenge of reaching more accurate quantum gates: it is well known that current quantum computations are still heavily affected by noise [10]. In tandem, the number of physical qubits incorporated in quantum computing devices still needs to grow. Next, a very steep learning curve is assumed to be required for any programmer to become (even if minimally) productive in developing software that can leverage the quantum computing potential. In this chapter, we attempt to shed light on this second hurdle.

The main hypothesis for our work is that *a programmer can build on already existing quantum computing frameworks* such as IBM's *Qiskit*[2] or Google's *Cirq*[3] *to significantly accelerate the development of deep learning-based applications*.

Our vision is that, in order to achieve real-world application of quantum neural networks, or hybrid quantum-classical neural networks, mature tools, frameworks and libraries must be readily available [11]. This actually comes as no surprise in the classical context: such libraries and tools do exist for implementing classical workflows.

---

[2]https://qiskit.org/

[3]https://quantumai.google/cirq

The creation of frameworks or libraries that interact and abstract many gruesome processes within neural networks, such as backpropagation, loss calculation and evaluation, and many others, is vital for the future adoption of quantum deep learning. Libraries such as *PyTorch* [12] and *Tensorflow* [13] have propelled classical deep learning into wide adoption both in research and industry. The same adoption in the area of quantum-classical deep learning must be achieved in order to further advance the knowledge state and to cement its position as a truly disruptive field in application.

In our work, we therefore assume the mindset of a deep learning (classical) programmer who wants to leverage quantum computing components in their work. With this mindset, we designed and conducted an empirical study comparing *Qiskit* and *Cirq*, two highly popular frameworks that enable parametrized circuit construction. We compare their libraries and characteristics for hybrid model development from the perspective of a classical deep learning engineer or scientist.

Concerning libraries and tools for quantum-classical development, *Qiskit* offers integration with *PyTorch* [12], a tool already widely used in research on classical deep learning. On the other hand, *Cirq* integrates a framework, *Tensorflow Quantum* [14], which facilitates the development of circuit-based models while maintaining the structure of *Tensorflow* [13], another competitor tool widely used in the research and production of classical workflows.

We focus our comparative study on two widely adopted and validated architectures: generative adversarial neural networks (GANs) and convolutional neural networks (CNNs). We choose a generative modelling architecture due to its natural fit to quantum information theory. It is believed that GANs can be largely improved by the capabilities of quantum computers (e.g., [15]). On the other hand, we also choose convolutional neural networks since they are one of the building blocks of current deep learning research and provide state-of-the-art results on a wide range of tasks.

The main contributions of our chapter can be highlighted as:

- We study readily available infrastructures for the development of hybrid convolutional neural networks and generative adversarial neural networks on both Qiskit and Cirq, taking a classical-computing scientist perspective.
- We implement both deep learning architectures in both quantum computing frameworks.
- We compare the two frameworks for such implementation.

Overall, we seek to answer the following general research questions:

RQ1. What is the effort that a deep learning scientist needs to undertake to leverage quantum computing using readily available quantum components?

RQ2. What is the relative power and ease of use of two of the most popular quantum computing frameworks in the implementation of typical deep learning architectures?

From our work, we were able to synthesize the following conclusions:

- *Qiskit* enables an easier introduction for users with no quantum knowledge as they can replicate small models known to them and understand the majority of the process.
- *PyTorch* users also have an advantage when using *Qiskit* for model development as the workflow is seamlessly transferred.
- *Cirq* and *Tensorflow Quantum* present better structure and organization, thus being more intuitive for advanced development. We also find *Tensorflow Quantum* tutorials to provide more insight.
- *Tensorflow* users also have an advantage when transferring to *Tensorflow Quantum* as the workflow is the same.
- *Qiskit* includes a wide panoply of abstractions that allow for swift prototyping of applications. Nevertheless, versioning issues might be an obstacle for newcomers even when navigating the wide range of available tutorials.

To foster reproducibility, the code platform we developed is publicly available at https://github.com/FilipaRamos/QuantumComputingDeepLearning.git.

This chapter is organized as follows. In Sect. 15.2, we enumerate some available quantum frameworks, providing a more in-depth description of both *Qiskit* and *Cirq*, focusing on the libraries that are necessary for hybrid-classical deep learning development. In Sect. 15.3, we present a summary of previous studies on generative adversarial and convolutional neural networks, both in the quantum and classical context, including an analysis on research that analyses quantum frameworks and tools. Section 15.4 describes the implementation process of the chosen networks on both frameworks, including the description of implementation details with the highlighting of the most important abstractions and structures available. In Sect. 15.5, we delineate the evaluation parameters and proceed to describe our experience with both frameworks. Finally, in Sect. 15.6, we summarize the results stemming from the carried evaluation, with the identification of both advantages and disadvantages for each framework and respective deep learning library while finalizing with some directions for future work.

15.2 Quantum Computing Background

The advent of quantum computing has been accompanied by the insurgence of several languages and frameworks that allow the creation of parametrized circuits and thus propel innovation in the field. While the dawn of quantum computing was associated with the creation of new stand-alone languages, such as the pioneer Quantum Computation Language (QCL) [16, 17], current research has been focused on using an already existent and established language, Python, for which several framework-style quantum computing packages have been created.

The division of available tools for quantum computing can thus be delineated in two distinct groups—that of stand-alone languages and that of packages for the existent Python language. Within the stand-alone languages, one can find diversified types such as imperative, functional, and multi-paradigm languages. QCL, previously mentioned, falls within the imperative paradigm, as well as QGCL [18], a self-entitled extension of Dijkstra's GCL. On the functional paradigm, QML [19] and Quipper [20] can be highlighted. As for multi-paradigm languages, Q# [21], from Microsoft, and more recently Silq [22] can be found. As for Python-based package frameworks, the aforementioned *Cirq* and *Qiskit* are the standouts; however, there are other existent packages such as Ocean[4] from D-Wave.

We focus our research on *Qiskit* and *Cirq* not simply due to their increased popularity and accessibility, but especially due to their interaction with two of the most widely used classical deep learning libraries, *Pytorch* and *Tensorflow*. This stems from the fact that we aim to provide an introductory outlet for classical deep learning scientists into the world of quantum computing, and thus, the existence of previously known classical structures in the quantum computing world may be critical for adoption.

Qiskit[5] is officially labelled as an open-source SDK for working with quantum computers either at an application level (e.g., hybrid deep learning development) or at a lower, hardware-targeted use for investigation in the area of pulses and circuit building. The SDK includes access to several simulators available for the modelling and testing of the developed functions. More than this, *Qiskit* enables public access to IBM's physical quantum hardware, spanning a multitude of different architectures, from superconducting qubits to trapped ions. Even though the availability of real, physical quantum computing hardware is a strong advantage of *Qiskit*, the current limitations on qubit technology dictate that their use be restricted to only small-sized problems.

In particular, *Qiskit*'s application level aims to enable research activities and quick prototyping of algorithms for a variety of different tasks, ranging from the fields of machine learning to optimization, finance, and chemistry. Because of these characteristics that are central to the SDK, *Qiskit* has a wide library of algorithms already available, with abstractions and tutorials ready to be employed on the aforementioned areas of investigation.

Cirq,[6] on the other hand, is officially named an open-source framework, made available to the general public as a Python library. The framework is focused on the writing, manipulation, and optimization of quantum circuits, for execution on either simulators or physical computers. Distinguishing from *Qiskit*'s approach, abstractions developed on *Cirq* are tuned to deal with the noisy characteristics of quantum hardware, with a clear target of enabling users to achieve more facilitated state-of-the-art results.

In terms of accessibility to simulators and hardware platforms, *Cirq* enables the use of several types of simulators, with qsim being considered the current state-of-the-art for wave function simulating. Access to a physical quantum computer is

---

[4] https://docs.ocean.dwavesys.com/en/stable/

[5] https://qiskit.org/

[6] https://quantumai.google/cirq

authorized and only possible through other services (e.g., quantum computing service[7]). Nevertheless, for researchers, the class Device represents an abstract concept that can represent constraints of an actual quantum processor. Further than this, *Cirq* recently presented a new tool, *ReCirq*, with the aim of easing the development of novel research experiments through the availability of templates.

15.3 Deep Learning Background

In this section, some deep learning background is layered out, starting with a brief description of the architectures considered for the comparative analysis of *Qiskit* and *Cirq*. Furthermore, some related work in the area is mentioned, including both recent classical and hybrid applications of these architectures. Lastly, we describe possibly related research that focuses on either frameworks or tools for hybrid quantum-classical deep learning.

15.3.1 *Generative Adversarial Neural Networks*

Generative adversarial neural networks were proposed by Goodfellow et al. [23] and have become popular due to their capabilities to model complex distributions. The basic structure of a GAN is composed of a pair of networks—a generator, which is tasked with generating samples, and a discriminator, which tries to distinguish between real and generated samples. Both networks are typically trained in a min-max game until they reach Nash equilibrium. Naturally, the generator will learn to emulate the target distribution as the discriminator will keep classifying its samples as fake unless they are rather close to the target ones. Some examples of applications where GANs have been widely successful are image-to-image translation [24], 3D object generation [25], and super resolution [26], among many others.

Concerning quantum GANs, ever since their theoretical feasibility was discussed, many authors have focused on delivering possible implementations [27–29]. Situ et al. [29] focus on modelling discrete distributions, while works like [28] have tackled continuous distributions with a variational generator. In this area of application, Zoufal et al. [6] propose the first qGAN that loads probability distributions into quantum states, thus taking the first step into producing a generator that learns to represent the distribution itself within the quantum space.

---

[7] https://quantumai.google/cirq/tutorials/google/start

15.3.2   Convolutional Neural Networks

Convolutional neural networks are able to extract meaningful features from many different types of data, which makes them resourceful for many applications. Coupling high adaptability with high accuracy, CNNs have wide adoption and are the current state of the art on many tasks, especially visual-driven ones, such as object detection [30], face recognition [31], and personality feature identification [32], just to name a few.

On the field of quantum convolutional neural networks, [33] demonstrate a possible implementation and discuss potential experimental realizations and generalizations. Concerning hybrid models, [5] propose an architecture with convolutional filtering as a quantum circuit followed by traditionally fully connected layers. On the other hand, [34] demonstrates a methodology for gradient calculation in quantum fully connected layers. This methodology is generally coupled with a classical convolutional module.

15.3.3   Frameworks and Tools for Hybrid Deep Learning

On the topic of studies of hybrid deep learning, we have found several authors that focus on demonstrating the available methods and possibilities from an algorithmic perspective, such as [35–37].

On the specific topic of framework analysis, we found studies targeted at each single framework, such as [38] and [39] for Qiskit and Cirq, respectively.

Especially related to hybrid deep learning, as far as we are aware, there are at the moment no studies equivalent to the one we are conducting.

15.4   Methods and Materials

In this section, the methodology that was employed for the analysis of both *Qiskit* and *Cirq* is thoroughly described, including relevant implementation details. We carry out the comparative study of the implementation of the aforementioned neural network architectures—convolutional and generative adversarial networks—in a quantum-classical, or hybrid environment in phases, as described in Fig. 15.1.

Each phase consists of:

Phase 1 Implementation of a sample hybrid generative adversarial network using *Qiskit* (1. on Fig. 15.1)

Phase 2 Implementation of a sample hybrid generative adversarial network using *Cirq* (2. on Fig. 15.1)

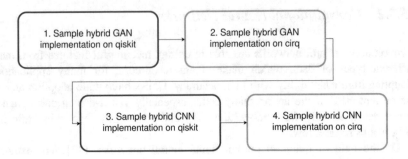

Fig. 15.1 Phases of implementation for the sample architectures on both frameworks

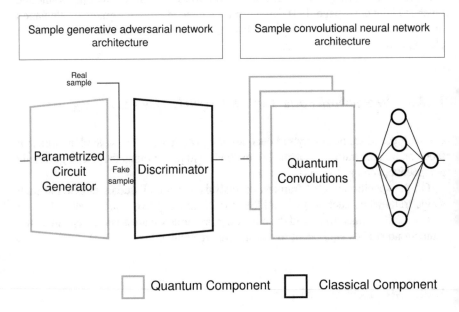

Fig. 15.2 General architectures considered for a proof-of-concept implementation

Phase 3 Implementation of a sample hybrid convolutional neural network using *Qiskit* (3. on Fig. 15.1)

Phase 4 Implementation of a sample hybrid convolutional neural network using *Cirq* (4. on Fig. 15.1)

All phases are described in the following subsections, including the implementation details. Since the focus of this chapter is to provide insight into the aforementioned frameworks, we implement simple architectures, regardless of their quantum utility, as a proof of concept. The general architectures that were considered for framework testing purposes are described in Fig. 15.2.

Overall, the generative adversarial network consists of a simple parametrized circuit as a generator followed by a classical discriminator. Likewise, the convolutional neural network sports a quantum convolutional layer followed by a fully connected layer.

15.4.1   Generative Adversarial Network

We adopt a simple approach for a proof of concept of a generative adversarial network on both frameworks. The generator is entirely quantum and consists of a parameterized circuit. The discriminator, on the other hand, is a simple classical model. On both, we set the objective as the modelling of a log-normal distribution.

Qiskit In *Qiskit*, the implementation of a qGAN is rather simple due to the already existent abstractions. The qGAN abstraction accepts as arguments a generator circuit and a discriminator model from *Pytorch* and, as such, allows for the complete control over the architectures, encapsulating only the training procedures such as gradient and loss calculation. The class, with all possible arguments, is shown in Listing 15.1.

The creation of a generator circuit, described in Listing 15.2, can also be easily achieved using *Qiskit*'s circuit library. In particular, *Qiskit* provides a couple of ansatz circuits[8] by design, facilitating even further this development. We utilize the TwoLocal ansatz with two qubits, rotation over y and entanglement with a Z gate for proof of concept.

For the discriminator, we can load PyTorchDiscriminator from qiskit.aqua or create a simple model from scratch in a classical manner, making use of nn.Module.

After the training is finished, the losses of both the generator and discriminator can be conveniently accessed through qgan.gloss and qgan.dloss. Relative entropy is also accessible on the parameter qgan.relentr. In order to plot and visualize the resulting distribution that is being modelled, qgan.generator. getoutput(qgan. quantuminstance, shots=10000) can be called, returning both generated samples and probabilities.

Cirq On *Cirq*, we have not found a direct abstraction that facilitates the development of a Generative Adversarial Neural Network. Instead, it is possible to encapsulate GANs training procedures through the use of *tensorflow-gan*, an open-source lightweight library that is maintained by *Tensorflow*. We replicate the same setting as described for *Qiskit* as much as possible for *Cirq*.

---

[8]In the context of variational circuits, an ansatz usually describes a subroutine consisting of a sequence of gates applied to specific wires. Similar to the architecture of a neural network, this only defines the base structure, while the types of gates and/or their free parameters can be optimized by the variational procedure.

```
# Create a Quantum Instance
q_instance = QuantumInstance(
            backend=
BasicAer.get_backend('statevector_simulator'),
            seed_transpiler=seed,
            seed_simulator=seed)

# Create a QGAN object
qgan = QGAN(data,
            bounds=np.array([0., 3.]),
            num_qubits=[2],
            batch_size=100,
            seed=71,
            num_epochs=20,
            discriminator=PyTorchDiscriminator(len(num_qubits)),
            generator=g_circuit,
            tol_rel_ent=None,
            snapshot_dir=None,
            quantum_instance=q_instance)
```

Listing 15.1 Creation of a quantum instance and the QGAN abstraction on Qiskit

```
# Qubits
num_qubits = [2]

# Setting the ansatz
ansatz = TwoLocal(int(np.sum(num_qubits)),
    'ry', 'cz', entanglement=[[0,1]], reps=1)

# Setting initial random parameters
init_params = np.random.rand(ansatz.
    num_parameters_settable) * 2 * np.pi

# Compose circuit
g_circuit = ansatz.compose(
    UniformDistribution(sum(num_qubits)),
    front=True)
```

Listing 15.2 A simple circuit-based generator on Qiskit

Cirq enables the creation of qubits on a grid or line through the abstractions cirq. GridQubit (row, col) and cirq.LineQubit(x). Since we aim at characterizing the interfaces provided by *Cirq* and we have no access to a real quantum computer from Google, we run all experiments on a simulator, and thus, the use of either qubits on a grid or line is irrelevant. We choose grid qubits to easily be able to support 2D

```
# Qubit parameters
num_qubits = 2
theta = sympy.symbols(f'a0:{num_qubits}')

# Create qubits
qubits = [cirq.GridQubit(x, 0)
                 for x in range(num_qubits)]
```

Listing 15.3 Interface for qubit creation on Cirq

data with minimal code changes on other experiments. *Cirq* demands the specification of qubit parameters through sympy, as described in Listing 15.3.

We replicate the generator by hand through the construction of the same simple circuit with two qubits, rotation on y and entanglement with a Z gate. The workflow is rather similar to classical *Tensorflow* development, and, as such, an input layer and a Model must be defined, as described in Listing 15.4.

As for the discriminator, we are able to replicate the PyTorchDiscriminator from *Qiskit* with *Keras*, as showcased in Listing 15.5.

Finally, the abstraction from tensorflow-gan can be employed, passing only the custom generator and discriminator as arguments, as seen in Listing 15.6. The training loop needs to be constructed by the programmer; however, the GANEstimator class has a method for evaluation and extraction of predictions built-in, accessible through gan.evaluate(data, steps) and gan.predict(data).

15.4.2   Convolutional Neural Network

As for the convolutional neural network, we test two different layouts on both frameworks: a parameterized circuit followed by convolutional layers and the inverse, meaning convolutional layers followed by a parameterized circuit. The description in the following subsections will be more focused on the essential abstractions and methods available for the construction of said architectures. Whenever necessary, we focus on the quantum followed by classical architecture since this is the most demanding implementation since data needs to be loaded into a quantum space.

For completeness, we run the proof of concept on two popular benchmark datasets—mnist [40] and olivetti [41]. For both, classification is kept binary, and as such, the data from two single classes is extracted from the original datasets. When the data is fed directly to a parameterized circuit, the images are resized from

```python
# Replicate ansatz with rotation over y
# and entanglement with a Z gate
param_circ = cirq.Circuit(cirq.Moment([
                    cirq.ry(t)(q) for t, q
                        in zip(theta, qubits)]
                    ))
entangled_circ = cirq.Circuit([cirq.CZ(qubits[0], qubits[1])])

# Join both circuits to create the ansatz
ansatz = param_circ + entangled_circ

# Create a readout qubit
readout = sum(
            (cirq.Z(qubits[i]) + 1) / 2 * 2 ** i
                for i in range(num_qubits))

# The model input must be defined, following Tensorflow's
    worflow
input_layer = tf.keras.Input(shape=(),
                    dtype=tf.dtypes.string)

# Create a parameterized circuit layer that can interact with
    classical layers
pqc = tfq.layers.PQC(ansatz, readout,
                    repetitions=1)(input_layer)

# The compiled model is saved on a variable
model = tf.keras.Model(inputs=[input_layer],
                    outputs=[pqc])
```

Listing 15.4 Building a simple circuit-based generator using *Cirq*

their original size into a 4 × 4 array. We represent each pixel with a qubit, influencing the state with the pixel value, in the fashion of [7].

Qiskit For the development of a qCNN, we start by creating a parameterized circuit. We encapsulate the general circuit on a class. We do not replicate the circuit in Listing 15.7 due to space constraints and instead choose to represent the most relevant aspects to match the general logic demonstrated in Cirq.

Model encapsulation is then achieved in a classical manner, following *Pytorch's* workflow. We leave an example of the model creation in Listing 15.8. We do not include the parameters in the Listing in order to simplify the demonstration of the workflow.

```
# Create a Sequential object and add layers
model = tf.keras.Sequential()
model.add(tf.keras.Input(
                    shape=(sample_size,)
                    ))

model.add(tf.keras.layers.Dense(512))
model.add(tf.keras.layers.LeakyReLU(
                    alpha=0.2
                    ))

model.add(tf.keras.layers.Dense(256))
model.add(tf.keras.layers.LeakyReLU(
                    alpha=0.2
                    ))

model.add(tf.keras.layers.Dense(
                    1, activation='sigmoid'
                    ))
```

Listing 15.5 Replicating PyTorchDiscriminator from *Qiskit* on *Tensorflow*

```
gan = tfg.estimator.GANEstimator(
    generator_fn=generator,
    discriminator_fn=discriminator,
    generator_loss_fn=
        tfg.losses.modified_generator_loss,
    discriminator_loss_fn=
        tfg.losses.modified_discriminator_loss,
    generator_optimizer=
        tf.compat.v1.train.AdamOptimizer(
                    gen_lr),
    discriminator_optimizer=
        tf.compat.v1.train.AdamOptimizer(
                    disc_lr),
    get_eval_metric_ops_fn=get_eval_metrics
)
```

Listing 15.6 The GANEstimator class from tensorflow-gan

Further than this, we define a forward function for the propagation through the model and the training loop, on which losses are calculated and the forward and backward methods are readily available for the abstraction of the internal training procedures.

```
circuit = qiskit.QuantumCircuit(num_qubits)
theta = [qiskit.circuit.Parameter('theta{}'.format(i)) for i in
    range(num_qubits)]

# Build the circuit
for i in range(num_qubits):
    circuit.rx(theta[i], i)
```

Listing 15.7 Creating a parameterized circuit layer

```
# Parameters not included
class Net(nn.Module):
    def __init__(self):
        super(Net, self).__init__()
        self.quanv = QuantumCircuitModel()
        self.conv = nn.Conv2d()
        self.fc1 = nn.Linear()
        self.fc2 = nn.Linear()
```

Listing 15.8 Creating a parameterized circuit layer

```
# Omitting the qubits and readout creation since it is showcased
    previously
circuit = cirq.Circuit()

# Build the circuit
for i, qubit in enumerate(qubits):
    symbol = sympy.Symbol(prefix + '-' + str(i))
    circuit.append(cirq.XX(qubit, readout)**symbol)
```

Listing 15.9 Creating a parameterized circuit layer

Cirq Following the previously described logic, a parameterized circuit can be created, as described in Listing 15.9.

This circuit is then encapsulated on a Sequential, as exemplified in Listing 15.10, or on a Model object from *Tensorflow*. Classical layers can then be added at will on the same object, facilitating the creation of the hybrid model. As previously described, we do not include the parameters in the Listing in order to simplify the demonstration of the workflow.

Model parameterization can be achieved in the same manner as in classical deep learning development. The compile and fit methods are seamlessly available for this purpose.

```
model = tf.keras.Sequential([
    tf.keras.layers.Input(shape=(), dtype=tf.string),
    tfq.layers.PQC(model_circuit, model_readout),
    tf.keras.layers.Conv2D(),
    tf.keras.layers.Dense(),
    tf.keras.layers.Dense()
])
```

Listing 15.10   Encapsulating the network on a Sequential object

15.5   Results and Discussion

In this section, we evaluate the experience we had with both frameworks, *Qiskit* and *Cirq*, and their respective tools for hybrid deep learning development. We will focus on three main aspects: *(1)* the creation of parameterized circuits, *(2)* the integration of parameterized circuits with classical layers, and *(3)* the training procedure.

This evaluation is targeted at qualifying the ease of introduction of classical scientists into quantum-classical networks provided by both frameworks and respective libraries. In this context, we consider the following factors when evaluating the learning curve of:

- **Readability.** How easy can the code be written and understood.
- **Expressiveness.** Due to their usability, on this criterion, we consider only the availability of abstractions and their quality.
- **Effort.** Effort in time needed for the initial development of the architectures.
- **Documentation.** Quality and accessibility of the documentation.

1. Creation of Parameterized Circuits

About structuring and parameterizing circuits, both frameworks offer several tools of interest.

We argue that, in terms of the parameterization of circuits, *Qiskit* presents a slightly more confusing interface as the definition of qubits and parameters changes depending on the abstraction being used. On the other hand, on *Cirq*, parameterization must be constructed through simply definitions, which gives it a more homogeneous structure. This may be due to the fact that *Cirq* is a framework focused on circuit building, while *Qiskit* is more general in its purpose.

In terms of general readability, we feel that *Cirq* has the advantage as the qubit creation and parameterization interfaces are more structured and homogeneous. This makes the code more readable and easier to write in a coherent manner.

Regarding expressiveness, *Qiskit* has some advantages in its wide availability of circuit abstractions. However, the interface to these abstractions changes slightly between them and even more between *Qiskit* versions. We consider this to be a negative point to the quality of the provided abstractions. On the other hand, *Cirq*

Table 15.1 Implementation time for circuit construction on both frameworks and architectures

Architecture	Time for implementation on *Qiskit* (h)	Time for implementation on *Cirq* (h)
qGAN	0.25	1
qCNN	1	1

focuses on maintaining its structure and logic, which can be positive for seasoned developers, but harder to tackle from the perspective of newer ones.

In terms of time, for the creation of the circuits, in both cases, we summarize an estimate in Table 15.1. Deriving from the previously enumerated characteristics, we find that the implementation on *Cirq* takes consistent time throughout architectures (1 h), while on *Qiskit*, it is highly dependent on the existent abstractions (from 0.25 h to 1 h on qCNN).

With regard to documentation, both provide suitable and complete sources. We have found no issues navigating both circuit-building documentations. Several tutorials of interest are also provided, with *Cirq* offering more directed, research-oriented tutorials for advanced users. Nevertheless, the same information can be roughly matched on several *Qiskit* tutorials.

2. Integration of Parameterized Circuits with Classical Layers

As for the integration of circuits with classical layers or models, we have found completely opposite experiences with both architectures.

We find that the simple structure of *Cirq* in conjunction with *Tensorflow Quantum*'s functionality makes for seamless and easy development, even the more relevant for *Tensorflow* users. On *Qiskit*, we also see advantages for *Pytorch* users as the translation is almost as seamless. However, we believe that it is necessary to produce more code on *Qiskit* to achieve the same result when there is no abstraction available, such as qCNN. Overall, from our experience, we see the easiness of developing with *Qiskit* somewhat dependent on the existent abstractions.

Concerning readability, we consider both easily interpretable and see advantages in their model construction. The slight differences between both seem to be derived from the differentiation found between *Pytorch* and *Tensorflow* workflows. We believe that users coming with experience on either will have no difficulties in understanding the integration of the hybrid layers. We want to single out the abstraction from *Tensorflow Quantum*, PQC which we believe is paramount to the easiness of integration between both layers and the readability of the final model.

When it comes to expressiveness, as previously mentioned, in our experience, we level both frameworks similarly as the available abstractions come mostly directly from *Pytorch* and *Tensorflow*.

Considering the time needed for an introductory construction of each architecture, we again summarize an estimate in Table 15.2. As expected, the implementation of the qGAN is very much facilitated on *Qiskit* as a newcomer, while on *Cirq*, it takes a much longer time for finding available structures and replicating the circuits by hand.

Table 15.2 Estimated implementation time for model construction on both frameworks and architectures

Architecture	Time for implementation on *Qiskit* (h)	Time for implementation on *Cirq* (h)
qGAN	0.5	1.5
qCNN	1.5	0.5

For qCNN, we find that *Keras* facilitated development, thus reducing the model construction time.

Further than this, we have found *Tensorflow Quantum*'s documentation easier to handle. This is due to the fact that *Qiskit*'s documentation requires the consultation of specific versions for all packages since abstractions and methods are moved and changed in between them. Further than that, it is necessary to know in which package the desired functions are. Matching versions would be important for new developers coming into *Qiskit*, as we found that certain functionalities do not work on specific versions.

3. Training Procedures

Relating to training procedures, our analysis corroborates the previously described characteristics.

Due to the existent qGAN abstraction in *Qiskit*, which completely encapsulates the training procedure, on this architecture, the framework enables eased development, especially for newer users. On the other hand, using *Cirq* and *Tensorflow Quantum*, we had to employ an abstraction from another library to obtain a comparable level of training encapsulation. This implicates the installation of another package to the environment, which may be less desirable for certain users. Further than this, the GANEstimator abstraction is not as automatized as *Qiskit*'s qGAN, which means that more code is necessary to achieve the same result. Without using the library, users have to manually program the entire training procedure.

Concerning the qCNN architecture, no abstractions can be used in either framework, which leads to the gap between *Pytorch* and *Tensorflow/Keras* to be seen as differentiation factors.

Relating to our criteria, we classify readability as being slightly higher on *Tensorflow Quantum* due to *Keras'* inherent easiness of model compilation and fitting. On *Qiskit*, even with the qGAN abstraction, the training procedure becomes entirely encapsulated, which might be considered as less interpretable from a new user's perspective.

Pertaining to the previously described aspects of both frameworks and respective abstractions, we classify *Qiskit*'s expressiveness related to training procedures as slightly superior.

As for development time, again summarized in Table 15.3, we find results to be coherent with the previously described characteristics. Deriving from the existent

Table 15.3 Estimated implementation time for training procedures on both frameworks and architectures

Architecture	Time for implementation on *Qiskit* (h)	Time for implementation on *Cirq* (h)
qGAN	0.2	0.5
qCNN	1	0.2

abstractions, the estimated development time in *Qiskit* is highly reduced in qGAN, while Keras enables faster implementation on qCNN.

In terms of documentation, it is impossible to separate model creation from training procedures, and, as such, we stand by the observations made in the previous subsection.

15.5.1 Main Take-Aways

Building upon the aforementioned analysis, we draw the following take-away messages, which may be considered as the main results of our study:

- *Qiskit* enables an easier introduction for users with no quantum knowledge as they can replicate small models known to them and understand the majority of the process.
- *Pytorch* users also have an advantage when using *Qiskit* for model development as the workflow is seamlessly transferred.
- *Cirq* and *Tensorflow Quantum* present better structure and organization, thus being more intuitive for advanced development. We also find *Tensorflow Quantum* tutorials to provide more insight even for beginner developers.
- *Tensorflow* users also have an advantage when transferring to *Tensorflow Quantum* as the workflow is identical.
- *Qiskit* includes a wide panoply of abstractions that allow for swift prototyping of applications. Nevertheless, versioning issues might be an obstacle for newcomers even when navigating the wide range of available tutorials.

In particular, accounting for the adopted criteria for validation—*readability, expressiveness, effort*, and *documentation*—we sum up the following aspects:

- **Readability** *Cirq* showcases higher readability throughout the tested architectures, with strong structure and homogeneity. When abstractions are available, for example, qGAN, *Qiskit*'s training procedures and structure can be entirely altered, which can be a negative aspect for readability.
- **Expressiveness** *Qiskit* provides a wide range of abstractions that enable the encapsulation of several processes, while *Cirq* lacks such functions. Nevertheless, interfaces to *Qiskit*'s abstractions might be entirely dependent on the used version which can become a hurdle for continued projects.
- **Effort** The effort that is needed for implementation depends on the existence and usability of the available abstractions. Implementation effort on *Qiskit* is highly

dependent on the employed abstraction, while on *Cirq*, with less abstractions, a more constant period of time is required.

- **Documentation** We find that both *Qiskit* and *Cirq* showcase good documentation with eased access, including a wide range of informed tutorials. *Cirq*'s tutorials can be considered as slightly more informative, with the same details having to be matched in several places within *Qiskit*'s documentation.

15.6 Conclusion

In this chapter, we analyze and compare two frameworks, *Qiskit* and *Cirq*, and their respective hybrid deep learning libraries and tools in the context of the introduction of classical scientists to the field of quantum-classical deep learning.

After targeting the development of two very prominent architectures, generative adversarial and convolutional, we discuss strong and weak points for both environments.

The conclusions that we reached are grounded on the fact that *Qiskit*, with its plenty availability of abstractions, eases the ability to start implementing simple networks, while *Cirq* seems harder to tackle at first, however, presents very good structure that is seamless for scientists that are comfortable with *Tensorflow*.

To the best of our knowledge, our study is novel in its aim and presents relevant conclusions. To further advance the field of hybrid quantum-classical deep learning, it is of paramount importance to captivate classical scientists that bring knowledge from classical networks.

Moreover, classical deep learning has captivated several scientists due to the availability of frameworks with an acceptable learning curve. Quantum computing would significantly benefit from a similar infrastructure.

We argue that it would be interesting to tackle the implementation of other types of relevant architectures, such as those based on deep reinforcement learning, within quantum computing. This would bring even more value for scientists and engineers from the classical computing paradigm who are entering the quantum-classical space.

The implications of our work for a classical deep learning developer are as follows. Firstly, we enable a faster learning curve to the hybrid quantum-classical deep learning world since we discuss the most widely used tools in this context, *Qiskit* and *Cirq*.

Secondly, we present some insight into the internals of these frameworks, detailing the development of two of the most popularized network architectures, GANs and CNNs. On this note, we foster reproducibility and encourage development by making our code platform publicly available. We believe these can soften the learning curve of these tools.

Finally, we provide valuable information to new quantum-classical deep learning scientists who are looking to select a framework to initiate their research work since we present a comparative analysis of their attributes. With these details, newcoming scientists can easily discern where to find the qualities they seek, either on *Qiskit* with *PyTorch* or with *Cirq* and *Tensorflow Quantum*.

Moving forward, we intend to extend this study to other possible available frameworks, evaluating whether there are other relevant tools for hybrid model development. Tackling the aforementioned improvements, we also intend to invest on building a sample deep reinforcement learning proof of concept.

Furthermore, we aim at delving deeper into both studied frameworks, starting with the replication of widely known, complex classical models on a hybrid setting to evaluate the scalability of both frameworks on more intricate scenarios.

Acknowledgments The work described in this chapter was supported in part by Fundaçao para a Ciência e a Tecnologia (FCT) under Grants CMU/TIC/0064/2019 (a project funded by the Carnegie Mellon Portugal Program), FaultLocker Project (ref. PTDC/CCI-COM/29300/2017), and UIDB/50021/2020. The work was also supported by the Artificial Intelligence and Computer Science Laboratory, University of Porto (LIACC), FCT/UID/CEC/0027/2020, funded by national funds through the FCT/MCTES (PIDDAC).

References

1. Moller M, Vuik C (2017) On the impact of quantum computing technology on future developments in high-performance scientific computing. Ethics Inf Technol:1–17. https://doi.org/10.1007/s10676-017-9438-0
2. Bertels K, Sarkar A, Krol A, Budhrani R, Samadi J, Geoffroy E, Matos J, Abreu R, Gielen G, Ashraf I (2021) Quantum accelerator stack: a research roadmap. arXiv preprint arXiv:2102.02035
3. Arute F, Arya K, Babbush R, Bacon D, Bardin JC, Barends R, Biswas R, Boixo S, Brandao FGSL, Buell DA, Burkett B, Chen Y, Chen Z, Chiaro B, Collins R, Courtney W, Dunsworth A, Farhi E, Foxen B, Fowler A, Gidney C, Giustina M, Graff R, Guerin K, Habegger S, Harrigan MP, Hartmann MJ, Ho A, Hoffmann M, Huang T, Humble TS, Isakov SV, Jeffrey E, Jiang Z, Kafri D, Kechedzhi K, Kelly J, Klimov PV, Knysh S, Korotkov A, Kostritsa F, Landhuis D, Lindmark M, Lucero E, Lyakh D, Mandra S, McClean JR, McEwen M, Megrant A, Mi X, Michielsen K, Mohseni M, Mutus J, Naaman O, Neeley M, Neill C, Niu MY, Ostby E, Petukhov A, Platt JC, Quintana C, Rieffel EG, Roushan P, Rubin NC, Sank D, Satzinger KJ, Smelyanskiy V, Sung KJ, Trevithick MD, Vainsencher A, Villalonga B, White T, Yao ZJ, Yeh P, Zalcman A, Neven H, Martinis JM (2019) Quantum supremacy using a programmable superconducting processor. Nature 574(7779):505–510. https://doi.org/10.1038/s41586019-1666-5
4. Rinott Y, Shoham T, Kalai G (2020) Statistical aspects of the quantum supremacy demonstration. arXiv
5. Henderson M, Shakya S, Pradhan S, Cook T (2020) Quanvolutional neural networks: powering image recognition with quantum circuits. Quantum Machine Intell 2(1):2. https://doi.org/10.1007/s42484-020-00012-y
6. Zoufal C, Lucchi A, Woerner S (2019) Quantum generative adversarial networks for learning and loading random distributions. NPJ Quantum Inf 5(1):103. https://doi.org/10.1038/s41534-019-0223-2
7. Farhi E, Neven H (2018) Classification with quantum neural networks on near term processors. arXiv

8. Alcazar J, Leyton-Ortega V, Perdomo-Ortiz A (2020) Classical versus quantum models in machine learning: insights from a finance application. Machine Learn Sci Technol 1(3):035003. https://doi.org/10.1088/26322153/ab9009
9. Huang HY, Broughton M, Mohseni M, Babbush R, Boixo S, Neven H, McClean JR (2021) Power of data in quantum machine learning. Nat Commun 12(1):2631. https://doi.org/10.1038/s41467-021-22539-9
10. Preskill J (2018) Quantum computing in the NISQ era and beyond. Quantum 2:79. https://doi.org/10.22331/q-2018-08-06-79
11. Gomes C, Fortunato D, Fernandes JP, Abreu R (2020) Off-the-shelf components for quantum programming and testing. In: Proceedings of the 1st International Workshop on Software Engineering & Technology (Q-SET'20), co-located with IEEE International Conference on Quantum Computing and Engineering (IEEE Quantum Week'20), pp 14–19
12. Paszke A, Gross S, Massa F, Lerer A, Bradbury J, Chanan G, Killeen T, Lin Z, Gimelshein N, Antiga L, Desmaison A, Kopf A, Yang E, DeVito Z, Raison M, Tejani A, Chilamkurthy S, Steiner B, Fang L, Bai J, Chintala S (2019) PyTorch: an imperative style, high-performance deep learning library. arXiv
13. Abadi M, Barham P, Chen J, Chen Z, Davis A, Dean J, Devin M, Ghemawat S, Irving G, Isard M, Kudlur M, Levenberg J, Monga R, Moore S, Murray DG, Steiner B, Tucker P, Vasudevan V, Warden P, Wicke M, Yu Y, Zheng X (2016) TensorFlow: A system for large-scale machine learning. 12th USENIX Symposium on Operating Systems Design and Implementation
14. Broughton M, Verdon G, McCourt T, Martinez AJ, Yoo JH, Isakov SV, Massey P, Niu MY, Halavati R, Peters E, Leib M, Skolik A, Streif M, Von Dollen D, McClean JR, Boixo S, Bacon D, Ho AK, Neven H, Mohseni M (2020) TensorFlow quantum: a software framework for quantum machine learning. arXiv
15. Stein SA, Baheri B, Tischio RM, Mao Y, Guan Q, Li A, Fang B, Xu S (2020) QuGAN: a generative adversarial network through quantum states. arXiv
16. Omer B (2003) Quantum programming in QCL. THESIS.MASTER, TU Vienna. http://tph.tuwien.ac.at/~oemer/doc/quprog.pdf
17. Omer B (2003) Structured quantum programming. THESIS.DOCTORAL, TU Vienna. http://tph.tuwien.ac.at/~oemer/doc/structquprog.pdf
18. Ying M, Yu N, Feng Y (2014) Alternation in quantum programming: from superposition of data to superposition of programs. arXiv
19. Grattage JJ (2006) A functional quantum programming language. THESIS.DOCTORAL, University of Nottingham. http://eprints.nottingham.ac.uk/10250/1/thesis.pdf
20. Green AS, Lumsdaine PL, Ross NJ, Selinger P, Valiron B (2013) Quipper. ACM SIGPLAN Notices 48(6):333–342. https://doi.org/10.1145/2499370.2462177
21. Svore K, Roetteler M, Geller A, Troyer M, Azariah J, Granade C, Heim B, Kliuchnikov V, Mykhailova M, Paz A (2018) Q# enabling scalable quantum computing and development with a high-level DSL. ACM Press, New York, NY, pp 1–10. https://doi.org/10.1145/3183895.3183901
22. Bichsel B, Baader M, Gehr T, Vechev M (2020) Silq: a high-level quantum language with safe uncomputation and intuitive semantics. In: Proceedings of the 41st ACM SIGPLAN Conference on Programming Language Design and Implementation. ACM, New York, NY, pp 286–300. https://doi.org/10.1145/3385412.3386007
23. Goodfellow I, Pouget-Abadie J, Mirza M, Xu B, Warde-Farley D, Ozair S, Courville A, Bengio Y (2014) Generative adversarial nets. Adv Neural Inf Process Syst
24. Zhu JY, Park T, Isola P, Efros AA (2017) Unpaired image-to-image translation using cycle-consistent adversarial networks. In: 2017 IEEE International Conference on Computer Vision (ICCV). IEEE, pp 2242–2251. https://doi.org/10.1109/ICCV.2017.244
25. Wu J, Zhang C, Xue T, Freeman B, Tenenbaum J (2016) Learning a probabilistic latent space of object shapes via 3D generative-adversarial modeling. Adv Neural Inf Process Syst

26. Ledig C, Theis L, Huszar F, Caballero J, Cunningham A, Acosta A, Aitken A, Tejani A, Totz J, Wang Z, Shi W (2017) Photo-realistic single image superresolution using a generative adversarial network. In: 2017 IEEE Conference on Computer Vision and Pattern Recognition (CVPR). IEEE, pp 105–114. https://doi.org/10.1109/CVPR.2017.19

27. Hu L, Wu SH, Cai W, Ma Y, Mu X, Xu Y, Wang H, Song Y, Deng DL, Zou CL, Sun L (2019) Quantum generative adversarial learning in a superconducting quantum circuit. Sci Adv 5(1): eaav2761. https://doi.org/10.1126/sciadv.aav2761

28. Romero J, Aspuru-Guzik A (2021) Variational quantum generators: generative adversarial quantum machine learning for continuous distributions. Adv Quantum Technol 4(1): 2000003. https://doi.org/10.1002/qute.202000003

29. Situ H, He Z, Wang Y, Li L, Zheng S (2020) Quantum generative adversarial network for generating discrete distribution. Inf Sci 538:193–208. https://doi.org/10.1016/j.ins.2020.05.127

30. Yuan T, Wan F, Fu M, Liu J, Xu S, Ji X, Ye Q (2021) Multiple instance active learning for object detection. In: Conference on Computer Vision and Pattern Recognition

31. Chrysos G, Moschoglou S, Bouritsas G, Deng J, Panagakis Y, Zafeiriou SP (2021) Deep polynomial neural networks. In: IEEE transactions on pattern analysis and machine intelligence. https://doi.org/10.1109/TPAMI.2021.3058891

32. Fatimah SH, Djamal EC, Ilyas R, Renaldi F (2019) Personality features identification from handwriting using convolutional neural networks. In: 2019 4th International Conference on Information Technology, Information Systems and Electrical Engineering (ICITISEE). IEEE, pp 119–124. https://doi.org/10.1109/ICITISEE48480.2019.9003855

33. Cong I, Choi S, Lukin MD (2019) Quantum convolutional neural networks. Nat Phys. https://doi.org/10.1038/s41567-019-0648-8

34. Crooks GE (2019) Gradients of parameterized quantum gates using the parameter-shift rule and gate decomposition. arXiv

35. Fastovets DV, Bogdanov YI, Bantysh BI, Lukichev V (2019) Machine learning methods in quantum computing theory. arXiv

36. Li R, Xu J, Yuan J, Li D (2021) An introduction to quantum machine learning algorithms. In: Liu Q, Liu X, Li L, Zhou H, Zhao HH (eds) Proceedings of the 9th international conference on computer engineering and networks, Advances in intelligent systems and computing, vol 1143. Springer Singapore, Singapore, pp 519–532. https://doi.org/10.1007/978-981-15-3753-0-51

37. Martın-Guerrero JD, Lamata L (2020) Quantum machine learning. European Symposium on Artificial Neural Networks, Computational Intelligence and Machine Learning

38. Wille R, Van Meter R, Naveh Y (2019) IBM' qiskit tool chain: Working with and developing for real quantum computers. In: 2019 Design, Automation & Test in Europe Conference & Exhibition (DATE). IEEE, pp 1234–1240. https://doi.org/10.23919/DATE.2019.8715261

39. Cirq quantum software framework review – quantum computing report. https://quantumcomputingreport.com/review-of-the-cirq-quantum-software-framework/

40. LeCun Y, Cortes C (2010) MNIST handwritten digit database. http://yann.lecun.com/exdb/mnist/

41. Face recognition on olivetti dataset |kaggle. https://www.kaggle.com/serkanpeldek/face-recognition-on-olivetti-dataset

Printed in the United States
by Baker & Taylor Publisher Services